CW01214683

BIRDS OF VANUATU

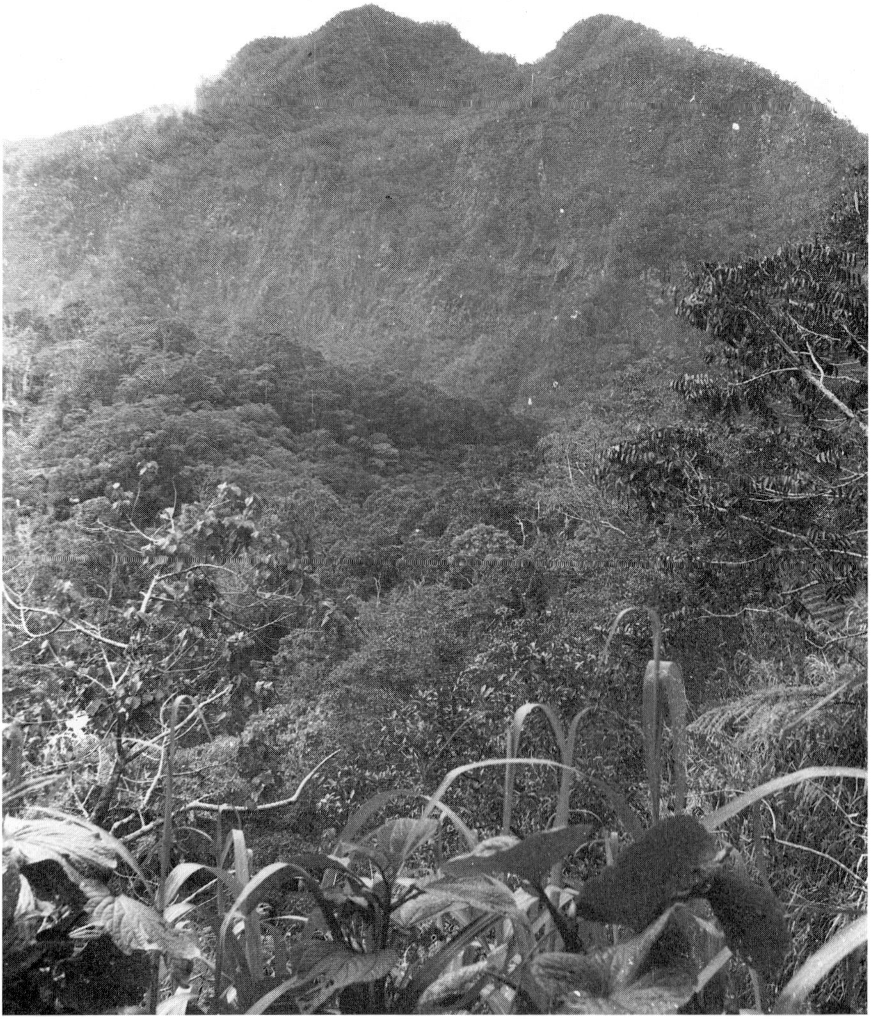

Heinrich L Bregulla

Birds of Vanuatu

Anthony Nelson

© Heinrich L Bregulla

First published in 1992 by Anthony Nelson
PO Box 9, Oswestry, Shropshire SY11 1BY, England
on behalf of the Board of Management of the Port-Vila
Cultural Centre, Vanuatu

Publication of this book would not have been possible
without a very generous grant from the German government
for which the Author and the Cultural Centre Board are
deeply grateful.

All rights reserved. No part of this book may be
reproduced, stored in a retrieval system, or
transmitted in any form or by any means, electronic,
mechanical, photocopying or otherwise, without the
permission of the publisher.

ISBN 0 904614 34 4

Designed by Alan Bartram
Typeset in Linotron Janson Text
by Nene Phototypesetters, Northampton
Printed by The Bath Press, Avon, England

FRONTISPIECE
Mount Tabwemasana,
the highest peak in Vanuatu at 1879 m
seen from Nokovula village, Santo

Contents

List of colour plates   7
List of black and white illustrations   9
FOREWORD 1   11
FOREWORD 2   13
PREFACE   15
ACKNOWLEDGEMENTS   17
Map of the southwest Pacific   19
Map of Vanuatu   20
INTRODUCTION BY MARCUS CHAMBERS   21
Table 1. List of islands   27
THE AVIFAUNA OF VANUATU AND CONSERVATION   44
CHECKLIST OF VANUATU BIRDS   56
CLASSIFICATION   62
Topography of a bird and shapes of eggs   65
HINTS FOR BIRDWATCHERS IN VANUATU AND NOTES ON THE TEXT   66
Table 2. Distribution of breeding birds   71
ORDERS, FAMILIES AND SPECIES ACCOUNTS   77
Podicipediformes   77
   Grebes   *Podicipedidae*   77
Procellariiformes   79
   Albatrosses   *Diomedeidae*   80
   Fulmars, Petrels, Prions and Shearwaters   *Procellariidae*   81
   Storm-Petrels   *Oceanitidae*   92
Pelecaniformes   95
   Pelicans   *Pelecanidae*   95
   Boobies and Gannets   *Sulidae*   96
   Cormorants   *Phalacrocoracidae*   101
   Frigatebirds   *Fregatidae*   102
   Tropicbirds   *Phaethontidae*   105
Ciconiiformes   108
   Herons   *Ardeidae*   109
Anseriformes   115
   Ducks, Geese and Swans   *Anatidae*   115

Accipitriformes   122
  Kites, Harriers, Hawks and allies   *Accipitridae*   122
Falconiformes   127
  Falcons   *Falconidae*   128
Galliformes   130
  Megapodes   *Megapodiidae*   131
  Pheasants, Fowls and allies   *Phasianidae*   135
Gruiformes   137
  Rails, Crakes, Swamphen and Coots   *Rallidae*   137
Charadriiformes   144
  Thick-knees   *Burhinidae*   146
  Oystercatchers   *Haematopodidae*   147
  Plovers, Lapwings and Dotterels   *Charadriidae*   148
  Curlews, Godwits, Sandpipers and allies   *Scolopacidae*   151
  Gulls, Terns and Noddies   *Laridae*   159
Columbiformes   170
  Pigeons and Doves   *Columbidae*   171
Psittaciformes   188
  Parrots   *Psittacidae*   188
Cuculiformes   193
  Cuckoos, Koels and Coucals   *Cuculidae*   193
Strigiformes   198
  Barn Owls and allies   *Tytonidae*   199
Apodiformes   201
  Swifts and Swiftlets   *Apodidae*   201
Coraciiformes   207
  Kingfishers   *Alcedinidae*   207
Passeriformes   213
  Swallows and Martins   *Hirundinidae*   214
  Cuckoo-shrikes   *Campephagidae*   217
  Thrushes   *Turdidae*   221
  Australian Robins, Whistlers and allies   *Pachycephalidae*   225
  Monarch Flycatchers   *Monarchidae*   229
  Fantails   *Rhipiduridae*   234
  Australian Warblers   *Acanthizidae*   238
  Honeyeaters   *Meliphagidae*   242
  White-eyes or Silvereyes   *Zosteropidae*   249
  Finches   *Fringillidae*   253
  Sparrows   *Passeridae*   254
  Waxbills, Mannikins and allies   *Estrildidae*   256
  Starlings and Mynahs   *Sturnidae*   266
  Woodswallows   *Artamidae*   272

GLOSSARY   275

BIBLIOGRAPHY   279

INDEX   287

Colour plates

Between pages 96 and 97

Plates 1 to 9 and 11 to 15 were painted by Hilary Forster and plate 10 by Ola Reeve. All photographs were taken by the author unless otherwise stated.

PLATE 1
Brown Booby *Sula leucogaster*
Masked Booby *Sula dactylatra*
Red-footed Booby *Sula sula*
Royal Albatross *Diomedea epomophora*
Least Frigatebird *Fregata ariel*.

PLATE 2
White Tern *Gygis alba*
Common Noddy *Anous stolidus*
Black-naped Tern *Sterna sumatrana*
Red-tailed Tropicbird *Phaethon rubricauda*
White-tailed Tropicbird *Phaethon lepturus*
Tahiti Petrel *Pseudobulweria rostrata*
Fluttering Shearwater *Puffinus gavia*

PLATE 3
Eastern Reef Heron *Ardea sacra*
White-faced Heron *Ardea novaehollandiae*
Little Heron *Butorides striatus*

PLATE 4
Australian Grebe *Tachybaptus novaehollandiae*
Little Pied Cormorant *Phalacrocorax melanoleucos*
Australian White-eyed Duck *Aythya australis*
Pacific Black Duck *Anas superciliosa*
Grey Teal *Anas gibberifrons*

PLATE 5
Barn Owl *Tyto alba*
Brown Goshawk *Accipiter fasciatus*
Peregrine Falcon *Falco peregrinus*
Swamp Harrier *Circus approximans*

PLATE 6
Spotless Crake *Porzana tabuensis*
White-browed Crake *Poliolimnas cinereus*
Purple Swamphen *Porphyrio porphyrio*
Buff-banded Rail *Gallirallus philippensis*
Incubator Bird *Megapodius freycinet*
Red Jungle Fowl *Gallus gallus*

PLATE 7
Pacific Golden Plover *Pluvialis fulva*
Ruddy Turnstone *Arenaria interpres*
Beach Thick-knee *Esacus magnirostris*
Whimbrel *Numenius phaeopus*
Wandering Tattler *Heteroscelus incanus*

PLATE 8
White-throated Pigeon *Columba vitiensis*
Vanuatu Mountain Pigeon *Ducula bakeri*
Pacific Imperial Pigeon *Ducula pacifica*
Vanuatu Fruit Dove *Ptilinopus tannensis*
Red-bellied Fruit Dove *Ptilinopus greyii*
Rufous-brown Pheasant-Dove *Macropygia mackinlayi*
Santa Cruz Ground Dove *Gallicolumba sanctaecrucis*
Green-winged Ground Dove *Chalcophaps indica*

PLATE 9
Vanuatu White-eye *Zosterops flavifrons*
Grey-backed White-eye *Zosterops lateralis*
Silver-eared Honeyeater *Lichmera incana*
Vanuatu Mountain Honeyeater *Phylidonyris notabilis*
Cardinal Honeyeater *Myzomela cardinalis*
Green Palm Lorikeet *Charmosyna palmarum*
Rainbow Lorikeet *Trichoglossus haematodus*

PLATE 10
Long-tailed New Zealand Cuckoo *Eudynamis taitensis*
Shining Bronze-Cuckoo *Chrysococcyx lucidus*
Fan-tailed Cuckoo *Cacomantis pyrrhophanus*

PLATE 11
Uniform Swiftlet *Aerodramus vanikorensis*
White-rumped Swiftlet *Aerodramus spodiopygius*
White-bellied Swiftlet *Collocalia esculenta*
Pacific Swallow *Hirundo tahitica*

PLATE 12
Melanesian Cuckoo-shrike *Coracina caledonica*
Long-tailed Triller *Lalage leucopyga*
Polynesian Triller *Lalage maculosa*
Vanuatu Kingfisher *Halcyon farquhari*
White-collared Kingfisher *Halcyon chloris*
Santo Mountain Starling *Aplonis santovestris*
Rusty-winged Starling *Aplonis zelandicus*
Indian Mynah *Acridotheres tristis*

PLATE 13
Spotted Fantail *Rhipidura spilodera*
Grey Fantail *Rhipidura fuliginosa*
Fantail Warbler *Gerygone flavolateralis*
Thicket Warbler *Cichlornis whitneyi*
Island Thrush *Turdus poliocephalus*

PLATE 14
Scarlet Robin *Petroica multicolor*
White-breasted Woodswallow *Artamus leucorhynchus*
Vanuatu Flycatcher *Neolalage banksiana*
Golden Whistler *Pachycephala pectoralis*
Southern Shrikebill *Clytorhynchus pachycephaloides*
Broad-billed Flycatcher *Myiagra caledonica*

PLATE 15
Chestnut-breasted Mannikin *Lonchura castaneothorax*
Common Waxbill *Estrilda astrild*
Black-headed Mannikin *Lonchura malacca*
Red-throated Parrotfinch *Erythrura psittacea*
Royal Parrotfinch *Erythrura cyaneovirens*
Blue-faced Parrotfinch *Erythrura trichroa*
Redpoll *Carduelis flammea*
House Sparrow *Passer domesticus*

PLATE 16
Little Pied Cormorant *Phalacrocorax melanoleucos*
Eastern Reef Heron *Ardea sacra*
Pacific Black Duck *Anas superciliosa*
Common Waxbill *Estrilda astrild*

PLATE 17
Vanuatu Mountain Pigeon *Ducula bakeri*
White-throated Pigeon *Columba vitiensis*
Rufous-brown Pheasant-Dove *Macropygia mackinlayi*
Green-winged Ground Dove *Chalcophaps indica*
Santa Cruz Ground Dove *Gallicolumba sanctaecrucis*
Rainbow Lorikeet *Trichoglossus haematodus*

PLATE 18
White-collared Kingfisher *Halcyon chloris*
Vanuatu Kingfisher *Halcyon farquhari*
(H Schroeder-Born)

PLATE 19
Broad-billed Flycatcher *Myiagra caledonica*
Fantail Warbler *Gerygone flavolateralis*
Thicket Warbler *Cichlornis whitneyi*

PLATE 20
Vanuatu Mountain Honeyeater *Phylidonyris notabilis*
Vanuatu White-eye *Zosterops flavifrons*

PLATE 21
Buff-banded Rail *Gallirallus philippensis*

PLATE 22
Blue-faced Parrotfinch *Erythrura trichroa*
Royal Parrotfinch *Erythrura cyaneovirens*

PLATE 23
Mountain slopes covered with a mosaic of light forests and savannah
Mangroves in the Maskelyne Islands
(M Chambers)

PLATE 24
Evergreen tropical rainforest in the mountainous interior of Vanuatu

Black and white illustrations

Mount Tabwemasana, the highest peak in Vanuatu at 1879m   *Frontispiece*

Heinrich Bregulla with villagers at Nokovula   23

Fallen trees and almost impenetrable undergrowth   26

Evergreen upland forest rich in epiphytes and tree ferns   30

Erakor Island near Efate   33

Lowland forest cleared for agriculture   35

Coast of Efate with fringing reefs   40

Monument Rock (Etarik) in the Shepherd Islands   45

Beach at Malapoa Peninsula, Efate (Euan Macdonald)   46

Open parkland by the River Colle, Efate (Euan Macdonald)   50

View of Mount Kotamtam, tropical rainforest and cloud forest   51

Little Duck Lake, Efate, part of the proposed Nature Reserve   55

Laika Island, breeding grounds of the Wedge-tailed Shearwater   55

Wedge-tailed Shearwater with chick in a burrow on Laika Island   88

Audubon's Shearwater which breeds in the mountains of Vanuatu   91

White-tailed Tropicbird   107

Reef Heron chicks in their nest   112

Nest of the Swamp Harrier hidden in dense vegetation   126

Peregrine Falcon with a Rainbow Lorikeet   129

The chick of the Incubator Bird, independent on hatching   133

Nest of the Buff-banded Rail with black downy chicks   139

The Red-bellied Fruit Dove, primarily a forest bird   173

Interlocking twigs form the nest of the Red-bellied Fruit Dove   174

The endemic Vanuatu Fruit Dove feeding in a tall fig tree   176

Young Pacific Imperial Pigeon about to leave the nest   178

Green-winged Ground Dove which has benefited from agriculture   185

Nests of the White-bellied Swiftlet glued to a cave wall   204

White-collared Kingfisher chicks in their nesting burrow   210

Nest of the Island Thrush thickly covered with green moss   223

Deep, cup-shaped nest of the Golden Whistler with 2 eggs   228

The nest of the endemic Vanuatu Flycatcher   233

Two young Grey Fantails almost ready to fly   236

Silver-eared Honeyeater nest suspended from a forked branch   245

The neatly woven nest of the endemic Vanuatu White-eye   252

Erratum, p 55. Top picture has been printed upside down.

Foreword 1

It gives me great pleasure to write a foreword to this book. I have followed with interest since 1985 its progress towards publication, and I have been happy, especially while I was Minister of Education, and even now with the portfolio of Tourism, to be in a position to give the project my support and encouragement.

The person who first introduced me to the project of this book, BIRDS OF VANUATU, is Keith Woodward, a former political secretary with British National Service. I am grateful to him for the privilege of being associated with the development towards its publication. During his retirement Keith has maintained interest in getting the book published.

It was fortunate that the affection which our country and its wildlife inspired in Heinrich Bregulla led him to make Vanuatu his home for so many years, for we benefited much from his stay amongst us. Soon after the Vanuatu Cultural Centre was established, the young German ornithologist, as he then was, devoted immense care to collecting and mounting the numerous birds, bats and snakes now exhibited in the Museum. He became a member of the Cultural Centre Board, and was its adviser on all wildlife matters. Herr Bregulla has always been interested in conservation, and Vanuatu's law giving protection to many species of birds was based on his detailed recommendations.

Above all, however, we are indebted to the author for the dedication to our bird-life which has borne fruit in this book. There is no need for me to dwell on its merits; they have been highlighted by Professor Peters, and will be obvious to all who read it.

I hope many of our people will read this book because it was written specially for them. It is clear from the long list of villages and individual ni-Vanuatu thanked by Heinrich Bregulla for hospitality and assistance, that many people became interested in his field-work, and that it could hardly have been possible without their co-operation. He became keenly aware of the close relationship between most ni-Vanuatu and their rural environment. It is his great hope that his book will both deepen the interest in birds (and wildlife in general) amongst those of us who already realise their value and stimulate the interest of those who as yet may not, especially our young people.

Thus I feel it is very desirable that as many people as possible in Vanuatu should be able to read this book, and particularly that each of our schools should receive a copy. I extend my personal thanks to the German Government for the very large grant without which this book could not have been published.

HON. S J REGENVANU
Minister of Finance, Housing and Tourism, Port Vila, Vanuatu   July 1991

Foreword 2

It gives me great pleasure to introduce this new field guide, which is the first book dealing exclusively with the avifauna of Vanuatu. Ernst Mayr's valuable guide to the Birds of the South-West Pacific, covering also the islands of Vanuatu, was published in 1945. Since then many things have changed dramatically, and much new information has been accumulated. A great part of this was reflected in *The Field Guide to the Birds of Hawaii and the Tropical Pacific*, published in 1987 by Pratt, Bruner and Berrett. However, Vanuatu was not included. Thus this book fills the gap in the ornithological literature, and is most welcome.

When the author, Heinrich Lorenz Bregulla, left Berlin for the tropical Pacific in 1959, he intended to spend nine months there. In fact he stayed for more than 20 years, mostly in Vanuatu, from where he undertook expeditions to other parts of the vast Pacific area. Starting as a collector of animals for museums, he soon realised that the fauna and flora of the islands were highly vulnerable. Consequently, he made great efforts to promote the protection of their plants and animals, and this book is in part the result of these efforts. Bregulla is strongly convinced that protection measures can only be successful if they are accepted by the local people. Thus the main goal of this new field guide, which has been commendably supported by the Government of Germany, is to demonstrate to the people of Vanuatu the richness and beauty of their native bird-life. It is for this educational reason that the text of this book is more extensive than in most other field guides. It can be used outdoors as well as in schools or other educational establishments. Based as it is on first-hand information that is not readily available elsewhere, the value of this book can hardly be exaggerated, and it will be applauded, not only in Vanuatu, but – I am sure – by people interested in birds all over the world.

PROFESSOR DOCTOR D STEFAN PETERS
Department of Vertebrates – Ornithological Section
Senckenberg Museum of Natural History
Frankfurt-am-Main, Germany

TO MY MOTHER

Preface

The study of the distribution, ecology, and behaviour of birds embraces such a complex network of research that it is becoming increasingly difficult to compile comprehensive works of a national or continental avifauna. If the scope is restricted, the task becomes more practicable. This book provides a field guide and a summary of present knowledge about the lives of all the species inhabiting the islands and, as far as is known at present, the seas of Vanuatu. The knowledge of the resident sea birds and common passage migrants in Vanuatu seas is still incomplete and there is much to be learned about the rarer migrants and vagrants in this region.

The Vanuatu avifauna has received little attention, apart from taxonomy, although in the tropical southwest Pacific archipelagos east of New Caledonia, it is only exceeded in area and matched in number of bird species by Fiji. The results of ornithological field work up to 1937, including the work of the Whitney South Sea Expedition which toured the Pacific from 1921 to 1939, were summarised by Ernst Mayr in *Birds of the Southwest Pacific* (1945). Earlier technical papers by Mayr, who was for a time the curator of the Whitney-Rothschild Collection at the American Museum of Natural History, are fundamental to understanding the avifauna. Since 1944 further information on distribution, ecology and biology has been obtained, mainly by the author during more than a decade of residence from 1959, by Ziswiler during a brief visit in 1970 to Efate and Emae, by the Royal Society Expedition which in 1971 spent four months on six islands, and by Diamond in the course of five short stays on Efate and Santo between 1969 and 1976. More recently the work of Richard Pickering, for several years editor of *Naika*, the journal of the Vanuatu Natural Science Society, in studying birds and recording ornithological data has done much to promote interest in the study of the birds of Vanuatu.

Many of the aspects of Vanuatu ornithology are still in the formative stage and further research is required on a good number of species. For example, as records on the breeding season are fragmentary, and only those from Efate cover the complete annual cycle, conclusions drawn might be misleading. In tropical regions birds may be found breeding at all times of the year. For many species in Vanuatu seasonal breeding seems likely. It is important to appreciate, however, that in an archipelago extending from 13°S to 22°S the climate varies significantly from north to south. Therefore as more information becomes available it might be discovered that breeding data apply only to the northern or southern populations of a species. For most birds throughout the world the main factor which controls the timing of the breeding cycle is the availability of the food needed to raise the most young. In temperate zones, increasing day length is considered to be the other important factor but in Vanuatu, where the day length varies only by a small amount, this factor can be discounted and it is the seasonal pattern of rainfall which appears to be the controlling influence. The majority of the land birds in Vanuatu start breeding at the end of the dry season taking advantage of the new vegetation and the resulting increased abundance of insects, nectar, fruit and seeds.

Another problem in Vanuatu is that of nomenclature. The local vernacular or common names of most birds are confusing because of the abundance of alternative names for most species on many islands or even in different parts of the same island. Therefore with very few exceptions I have not given local names. However, for some birds the Bislama names are given beside the accepted English and French names, if they are used throughout the archipelago. Where there are adequate data for each bird the headings used are: Identification, Distribution and Status, Field Notes, Voice, Food, and Nest and Breeding. If there are conservation issues for a particular species, notes have been included with the status in Vanuatu. For non-breeding migratory species or vagrants the information is less detailed and is generally given under two headings, Identification and Field Notes which includes relevant notes about voice and food, and Distribution and Status. In addition there is a general introduction to each Order and Family. Where the birds are particularly interesting the preliminary remarks are more extensive and some problems affecting these birds and their conservation are also discussed. Although I have strived to make this book as complete and accurate as possible, I have no illusions as to its perfection. I request therefore all those who find errors, or obtain new records of species, distribution and breeding, or have made observations on behaviour to communicate this data to the Vanuatu Cultural Centre or the Vanuatu Natural Science Society, both at Port Vila.

The photographs, some of rarely observed species, have been selected to show diagnostic features and, where possible, some characteristic posture or behaviour pattern. Most of the colour plates are based on photographs of living birds. Mounted specimens from the Cultural Centre at Port Vila were used for some plates. In conjunction with the written descriptions these illustrations should enable observers to recognise most Vanuatu birds in the field if enough sightings are obtained.

Beyond that, I hope that this book will stimulate further research particularly on the life history of all the endemic species. Most birds have not been studied in detail apart from the Rainbow Lorikeet and the Parrotfinches. If the status of most Vanuatu birds is to be maintained or improved, in the face of coming human expansion, development and deforestation, proper management based on sound scientific data will be essential in the future. Above all I hope that this book will awake a desire to further the protection and conservation of the Vanuatu wildlife heritage. Even at the cost of leaving some swamps unused, some wilderness areas undeveloped and some remnants of forest unfelled, these riches should be preserved for the enjoyment and study of future generations.

Acknowledgements
I should like to take this opportunity of expressing my thanks to the following for their willing co-operation and assistance in the field. The late Mr Ali, Senior, Port Havannah, Efate; the people of South Ambrym; the people of Anelghowat Village, Aneityum; Henri Daval, formerly of Messrs. Burns Philp, Efate; the people of Emau; the late Gabriel Frouin, Vila; Roger Garrido, Efate; W Hamlyn-Harris, formerly of Undine Bay, Efate; the late Auguste Henin, Tukutuku, Efate; Leon Langlois, formerly of Public Works Department, Vila; R Legall, formerly of the Agricultural Department, Tagabe; the people of South Maewo; Pastor Mahlon, Vatoko; Chief Pita Poilapa and the people of Mele Village, Efate; The Catholic Mission, Montmartre, Efate; Jacques Nicholls, SIP, Efate; the people of Paunangisu Village, Efate; J Paul Prevot, Teouma, Efate; Ernie Reid, Vila; the people of Sesake Village, Emae; the people of Sivi Village, Tanna; Apio Harry Sunday and his family, Pele Village, Tongoa; Chief Tom Tipoloamata, Tongoa; the late Rene Valin, formerly Chief Veterinary Officer; the people of the Catholic Mission on Walla Island, Malekula.

I also wish to thank for much hospitality and advice: the late Mr Celloki, Sivi Village, Tanna; Andre Colardeau, Les Lagunes, Efate; the late Lucien Houdie, Savaroy, Efate; the late Pastor Jansen and all other members of the Presbyterian Mission on Tangoa Island, Santo; the late A Krafft, Anelghowat Village, Aneityum; the people of Lesereplag Village, Ureparapara, Banks; J Leaney, Assistant British District Agent, Santo; Caroline Nalo, Noumea, New Caledonia; the Anglican Mission Lolowai, Ambae; the late Mrs C McCoy, formerly of Ambrym; the people and the Presbyterian Mission on Malo; Daniel Milne and family, Rentapao, Efate; the people of Mota Lava, Banks; the late Oscar Newman, Tisman Bay, Malekula; the late Henri Ohlen and family, Devil's Point, Efate; Andre Rolland, formerly of Messrs Burns Philp, Efate; the people of Sola and Mosina, Vanua Lava, Banks; Tapankai Sope, formerly of the Condominium Medical Department; Mr Wuli and sons, Nokovula Village, Tabwemasana, Santo; the people of Vusi Village and Kerepua Village, West Coast of Santo; Darvell Wilkins, former British District Agent, Southern Districts and CD2.

For providing me with much valuable information and literature I wish to extend my thanks to Dr W R P Bourne, University of Aberdeen, Scotland; E H Bryan Jr, Pacific Scientific Information Centre, Hawaii; Jared M Diamond, California; Noel Gove, Melbourne, Australia; Warren B King, Smithsonian Institution, Washington DC; and Dr Adrian G Marshall, University of Aberdeen, Scotland. The Earl of Cranbrook – for his interest and encouragement; R D Chancellor, formerly Hon Secretary to the British Section of the ICBP – for advice and assistance; Martin Horrocks, of the Vanuatu Natural Science Society – for research and liaison work; J Graeme Robertson, for the invaluable service of finding me a publisher, for compiling the preliminary checklist, and supplying records and references; Claude Mitride, of Port-Vila – for letting me use his photographic laboratory, and for much other help and Mr Schmidt and J-M Veillon, of the Office de la Recherche Scientifique et Technique d'Outre-Mer, New Caledonia, for identifying samples of food plants.

My very particular thanks go to Reece Discombe, Member of the Cultural Centre Board, to R J Makin, Director of Media Services, Vanuatu, and to Euan Macdonald of the Vanuatu Natural Science Society, for their quite exceptional, and ever-willing practical support in many different ways; to Keith Woodward, for many years Secretary to the Cultural Centre Board, for his indispensable services and unfailing encouragement since this book was first conceived by us both, and to his wife Elizabeth for her wholehearted support; to Hilary Forster, who devoted her great talent, and many hours of painstaking work, to the painting of most of the colour plates, and to Ola Reeve whose rich artistic gifts are also represented.

I am grateful indeed to the ornithologist and author, Robin Woods, and to his wife Anne, for updating the records by extensive examination of the published material, and for their very understanding and helpful editing of my manuscript; it was both a pleasure and privilege to work with them. I also express my gratitude to Dr Marcus Chambers, environmental adviser to the Government of Vanuatu from 1986-89, for providing the comprehensive Introduction which sets the context in which Vanuatu's avifauna can be better appreciated.

Finally, I should like to thank my wife Jeannette, and my daughter Michele, for typing and retyping my various drafts, and for their unwavering support over many years.

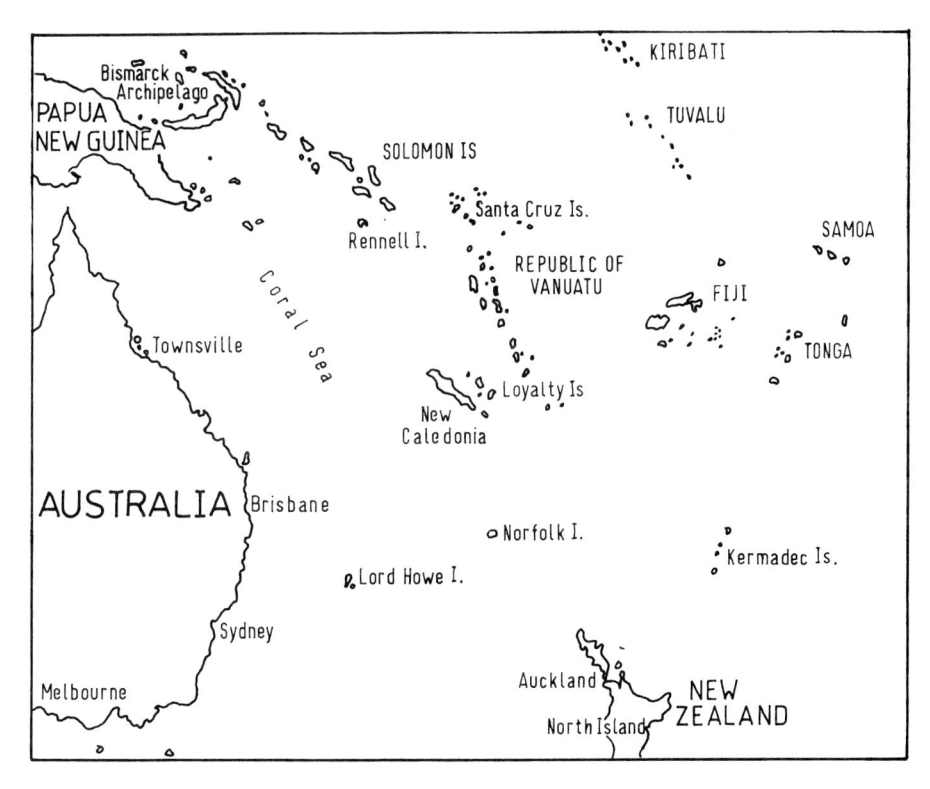

Southwest Pacific, showing location of Vanuatu

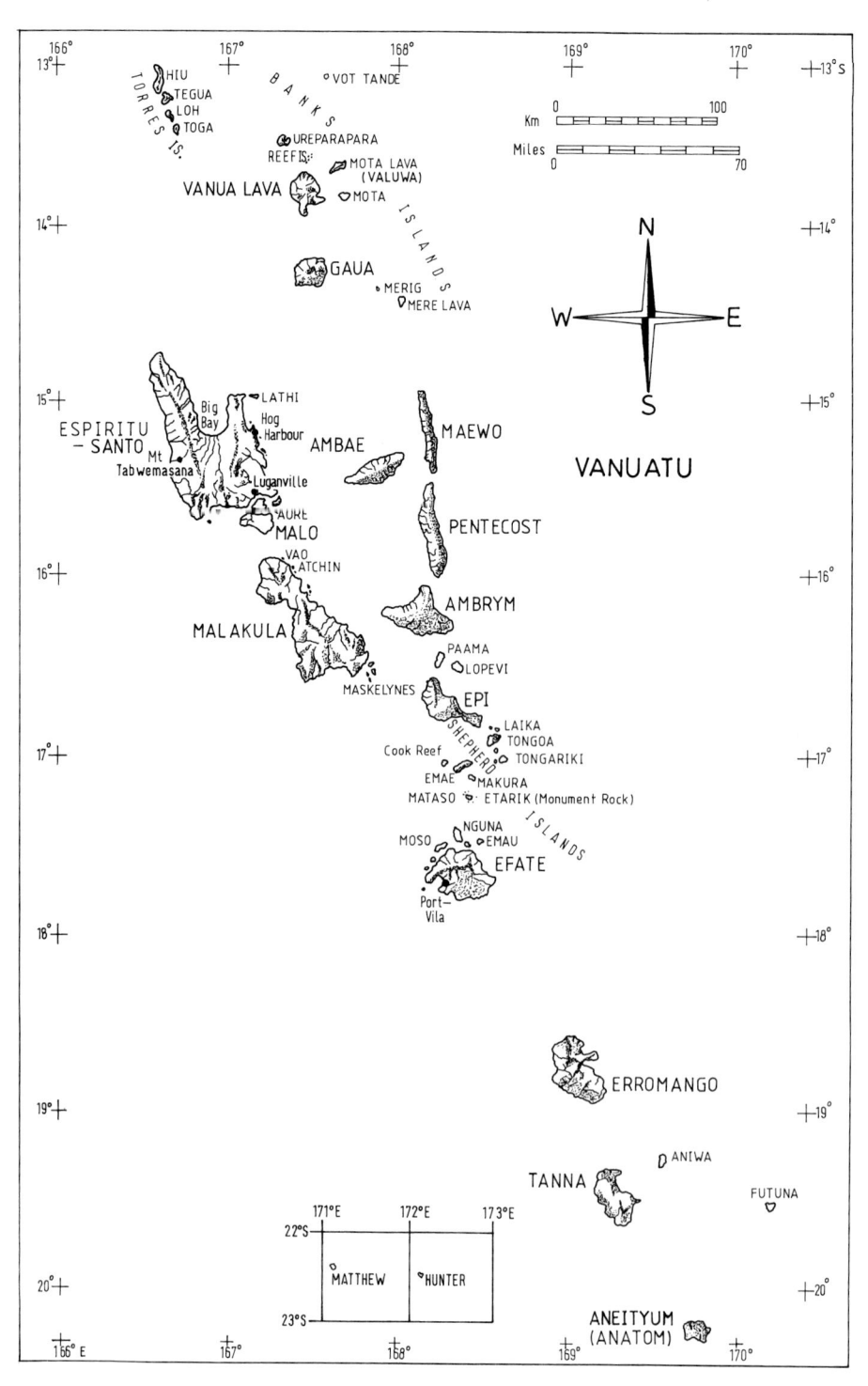

Vanuatu

Introduction *by Marcus Chambers*

Outside Vanuatu the islands and their people are little known. Even within the southwest Pacific region this is true and the further away one moves, the more the lack of knowledge is apparent. The islands were first discovered by Melanesian peoples at least 3,000 years ago at a time of great seafaring activity and exploration amongst Pacific islanders. Following initial and probably further settlements the Melanesians, together with small numbers of Polynesians, established themselves throughout the archipelago. On these rugged and isolated islands, subject to the violent forces of nature to a degree that few other places experience, an amazing variety of cultures proceeded to develop. This process continued uninterrupted until the first Europeans, led by the explorer de Queiros, landed at Big Bay, Santo, in 1606. He thought he had found the great southern continent Terra Australis, at that time unknown but which was believed to exist. Had he taken the trouble to explore further he could easily have sailed around the island and realised his error. This first European contact was not entirely successful from anyone's point of view and after a few weeks the expedition sailed away. The next major European contact was by the Frenchman, Louis de Bougainville, who mapped some of the northern islands in 1768. Captain James Cook was the first European to navigate and map the whole archipelago (except for the southernmost islands of Matthew and Hunter) in 1774 and he named them the New Hebrides. Following the discovery of sandalwood in 1825, traders, agriculturalists and missionaries settled the islands in increasing numbers. In 1906 the New Hebrides became a joint colony, a condominium, administered by both France and Great Britain. In 1980 independence was achieved under the name of Vanuatu.

The following chapters describe the natural environment of Vanuatu, its wildlife and conservation and, hopefully, set the context in which the nation's bird fauna can be described and appreciated.

Geography

Vanuatu ('Our Land') is a Y-shaped chain of about 100 ash and coral islands and islets situated between the Equator and the Tropic of Capricorn. They stretch from the sparsely inhabited raised reef terraces of the Torres Islands in the north to the remote, uninhabited and actively volcanic islands of Matthew and Hunter in the south, a total distance of about 1,100 km. The capital is Port Vila on the island of Efate and it is about 1,900 km northeast of Brisbane, Australia. The nearest surrounding countries are the Solomon Islands 400 km to the northwest, New Caledonia 400 km to the west and Fiji 800 km to the east.

The islands of Vanuatu are varied and differ enormously from one another in many ways. The largest is Santo with an area of 3,900 km² or 32% of the total land area of 12,190 km². Other major islands are Malakula, Efate, Erromango, Ambrym, Tanna, Epi, Pentecost, Ambae and Vanua Lava, which together make up 55% of the land. Most islands are mountainous and extremely rugged. The highest peak is Mount Tabwemasana on Santo (1,879 m). It has been climbed very few times, probably less than on ten occasions by foreigners at least. The largest 10 islands all rise to at least 647 m (Efate). Some of the smaller islands, for example, Lopevi, Mere Lava, Futuna and Mataso must be amongst the most mountainous, size for size, anywhere in the world. At the other extreme, some islands are of low altitude. The Reef Islands, sandy atolls perched in the middle of a large submerged reef, are only 2 m high whilst Aniwa, a raised limestone reef, is 42 m high.

Rivers in Vanuatu are short and usually fast flowing, often with little or no development of alluvial flood plains. The only extensive flood plain area in Vanuatu is formed by the rivers which drain the Mount Tabwemasana range and flow northeast into Big Bay. Swamp forests predominate here and the area is rich in bird life. Many rivers, for example the Teouma river on Efate and the Matenol of south Malakula, flow through spectacular and near-inaccessible gorges for much of their length. Some rivers, particularly in areas made up largely of raised reefs like east Santo, coastal Efate and the Torres Islands, flow only at times of heavy rain. Such areas have little or no surface water for all or much of the year as the rainfall percolates rapidly down through the porous rock.

There are about 25-30 freshwater lakes in Vanuatu. By far the largest and most impressive is Lake Letas on Gaua Island. This lake, 19 km² in area and 350 m deep, occupies the caldera of the active volcano Mount Garet. Excluding those in Papua New Guinea, New Zealand and Australia it is the largest, natural freshwater lake in the South Pacific. The caldera lakes of Ambae's active volcano Waivundolué, Manaro Lakua and Vui, are the highest in the South Pacific at over 1,300 m. Many freshwater lakes, however, are in coastal areas, for example Lake Otas on east Efate and Lakes Halékar and Haléwogh on Thion Island, northeast of Santo. There are also a number of brackish water and seawater lagoons in the coastal areas of some islands such as north Efate and south Santo and Lake Naléma on east Epi. The importance of Vanuatu's lakes and coastal lagoons to resident and migratory birds has yet to be evaluated.

The population of Vanuatu was estimated to be 140,154 in 1986. Most people live in small villages around the coastal areas of the 70 or so inhabited islands. The rural population, about 120,000, live in an estimated 790 villages with an average population of 152. The remainder live in the two urban centres of Port Vila on Efate and Luganville on Santo. The most populated island is Efate with more than 20,000 people, while the least inhabited is probably Metoma, in the Torres, with two people. The overall population density is very low, about 10 per square kilometre in rural areas. However, many small islands are more thickly populated. Kolivu in the Maskelynes has 500 per km², Vao has 758 per km² and Atchin 1,024 per km². Traditionally, many people have lived on small offshore islands as a defence against mosquitoes and marauding neighbours. On many of the larger islands such as Vanua Lava, Gaua, Santo, Ambrym, Epi, Efate, Erromango and Aneityum, the central areas are either completely uninhabited or only very sparsely populated. Thus the coastal

Heinrich Bregulla with villagers at Nokovula

areas in general are more densely populated than the national rural average. Among the larger islands, Tanna is the only one that is densely populated in the interior.

Archaeological evidence presently puts the arrival of humans in Vanuatu at about 3,000 years ago. In this time an enormous variety of cultures has developed, so much so that today 105 distinct languages are spoken in the islands, some by only a handful of people. This makes Vanuatu one of the most culturally complex and diverse countries in the world. During these few thousand years, human presence has had many effects on the natural environment. On birds however, the effect is probably small compared to many countries. No extinctions are known and no birds are believed to be endangered by human activities. There are ten introduced bird species but they are believed to have had little effect on either the indigenous birds or on other components of the fauna and flora. Little is known about the cultural importance of birds to the complex traditional societies of Vanuatu.

Geology

Vanuatu occurs in one of the geologically most active areas of the world, resulting in a complex and varied geological history. The archipelago is part of a continuous island arc system stretching from New Britain Island (Papua New Guinea) and the Solomon Islands to Vanuatu, Fiji and Tonga. Most of the islands are formed from the summit regions of mountain ranges which rise from the deep ocean floor. The whole region, particularly around Vanuatu, is an area of pronounced volcanic and earthquake activity, part of the so-called Pacific Rim of Fire. Vanuatu is situated on the western, leading edge of the Pacific tectonic plate, a huge portion of the earth's crust that is moving slowly westwards. This is located above the eastern, leading edge of the Australasian tectonic plate, another huge portion of the earth's crust that is moving eastwards and at the same time is being forced (subducted) below the Pacific plate. This subduction zone just to the west of Vanuatu, has formed a deep ocean trench, the New Hebrides Trench, which in places is more than 6,000 m deep. It is the collision of these two tectonic plates that has resulted in the formation of the Vanuatu archipelago and is responsible for the volcanic and earthquake activity of past and present times. Vanuatu has tens of thousands of earthquakes each year, which may be occasionally damaging to buildings and trigger many landslides on steep mountain slopes. The severest earthquakes in historical times occurred in south Vanuatu between 28-30 March 1875. Buildings were destroyed on Aneityum, a major harbour, Port Resolution, was blocked in Tanna and accompanying tsunamis (tidal waves) of 3-4 m height caused extensive damage. In more recent times the village of Marino on Maewo was destroyed by a 3-4 m tsunami in 1948. A severe earthquake is liable to occur at any time anywhere in Vanuatu.

The islands of Vanuatu are young in geological terms and their formation has occurred in four distinct phases of volcanic activity (Mallick, 1975). The first phase produced the Torres Islands, Santo and Malakula and the oldest rocks on these islands were formed 22 million years ago. The next oldest islands are Maewo and Pentecost, formed between four and eleven million years ago and then the smaller ones of Futuna and Mere Lava between two and five million years ago. All the remaining islands and island groups (the Banks, Ambae, Ambrym, Paama, Lopevi, Epi, the Shepherds, Efate, Erromango, Aniwa, Tanna, Aneityum, Matthew and Hunter) were formed between three million years ago and the present time.

Up until about two million years ago, most or all the islands were very much smaller and in total, they covered only about 5% (about 600 km^2) of their present area. In these last two million years a combination of continuing volcanic activity and gradual uplifting of the land with the emergence of fringing coral reefs has caused the increase and produced the present-day archipelago. These processes are continuing to the present time. Generally the more recently formed islands have few areas of raised reefs but Aniwa, Erromango and Efate are exceptions. On Efate for example, reefs have been uplifted at an average rate of one millimetre per year over the last 200,000 years, a rise of 200 m, and raised reefs cover about 60% of the island. On Pentecost raised reefs are found at 950 m. This lifting does not occur at an even, steady rate. It happens as a series of relatively rapid uplifts, followed by quiescent periods, which give rise to a series of stepped limestone cliffs that are easily discernible on many islands. Within recent years major uplifts of corals have been recorded on Malakula (60 cm during a 1965 earthquake), Santo (60 cm from 1945-80) and Ureparapara (20 cm in the last decade). Overall, about 20% of Vanuatu's land surface has developed in the last 200,000 years and 50% over the last 400,000 years, mainly due to the uplift of raised reefs which have formed a veneer over the underlying volcanic rocks. In contrast to the general trend some islands, like Ambrym, are slowly sinking into the Pacific Ocean.

New rocks and land are also being formed around the currently active volcanoes of Vanua Lava, Gaua, Ambae, Ambrym, Lopevi, Tanna, Matthew and Hunter. There were extensive new lava flows on Ambrym in 1988 and major eruptions of Lopevi in 1956 caused the permanent evacuation of the entire population. In addition there are several submarine volcanoes. One of these, Karua off east coast Epi, has emerged from the sea three times this century, in 1901, 1948 and 1959. On each occasion an ephemeral island was formed, the largest attaining a size of 1.5 km long by 100 m high before it was eroded away by the sea. There is little doubt that at some stage in the future new islands will be added to the archipelago. It is also possible that, in the near future, some islands will disappear by submersion or erosion if predictions of rising sea levels are borne out.

Present landscapes have been produced by weathering, the physical and chemical action of wind and rain leading to the erosion of the rocks. These processes are assisted by biological agents, chiefly the roots of trees burrowing into and fragmenting the underlying rocks. The products of weathering, either in solution or as particles are then carried away to the sea or river flood plains by flowing water. The raised reefs generally form terraces or gently sloping plateaux. The younger ones are little affected by erosion but the older ones are frequently dissected by steep ravines and gorges. In some areas the resultant landforms are all but impenetrable, like the so-called 'badlands' areas of Efate and Malakula. Badlands may also result from pronounced water erosion of thick ashfalls, downwind of the Ambrym volcano for example. Continued erosion of the older volcanic rocks has resulted in deep V-shaped valleys separated by sharp ridges as on Santo and Malakula. Landslides, often caused by earthquakes or heavy rain, are common in such areas and speed up the erosion of the land. By contrast, the more recent volcanic areas may be little eroded. Lopevi Island, for example, is a classic volcanic cone rising straight up out of the sea to a height of 1,413 m.

Climate

Vanuatu has a wet, tropical climate in the north gradually changing to sub-tropical in the south of the country and varying within an island according to altitude and exposure to the prevailing southeasterly winds. Dominating the general and often benign climate is the annual occurrence of tropical cyclones or hurricanes, often extremely damaging.

The north of Vanuatu is both wetter and warmer than the south. The mean (30-year averages) annual rainfall at east Vanua Lava, Port Vila and south Aneityum is 4,210, 2,270, and 2,155 mm respectively (approximately 170, 90 and 86 in). The mean annual maximum temperature at the same meteorological stations is 29.2°C, 28.7°C and 27.1°C whilst the minimum is 23.3°C, 21.6°C and 20.5°C. The climate in the northern islands is also less seasonal than in the south. Thus at Vanua Lava, the rainfall in the wettest month is twice that in the driest month whilst in Aneityum it is nearly 5 times greater. There is little variation in the mean monthly temperatures throughout the year in northern Vanuatu but in the south the winter months are decidedly cooler than the summer months. Excessive temperatures have never been recorded in Vanuatu due to the ameliorating presence of the sea. The maximum temperature ever recorded is only 35°C. Rainfall however may be very high on occasions and 250 mm (10 in) was recorded in a 3-hour period at south Efate on 1 August 1988. The island's main bridge was swept away by the resulting flood.

With regard to climatic differences within a single island, the lowland, southeast, windward sides of large islands are invariably wetter than the leeward sides. Thus island areas exposed to the prevailing southeasterlies have rainfall figures varying from

Fallen trees and almost impenetrable undergrowth on the slopes of Mount Tabwemasana

about 2,000 mm (80 in) per year in the south to about 4,200 mm (170 in) in the north of the country. On the northwest, leeward slopes however, in the rain-shadow of the high, central mountains, rainfall is generally less than 2,000 mm (80 in), considerably so in the south. Additionally such sheltered areas often have a distinct dry season of two or more months in the winter season, whereas this is not generally so in exposed areas. At higher altitudes climatic data are generally lacking in Vanuatu. However, above about 500 m in the south and 300 m in the north, the climate is predominantly misty and highly humid for much of the time. Rainfall is probably well in excess of 5,000 mm (200 in) per year, certainly in the north, and with little or no seasonality. This high rainfall is orographic, resulting from the expansion and cooling of moist air, with subsequent precipitation, as it rises up the mountain slopes. Frosts probably occur at the highest altitudes. In general for every 100 m increase in altitude a 1°C decrease in temperature will occur.

Cyclones are the greatest of the natural hazards that affect Vanuatu. They have been responsible for much death, destruction and damage. They occur regularly at any time from November to April, with an average frequency of 2.6 per year over the last 40 years. It is chiefly the high winds associated with the areas close to the eye of the cyclone that cause the damage. On average, any particular area of Vanuatu is struck full-force once in about every 30 years. At such times damage to forests, buildings, crops and coral reefs is enormous. In between such disasters, all areas are affected each year by the stormy outer edges of cyclones. The heavy rainfall that is always associated with cyclones may in itself cause damage through flooding, by triggering landslides on steep slopes or pulverising crops. There is no doubt that cyclones, with the enormous economic damage and diversion of scarce workforce resources that they entail, have hindered the development of Vanuatu. If the recent predictions of increased cyclone frequency and intensity due to global warming are borne out, this will surely have serious consequences for Vanuatu.

Table I. The islands of Vanuatu

Islands marked * were uninhabited during the 1979 national census. Some small islets, habited and uninhabited are not included. Islands are listed in order of increasing latitude, that is from north to south.

ISLAND	AREA (KM^2)	HIGHEST POINT (M)	
Torres islands			
Hiu	50	366	Mt Wonvarra
Metoma	3	115	
Tegua	31	240	Mt Repugura
Linua*	4	8	
Loh	13	155	
Toga	19	240	Mt Lemeura
Banks islands			
Vot Tande*	<1	64	
Ureparapara	39	764	Mt Tow Lap
Reef Islands*	≃1	2	
Mota Lava (Valua)	31	411	Mt Wungol
Ra	<1	<40	
Vanua Lava	331	946	Mt Tow Lava
Ravenga*	<1	15	
Mota	15	411	Mt Tawe
Kwakea	<2	7	
Nawila*	<1	<40	
Gaua (Santa Maria)	310	797	Mt Garet
Merig	<1	120	
Mere Lava (Star Peak)	15	883	Mt Teu
Santo and offshore islands			
Santo	3900	1879	Mt Tabwemasana
Lathi	≃11	109	
Thion*	≃3	190	
Lathu	≃2	177	
Lataro	≃3	97	
Lataroa	≃2	68	
Mavea	≃4	48	
Aese	≃10	19	
Aore	60	99	
Tutuba	14	36	
Bokissa	<1	5	
Tangoa	<1	<40	
Urelapa	<1	5	
Araki	≃3	227	
Malo	180	326	
Malokilikili	≃2	2	

Maewo (Aurora)	270	811	Mt Tavut Gagaro
Ambae (Aoba)	400	1496	Mt Waivundolué
Pentecost	439	946	Mt Vulmat
Malakula and offshore islands			
Malakula	2030	879	Mt Penot
Vao	≃1	<20	
Atchin	≃1	23	
Wala	≃1	26	
Rano	≃2	24	
Norsup	<1	44	
Uripiv	≃1	38	
Uri	≃2	<20	
Maskelyne islands	≃10	102	
Arseo	<1	<20	
Akhamb	≃1	30	
Tomman	≃3	84	
Ambrym	665	1270	Mt Marum
Paama	33	544	Venhuovae
Lopevi*	30	1413	
Epi and offshore islands			
Epi	445	833	Mt Pomare
Lamen	≃1	<40	
Namuka*	<1	184	
Shepherd islands			
Laika*	<1	87	
Tongoa	42	487	Tafa ni Urata
Ewose*	≃1	319	
Falea	<1	100	
Tongariki	6	521	Mele In
Buninga	1.5	216	
Emae	33	644	Maunga Lasi
Makura	1.7	297	
Mataso	1	494	
Efate and offshore islands			
Efate	915	647	Mt MacDonald
Nguna	25	593	
Emau	8	448	
Pele	5	198	
Moso	25	116	
Lelepa	8	202	
Eretoka	≃1	90	
Iririki	<1	40	
Ifira	<1	20	

Erakor	<1	<20	
Eratap*	<1	<20	
Erueti*	<1	<20	
Erromango	900	886	Mt Santop
Aniwa	8	42	
Tanna	572	1084	Mt Toukosmereu
Futuna	11	666	Mt Tatafu
Aneityum and offshore island			
Aneityum	160	859	Mt Inrera
Inyeug*	<1	<20	
Matthew	<1	177	
Hunter	<1	260	

Flora

The characteristic vegetation of Vanuatu is evergreen rainforest which covers about 75% of the country. All the typical rainforest plants (large buttressed trees, shrubs, herbs, climbers, stranglers, epiphytes and saprophytes) are present. Most of the species are the same or similar to those which occur in the rainforests of south and southeast Asia and New Guinea. There are fewer species in Vanuatu however than in these other regions: due to the isolation and youth of the islands it has been difficult for plants to get to Vanuatu (Chew, 1975). Thus in Vanuatu there are about 900 species of flowering plants. This is much less than in neighbouring areas like Fiji (1,600 species in 18,000 km^2) and New Caledonia (3,100 species in 24,000 km^2). Most plant species in Vanuatu have probably arrived by way of Fiji, as their floras more closely resemble each other. In earlier times Vanuatu was much closer to Fiji. Movements of the earth's crust have in the past carried Vanuatu westwards away from Fiji and in fact are still doing so at the rate of about 10 cm per year.

There are comparatively few endemic plant species, about 135 or 15% of the plants in Vanuatu. There are no endemic families or genera. This proportion is much lower than in neighbouring island groups which again, illustrates the youth of the islands: there has been little time for speciation to occur. The highest proportion of endemics occurs in the orchid family, where about 40 species out of 90 are found only in Vanuatu. Undoubtedly more endemic species are awaiting discovery: botanical expeditions to Santo and Ambae in 1988 discovered six and one new species of orchid, respectively from these islands. The fern flora of Vanuatu, unlike the flowering plants, is comparatively rich compared to neighbouring islands. About 250 species are known, of which 11 are endemic, a rather low proportion (Braithwaite, 1975). There has been little study of the mosses and lichens of the islands.

Within the islands, the composition of the vegetation depends on a number of factors: situation on the windward or leeward slopes, altitude, climate, geology, topography, soils and the effect of human activity. With respect to situation, on the larger mountainous islands at least, three major categories of vegetation can be readily recognised. These are:

The evergreen upland forests on the slopes of Mount Tabwemasana; here the cooler, wetter climate results in forests of smaller trees rich in epiphytes and tree ferns

(1) the evergreen tropical rainforests of the lowland, warm, wet, windward slopes

(2) the semi-deciduous forests and fire-induced savannahs and grasslands of the lowland, warm, drier, leeward slopes

(3) the evergreen forests of upland and summit areas where the cooler, wetter and more humid climate results in a forest of smaller trees rich in epiphytes such as orchids, ferns, mosses, lichens and clubmosses.

On Efate, the characteristics of these three areas are as follows (Quantin, 1977). On lowland leeward slopes there are extensive areas of savannah and open woodland, dominated by *Acacia, Leucaena glauca, Psidium goyava* and *Lantana camara*. Common grasses include *Imperata cylindrica*, and *Paspalum orbiculare*, with *Themeda* on other islands such as Malakula and Santo. These communities probably developed through human activity, clearing and burning the land, readily feasible only in such leeward areas with a dry season. Occasional burning is probably required to prevent them from reverting to a more closed forest. On lowland, windward slopes a much richer evergreen forest prevails. The canopy layer, up to 30 m high, is dominated by *Antiaris toxicaria*, frequently associated with *Laportea, Pangium* and *Kleinhovia*. Beneath this top layer is an understorey layer and below this a shrub layer. Throughout the forest climbing lianes are abundant, and tall (up to 40 m) large-crowned banyan trees (*Ficus*) occur regularly. At altitudes above 300-400 m, species composition changes and the trees become smaller, with a canopy height from 15-20 m or less on exposed ridges and summits. At these altitudes the trees are characterised by broad, short trunks with large, tufted and bushy canopies, for example, *Metrosideros*, and narrow leaves and stilted roots, for example, *Myristica inutilis*. The commonest canopy trees at these higher altitudes are *Elaeocarpus, Thieogomapanax, Hernandia, Ficus* and *Calophyllum*. Beneath this canopy is an understorey of smaller trees including *Pandanas* (the screw palm) and *Cyathea* and *Dicksonia* (tree ferns). The latter may be very common especially on steep slopes. The ground layer of the montane forest consists mainly of a dense carpet of ferns and clubmosses. The trunks and branches of all trees are densely clothed in a variety of epiphytes, particularly mosses, lichens, ferns and orchids. The highest areas, above 500-600 m are generally too cold and wet for human habitation and the soils too poor for agriculture. Consequently the vegetation and its associated fauna are little disturbed.

A further differentiation of the flora is that between the northern and southern islands of the archipelago. This is chiefly related to climatic differences and expresses itself as different frequencies of some species and the occurrence at higher altitudes in the north of species found at lower altitudes in the south. Thus some species such as *Myristica fatua* and *Veitchia joannis* are common in the northern islands but are rare in the south. Conversely some species, *Calophyllum neo-ebudicum* and *Serianthes melanesica* for example, are common in the south but are rare in the north. Concerning altitude, species such as *Metrosideros* and *Weinmannia* are abundant at heights of 500-700 m in the south but are uncommon below 1,200 m in the north. Similarly, epiphytic orchids are much commoner at lower altitudes in the south than the north. Such differences are undoubtedly due to the cooler climate in the south.

In Vanuatu, the forest canopy is usually at a lower height and more open than in other rainforest regions. This is due to cyclone damage. Large tracts of the forest can be almost completely flattened by strong winds as the centre of the cyclone passes over them. On average this occurs about every 30 years in any one locality. There is insufficient time, between successive flattenings, for a full-sized, mature forest to develop. Consequently Vanuatu's forests are generally sub-climax and successional in nature. This cycle of forest destruction and regrowth must affect the bird population, both by killing birds during cyclone passage and by producing a mosaic of different-aged forest communities, with associated bird communities, over any given large area. Some forest trees however are noticeably resistant to cyclone damage. The best known of these is the kauri *Agathis macrophylla* which occurs on Aneityum, Erromango and Santo. Very large and old specimens of this tree, often with a trunk diameter of 3 m, can be found on these islands. A particularly severe cyclone swept over Erromango in February 1987, destroying great swathes of forest. Only the kauri trees survived intact.

Mangroves form the main wetlands vegetation in Vanuatu. In total, they cover an estimated 25-35 km^2, some 0.2-0.3% of the land area. The main mangrove forests are in Hiu (Torres Islands), Ureparapara, Mota Lava, Vanua Lava, Pentecost, Malakula, Epi, Emae, Efate and Aniwa. By far the most extensive (19 km^2) occur around the Port Stanley and Crab Bay areas of east coast Malakula and the southeast coasts of Malakula and the neighbouring Maskelyne Islands. The dominant species are *Rhizophora stylosa* and *Ceriops tagal*, but the mangroves of Vanuatu contain few species with poorly developed zonation patterns compared to the forests of southern Asia and New Guinea. Additionally many of the forests are rather scrubby in nature with little development of tall trees. On other islands mangroves are either absent from much of the coast or occur only as a narrow belt. The mangrove forests do not support any bird species that does not also occur in terrestrial habitats and support fewer species than are found in such areas. Seagrasses occur on shores and the shallow sublittoral (rarely more than 2 m deep) throughout the archipelago. In some places, for example, Ureparapara, east and southeast Malakula and the Maskelynes, north Efate and Moso, there are extensive and dense intertidal beds with comparatively rich invertebrate fauna which may provide important feeding areas for shore birds. Generally though, Vanuatu's coasts are inhospitable places for mangroves and seagrasses, being too rocky and/or exposed. Terrestrial swamp forests or marshes are generally small and few in number. They occur as fringing areas around lakes as on Efate and Thion Island (northeast Santo), in depressions on plateaux as on Gaua, Maewo, Epi and Efate, in extinct volcanoes like Vanua Lava or on major flood plains like that of the Jordan River on Santo. The importance of such swamp lands for birds should not be underestimated though detailed work on bird populations has yet to be done.

Fauna

Just as so much of the flora of Vanuatu is species-poor, so are the components of the terrestrial fauna and for the same reasons, the isolation and youth of the islands. It has been difficult for many animals to reach Vanuatu and little time for this to be achieved. Many groups of animals therefore, particularly terrestrial vertebrates, have few species compared to the older, neighbouring islands of Fiji, the Solomons and New Caledonia. Some groups found in those countries are completely absent from Vanuatu, for example, amphibians although there are two introduced species.

The only naturally occurring mammals in Vanuatu are bats (Medway and Marshall, 1975). There are 12 species comprising four flying-foxes (fruit bats) and eight small insectivorous species. Only one species, the white flying-fox *Pteropus anetianus*, is endemic. In addition to feral domestic animals (cattle, horses, pigs, goats and cats) the only other mammals are three species of rats and the house mouse *Mus musculus*, all introduced at one time or another. There are only two species of snake, neither of which is poisonous, the naturally occurring Pacific boa *Candoia bibroni* and a small

Erakor Island near Efate

introduced burrowing snake. There are 19 species of lizard, mostly belonging to the skink (13) or gecko (5) families. Of these, only three skinks are endemic whilst several gecko species have probably been introduced during early human colonisation. An iguanid lizard has been accidentally introduced recently. One of the geckos is especially interesting; the southwest Pacific bent-toed gecko *Nactus arnouxii* is found equally as males and females in the north of the country, but south of Efate it occurs mainly as only females which reproduce parthenogenetically. Vanuatu is fortunate that it has escaped some of the harmful vertebrate introductions like the mongoose, introduced throughout much of the Pacific and causing tremendous damage to birds and other fauna. Rats however may cause considerable damage to nesting birds and to coconuts and other crops.

The terrestrial invertebrates, in contrast to vertebrates and land plants, are well represented when compared to neighbouring countries (Gross, 1975). Additionally their proportions of endemic species are often, though not always, high. The numbers of species in selected groups, with the percentage of endemics are:

22 earthworms, 50%; 12 termites, 42%; 16 earwigs, 31%; 124 bugs, 35%;
64 butterflies, 6% and 73 land snails, 78%.

Most invertebrate species appear to have migrated from east Asia and New Guinea by way of the Solomon Islands. Perhaps the invertebrates, more easily dispersed by wind, on floating logs and trees and by birds, arrived early on in the development of the islands and have been able to diversify into many new species during this time.

Much of the coastline of Vanuatu is ringed by a narrow, fringing coral reef rarely more than 200m wide and beyond the edge of the reef there is a sharp drop to great depths. Shores are generally steep and rocky with few beaches. Within the narrow fringing reef there is a very rich marine fauna. A total of 295 stony coral species are known and 469 species of reef fish. Two interesting components of the marine fauna are the dugong *Dugong dugon* and the estuarine crocodile *Crocodylus porosus*. For both of these species, Vanuatu is the easternmost limit of their extensive distribution along tropical coastlines and islands. The dugong occurs throughout the archipelago, but only one breeding population of the crocodile is known from eastern Vanua Lava. There are few records of the crocodile attacking humans, but dogs and cattle are not so fortunate. Recent studies have shown that very few crocodiles remain and breeding has apparently ceased. This decline appears to have been caused by mortality from cyclones and hunting. The crocodile may be on the verge of extinction from Vanuatu (Chambers and Esrom, in press). Little is known about turtles in the country, although the green turtle *Chelonia mydas*, hawksbill *Eretmochelys imbricata*, loggerhead *Caretta caretta* and leatherback *Dermochelys olivacea* all occur and nest in the islands. There are few large sandy beaches however, so breeding populations may be small. The coconut (or robber) crab *Birgus latro* is common in some parts of Vanuatu, noticeably the Torres Islands and the east coast of Santo. It can live for more than 50 years and grows up to one metre in size (leg span). This culinary delicacy, the world's largest land crab (although the initial larval stages take place in sea water), has been decimated or eliminated from many areas throughout its widespread tropical distribution, including other Pacific islands. Its name derives from its liking for, and ability to open, coconuts. However, as the latter process takes a large crab three weeks to accomplish, it is not a serious economic liability. The freshwater fauna of Vanuatu has been little studied and is virtually unknown.

Agriculture and forestry resources

Agriculture is the mainstay of Vanuatu. About 90% of the population live in the rural areas and most of them are engaged in subsistence farming. There is also some commercial farming with plantations, mainly of coconuts. In total, these two sectors provide 95%, by value, of Vanuatu's export revenue. The fact that most of the population provides all or most of its own food, considerably reducing import costs, means that agriculture is of tremendous economic significance. By comparison, forestry is of lesser importance, but it is still a major concern.

Vanuatu is fortunate in having large amounts of fertile land, for its dependence on agriculture (Quantin, 1977). There are 4,970 km^2 of land classified as of average to optimum agricultural capability, some 41% of the total land area. These are soils requiring little or no fertilisation and with minimal erosion risk. With fertilisation and erosion control measures, more land could be used if need be. The best agricultural land, however, is not evenly spread around the islands. Aneityum and Ambrym have only 10% and 20% respectively of good arable land whilst Torres and Efate have 81% and 65%. Most of this good land is in lowland, coastal areas, often on the raised limestone terraces. These extensive areas have long acted as collecting pans for the volcanic ashes emitted from the country's active volcanoes and consequently the soils are very fertile. The soils are also young, again enhancing their fertility. At the present time, due to the low, rural population density, only about 2,200 km^2 (44%) of the best potentially cultivable land is used. Generally, land shortage is not a major issue in Vanuatu, though it is becoming a problem in some more crowded islands.

Along the coasts of many islands the lowland forest has been extensively cleared for agriculture

The main crop grown by subsistence farmers are food crops such as taro, yam, cassava (manioc) and kumala (sweet potato). These are supplemented by a number of leafy green vegetables. Typically, all crops are grown in a garden cut from the nearby forest and used for one or two years before soil fertility declines and yields decrease. The land is then left fallow for about 15 years and a new garden is created in the forest. Crops are often grown in rotation in the garden, thereby increasing its period of usefulness and decreasing the chance of pest or disease in any one crop. The average garden size in Vanuatu is 0.22 ha (0.6 acres); with a range from 0.14 to 0.38 ha. Thus with a fallow period of 15 years, the average household will garden regularly on about 3.3 ha. In total, about 1,150 km^2 are used for subsistence agriculture. In some of the smaller and more crowded islands, for example Paama, population pressures have reduced the fallow period to two or three years. Most subsistence farmers supplement their gardening activities with hunting and gathering. Pigs, fruit bats and birds are hunted in the forest and fish, turtles, molluscs and crustaceans are collected from rivers and reefs. The coconut crab is also collected from those forested areas where it occurs. Forest plants are extensively gathered and used for building materials, boats, clothing, medicine, food, weapons, ceremonial items and cultural artefacts. The forest, in particular, with it numerous resources, is the great provider for most of the population. Most of these farmers also grow crops for sale including coconuts (copra), coffee, and kava from which an intoxicating liquor is made. They also keep cattle for their own use and for sale. Around the urban areas of Port Vila and Luganville such cash-cropping activities are more important than in rural areas.

The commercial agricultural sector, has been operating in Vanuatu for over 100 years. Perennial crops such as coconut, coffee and cocoa cover about 660 km^2 (13.3%) of the best cultivable land and coconut (650 km^2) is by far the most important. Cattle ranches, with mainly beef herds, occupy about 380 km² of pasture, of which about 100 km² are also under coconut. The national herd is about 110,000 head of cattle and 73,000 pigs. Most of the latter are kept, mainly for their cultural importance, by subsistence farmers. To obtain the best beef yields the pastures have to be improved by the planting of exotic grass species and legumes. At the present time the plantation sector is being encouraged by the government to diversify and expand and large new plantations of cocoa on Malakula and coffee on Tanna have recently started. Tea is being grown on an experimental basis on Efate. Between 1981 and 1986, copra exports varied from 34,000 to 48,000 tonnes per year, cocoa from 500 to 1,300 tonnes and coffee from 50 to 60 tonnes.

The commercial forestry resources of Vanuatu are not well known at the present time. A major economic inventory of these resources is due for completion by 1991 and will provide a good data base for their rational exploitation. Inventories carried out to date in better areas of forest give estimates of 15-25 m³ of useful timber per hectare, not high values. The overall value of forest resources is limited by a number of factors: large areas of land that are too steep for logging; few commercial species; small tree size and timber volume; cyclone damage and shifting cultivation. In addition the isolation of the islands and the frequently rough terrain makes commercial exploitation expensive. The main commercial species are kauri *Agathis macrophylla*, milktree *Antiaris toxicara*, blackbean *Castanospermum australe*, whitewood *Endospermum medullosum* and natora *Intsia bijuga*.

It is currently estimated that sufficient exploitable natural forest exists to supply domestic demand for at least 20 years. In addition to natural forests, a number of plantations have been established in past years to supply local demand and for export. These plantations total about 2,200 ha and consist of the hardwood *Cordia alliodora* and the softwood *Pinus caribaea*. New plantations of several thousand hectares are planned for Santo and should help to take the pressure off the natural forests. Between 1980 and 1986, some 119,000 m³ of timber were harvested in commercial operations, and an unknown amount for use in the subsistence sector. About half of the commercially cut timber was exported and the rest was used to supply the domestic market.

Wildlife conservation

Although Vanuatu consists of many beautiful islands, it is not quite the paradise described in the travel brochures. For certain, there are spectacular beaches lined with reclining palm trees and washed by warm seas in which abound multitudes of colourful fish playing amongst coral gardens and reefs. There are lofty, misty mountains and smoking volcanoes clothed with dense forests that support interesting and varied wildlife. There are sparkling rivers and deep lakes all pretty much in a natural and pristine condition. But this arcadia is under constant threat, most immediately from natural disasters and in the long term from human intervention.

The most serious and regular threat of destruction is from cyclones. Storm damage to buildings, forests, reefs and crops is frequently total. Buildings can be built quickly and for free from forest materials, at least in rural areas. Destruction of food gardens means hard times for rural people and their cash crops are also lost. In the past, cyclones have caused the complete destruction and subsequent abandonment of villages on small islands such as the Reef Islands (Banks) and Eratap and Mele Islands around Efate. Destruction of the forest causes loss of timber and subsistence resources. The forest reverts to an early stage of succession, becoming weedy, scrubby, vine-entangled and virtually impenetrable for years. The heavy rains from cyclones, and at other times too, pulverise crops and lead to substantial losses. These same rains cause massive erosion on unprotected soils, a danger with excessive forest clearance.

Volcanoes are also a constant threat. Eruptions and lava flows on Lopevi in 1956 led to the evacuation of the island. Major emissions of smoke and ash from Mt Yasur on Tanna in 1987-88 caused acid rainfall over large regions downwind of the volcano with the subsequent death of considerable areas of forest and food gardens. Six thousand people had their livelihood destroyed and the government considered evacuating them to another island. All the people at present living around Vanuatu's eight active volcanoes are at some peril from catastrophic eruptions.

A serious earthquake can happen at any time and place in Vanuatu. Considerable structural damage would occur only in urban areas, for traditional rural buildings can better withstand such forces. Landslides, associated with earthquakes, cause most problems in the rural areas removing gardens and houses from steep slopes to the valleys below. The hillsides of Vanuatu are scarred from the earthslips of the past. Earthquakes also cause upliftings of the ground and in Malakula this is leading to the slow death of large tracts of mangrove forests. The trees, very sensitive to their position on the shore, have been lifted out of the tidal regime needed to complete their life cycle and no young trees are replacing those that die.

Despite the heavy rainfall, large scale flooding is not a major problem. River floodplains are usually narrow and villages are not generally built in vulnerable areas. Rather perversely, water shortages can cause serious problems on occasion. In many areas there is little or no surface water and during periods of drought, especially in limestone areas, the wells, boreholes and springs dry up. At such times water has to be brought in by boat or road to the affected villages.

Agricultural impacts of both the subsistence and commercial sectors are not generally severe as there is currently a surplus of land. Clearly however, such activities are damaging to the natural environment. Large plantations involve the complete removal of the natural forest and subsistence gardening to its major alteration, though forest is still retained in most instances. Over the coming years however, with an increasing population and encouragement of the plantation sector, pressure on land and increasing land degradation will occur. On some small islands virtually all the natural vegetation has gone and even on some of the larger, more densely populated islands like Paama, most of the good land has already been converted to subsistence agriculture. In some areas soil erosion is already a problem and instances can be expected to become more common in the coming years. Perhaps in 50-100 years much or all of the good lowland farming land will be in use. This will inevitably lead to the loss or modification of natural flora and fauna. The use of these lowland areas for agriculture cannot, and should not, be stopped. However, it must be planned to proceed in ways in which the soil, flora, fauna and water resources are utilised with maximum efficiency and degradation is kept to a minimum. The dependence of all the people in Vanuatu on their natural resource base is so complete that its loss or severe degradation would lead to an unacceptably poor quality of life. This dependence will remain for the foreseeable future.

The exploitation of forest timber resources has been rather wasteful and unplanned until recent times. Two species, the kauri *Agathis macrophylla* and sandalwood *Santalum austrocaledonicum* have particularly suffered. The kauri, occurring only on Aneityum, Erromango and Santo, has been badly exploited in the past. Stocks on Aneityum are virtually extinct and logging has taken place in Erromango but there are plans to establish a kauri reserve. On Santo the kauri is sparsely distributed in rough terrain and this may ensure its survival. Sandalwood was first discovered in Erromango in 1825 (it appears to be absent or sparse on other islands), and this led to its exploitation. Well before the end of the 19th century the stock was virtually eliminated, and the efforts of a missionary to establish a reserve were not successful. After this rapid depletion, sandalwood trading continued at a low level until 1987, when a 5-year moratorium on exports commenced. Hopefully, this will enable stocks to recover and studies to be made that will ensure a form of rational and sustainable exploitation in the future. Logging for other species has generally been carried out at a fairly low level on a few islands chiefly Hiu, Santo, Malakula, Efate and Tanna. Logging is selective with a few species above a minimum girth size being taken. Plans have recently been announced for large-scale logging on Malakula which could cause extensive environmental damage to the forest resource, soil and neighbouring rivers and reefs. At the present time, kauri and sandalwood apart, most of the forests in Vanuatu are generally in good condition. Due to cyclone damage however, all forests are rather poor in stature compared to those in other tropical regions.

In coming years the lowland natural forests will decrease in size as the land is taken over for agriculture, building, roads and commercial forest plantations. One result of the forest resource inventory should be to identify good lowland forest areas for protection from all but minor developments and activities. The upland and cloud forests of the islands above about 500m will probably escape major degradation and their flora and fauna survive more or less intact. Below these altitudes, initially in areas of fertile soils, major changes involving significant reductions in natural vegetation and perhaps some species loss can be expected.

The need to conserve and rationally exploit Vanuatu's resource base is recognised in the Constitution: *'Every person has the fundamental duty to himself and his descendants and to others to protect Vanuatu and to safeguard the national wealth, resources and environment in the interests of the present generation and of future generations'*.

This constitutional requirement is echoed in one of the objectives of the current 5-year development plan: *'to ensure that Vanuatu's unique environmental and cultural heritage is not damaged in the process of economic development and change'*.

Realistically, some damage must occur but hopefully the damage will be at a level acceptable to all and this is indeed the stated objective of resource management and development agencies within the government.

Vanuatu at present has an inadequate set of environmental laws to assist with the constitutional directive. Many birds are protected from hunting, egg collecting, sale and export. However the law is not widely regarded and although there is little sale and no export of birds, hunting and egg collecting continue in many rural areas. There is no recent information on how or which bird populations are affected, but on most islands it is necessary to go away from the villages and some distance into the forest before many birds appear or become abundant. Many marine species are protected by law: all marine mammals are totally protected; explosives and poisons cannot be used to capture fish; it is illegal to take turtle eggs or to sell or purchase the hawksbill turtle shell *Eretmochelys imbricata*; removal of living coral is restricted; rock lobsters *Panulirus*, slipper lobsters *Parribacus caledonicus*, coconut crab *Birgus latro*, green snail *Turbo marmoratus*, trochus snail *Trochus niloticus*, trumpet shell *Charonia tritonis* are all protected by limits on sizes that can be taken and/or prevention of capturing egg-bearing females; and export permits must be obtained for all crustaceans, aquarium fish and bêche-de-mer. Despite these laws, turtle eggs are extensively collected and the coconut crab has been eliminated from many islands by over-collecting. There is only one small protected area in Vanuatu, centred around the wreck of the ss *President Coolidge* on the south Santo coast. More reserves need to be established, but the present legislation is inadequate. Any new legislation would have to take full cognisance of the fact that nearly all the land (more than 99%) in Vanuatu, and the coastal reefs and lagoons, are owned by the village people themselves. No land or sea areas can be taken from them for any purpose or by any means whatsoever. Any parks or reserves therefore could only be declared with the full co-operation of the many people who own a particular area. The most pressing needs for parks and reserves will arise in the lowland, fertile areas so that good representative portions of their flora and fauna can be protected. Upland areas and most marine areas are under little actual or perceived threat so there is less urgency but pressures will develop in all but the highest and most remote regions and the most inaccessible coasts in the coming years. The legislative deficiencies in protecting both vulnerable species and valuable land habitats for future generations are well recognised in the country and a thorough review of environmental legislation is currently in progress.

Vanuatu joined the Convention on International Trade in Endangered Species of Wild Fauna and Flora (CITES) in 1989, the 103rd country to do so. CITES has important legal provisions for controlling and in some cases prohibiting international trade in those plants and animals and their products which are threatened with extinction. This will increase protection to those of Vanuatu's birds on the CITES lists, namely the Peregrine Falcon *Falco peregrinus* on Appendix I and the Rainbow Lorikeet *Trichoglossus haematodus*, the Green Palm or Vanuatu Lorikeet *Charmosyna palmarum* and the Barn Owl *Tyto alba* on Appendix II, and increase protection to the fauna and flora generally.

Fauna, flora and their habitats, are natural resources that must be studied and evaluated before sensible plans can be devised for their use and management. A number of studies have been conducted in recent years throughout the country on the dugong, coral reefs, coconut crab and fruit bats and others, on the forest resources, crocodiles and turtles are in progress or planned. It is the objective of all these studies to evaluate the resource base and if such needs are identified to devise plans for management.

The dugong occurs widely throughout Vanuatu, from Aneityum in the south to Torres in the north (Chambers *et al*, 1989). It is not abundant anywhere, generally occurring in groups of two or three animals and rarely more than ten. The dugong's preferred habitat, shallow, sheltered water is not common and such small group sizes are not surprising. Many of the country's little coves and bays support dugong and they find sufficient food (seagrasses) there and in the lagoons behind the fringing

Coast of Efate with fringing reefs

reefs. Very few people hunt the dugong in Vanuatu and there is little threat from pollution or loss of habitat and food supply. This is in stark contrast to the situation in most countries where it occurs and where it is becoming an endangered species. It is not immediately necessary to conserve the dugong in Vanuatu but when marine reserves are declared in the future, major dugong areas should be strongly considered. There are a number of traditional stories and customs about the dugong. At Lamen Bay on Epi, where the dugong is regularly hunted, women are not allowed to swim in the sea for two months before the planned capture. The men are forbidden to throw stones, spears or arrows into the sea and those who are to capture the dugongs must live in the forest and make a net up to 550m long from creepers, vines and thorny branches. This net is then used to surround the dugongs as they feed in the shallow lagoons. At Paonangisu village in north Efate, there is a tradition that some families are descended from fish. If a member of the fish family dies, or is to become a chief, then a meat feast must be provided. If the family has no meat then a fish from the sea will provide a large fish, turtle or dugong for capture. A dugong would only be caught occasionally for such a traditional ceremony.

The reef resources of Vanuatu were surveyed for the first time in 1988 (Done and Navin, 1989). A large number of fringing and patch reefs between Aneityum and Ureparapara were studied for their coral, fish, shellfish, bêche-de-mer and seagrass resources. Coral and fish communities were often rich in species and spectacularly beautiful. A number of reefs however, have been degraded by various causes such as the crown-of-thorns starfish, predatory snails, cyclones, earthquakes or smothering by sediments. The deposition of sediments could be controlled to some extent by ensuring that land-based developments do not lead to unacceptable levels of soil erosion. Severe cyclones can destroy living coral down to 20m or more, and some examples were found on the survey. Cyclones may also damage reefs without physically destroying them. This occurs when the corals are subjected to stress through severe wave action, dilution of shallow seawater by prolonged heavy rain or direct exposure to heavy rain. At such times the symbiotic algae in living corals are killed off, the coral becomes bleached and usually, slowly dies. Thus in Vanuatu the coral reef communities at any one locality are those which have developed since the last damaging cyclone. Recently damaged communities are sparse and comprise invader and pioneer species which are subsequently replaced by others as the communities move towards their mature formation. Coral reefs, like the forests in Vanuatu are highly modified by cyclones. The best reefs are probably those which have escaped cyclone damage for the longest time. In the nature of things their turn will unfortunately come. Earthquakes sometimes affect reefs by lifting them out of the sea and killing the marine organisms that produce the coral. Large areas of Vanuatu are covered in raised reef limestone. On a reduced scale, earthquakes may lift reefs by just a few centimetres so that the tops of the corals die off through increased exposure to air, rain and sunlight whilst the lower parts are unaffected. During the survey several such areas were seen on the islands of Moso and Ureparapara.

The shellfish of the reefs are an important subsistence and cash resource. Several species of giant clam were studied during the survey. The most interesting was the horse-shoe clam *Hippopus hippopus* which was found to be abundant on several reefs. In many parts of the Pacific this clam has become extinct or rare through over-collecting for food. It is also eaten in Vanuatu but the isolation of some reefs may protect it here from such a fate. Other shellfish such as trochus and the green snail are both eaten and their shells are sold for mother-of-pearl. Bêche-de-mer is not eaten in Vanuatu but a small export trade exists. It is not a large resource due to the small areas of suitable habitat. A total of nine species of seagrass were found on the survey, four less than exist on the Great Barrier Reef of Australia. This again demonstrates the general paucity of many types of flora in Vanuatu. Seagrasses are an important resource providing shelter and feeding areas for subsistence fisheries, protection of coastlines from erosion and food for dugongs and green turtles. In general there is little human interference and the reef resources of Vanuatu are in good condition. The major threats are from natural catastrophes.

The coconut crab, the world's largest land crab, has suffered in Vanuatu. Heavy collecting has caused it to disappear from some islands, to become rare in others and to be abundant in only few areas. The crabs are very slow growing, taking about 15 years to reach the legal size limit for harvesting but even strict enforcement of this control may not provide sufficient protection. Breeding success is sporadic and many years may pass without young animals being recruited to the population. With this combination of slow growth and poor breeding, it is possible the animal could become extinct even with conservation measures. However, voluntary controls are in operation that limit the numbers collected from the Torres Islands, the remaining stronghold, and one small island there has become a breeding reserve from which no collecting is allowed. In contrast to the damaging effects of cyclones on much of

Vanuatu's fauna and flora, such events may assist the coconut crab. After the passage of a cyclone, the forests become virtually inaccessible to humans for some years, the coconut crab is safe from predation and numbers may recover.

Flying-foxes occur abundantly throughout Vanuatu and are an important food (Chambers and Esrom, 1989). Virtually everyone in rural areas eats them at least occasionally, and they are also served as delicacies in tourist hotels. The most common species is the black flying-fox *Pteropus tonganus*. It is easily caught whilst feeding at fruit trees and is one of the most readily available forms of animal protein for many people, particularly inland. Whole colonies of flying-foxes may be blown to the ground during cyclones and are either killed by villagers or are unable to regain the air. The hunting pressure on the bats does not seem to have affected their numbers.

Folk tales about these bats abound, many involving their interaction with birds. One story, from Pongkil in Erromango relates how the black flying-fox obtained its colours. One day, the flying-fox and the rainbow lory were sitting together on the branch of a tree. The flying-fox told the lory that they should try to make themselves beautiful. The bird agreed and asked the bat to paint her first. The flying-fox painted the lory with many pretty colours finishing with bright red on the neck. The bird was pleased and asked the bat to go to sleep so that she could paint her. When the flying-fox was asleep, the lory got a black pen and painted her friend and then flew away. When the flying-fox awoke, she was horrified at her appearance and went off and hid herself. Thus the bat now only comes out at night and is no longer friendly with the lory. Another story, this time concerning the barn owl comes from Loltong, north Pentecost. One day, there was a heavy rain, so the owl hid in a hollow tree. A black flying-fox flew by and saw the owl inside the tree. The bat shouted out for all to hear, 'It's raining, and the owl is afraid to go out. He hides in a tree, with his eyes deep inside his head'. Whereupon the owl retorted, 'What are you saying! You hang upside down, you urinate upside down and you defaecate upside down. I am much better than you!'

Conclusion

After 3,000 years history of human settlement, the islands of Vanuatu now support about 150,000 people. All of these depend to a very significant extent upon the natural resources of soil, fauna, flora, river, lake, and reef. For most, this dependency is immediate and urgent providing essential food and shelter. The natural environment also provides the equally essential spiritual and cultural resources, to a degree that many other societies have abandoned or lost. Severe environmental degradation would undoubtedly result in physical and spiritual decline for most islanders.

At the present time the resource base is in generally good shape, with the major threats coming from natural hazards of one type or another. As the population increases and agriculture and forestry expand and perhaps mining and industrialisation commence, human activities will pose the greater problems. An important indicator of how Vanuatu will cope with these pressures and problems will be the fate of the avifauna described in this book.

References

Braithwaite, A F (1975): The phytogeographical relationships and origin of the New Hebrides fern flora. *Philosophical Transactions of The Royal Society of London*, Series B 272, 293-313.

Chambers, M R, Bani, E & Barker-Hudson, B (1989): The status of the dugong *Dugong dugon* in Vanuatu. *South Pacific Regional Environment Programme Topic Review No.37*. South Pacific Commission, Noumea, New Caledonia, pp.63.

Chambers, M R & Esrom, D (1989): The flying-foxes of Vanuatu with notes on their cultural and social importance. *Naika 30*, 6-13.

Chambers, M R & Esrom, D (in press): The status of the estuarine crocodile (*Crocydylus porosus* Schneider) in Vanuatu. *South Pacific Regional Environment Programme Topic Review*. South Pacific Commission, Noumea, New Caledonia.

Chew, W L (1975): The phanerogamic flora of the New Hebrides and their relationships. *Philosophical Transactions of The Royal Society of London*, Series B 272, 315-328.

Done, T J & Navin, K F, editors (1989): *The Marine Resources Survey of Vanuatu, March-April 1988*. Australian Institute of Marine Science, Townsville, Australia. pp.333.

Gross, G F (1975): The land invertebrates of the New Hebrides and their relationships. *Philosophical Transactions of The Royal Society of London*, Series B 272, 391-421.

Mallick, D I J (1975): Development of the New Hebrides archipelago. *Philosophical Transactions of The Royal Society of London*, Series B 272, 277-285.

Medway, Lord & Marshall, A G (1975): Terrestrial vertebrates of the New Hebrides: origin and distribution. *Philosophical Transactions of The Royal Society of London*, Series B 272, 423-465.

Quantin, P (1977): *Archipel des Nouvelles Hebrides. Atlas des Sols et quelques données du Milieu Naturel*. ORSTOM, Paris.

Climatological data was provided by Mike Longworth, Director of the Vanuatu Meteorological Service.

The avifauna of Vanuatu and conservation

The avifauna consists of about 121 species of birds. Of these, 32 species are seabirds of which few are resident, 15 species are shorebirds, and 74 species are land and freshwater birds.

More irregular visitors and vagrants have been recorded in recent years than was the case in the past. This reflects the presence of a greater number of knowledgeable observers during the last ten years.

Seabirds

Many of the 32 seabirds recorded in Vanuatu waters are widespread tropical species, some migrate from northern or southern temperate regions and a few disperse widely on circumpolar routes. The Procellariiformes are represented by 13 species in 3 families. Most are migrants or vagrants recorded on their journeys through Vanuatu, sometimes only glimpsed briefly as they skim over the waves or seen gliding effortlessly as they follow ships. Seven of these intriguing oceanic species are thought to breed in Vanuatu. Breeding has been confirmed for four; Collared/Gould's Petrel *Pterodroma leucoptera*, Wedge-tailed Shearwater *Puffinus pacificus*, Audubon's Shearwater *Puffinus lherminieri* and the Polynesian Storm-Petrel *Nesofregetta fuliginosa*. The Tahiti Petrel *Pseudobulweria rostrata*, White-necked Petrel *Pterodroma externa* and the Fluttering Shearwater *Puffinus gavia* may breed on uninhabited islands or in remote mountains on the larger islands. In these inaccessible regions it is difficult to confirm breeding as the adults are at sea during the day and return to their nesting burrows at night.

The order Pelecaniformes has 9 species in 4 families on the Vanuatu list. Five species are known to breed in Vanuatu, the Brown Booby *Sula leucogaster*, the Red-footed Booby *Sula sula*, the Least Frigatebird *Fregata ariel*, the Red-tailed Tropicbird *Phaethon rubricauda* and the White-tailed Tropicbird *Phaethon lepturus*. In some parts of the group, the Little Pied Cormorant *Phalacrocorax melanoleucos* seems to be present throughout the year and may breed.

The family Laridae in the order Charadriiformes has 10 species on the list. Only two, the Black-naped Tern *Sterna sumatrana* and the Sooty Tern *Sterna fuscata* are known to breed. Seven other terns have been recorded and 4 species may breed irregularly on coral reefs and sand cays. Terns are the seabirds most regularly seen close to the shore, often diving for fish or flying over estuaries, reefs and along the edges of mangroves.

The uncertainty surrounding the breeding status of the majority of seabird species in Vanuatu is due to the limited amount of attention this group of birds has received.

Rugged and inhospitable limestone islands like Monument Rock (Etarik) in the Shepherd Islands afford good protection for nesting and roosting seabirds

Garnett (1984) noted the same lack of information for seabirds breeding in all islands of the south Pacific region.

Shorebirds
Fifteen species in 4 families of the order Charadriiformes have been recorded in Vanuatu. Only one species, the very distinctive though elusive Beach Thick-knee *Esacus magnirostris* is thought to breed but this has not been confirmed. Almost all other shorebirds (waders) so far recorded in the group are species that breed in the northern hemisphere and visit Vanuatu regularly during their annual migrations. The large black and white South Island Pied Oystercatcher *Haematopus longirostris finschi* has been recorded once as a vagrant, from New Zealand. Shorebirds are most often seen at low tide on exposed reefs, beaches, mudflats and sandbanks, or on grassland near the coast. Long-distance migratory shorebirds often occur far outside their usual range and many more species could reach Vanuatu and stay for days, or longer in suitable habitats.

Land and freshwater birds
This group contains by far the majority of the bird species recorded in Vanuatu, with representatives of 14 Orders and 28 Families. However, as is characteristic for most

Beach at Malapoa peninsula, Efate; a good place to see curlews, plovers, sandpipers and other shorebirds at low tide or roosting on islets of dead coral at high water

oceanic islands, the landbird avifauna has fewer species than a continental area of similar size. On the more isolated and smaller islands, this difference is more pronounced. Of the 74 species of land and freshwater birds, 10 have been introduced, the Long-tailed New Zealand Cuckoo *Eudynamis taitensis* is a non-breeding visitor and 7 species have been recorded less than five times.

Vanuatu is important as a faunal crossroads where the three main streams of colonisation of Southwest Pacific birds (the Papuan, Australian and Polynesian) meet. Virtually all our resident species were derived at some stage from Australia or New Guinea or both, but only a few from Fiji or other unidentifiable sources and none from New Zealand or Micronesia. Diamond and Marshall (1976) give a detailed biogeographical analysis of the fascinating interplay of these colonising streams.

The isolation of the Vanuatu archipelago has led to the development of 7 endemic species, one of which belongs to an endemic genus. Others are only found on a few islands within the group though they also occur outside Vanuatu. Several species are confined mainly to the highlands and mountains of the larger islands. Most of the other species are widely distributed geographically in the archipelago and occupy a great variety of habitats, though the range of many species shows distributional gaps along the chain of islands (see Table 2 page 71).

A discontinuous distribution is found on many island-chains throughout the world, in which a particular species is widespread on all types of islands in one part of the group, yet is absent in nearby parts with similar islands. Ranges are subject to continuous modification by extinction and immigration, at rates of turnover that vary with the species. Several major fluctuations in distribution have been apparent within a century for the Green Palm Lorikeet *Charmosyna palmarum*, Fan-tailed Cuckoo

Cacomantis pyrrhophanus, Shining Bronze-Cuckoo *Chrysococcyx lucidus*, White-rumped Swiftlet *Aerodramus spodiopygius* and the Fantail Warbler *Gerygone flavolateralis*. Factors which appear to control the inter-island distribution of particular species and the number of bird species on an island include the isolation of the island in question, its size and its altitude. The last two factors control the number of distinct habitats that it supports.

The number of land and freshwater species breeding on each Vanuatu island increases with size from 20 to 30 on islands of 10 km^2 to 50 on the largest island, Santo. However the Banks Islands in the north and Erromango, Aniwa, Tanna, Futuna, and Aneityum in the south have fewer species than the central Vanuatu islands of equivalent size. Apart from their political inclusion, the Banks and Torres Island are *zoologically* part of Vanuatu because the same species of birds occur there. It is relevant here to mention the Santa Cruz Islands (politically part of the Solomon Islands) to the north. Of their 33 species of breeding birds, more are shared with Vanuatu than with the Solomons or Fiji, and in terms of avifauna, this group could be considered an impoverished outlier of Vanuatu with admixtures from the other two countries (Diamond and Marshall, 1976).

The introduced species, apart from the Red Jungle Fowl *Gallus gallus* are essentially birds of suburban and agricultural land and most are confined to the larger islands of the group. The Indian Mynah *Acridotheres tristis* was deliberately introduced in an attempt to control insect pests. The House Sparrow *Passer domesticus* was presumably brought in for sentimental reasons and the waxbills and mannikins have become established from birds which have been released or have escaped from aviaries. With all introduced species there is a possibility that they may increase to pest proportions but some of these introductions may still die out.

Habitat preferences

There are many factors which seem to be important in controlling the inter-island distribution of a species, apart from ecological diversity, and there is still much to be learned about specific conditions regulating the composition of the avifauna in Vanuatu.

Every bird species has preferences for the type of environment in which it lives. A few species, like the swiftlets and swallows, fly over all types of habitat and the air itself can be considered as their environment. Some, like the Green-winged Ground Dove *Chalcophaps indica*, are able to tolerate wide variations and can be found in most types of habitat in Vanuatu. Some species are more often found in one kind of habitat but are quite at home in several. The Rufous-brown Pheasant-Dove *Macropygia mackinlayi*, for example, lives mainly in the forest but it can be found in any other partly wooded habitat, including plantations.

Other species have narrow preferences and are rarely if ever found away from the particular kind of habitat they prefer. For example, the Vanuatu Mountain Pigeon *Ducula bakeri* and the Thicket Warbler *Cichlornis whitneyi* are almost restricted to the high mountain forests while the Spotless Crake *Porzana tabuensis* is virtually confined to swamps. However, extreme specialisation makes such species vulnerable and may prove fatal if a particular environment undergoes rapid degradation.

Species restricted to distinct small areas, such as the Santo Mountain Starling

Aplonis santovestris which lives only in the cloud forest on the highest mountain peaks, may have become intolerant of changes in their habitat, less adaptable, less resilient and perhaps less vigorous than the more mobile species. They are therefore more likely to be at risk of extinction. Except for the specialised bird species which prefer a particular type of habitat, a considerable number of species are likely to be found in the forest up to about 500 m. At the junction of two or more habitats, such as forest, open land, streams or lakes, a greater diversity of species and larger numbers of birds can be expected than in any single habitat.

Ecological isolation and specialisation
It is interesting to note the number of situations in Vanuatu where pairs of closely related species occur together. According to some theorists, following Steere (1894), such pairs of species avoid competition through isolation. It is generally recognised that ecological isolation can be maintained by one or more of three methods:

(a) Distinct range: members of competing species are confined to different islands in a group.
(b) Distinct habitat: occupation of different habitats although living on the same island.
(c) Distinct diet: closely related species feeding on different foods although occupying the same habitat.

The two *Ducula* pigeons are to some degree separated by range and by habitat preference. The Pacific Imperial Pigeon *Ducula pacifica* is found in the whole region from sea level up to about 1,000 m whilst the Vanuatu Mountain Pigeon is confined to some of the larger northern islands and frequents the mountain forests.

The two pairs of lorikeets and starlings are separated by habitat, foraging behaviour and probably difference in size. The Rainbow Lorikeet *Trichoglossus haematodus* is generally common only in the lowlands whereas the Green Palm Lorikeet appears to prefer the mountain forest. There is an obvious size difference and (possibly) feeding differences. The Santo Mountain Starling is confined to the cloud forest on Santo whereas the Rusty-winged Starling *Aplonis zelandicus* an active canopy feeder is found on many northern islands, mainly in the hill and mountain forest.

The three honeyeaters are separated either by range and habitat preferences or feeding and size differences. Although the three species do occur together on some islands, the Silver-eared Honeyeater *Lichmera incana* frequents the lowland and the hill forest, the Vanuatu Mountain Honeyeater *Phylidonyris notabilis* apparently prefers the higher mountain forest whilst the Cardinal Honeyeater *Myzomela cardinalis* co-exists with both other species and avoids competition by a marked difference in size and by adopting different feeding strategies.

The two parrotfinches are clearly separated by habitat and food preferences. Another strategy that appears to be relevant in Vanuatu is that a *generalist* species can co-exist with a more *specialist* species having a limited habitat tolerance and/or a specialist feeding technique. The following pairs of species could be distinguished on this basis: ducks, ground doves, kingfishers, trillers, fantails and white-eyes. The two fruit doves co-exist with each other but are possibly separated by feeding ecology and difference in size.

The breeding land and freshwater avifauna of Vanuatu were surveyed by Diamond and Marshall (1977a). In their comparison of the niches occupied by these birds, they found examples where the niche of a species had shifted by change of habitat, change of altitude or vertical foraging range in the same habitat, through competition from a close species.

Pressures on native birds

At present no Vanuatu species is known to have become extinct although there have been several distributional changes in island populations. It is now generally assumed that the record for one species, the Tanna Ground Dove *Gallicolumba ferruginae*, supposedly collected by Forster on Tanna in 1774, is based on an error and this species has never existed on Tanna (Diamond and Marshall, 1976). The status of many other species, whilst in no immediate danger, may be considered precarious. Foremost among them are birds found on only a few islands, such as the white-headed form of the Island Thrush *Turdus poliocephalus* from Erromango and Tanna, or the Vanuatu Kingfisher *Halcyon farquhari* and those species that are confined to small isolated areas, like the Santo Mountain Starling, White-browed Crake *Poliolimnas cinereus* and the Spotless Crake and some colonies of petrels. However some of these birds are fortunately widespread species elsewhere in the Pacific or the Australo-Papuan regions. The Pacific Imperial Pigeon and the Pacific Black Duck *Anas superciliosa* appear to be far less numerous now than in former times. This can be attributed to overhunting as unfortunately, the former colonial governments did not prevent the widespread use of firearms, especially on Efate and Santo. The greatest pressures on native birds in Vanuatu are likely to come from human expansion and development bringing changes in the natural vegetation.

The effects of habitat modification

Most of the native birds are adapted to living in forest except for some like the Pacific Swallow *Hirundo tahitica* and the herons which are coastal, estuarine or riverine species. Some of these species will probably not be able to adjust to vastly different habitats, modified by human activities during a relatively short period of time.

However, a number of species have in part adapted themselves to partly cleared forests or agricultural areas or pastures which are still amply supplied with trees and bushes. These are the Buff-banded Rail *Gallirallus philippensis*, Green-winged Ground Dove, Rainbow Lorikeet, Barn Owl *Tyto alba*, the swiftlets, White-collared Kingfisher *Halcyon chloris*, Long-tailed Triller *Lalage leucopyga*, Grey Fantail *Rhipidura fuliginosa*, Broad-billed Flycatcher *Myiagra caledonica*, Golden Whistler *Pachycephala pectoralis*, White-breasted Woodswallow *Artamus leucorhynchus*, Silver-eared Honeyeater and the white-eyes.

Several other species may also use these areas of partly cleared forest. These include the Brown Goshawk *Accipiter fasciatus*, Swamp Harrier *Circus approximans*, Peregrine Falcon *Falco peregrinus*, Red Jungle Fowl, Purple Swamphen *Porphyrio porphyrio*, the fruit doves, White-throated Pigeon *Columba vitiensis*, Rufous-brown Pheasant-Dove, the cuckoos, Melanesian Cuckoo-shrike *Coracina caledonica*, Fantail Warbler, Vanuatu Flycatcher *Neolalage banksiana*, Cardinal Honeyeater and the Royal Parrotfinch.

Most of these partly developed areas could be rendered significantly more attractive

Open park land by the River Colle north of Port Vila, used for cattle

for birds by selective clearing which leaves the flowering and fruit-bearing trees standing. The fig trees are important because the fruits of most of the 21 or so species in Vanuatu are an essential part of the diet of many birds and the flying-foxes. Fig trees have a special significance because a number of them have no set fruiting season and may bear fruit in any month of the year.

A few bird species however, have found the new habitats more suitable for their needs. The Blue-faced Parrotfinch *Erythrura trichroa* for instance, has considerably increased in numbers on islands with extensive pasture land, presumably because of the abundance of seeds from imported grasses and probably also through the provision of watering places for cattle. This species nevertheless keeps mainly to the junction between forest, secondary growth or high scrub and the pastures and apparently avoids moving too far away from the forest edge. The Barn Owl has also benefited. It appears to hunt more successfully in cleared areas than in the forest and also finds more prey in plantations.

Potential threats to the avifauna of Vanuatu

The birds of Vanuatu have so far been less affected by human interference than those of many other Pacific islands. Birds native to islands and endemic species are, however, especially vulnerable. At the World Conference, on the Conservation of Island Birds, of the International Council for Bird Preservation in 1982, Warren B King made the following statement: 'Since the seventeenth century, avian extinction has been largely an island phenomenon. Fully 93 percent of the 93 species and 83 subspecies of birds which have become extinct since 1600 have been island forms, and avian extinction on islands is far from a dead process.' He also noted that: 'extinctions in the Pacific Ocean have been recent, more having come in the first 50 years of this century than in any other 50 year period' (King, 1985).

At the present time the various habitats in Vanuatu have been little altered through

Distant view of Mount Kotamtam from Tabwemasana; dense tropical rainforest and cloud forest – at higher levels the haunt of the Santo Mountain Starling

human activities. However as the population increases, agriculture and commercial forestry expand and perhaps mining and industrialisation commence, the lowland natural forest will decrease in size until there will be only remnants of the once unbroken expanse of forest. Above 500m, the upland and cloud forests of the islands should escape major degradation and their avifauna survive more or less intact. Below this altitude, major changes through the significant reduction of natural vegetation will result in the decrease in populations of most bird species and may even cause the extinction of some. Habitat destruction on islands is largely an irreversible process. Though not so important in earlier decades, loss or deterioration of habitats will be the most significant dangers to the avifauna of Vanuatu in future years. The continued existence of sufficiently large and diverse habitats is essential if the birds that inhabit the archipelago are to survive in the long-term. Carefully selected representative areas of valuable habitats, especially in the lowlands, need to be set aside and managed as Reserves or National Parks. Although one can suppose that the rugged and mountainous terrain will ensure that a sizeable proportion of natural forest will be spared, fragmentation of the forest into isolated patches would eventually be equivalent to deforestation.

Apart from changes in habitat, other destabilising factors have been more important causes of decline or extinction in other parts of the world. According to King (1985), the 'single most important cause of extinction on islands has been predation by alien predators which have been introduced sometimes intentionally, sometimes inadvertently, by man. While this will remain a significant factor in extinctions for years to come, we are witnessing increasingly the gradual deterioration of many island habitats through the combined onslaught of selected browsing by introduced herbivores, excessive competition for space and light between native floras and vigorous introduced continental vegetation, and increased rates of utilisation of trees for firewood and building materials by expanding human populations. Avian disease may play a more insidious role here than previously supposed.' Of the additional factors mentioned by King, the following may be relevant for Vanuatu although, at the present time, there is little or no evidence available:

(a) Rats, cats and dogs are the most significant predators, especially on ground-nesting or ground-dwelling birds. Petrels and shearwaters at their nesting sites on small offshore islands are particularly susceptible to such predation. The nesting colonies can also be seriously affected by predation from pigs and by habitat deterioration through over-grazing by goats or other herbivores.

(b) Hunting has been an important cause of extinction of island birds and it continues to play a contributory role. In Vanuatu, hunting may become a serious factor in the decline of species that can be regarded as potentially endangered, like the relatively common Vanuatu Fruit Dove, or the Vanuatu Mountain Pigeon whose population is already restricted to limited areas.

(c) Competition with introduced birds for food or space, including nest sites, has been an important factor in the decline of some native island birds. However, recent studies suggest that, 'it was not competition from introduced species that caused declines in native species, but conversely, that declines in native birds permitted the establishment of introduced birds' (Diamond & Veitch, 1981). Nevertheless, as any introduced bird or animal could become a contributory factor in the decline or extinction of native birds, introductions should be generally discouraged if not banned.

(d) As far as avian disease is concerned, King (1985) comments that, 'the role of disease in causing extinctions of birds on islands has recently come under increasing scrutiny'. It has been suggested that mosquito-borne avian malaria and bird-pox are linked to the reduction or loss of some species. King states that 'until the deleterious effects of disease can be demonstrated, we should continue to think of disease as affecting birds only on the most isolated island groups, where the avifauna has evolved in the absence of disease vectors and thus has not had opportunity to develop immunity'. As avian malaria is known to have been introduced to Vanuatu there is a possibility that this may be affecting the Green Palm Lorikeet. A small number of these lorikeets were kept for observation without any difficulty for some weeks in the Santo highlands at the foot of Mount Tabwemasana. After transfer to the west coast of Santo and later to Port Vila, some died and the remainder stayed alive only after having been placed in mosquito-proof aviaries. The present reduced range of the Green Palm Lorikeet may be linked to its possible susceptibility to avian malaria.

Conservation

Fortunately, the government of Vanuatu are aware of the need for conservation of the natural flora and fauna. As far as the avifauna is concerned, given the considerable variety of potential problems outlined above, the following suggestions may be helpful:

(1) Ecology and conservation are already on the syllabus for island secondary schools and are taught in the primary schools. The provision of facilities for field studies and regular environmental and conservation education programmes for the general public would also increase awareness.

(2) The local people could be encouraged, possibly with the help of grants, to co-operate in setting aside and preserving large sections of marginal land, particularly forests, swamps, lakes and mangroves and the wildlife they support. The native landbirds are mainly forest species and most of them are unable to adapt to an agricultural or urban environment. Some species could be lost from islands unless carefully selected, representative areas with different intact or nearly intact ecosystems are set aside and managed as Reserves or National Parks. Before deciding on the size of any reserve, there is merit in looking carefully at the species-area factor. It is known that the larger the habitat fragment the larger the proportion of the original complement of species it will retain.

(3) Logging is generally on a small scale at present, except on Efate. On Malakula, permission to log large areas has recently been given. Greater consideration should be given to the ecological effects of logging and the introduction of foreign plant species. The enactment of legislation to control these activities would be beneficial.

(4) Pesticides and other synthesised chemicals are not widely used in Vanuatu (though Dieldrin, which is banned in many parts of the world because of its persistence, is mentioned by Weightman (1989) as one means of controlling the banana weevil). Where they are used, there are voluntary controls to avoid pollution of watercourses. If their use increases significantly in future, statutory pollution control measures may be necessary for streams, rivers, lakes, lagoons, mangroves and coastal waters. The excessive use of such chemicals could reduce food supplies for several species of waterbirds and indirectly lead to reduced fertility in birds of prey.

(5) At present only a few species of birds in Vanuatu are fully or partly protected by law. Most species of birds and their eggs should receive full legal protection with

exceptions for game-birds, and those which have been harvested traditionally, to allow limited killing at levels that their populations can withstand. Steel shot could be used in preference to lead shot which may poison rare species of waterbirds indiscriminately when they are feeding in lake mud. Restrictions on the possession and use of firearms and the supply of ammunition or a bag limit could reduce hunting pressure and be less likely to endanger populations of birds like ducks and pigeons. This threat could probably be reduced through conservation education programmes, as in 1974 when the author initiated a 'game-bird campaign'. Colour posters illustrating the game species and indicating the limited hunting season were distributed and shown in towns and villages throughout the archipelago.

(6) A conservation strategy should be adopted for Vanuatu, involving the establishment of protected areas and provision for research and monitoring as sound conservation can only be based on understanding. As a preliminary measure, the Duck-Lake Reserve on Efate and the reserve in the Reef Islands could be established, as proposed by Bregulla (1972), Bennett (1972) and Marshall (1973).

On Efate especially, there is a pressing need for Lowland Reserves. The lakes provide valuable food and breeding places for ducks and dabchicks. Likewise, the surrounding mature forest, worth preserving for itself, could soon become a most important refuge for the survival of the Incubator Bird *Megapodius freycinet* because this species needs nesting areas in the lowlands. In addition, throughout the archipelago the most important existing waterfowl habitats, such as Lake Siwi on Tanna, should be declared as sites for special protection. The wise use of all wetlands including lakes, ponds, rivers, creeks, swamps, and mangroves should be promoted as under the terms of the Ramsar Convention.

Atolls are uncommon ecosystems in Vanuatu. They are important mainly as resting and breeding refuges for seabirds and as spawning and nursery areas for a multitude of marine species. Atolls and reefs are potential tourist attractions and if tourism is managed sympathetically in conjuction with programmes of scientific research, this may prove beneficial for conservation. The Reef Islands are of scientific importance, with Cook Reef, as the only non-fringing reefs and atolls in Vanuatu (Naika 31:26-27). The Reef Islands are heavily infested by rats but have the advantage of being uninhabited. They are thickly covered with low, dense vegetation but clearing rats with rodenticides may be possible on such small land areas. Details of programmes for the eradication of rats from some island reserves in New Zealand are given in the ICBP Technical Publication No.3 (Moors, 1985). It should be noted, however, that declaring the Reef Islands as a Reserve to protect the avifauna, particularly nesting petrels, need not preclude their use as subsistence fishing grounds.

Similarly, many uninhabited offshore islands deserve protection, such as Laika Island in the Shepherds with colonies of breeding shearwaters, and Monument Rock off Mataso Island and Goat Island off Erromango used as roosting sites or breeding grounds for some of the rarer seabirds of Vanuatu. In selecting Island Reserves, priority should be given to safeguarding islands which are at present free of predators or alien herbivores.

Finally, conservation and natural history groups can create awareness in the people of the dangers to their wildlife and the importance of preserving wildlife for future

Top: Little Duck Lake on Efate; part of the proposed nature reserve with Pacific Black Duck coming in to roost

Above: Laika Island near Tongoa, is one of the better known breeding grounds of the Wedge-tailed Shearwater

generations. They can also be active in encouraging and assisting government agencies in setting up reserves or parks and adopting other conservation measures. As in the past, wildlife conservation campaigns like the game-birds poster, the wildlife stamps series designed by the author and several other successful projects as well as the Botanical and Ornithological Park at Malapoa, Efate which was proposed by the author, all promote interest in the flora and fauna of Vanuatu. Therefore the continued success and the strengthening of natural history organisations like the Vanuatu Natural Science Society is of the utmost importance.

Checklist of Vanuatu birds

Nomenclature generally follows Simpson and Day (1989) *Field Guide to the Birds of Australia* and the RAOU list (1983) or Pratt, Bruner and Berrett (1987) *The Birds of Hawaii and the Tropical Pacific*.

Status is shown by the following code letters or symbols:

- B Breeds in Vanuatu
- M Migrates regularly to and from the islands or adjacent waters
- N Non-breeding regular visitor
- V Vagrant species
- ? Status uncertain due to lack of information
- e Endemic species
- * Introduced species

			Plate no.	Text page
		Order PODICIPEDIFORMES		
		Family Podicipedidae		
1	B	Australian Grebe *Tachybaptus novaehollandiae leucosternos*	4	78
		Order PROCELLARIIFORMES		
		Family Diomedeidae		
2	V	'Great' Albatross *Diomedea* spp	1	80
		Family Procellariidae		
3	V	Antarctic Giant-Petrel *Macronectes giganteus*		82
4	B?	Tahiti Petrel *Pseudobulweria rostrata*	2	83
5	BM	White-winged/Collared Petrel *Pterodroma leucoptera brevipes* /Gould's Petrel *Pterodroma leucoptera leucoptera*		84
6	B?M	White-necked Petrel *Pterodroma externa cervicalis*		86
7	V	Antarctic Prion *Pachyptila desolata*		86
8	BM	Wedge-tailed Shearwater *Puffinus pacificus*		87
9	N?	Short-tailed Shearwater *Puffinus tenuirostris*		90
10	B?	Fluttering Shearwater *Puffinus gavia*	2	90
11	B	Audubon's Shearwater *Puffinus lherminieri gunax*		91
		Family Oceanitidae		
12	V	Wilson's Storm-Petrel *Oceanites oceanicus*		93
13	V	Black-bellied Storm-Petrel *Fregetta tropica*		93
14	B	Polynesian Storm-Petrel *Nesofregetta fuliginosa*		94
		Order PELICANIFORMES		
		Family Pelecanidae		
15	V	Australian Pelican *Pelecanus conspicillatus*		96
		Family Sulidae		
16	B	Brown Booby *Sula leucogaster*	1	97
17	B	Red-footed Booby *Sula sula*	1	99
18	V	Masked Booby *Sula dactylatra*	1	100
		Family Phalacrocoracidae		
19	B?N	Little Pied Cormorant *Phalacrocorax melanoleucos*	4	102
		Family Fregatidae		
20	V	Great Frigatebird *Fregata minor*		103
21	B	Least Frigatebird *Fregata ariel*	1	104
		Family Phaethontidae		
22	B	Red-tailed Tropicbird *Phaethon rubricauda*	2	106
23	B	White-tailed Tropicbird *Phaethon lepturus*	2	107

			Plate no.	Text page
		Order CICONIIFORMES		
		Family Ardeidae		
24	V	White-faced Heron *Ardea novaehollandiae*	3	110
25	B	Eastern Reef Heron *Ardea sacra*	3	111
26	V	Rufous Night Heron *Nycticorax caledonicus*		113
27	B	Little (Mangrove) Heron *Butorides striatus solomonensis*	3	114
		Order ANSERIFORMES		
		Family Anatidae		
28	*B?	Mallard *Anas platyrhynchos*		116
29	B	Pacific Black (Australian Grey) Duck *Anas superciliosa pelewensis*	4	117
30	B	Grey Teal *Anas gibberifrons gracilis*	4	119
31	B	Australian White-eyed Duck *Aythya australis*	4	121
		Order ACCIPITRIFORMES		
		Family Accipitridae		
32	V	Brahminy Kite *Haliastur indus*		123
33	B	Brown (Australian) Goshawk *Accipiter fasciatus vigilax*	5	123
34	B	Swamp Harrier *Circus approximans approximans*	5	125
		Order FALCONIFORMES		
		Family Falconidae		
35	B	Peregrine Falcon *Falco peregrinus nesiotes*	5	128
		Order GALLIFORMES		
		Family Megapodiidae		
36	B	Incubator Bird *Megapodius freycinet layardi*	6	132
		Family Phasianidae		
37	*B	Red Jungle Fowl *Gallus gallus*	6	136
		Order GRUIFORMES		
		Family Rallidae		
38	B	Buff-banded (Banded) Rail *Gallirallus philippensis sethsmithi*	6	138
39	B	Spotless Crake (Sooty Rail) *Porzana tabuensis tabuensis*	6	140
40	B	White-browed Crake *Poliolimnas cinereus tannensis*	6	142
41	B	Purple Swamphen *Porphyrio porphyrio samoensis*	6	143
		Order CHARADRIIFORMES		
		Family Burhinidae		
42	B?	Beach Thick-knee *Esacus magnirostris*	7	146
		Family Haematopodidae		
43	V	South Island Pied Oystercatcher *Haematopus longirostris finschi*		147

			Plate no.	Text page
		Family Charadriidae		
44	N	Pacific Golden Plover *Pluvialis fulva*	7	149
45	V	Mongolian Plover *Charadrius mongolus*		150
46	V	Oriental Plover *Charadrius veredus*		151
		Family Scolopacidae		
47	N	Ruddy Turnstone *Arenaria interpres*	7	152
48	N?	Far Eastern Curlew *Numenius madagascariensis*		153
49	N	Whimbrel *Numenius phaeopus*	7	153
50	N	Siberian Tattler *Heteroscelus brevipes*		154
51	N	Wandering Tattler *Heteroscelus incanus*	7	155
52	N	Common Sandpiper *Actitis hypoleucos*		156
53	N	Bar-tailed Godwit *Limosa lapponica*		156
54	N	Sharp-tailed Sandpiper *Calidris acuminata*		157
55	V	Pectoral Sandpiper *Calidris melanotos*		158
56	N	Red-necked Stint *Calidris ruficollis*		158
		Family Laridae		
57	N	Silver Gull *Larus novaehollandiae*		159
58	N?	Common Tern *Sterna hirundo*		162
59	V	Roseate Tern *Sterna dougallii*		162
60	B	Black-naped Tern *Sterna sumatrana*	2	163
61	B	Sooty Tern *Sterna fuscata*		164
62	V	Bridled Tern *Sterna anaethetus*		165
63	B?	Great Crested Tern *Sterna bergii*		166
64	B?	Common Noddy *Anous stolidus*	2	167
65	B?	Black Noddy *Anous minutus*		168
66	B?	White Tern *Gygis alba*	2	169
		Order COLUMBIFORMES		
		Family Columbidae		
67	N	Red-bellied Fruit Dove *Ptilinopus greyii*	8	172
68	eB	Vanuatu (Yellow-headed) Fruit Dove *Ptilinopus tannensis*	8	175
69	B	Pacific Imperial Pigeon *Ducula pacifica pacifica*	8	177
70	eB	Vanuatu Mountain Pigeon *Ducula bakeri*	8	180
71	N	White-throated Pigeon *Columba vitiensis leopoldii*	8	181
72	B	Rufous-brown Pheasant-Dove *Macropygia mackinlayi mackinlayi*	8	183
73	B	Green-winged Ground (Emerald) Dove *Chalcophaps indica sandwichensis*	8	184
74	B	Santa Cruz Ground Dove *Gallicolumba sanctaecrucis*	8	186

			Plate no.	Text page
		Order PSITTACIFORMES		
		Family Psittacidae		
75	B	Rainbow Lorikeet *Trichoglossus haematodus massena*	9	189
76	B	Green Palm (Vanuatu) Lorikeet *Charmosyna palmarum*	9	191
		Order CUCULIFORMES		
		Family Cuculidae		
77	B	Fan-tailed Cuckoo *Cacomantis pyrrhophanus schistaceigularis*	10	194
78	B	Shining Bronze-Cuckoo *Chrysococcyx lucidus layardi*	10	195
79	N	Long-tailed New Zealand Cuckoo *Eudynamis taitensis*	10	197
		Order STRIGIFORMES		
		Family Tytonidae		
80	B	Barn Owl *Tyto alba*	5	199
		Order APODIFORMES		
		Family Apodidae		
81	B	White-bellied (Glossy) Swiftlet *Collocalia esculenta uropygialis*	11	203
82	B	White-rumped Swiftlet *Aerodramus spodiopygius*	11	204
83	B	Uniform (Vanikoro) Swiftlet *Aerodramus vanikorensis vanikorensis*	11	206
		Order CORACIIFORMES		
		Family Alcedinidae		
84	B	White-collared Kingfisher *Halcyon chloris*	12	208
85	eB	Vanuatu (Chestnut-bellied) Kingfisher *Halcyon farquhari*	12	212
		Order PASSERIFORMES		
		Family Hirundinidae		
86	B	Pacific Swallow *Hirundo tahitica subfusca*	11	215
		Family Campephagidae		
87	B	Melanesian Cuckoo-shrike (Graybird) *Coracina caledonica*	12	217
88	B	Polynesian Triller *Lalage maculosa*	12	218
89	B	Long-tailed Triller *Lalage leucopyga*	12	220
		Family Turdidae		
90	B	Island Thrush *Turdus poliocephalus*	13	222
91	V	Song Thrush *Turdus philomelos*		224
		Family Pachycephalidae		
92	B	Scarlet Robin *Petroica multicolor*	14	225
93	B	Golden Whistler *Pachycephala pectoralis*	14	227

			Plate no.	Text page
		Family Monarchidae		
94	B	Southern Shrikebill *Clytorhynchus pachycephaloides grisescens*	14	230
95	B	Broad-billed Flycatcher *Myiagra caledonica*	14	231
96	eB	Vanuatu (Buff-bellied) Flycatcher *Neolalage banksiana*	14	232
		Family Rhipiduridae		
97	B	Grey (Collared) Fantail *Rhipidura fuliginosa brenchleyi*	13	235
98	B	Spotted Fantail *Rhipidura spilodera spilodera*	13	237
		Family Acanthizidae		
99	B	Fantail Warbler *Gerygone flavolateralis correiae*	13	239
100	B	Thicket Warbler *Cichlornis whitneyi whitneyi*	13	241
		Family Meliphagidae		
101	eB	Vanuatu Mountain (White-bellied) Honeyeater *Phylidonyris notabilis*	9	243
102	B	Silver-eared Honeyeater *Lichmera incana*	9	245
103	B	Cardinal Honeyeater *Myzomela cardinalis*	9	247
		Family Zosteropidae		
104	eB	Vanuatu (Yellow) White-eye *Zosterops flavifrons*	9	250
105	B	Grey-backed White-eye (Silvereye) *Zosterops lateralis*	9	252
		Family Fringillidae		
106	V	Redpoll *Carduelis flammea cabaret*	15	253
		Family Passeridae		
107	*B	House Sparrow *Passer domesticus*	15	255
		Family Estrildidae		
108	*B	Common Waxbill *Estrilda astrild*	15	256
109	*V	Red-browed Firetail *Neochmia temporalis*		258
110	*V	Red Avadavat *Amandava amandava*		258
111	*B	Chestnut-breasted Mannikin *Lonchura castaneothorax*	15	259
112	*B	Black-headed Mannikin *Lonchura malacca*	15	260
113	*B?	Red-throated Parrotfinch *Erythrura psittacea*	15	261
114	B	Blue-faced Parrotfinch *Erythrura trichroa cyaneifrons*	15	262
115	B	Royal Parrotfinch *Erythrura cyaneovirens*	15	264
		Family Sturnidae		
116	eB	Santo Mountain Starling *Aplonis santovestris*	12	267
117	B	Rusty-winged Starling *Aplonis zelandicus rufipennis*	12	268
118	V	European Starling *Sturnus vulgaris*		269
119	*B	Indian Mynah *Acridotheres tristis*	12	270
120	V	Papuan (Yellow-faced) Mynah *Mino dumontii*		271
		Family Artamidae		
121	B	White-breasted Woodswallow *Artamus leucorhynchus tenuis*	14	272

Classification of birds

Classification involves describing all species of plants and animals living in the world, giving them scientific names and sorting them into logical relationships based on their perceived evolutionary pattern. The theory and practice used by scientists to classify all living things (organisms) is called *taxonomy*. Another word used by scientists in studying the differences and relationships between organisms is *systematics*. Our present scientific names have their origins in the work of the Swedish naturalist Carl Linné (1707-78), who is generally known by the Latin name of Linnaeus. He introduced the system of giving at least two names to each species. The first name describes the group of similar species, the *genus* (plural genera), to which an organism belongs and the second name identifies the individual *species*. A third name may be given to denote the subspecies or *race*. The basic unit of classification is the species. Species must be distinctly determined and described before they can be assemble into genera, genera into families and families into orders in a way that taxonomists can claim to be phylogenetic.

In determining the genera, families and orders of birds, Linnaeus and his successors in the 18th century relied heavily upon similarities in such features as bill, wings, tail and feet as the major taxonomic characters. This practice has been modified with the realisation that these are the structures which are most likely to have been adapted to specific habitats and food-niches and are therefore extremely variable. Any apparent similarity among different species may be due to convergent evolution by members of quite separate avian groups. Once this was realised a quest began for characters which are less subject to specific adaptive changes and might prove fully reliable. Studies have been made of the structure of the bones of the palate, the scales on the legs, the texture and colour pattern of plumage and of eggs, the nature of both external and internal parasites, of song as analysed by sonagraph and of innate behaviour patterns. These are some of the aspects currently used which have been helpful as taxonomic characters, although none has proved to be reliable for all cases. Small differences of the skeleton, especially the skull, still form the basis of the major accepted groupings but recent biochemical studies comparing the DNA (genetic material) of different species, in egg-white proteins for example, have established similarities between some families which were previously thought to be unrelated. These studies are likely to bring about major changes in classification in the future.

Birds belong to the class AVES. Within this class the main categories are Orders, Families, Genera, Species and Subspecies (Races). These have been defined by systematists as follows:

ORDER: a grouping of related families (name ending with 'formes'). Modern classification of birds begins with the order which is considered to be the most primitive ancestral order and ends with the most highly evolved group. The birds of Vanuatu described in this book are arranged in this evolutionary sequence. The first orders represented in Vanuatu are Podicipediformes and Procellariiformes with some of the most primitive species in the world and the last order is Passeriformes. The characteristic features of the families comprising each order are described and common behaviour patterns are outlined.

FAMILY: a grouping of related genera (name ending with 'idae'). In this book the appearance, habitats and general behaviour of each family represented are described in some detail and brief notes are given on the members of the family found in Vanuatu. A knowledge of the family characteristics is a great help in identification. To see a bird and know that it is a heron, dove or swiftlet means that you are already well on the way to knowing the individual species.

GENUS (PLURAL GENERA): defined by Mayr (1942b) as 'a systematic unit (group) including one species or a group of species of presumably common phylogenetic origin which is separated from other similar units by a decided gap'. It is obligatory that every species be placed in a genus. The name of the genus, always written in italics and beginning with a capital letter, constitutes the first word of the scientific name of a species.

SPECIES: the category on which classification is based. The species is a *natural entity*, whereas classification in all other categories, lower and higher, is subjective. Amadon (1970) defines species as a freely interbreeding population whose members do not interbreed with those of other populations. For example, suppose that somewhere in Vanuatu, Red-bellied Fruit Doves *Ptilinopus greyii* are commencing nesting activities, and that in the same area Vanuatu Fruit Doves *Ptilinopus tannensis* are also breeding. If the two kinds of fruit doves always pair within their own groups and do not breed with members of the other group, they are separate species. However, as there are obvious similarities between them, both are placed in the same Genus *Ptilinopus* and with other pigeons and doves are included in the Family Columbidae and the Order Columbiformes.

SUBSPECIES OR RACE: where a given species exhibits definite taxonomic variations in different parts of its geographical range, it is sub-divided by taxonomists into races. Races may be found within a continuous distribution or they may be separated by biological or geographical barriers. In Vanuatu, geographical variation is a conspicuous feature of the avifauna. A geographically isolated race is a population of birds which is to some extent genetically different from the other populations of the species, though interbreeding is still possible. Races are found on continents where, for example, mountain ranges, deserts or wide rivers separate populations or they are separated when changes in vegetation take place. They occur particularly in archipelagos like Vanuatu, where populations are separated by wide expanses of sea. In such cases divergence from the parent stock frequently occurs. The extent of divergence in size, colour of plumage or shape of bill, for example, depends largely on the length of time the population has been isolated.

In polytypic species (where there is more than one race) the scientific name consists of the genus, species and race. The first race described, known as the nominate race, has the second name repeated. In New Caledonia the name of the Melanesian Cuckoo-shrike is *Coracina caledonica caledonica* whereas in Vanuatu the scientific name of the Melanesian Cuckoo-shrike is:

Coracina caledonica seiuncta for the southern population and
Coracina caledonica thilenii for the population found on the northern islands.

The Melanesian Cuckoo-shrike is grouped with trillers and cicadabirds in the family *Campephagidae*. This family is grouped with about 80 other families in the order Passeriformes, the perching-birds or songbirds. This and about 30 other orders are grouped in the class Aves, which comprises all birds. The full classification is therefore as follows:

Class: Aves
Order: Passeriformes
Family: Campephagidae
Genus: *Coracina*
Species: *caledonica*
First race: *seiuncta*, on Erromango
Second race: *thilenii*, on Santo, Malo and Malakula.

There is so much work in progress in different countries that ornithologists disagree about the number and sequence of orders and which families or species should be grouped together. They are constantly reclassifying birds in the light of new knowledge. In 1962 for example, during the examination of birds in Vanuatu, the author had some doubts about the validity of the standard classification of two species. At that time the Green Palm Lorikeet *Charmosyna palmarum* was placed in the genus *Vini*. Although this group of small parrots appeared to be closely related there were considerable differences in their external features and it seemed more logical to split them into two genera. This was confirmed by Forshaw (1973) when the two genera were defined as follows:

Genus *Charmosyna*: (14 species) unites all species with slender body and more gradated tail with narrow pointed feathers. Sexual dimorphism is present in most species.

Genus *Vini*: (5 species) all members have a stocky body and erectile crown feathers, and a short rounded tail in which the central feathers are longer than the lateral ones. There is no sexual dimorphism.

In the second case the author was concerned about the classification of the Royal Parrotfinch *Erythrura cyaneovirens*. This handsome species was then named the Red-headed Parrotfinch with the nominate race in Samoa and other races in Vanuatu and Fiji. However a revision of all species in the genus *Erythrura*, has shown that there are considerable differences in the general proportions, colour of plumage, habits and voice between the Fiji birds and the other two populations. It seems best to separate them and consider the Fiji population as a full species *Erythrura pealii* (Ziswiler, Güttinger and Bregulla, 1972).

The living birds of the world have been variously, scientifically arranged into 27 orders, with about 8,548 species (Mayr and Amadon, 1951), and 28 to 30 orders with some 9,300 species (Perrins, 1990). It is unlikely that the number will increase much, though new species of birds are still being discovered from time to time. With increasing human population and development pressures leading to worldwide degradation and destruction of habitats, the International Council for Bird Preservation estimate that about 1,000 species are threatened or endangered (Perrins, 1990).

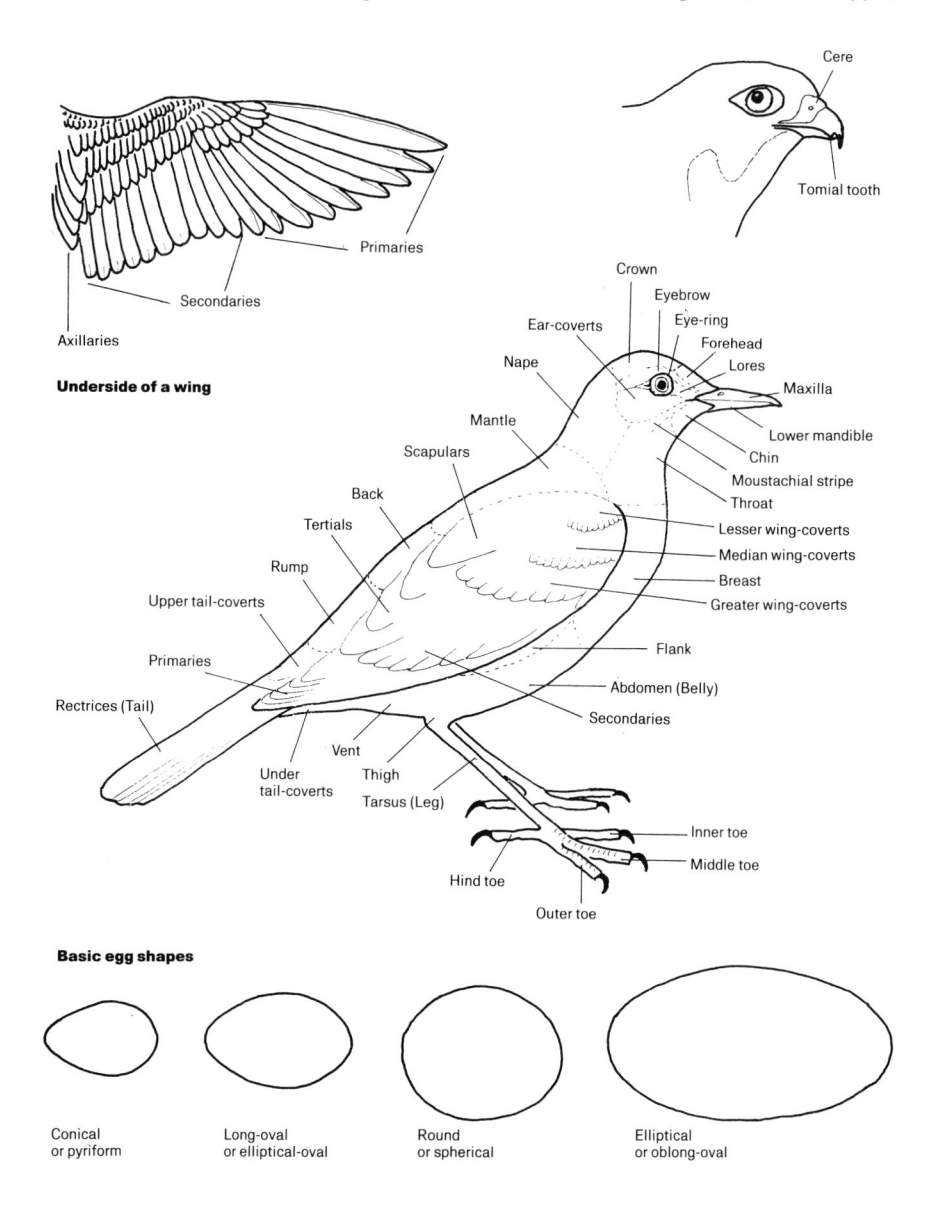

Topography of a bird and shapes of eggs

Hints for birdwatchers in Vanuatu and notes on the text

This book will help the birdwatcher to identify and name the birds seen and to discover which species can be expected on some islands. Identification of a bird seen for the first time is exciting for any birdwatcher. It is also the first step in discovering more about the life and behaviour of the species. In Vanuatu, very little is known about the lives of many of the resident birds and even less about some of the vagrant species or migrants. Any keen birdwatcher can make observations that will add to this store of knowledge. Many species journey through the islands annually, including shorebirds from Asia and Australia. Close observations of birds on beaches or mudflats will almost certainly reveal new species for the Vanuatu Checklist.

Birdwatching is not an expensive hobby as the basic equipment consists of a notebook and pencil or ballpen. If later you can afford a pair of binoculars your enjoyment will be increased immeasurably; a bird that is 80m away will appear to be only 10m away through a pair of 8x magnification binoculars and far more can be seen of its plumage and behaviour than at 80m.

Write down the date, place and the weather conditions before you start recording any birds that you see. This may be useful at some time in the future for studying their behaviour at different times of the year or their movements, whether they are sedentary, nomadic or migratory. When you see a bird that you don't recognise, look at it carefully for as long as possible. Sometimes this may be only a few seconds but you should still be able to keep a visual impression long enough to write what you saw. *Before* you start looking through the book, write as much as you can and sketch it, no matter how roughly, adding notes on patches of colour, shape and length of bill, shape of the wings and tail and anything you notice about the way it moves, whether hopping or running for example and the way that it flies. Compare the strange bird with your memories of similar-sized birds that you know. Then you are in a position to consult the pictures, look up the text and with luck, you will be able to name the new bird and add it to your list. Don't be too disappointed or surprised if you cannot identify this new bird. There will always be some birds that you cannot recognise.

For birds that breed in Vanuatu the following headings are used in the species accounts: Identification, Distribution and Status, Field Notes, Voice, Food, Nest and Breeding. For species that are vagrants or regular visitors and are not known to breed in Vanuatu the information is not so detailed. Information on voice or food, where relevant, and on breeding behaviour in other regions for species that could possibly breed in Vanuatu, is included under the combined heading of Identification and Field Notes.

In the IDENTIFICATION section the approximate body length from the tip of the bill to the tip of the tail is given. Where the tail is unusually long, this measurement is given separately. These are absolute measurements whereas the attributes 'large' and 'small' are relative and a small heron (40 cm) is of course bigger than a large flycatcher (19 cm). A description is given of the main plumage colours of adult male and female and immature, the colour of the iris, bill, legs and feet and some notes on the diagnostic features which should enable the birdwatcher to avoid confusion with similar species. One difficulty for the beginner is that birds do not have exactly the same plumage all through the year. The feathers tend to become worn and ragged with wear, especially on the tips, and the colours are also likely to fade somewhat. For these reasons the plumage is renewed periodically by the process of moult. Most adult birds moult twice a year: a partial moult, usually of the body plumage only, immediately preceding the breeding season (pre-nuptial moult) and a complete moult after breeding. In general, males tend to moult more than females and the pre-nuptial moult is less extensive in the female. The new breeding plumage is usually more brightly coloured and in some species includes special ornamental feathers. This plumage is replaced, in a complete moult, towards or at the end of the breeding season by what is generally termed the non-breeding plumage. This moult corresponds with the annual moult in species which only moult once a year and in these birds the pale tips of the feathers often wear to produce a darker breeding plumage. The regular moults of adults are preceded by a succession of nestling and immature plumages and moults. The down of the nestling is rapidly replaced by the first 'juvenile' plumage. This is frequently dark coloured, drab or at least less bright than adult plumage and lacks ornamentation. Streaked and spotted patterns are frequent features. The immature bird, especially in the larger species, may go through several plumage changes before the full adult plumage is attained and where this is known, some indication has been given in the text. In general, immature plumage is reminiscent of the female rather than the male adult plumage. Existing moulting records for Vanuatu are so few and fragmentary that a detailed account is not possible. Consequently, any birdwatcher can make useful observations on the extent of the moult and the time of year, particularly for the species in Vanuatu that have an extended breeding season.

DISTRIBUTION AND STATUS: gives information on the worldwide distribution of the species and its status in Vanuatu. A CONSERVATION section has been added here for some rare or possibly threatened species where there may be a need for conservation action. If there is some uncertainty about the classification or distribution of a species, comments are included here. The range of a species is an important aid to identification as this is determined by the availability of suitable habitat and food. Within their range, some species are sedentary throughout the year in one area. Others migrate between two regions or are nomadic. It may be worth consulting Table 2 page 71 to look up the known distribution of breeding birds in Vanuatu. It is always interesting to list the birds that you see on any island, particularly if you can estimate the numbers fairly accurately, and you may be lucky enough to have a new island record.

Another simple observation will help you to reduce the number of possibilities when looking at the book. Take note of where you saw the bird. Was it in lowland forest or in the mountains, in a village garden, in a marshy area or on the shore? As you will soon learn, every bird species likes to live in its own preferred environment. Some have narrow preferences and are found in very restricted areas but others can live in several different habitats. These are described in the FIELD NOTES in the book. This section also includes notes on many kinds of behaviour that are uniquely interesting. The characteristic flight is another useful clue. Is it direct, powerful or fluttering? Does the bird fly in rapid bursts or is its flight sustained? A bird may use its wings almost all the time in flapping flight or may glide on outstretched wings. It may hover, soar in thermals or have an undulating flight which is a fairly regular pattern of flapping and gliding. The size and shape of the wings, the speed at which they move and the depth of the wingbeats are also helpful in identification.

There is much that you can learn on your own by careful, quiet observation, especially about the birds which you see regularly but the quickest and easiest way to identify the birds in your area is to go out birdwatching with someone who knows them already. If you can find someone who is knowledgeable, you should also have a chance to develop the other essential skill for bird identification; recognition by call-notes and songs. The section on VOICE for each species includes information on the commonest call-notes and when they are used and for songbirds, when the species sings. In thickly wooded areas many more birds will be heard than seen. Most woodland and forest birds have distinctive calls, but they frequently sing from dense cover or in the tops of the trees. The best way to learn these calls on your own is to be persistent in trying to see a calling bird. If you can recognise it by sight and fit the call to the bird, the next time you hear the same call, you may be able to name the bird without seeing it. Learning bird-calls and songs takes time but, as with all skills, plenty of practice improves the skill and you will be surprised how quickly you can distinguish birds of very similar appearance or habits by their different calls.

Notes on feeding behaviour are included in the field notes and details of the diet, where known, are included in the FOOD section. Again, much useful information can be added by careful observation. Any further knowledge gained about their particular food preferences may help species at risk.

NEST AND BREEDING: gives information about the structure of the nest, the nest site, the clutch size and eggs. The clutch size is generally uniform within a range for each species but for some species, where food is unusually abundant, the clutch may be exceptionally large and in times of scarcity eggs may not be laid at all. Some aspects of breeding behaviour are discussed and the main breeding season is noted. Many bird species have distinct breeding seasons. In Vanuatu the majority of landbirds begin breeding at the end of the dry season and continue until the end of the wet season, taking advantage of the increased abundance of insects, fruit and seeds, thereby raising the most young.

In the species accounts the number given to every species known to have been recorded in Vanuatu may be useful in referring from one section of the book to another. The English vernacular name is followed by the scientific name and other common names are given where they are known. The scientific names look odd because they are in a special language, based on ancient Latin or Greek and you might think that a local name is quite good enough for you. The reason for having a scientific name is that it can be understood by any birdwatcher and if you are sending information about your birds to other people this name should be included. As an example, in Brazil one small bird is called 'Pardal', in France the same bird is known as 'Moineau domestique', and in Argentina as 'Gorrion' while in England it is called the 'House Sparrow'. Each name makes sense in these countries but birdwatchers and ornithologists throughout the world know immediately which species is being described if the name *Passer domesticus* is used.

Dead birds can also yield useful information. If the bird is in fairly good condition, take some notes on its plumage and have a go at measuring the length of the wing, bill, tail, tarsus and the body. If you find a dead bird with a metal band on its leg, you are immediately in a position to provide more knowledge for ornithology. Look carefully at the band and you will see a series of numbers and letters and an address. The serial number on each band is unique. When birds are banded, the number and place of banding are recorded. If you can remove the band without damaging the numbers, do so and then flatten the band and post it to the address shown. Enclose a note with your own name and address, the date and place where you found the bird and how you think it may have died. Some time later you should receive a letter telling you where and when the bird was banded. Your report, known as a 'recovery' to the banders, will help them to find out more about the bird's movements and how long it has lived. In Vanuatu from 1968 onwards, the author banded petrels on Laika Island and a good number of most of the small species of common birds during visits to Tanna and Santo and for several years on Efate. These bands were supplied by the Migratory Animal Pathological Survey of the APO US Forces, Bangkok, Thailand. In 1971, over 800 birds of 19 species were also banded at 11 sites in closed-canopy forest on the islands of Santo, Malakula, Efate, Erromango, Tanna and Aneityum (Medway and Marshall, 1975). It is unlikely that any of the small birds are still alive, though petrels have been known to live for 25 years or more. The nearest countries with large-scale schemes for banding birds are Australia and New Zealand but you may be lucky enough to find a shorebird that had been banded in one of the countries in the northern hemisphere or even a seabird from Antarctica.

Some birds live only in Vanuatu (endemic) and they are specially important as any *new* piece of information you have about their behaviour, nests or breeding will not be known to anyone else in the world, unless you tell them. The Vanuatu Natural Science Society and the Cultural Centre at Port Vila collect information about the flora and fauna of Vanuatu and will be pleased to receive any new records or, if they are in good condition, specimens of any unusual species that are found dead.

Since many features of the life-histories of most Vanuatu birds are insufficiently known, priority should be given to clarifying the following ecological aspects. What are the characteristics of the optimal habitat (most favourable conditions) for each species? For example, altitude and relief of the land surface; type, structure and composition of the vegetation; relative abundance of food sources, including identification of the trees or other plant species whose fruit, seeds, or nectar the birds like most; breeding season and the preferred nesting places. It is important to appreciate that, because of variations in climate and conditions in this long chain of islands, such data need to be obtained from at least the 12 major islands and from the Torres and

Banks Islands in the north and from islands at the southern end of the archipelago. Also that breeding records, which are at present few and fragmentary, should cover at least one complete annual cycle. As the knowledge of these factors is indispensable for the definition of successful conservation strategies or to increase the number of individual birds living in a given locality or reserve, any birdwatcher can make valuable observations that may indirectly help to save species and their habitats for the enjoyment of future generations.

Table 2. Distribution of the breeding land and fresh-water birds of Vanuatu

Island by island distribution of native and introduced species, extracted and adapted from Appendix 1 of the paper, *Origin of the New Hebridean Fauna* by J M Diamond and A G Marshall (1976). This information came from the following sources: critical evaluation of records published in the literature to 1975; the unpublished diaries and letters of the Whitney South Sea Expedition (1921-1939) and of L MacMillan in the American Museum of Natural History; observations by the author between 1959 and 1976; Diamond and Marshall's unpublished observations and specimens they examined in the collection of the AMNH; lists of parts of the New Hebridean collections in the British Museum (Natural History) and the Oxford University Museum, prepared by I C J Galbraith and J Hull respectively; and later records from *Naika*, the journal of the Vanuatu Natural Science Society. Refer to the main text for races and changes in distribution.

The table includes all the larger islands and all islands that have been well explored. A few records for wide-ranging species that occur on other small islands are not included.

e = Endemic   * = Introduced species

LIST OF ISLANDS FROM NORTH TO SOUTH

1	Torres group	11	Pentecost	21	Nguna
2	Ureparapara	12	Malakula	22	Emau
3	Mota Lava (Valua)	13	Ambrym	23	Efate
4	Vanua Lava	14	Paama	24	Erromango
5	Gaua	15	Lopevi	25	Aniwa
6	Mere Lava (Star Peak)	16	Epi	26	Tanna
7	Santo	17	Tongoa	27	Futuna
8	Malo	18	Tongariki	28	Aneityum
9	Maewo (Aurora)	19	Emae		
10	Ambae (Aoba)	20	Makura		

DISTRIBUTION

ISLANDS		1	2	3	4	5	6	7	8	9	10
01	Australian Grebe					■		■	■	■	■
25	Eastern Reef Heron	■	■	■	■	■	■	■	■	■	■
27	Little Heron	■	■		■	■		■			
28	*Mallard										
29	Pacific Black Duck					■		■			■
30	Grey Teal										
31	White-eyed Duck					■		■	■		■
33	Brown Goshawk										
34	Swamp Harrier	■	■		■			■	■	■	
35	Peregrine Falcon					■		■	■	■	
36	Incubator Bird	■	■	■	■			■		■	■
37	*Red Jungle Fowl							■			
38	Buff-banded Rail					■		■	■		
39	Spotless Crake										
40	White-browed Crake						■				
41	Purple Swamphen								■	■	■
67	Red-bellied Fruit Dove	■	■	■	■	■	■	■	■	■	
68	eVanuatu Fruit Dove				■	■	■	■	■		
69	Pacific Imperial Pigeon	■	■		■	■	■	■	■	■	■
70	eVanuatu Mountain Pigeon			■	■	■	■	■		■	■
71	White-throated Pigeon	■	■		■		■	■	■	■	■
72	Rufous-brown Pheasant-Dove		■	■	■	■	■	■	■	■	■
73	Green-winged Ground Dove	■	■	■	■	■	■	■	■	■	■
74	Santa Cruz Ground Dove							■			
75	Rainbow Lorikeet	■	■	■	■			■			
76	Green Palm Lorikeet			■	■	■	■		■		■
77	Fan-tailed Cuckoo			■	■	■	■		■		■
78	Shining Bronze-Cuckoo					■	■		■		
80	Barn Owl		■			■		■		■	
81	White-bellied Swiftlet	■	■	■		■		■	■	■	■
82	White-rumped Swiftlet		■					■	■		
83	Uniform Swiftlet	■			■	■		■	■	■	■
84	White-collared Kingfisher	■	■	■	■	■	■	■	■	■	■
85	eVanuatu Kingfisher							■	■		
86	Pacific Swallow	■						■	■	■	■
87	Melanesian Cuckoo-shrike							■	■		
88	Polynesian Triller							■	■		
89	Long-tailed Triller	■	■	■	■	■	■	■	■	■	■
90	Island Thrush		■		■	■	■	■	■	■	■
92	Scarlet Robin					■	■	■	■	■	■

13	14	15	16	17	18	19	20	21	22	23	24	25	26	27	28

DISTRIBUTION

ISLANDS		1	2	3	4	5	6	7	8	9	10
93	Golden Whistler		■		■	■		■	■	■	■
94	Southern Shrikebill	■	■	■	■	■	■	■	■	■	■
95	Broad-billed Flycatcher	■	■	■	■	■	■	■	■	■	■
96	eVanuatu Flycatcher					■			■	■	■
97	Grey Fantail	■	■	■	■	■	■	■	■	■	■
98	Spotted Fantail					■	■		■	■	■
99	Fantail Warbler					■	■		■	■	■
100	Thicket Warbler							■			
101	eVanuatu Mountain Honeyeater				■		■		■		■	■
102	Silver-eared Honeyeater										
103	Cardinal Honeyeater	■	■	■	■	■	■	■	■		■
104	eVanuatu White-eye	■			■	■	■	■	■	■	■
105	Grey-backed White-eye	■	■	■	■	■	■	■	■	■	■
107	*House Sparrow							■			
108	*Common Waxbill										
111	*Chestnut-breasted Mannikin							■			
112	*Black-headed Mannikin							■			
113	*Red-throated Parrotfinch										
114	Blue-faced Parrotfinch					■					■
115	Royal Parrotfinch					■			■		■
116	eSanto Mountain Starling							■			
117	Rusty-winged Starling	■				■		■	■		■
119	*Indian Mynah							■	■		
121	White-breasted Woodswallow					■		■	■	■	■

13	14	15	16	17	18	19	20	21	22	23	24	25	26	27	28

Orders, families and species accounts

Order PODICIPEDIFORMES
There is only one family in this order.

Grebes *Podicipedidae*
Grebes, past masters in the art of diving, are probably the most aquatic of birds. They feed, roost, and carry out their elaborate courtship display on water, and nest on floating vegetation. Grebes with short, thick, silky plumage look somewhat like ducks at a distance but can be distinguished by the slender pointed bill and tail-less appearance. They differ from other swimming birds in a number of ways. Their feet are very different: instead of being webbed with leathery skin as in most water birds, each of their toes is separately fringed with stiff, horny flaps or lobes. Another characteristic is their lack of a functional tail. The few, soft very short tail feathers are useless for steering and therefore, in the water and the air, grebes steer with the feet which trail behind them conspicuously in flight.

Although grebes are weak fliers and several are practically flightless some species migrate long distances. They are not highly gregarious birds but may travel in small flocks or nest in loose breeding colonies. Grebes have a variety of trumpeting calls, shrill whistles and piercing wails and they chatter to each other in quacks, chuckles and whinnies. Grebes are famous for their intricate and spectacular courtship-dances which precede mating. Both sexes of some species have decorative nuptial plumes, horns, ears or collars which they display to each other. All grebes breed on fresh water but some species are often found in estuaries and coastal waters. The nest containing 3-10 eggs, is built of pieces of reeds, rushes and other water plants matted together and floating in shallow water or anchored to a convenient clump of reeds. The incubation period varies from 20 to 30 days and the chicks have longitudinal stripes on the head and neck. Most grebes carry their downy young about, either in the open on their backs or concealed under their feathers with just the young bird's head visible. The parent birds even dive with the chicks tucked away under their wings or among their back feathers. Grebes obtain their food by diving, feeding on small fish and aquatic invertebrates. They have one peculiar habit which has yet to be explained satisfactorily: they eat quantities of their own body feathers and even feed them to their young. As feathers have very little or no nutritive value, it may be that wads of feathers protect the intestines from sharp fish bones. Their lustrous plumage was formerly in demand for decorating hats and this seriously jeopardised the survival of some species. The birds are now protected by law and grebes are no longer killed for their feathers.

Grebes comprise a cosmopolitan family of 22 species in 8 genera. Only one species, the Australian Grebe occurs in Vanuatu and breeds locally on lakes and ponds.

1. Australian Grebe *Tachybaptus novaehollandiae leucosternos*   PLATE 4
Other name: Dabchick
French name: Grèbe australien   or locally: Plongeur

IDENTIFICATION
Length about 27 cm. A small grebe with a rounded plump body, long thin neck and a very short hardly visible tail. *Adult male:* upperparts blackish-brown with breast and flanks mottled with brown, underparts mostly silky white. Head black, slightly glossy, with a chestnut-brown stripe extending from behind the eye to the side of the head and separating the black crown and nape from the black chin and throat. These colours are probably duller in the non-breeding season. Iris: yellow. Bill: black with a light tip and a yellow, oval patch of bare skin at the base. Legs and feet: light olive-yellow with irregular dark brown patches. *Adult female:* like the male but slightly smaller; head and neck colours are duller. *Immature:* similar to adult but colours, particularly the black and brown on the head and neck, are much duller and it may have stripes on the head. Iris is ochre not yellow. The dark grey downy young have light stripes along the upperparts.

DISTRIBUTION AND STATUS
The Australian Grebe is found throughout Australia and in Java, Timor, the Talaud Islands, New Guinea, Rennell Island in the Solomons and New Caledonia. It is a vagrant in New Zealand. In Vanuatu the race *leucosternos* was thought to occur only on freshwater lakes on Santo and Gaua but it has been recorded by the author on Efate, Ambae and Maewo and by Diamond and Marshall (1976) on Malo. It probably occurs throughout the group wherever suitable habitat exists, usually on freshwater though it visits coastal waters occasionally. This race also occurs in New Caledonia.

FIELD NOTES
At first sight it may look like a small duck but the lack of tail, the pointed bill, the long thin neck and the way that it rides high in the water are good distinguishing features. The neck is held erect and turned frequently from side to side. They are seen in pairs during the breeding season but at other times may associate in small, loose flocks and are fairly common on quiet, little disturbed lakes, ponds and swamps, mainly inland. Usually rather sedentary they are sometimes reported from flooded areas only to disappear once the floods subside. As changes of locality are usually made at night the birds are seldom seen flying. Flight is direct with head and neck held stiffly forward rather below body level and wings showing a white bar. They are shy birds, easily overlooked and often only revealed by their characteristic trilling. If a bird is disturbed near the shore it will swim out to the centre of a large lake or to the other side of a pond where it soon becomes lost in the vegetation. Grebes dive frequently when feeding: they are incredibly agile and normally do not stay under water for long. They also dive to escape danger (such as being shot) rather than take wing. It is almost impossible to induce them to fly and they can swim for considerable distances under water. They have the ability to expel air from within their bodies and from under the feathers, increasing their specific gravity, and slowly sink below the surface. They are difficult birds to observe: when suspicious of danger they often swim about with just the head exposed.

VOICE
The most frequently heard call is a repeated piercing trill. Single sharp notes and twittering in duet have also been recorded but they are not noisy birds.

FOOD
They dive for much of their food which consists mainly of insects and their larvae, crustaceans, small fish, tadpoles and other small aquatic creatures living amongst the sedges and other water plants growing in shallow water.

NEST AND BREEDING
The nest is a floating platform of aquatic plants, often anchored to surrounding vegetation or hidden in dense cover. In a depression on the top of this sodden mound 3-6 whitish to pale-blue eggs (about 35 × 25 mm) are laid and incubated by both sexes for about 20 days. When leaving the nest the birds cover the eggs with wet nest material to keep them warm and to conceal them from predators. Chicks take to the water soon after hatching but frequently ride on the backs of their parents. In Vanuatu, the Australian Grebe probably breeds from July to December or January and may have more than one brood each season.

Order PROCELLARIIFORMES
The 4 families of albatrosses, shearwaters, storm-petrels and diving-petrels are closely related and are placed in the order Procellariiformes. This group is also known as tubenoses (formerly Tubinares) as all the 100 or so species have their nostrils opening into tubes on the bill. Sometimes the tubular nostrils are united on top of the upper mandible but in albatrosses they are on the sides and are not so obvious. In tubenoses the nasal olfactory organ is larger than in other seabirds and it is thought that they have a highly developed sense of smell. The bill is hooked and the horny covering is divided into plates separated by distinct grooves. The wings are mostly long, always with 11 primaries (10 functional, the outer is minute) but a varying number of short secondaries. The 3 front toes are fully webbed; the hind toe is vestigial. The sexes are generally similar in size and plumage though in some species the male is slightly larger, especially the bill. Some species have a light and dark phase, the underparts in some individuals being more or less white and in others dusky, or with melanistic or albinistic forms. The chick is hatched covered in thick down. The juvenile plumage is often similar to that of the adult but in the larger albatrosses and the giant-petrels tends to have paler edges to the feathers. The tubenoses are excellent fliers and all are pelagic spending most of the year as ocean-wanderers and coming to land only to breed.

Most species nest in colonies, on small islands, on promontories almost surrounded by the sea or in the mountains. The albatrosses, giant-petrels and some tropical shearwaters build an open nest on the ground. A few nest on cliffs but most, characteristically, nest underground in burrows or concealed hollows under tussocks or rocks. Almost all tubenoses are at sea during the day and only active at their breeding grounds at night. The incubation and nestling stages are noticeably prolonged, with many adults travelling long distances in search of food. The development to breeding adult takes considerably longer than with most other birds.

Only one egg is laid, which is large for the size of the bird and white in colour though in many species there may be fine spots. Both sexes share in the incubation of the egg and care of the young which when big enough are left unattended. All tubenoses feed their young by regurgitation. Many adults also have a clear orange or yellow stomach oil which they feed to the young. This oil has a very strong smell and can be spat out at will if the bird is disturbed or attacked. As many ornithologists know, clothing which has been sprayed and museum skins and egg-shells may retain their distinctive musky odour for years.

These and other features of anatomy and behaviour set the Procellariiformes apart from all other groups. There are more tubenoses in the southern than northern hemisphere, but some make trans-equatorial migrations. There are fewer tropical species. The albatrosses (70 to 140cm in length) are among the largest seabirds and the storm-petrels (12 to 25cm) the smallest. Each of the families is fairly distinctive and, with minor exceptions, can be identified by size but separating the species is often difficult. Approximately 50 species of tubenoses can be encountered in the tropical south Pacific and 13, in 3 families, have been recorded in Vanuatu. Of these, 4 species are known to breed and 3 more probably breed within the islands. The others may be seen on migration or occur as vagrants.

Albatrosses *Diomedeidae*
The largest pelagic seabirds, albatrosses are easily recognised and most impressive in flight. They may follow ships for days at a time, often circling or crossing the vessel and some species take refuse from ships. Their long narrow wings are perfect for gliding flight in strong winds but are inefficient for flapping in still air and on calm days they may rest on the sea. Nine or 10 species are mainly confined to the southern oceans in the belts of high winds associated with low pressure systems moving from west to east between the southern tips of the continents and the antarctic ice. All albatrosses have a large rounded head and a stout body. The tail is either short, broad and square as in the 3 species of great albatrosses and 9 species of the smaller mollymawks or long and wedge shaped as in the two species of sooty albatrosses. Albatrosses can live for 40 or more years and banding records also show that young birds disperse widely. A bird found 110 km north of Fremantle, Western Australia, in early autumn had been banded as a nestling at an island 480 km south of New Zealand in mid-September the previous year. It is possible that it had circumnavigated the globe. Albatrosses are rare vagrants in Vanuatu waters having an approximate northerly limit of 20°S, except for 3 species occurring in the north Pacific and one found on the equator. Those reported once off the west coast of Santo were probably one of the species of great albatrosses.

2. 'Great' Albatross   *Diomedea* spp
Wandering Albatross   *Diomedea exulans*
Royal Albatross   *Diomedea epomophora*
Amsterdam Island Albatross   *Diomedea amsterdamensis*
All three species are closely related but there is inter-population variation in size, weight and colour of plumage which roughly follows latitude; the northern birds being generally smaller and darker (Jouventin *et al*, 1989). Specific identification at sea is very difficult particularly in some stages of plumage; see Simpson and Day (1989).

Wandering Albatross (or Wanderer)   *D. exulans*
French name: Albatros hurleur
Length up to 135 cm with a wingspan of 300 cm or more; weight averaging 8 kg. There are a number of intermediate, mottled phases each progressively whiter between the almost complete dark brown immature plumage (except for white face and underwing) and the final adult plumage, pure white with a black trailing edge to the wing. Upperwing shows increasing white with age, spreading outwards from the *centre* of the wings. Seven stages are described in Harrison (1983). Adult plumage also varies with some birds of the southern populations breeding while still in mottled plumage. Bill: pink, with a horn-coloured tip. Legs and feet: pale flesh-coloured. It breeds on subantarctic islands and ranges the southern oceans straying north fairly frequently to about 20°S in the tropical Pacific and reaching 10-15°S in the Humboldt Current.

Royal Albatross   *D. epomophora*   PLATE 1
French name: Albatros royal
The Royal Albatross is similar in size to the commoner and more widely distributed Wanderer. Plumage varies little with age: juveniles have light mottling on the crown and back and a narrow black tip to the tail that is not present in adults. Body and tail are white. In the southern race *D. e. epomophora* white develops from the *leading edge* of the upperwing but in the northern race *D. e. sanfordi* the upperwing is wholly black. Bill: flesh-coloured. Legs and feet: bluey-white with blue-grey webs. *D. e. epomophora* breeds in the sub-antarctic on Campbell Island and the Auckland Islands south of New Zealand. The northern race, *sanfordi* breeds at Chatham Islands and on Taiaroa Head near Dunedin. It is found mainly in cool waters but strays occasionally into the tropical zone. Birds have been recovered off the coast of Australia and it occurs off South America to 10°S off Peru and 23°S off Brazil.

The very small population of the Amsterdam Island Albatross *D. amsterdamensis* breed in a dark plumage stage similar to that of immature and some adult Wanderers from Antipodes and Campbell Islands. The Royal and the Amsterdam Island Albatross both have a distinct dark line on the cutting edge of the upper mandible, visible at close range, which is not a feature of the Wanderer. In addition, characteristically, the hook of the mandible in the Amsterdam Island birds is darker than the rest of the bill and the lower mandible shows an even darker patch at the tip which extends laterally (Jouventin *et al*, 1989).

Fulmars, Petrels, Prions and Shearwaters   *Procellariidae*
Often simply called 'petrels', this family is the most diverse group of the order with about 55 species in 12 genera comprising four natural groups. The first group of 7 species, includes two fulmars and the giant-petrels. The gadfly-petrels are a group of about 22 species of medium-sized petrels, the northern genus, Bulweria, *being lightly built and* Pterodroma, *sturdy with forceful flight. The gadfly-petrels are perhaps the most graceful, with stubby, black, hooked bills, short necks and long wings. The prions, 12 closely related species and races, are specialised petrels with attractive blue-grey plumage and the shearwaters, or muttonbirds, are a large, variable group of some 15 species, with long slender bills and fluttering, sometimes*

gliding flight. Apart from the giant-petrels, which are the size of the smaller species of albatross, most are medium-sized birds, about the size of small gulls or terns with slender streamlined bodies and long, pointed, tapering wings. The nostrils are dorsally placed on the culmen, within a single tube but separated by an internal septum. The plumage is darkish-brown to black and white except for the prions. The iris is brown. The colour of the feet, varying from whitish-flesh or pink to black and bright blue, is an important guide to identification in the hand. Sexes have similar plumage and, with the exception of the giant-petrels, immatures resemble the adults. These birds are widespread and found throughout the oceans of the world but do not usually follow ships. They feed on a variety of marine organisms, small crustaceans, marine worms, cephalopods (squid, cuttlefish, octopus) and occasionally fish. Some obviously have a very specialised diet but there have been few studies. Many travel vast distances. The Short-tailed Shearwater Puffinus tenuirostris *migrates in a great loop from Australia to the north Pacific. Flying over the Tasman Sea towards New Zealand the birds move clockwise into and around the north Pacific, crossing the equatorial waters of the central Pacific and making a landfall on the coast of Australia before moving on to the breeding grounds on small islands in the Bass Strait. One bird, banded at Cedua, South Australia was recovered some six weeks later in the Bering Sea, after a journey of about 15,300 km. Petrels usually visit land only to breed, typically in colonies on remote, wind-swept islands, peninsulas or coastal mountains where there are few predators. Most species nest in burrows or in crevices between rocks, except for the giant-petrels which nest on the ground. Usually quiet at sea, most petrels are extremely noisy in their breeding colonies making weird, cooing, wailing or screeching noises from dusk to dawn.*

Several species of shearwaters, the muttonbirds, have been exploited commercially and for food in Australia and New Zealand and to a lesser degree in the Pacific islands. Sometimes adults but mainly the fat and oily chicks are taken from their burrows and salt-cured for food with the by-products including pro-ventricular oil used for cosmetics and suntan lotions, fat used mainly as a food supplement for dairy cows and down feathers used for padding and upholstery. Rigorous protection regulations were imposed by the two governments early in this century but chicks may still be taken for a limited period under licence. The eggs and adult birds are strictly protected.

Nine species in the family Procellariidae have been recorded in Vanuatu. Two very different species, a giant-petrel and a prion, are migrants from their breeding grounds in the antarctic and subantarctic which have occurred as vagrants. One shearwater, breeding in Australia and migrating across the Pacific to the Bering Sea, is probably a regular visitor to Vanuatu waters. Three other shearwaters and a gadfly-petrel have been recorded as breeding in Vanuatu and 2 other gadfly-petrels may possibly breed in the group.

3. Antarctic Giant-Petrel   *Macronectes giganteus*
French name: Pétrel géant

IDENTIFICATION AND FIELD NOTES
Length 85 to 90 cm. The Antarctic Giant-Petrel is the size of a small albatross, with a massive horn-coloured bill, heavier build, shorter wingspan, less graceful, stiff-winged flight and diagnostic, single, prominent nasal tube. Plumage is variable with dark and light phases. *Adult male:* the common dark greyish-brown birds develop a pale grey to whitish head with age and the leading edges of the wings become mottled with pale

feathers; some individuals have rather mottled, light grey and brown plumage and almost white forehead. White phase birds (≃5% of the population) are white with a few scattered dark feathers on body and wings. Iris: dark brown to pale grey with age. Legs and feet: blackish-grey, may be flesh-coloured in light phase birds. *Adult female:* similar to male but appreciably smaller. *Immature:* dark phase birds entirely dark brown, becoming paler with age; white phase individuals are like the adults.

The closely related Hall's Giant-Petrel *Macronectes halli* has no white phase. The plumage ranges from sooty-brown to dark grey with increasing age and the face and throat become paler. Immature has a dark crown and appears capped. The tip of the bill is reddish-brown in the immature and adult Hall's Giant-Petrel but dark greenish in the Antarctic. This difference can only be seen at close range and is rarely apparent at sea. In good viewing conditions, the leading edge of the innerwing viewed from below is very dark.

The Giant-Petrel is generally observed alone or in small numbers. It is bold, follows ships closely and when garbage is thrown overboard will congregate around it uttering low guttural noises.

DISTRIBUTION AND STATUS

The Antarctic Giant-Petrel *M. giganteus* breeds colonially on the Antarctic mainland and coastal islands, on the islands of the Scotia Arc north to South Georgia and the Falklands. Most adults probably disperse to neighbouring seas but the young birds are highly migratory. Juveniles banded at South Georgia have been recovered in Western Australia and New Zealand, distances of over 16,000 kms, within five weeks. The first few years are spent at sea taking advantage of the steady westerly winds to circle around the world, ranging north to 10°S in the colder currents and regularly reaching the tropics. It was these dark immatures that were found alive off Efate, in Vanuatu in 1973. Hall's Giant-Petrel *M. halli* breeds at the Chatham, Auckland, Antipodes, Campbell, Stewart, Macquarie, Kerguelen, Crozet, Marion and Gough Islands (Bourne and Warham, 1966). Juvenile *M. halli* banded on Macquarie and Crozet have been recovered in Australia and New Zealand. Both species breed on South Georgia, Kerguelen, Crozet and Marion Islands and nest within sight of each other at Macquarie.

4. Tahiti Petrel *Pseudobulweria rostrata* PLATE 2
French name: Pétrel de Tahiti

IDENTIFICATION AND FIELD NOTES

Length 38 to 40 cm. A medium-sized gadfly-petrel, with a bulbous black bill and wedge-shaped tail. It is mainly deep blackish-brown except for a sharply defined white lower breast, belly and undertail-coverts. Iris: dark brown. Legs and feet: flesh coloured or pink, usually with the outer half of the toes and webs black. In Vanuatu this species may be distinguished from all other black and white petrels by its larger size and heavier bill.

The Tahiti Petrel is usually seen singly or in flocks with other species feeding in pelagic waters. Rising and falling low over the water, this petrel is seldom seen above the horizon. Banking arcs and glides are interspersed with loose, deep wingbeats with wrists bent. Flight is not so erratic as the small Gould's Petrel *P. leucoptera* or as graceful and acrobatic as the White-necked Petrel *P. externa*.

DISTRIBUTION AND STATUS
It breeds in the Society Islands, the Marquesas, New Caledonia and possibly Rarotonga (Cook Is); a much smaller race *P.r.becki*, (29 cm), is known from the Solomon Islands and the Bismarck Archipelago. Abundant in the vicinity of its breeding grounds, small numbers disperse to the north and west reaching the eastern coast of Australia. The Tahiti Petrel, first recorded on Aneityum in 1961, is a vagrant in Vanuatu waters. There is a record in March 1985 that several were observed 'recently ... off the northern islands' (Naika 17:12). It has been recorded across the equator in the central Pacific during the southern winter.

5. The two races of *Pterodroma leucoptera* are considered separately.

White-winged Petrel   *Pterodroma leucoptera brevipes*
Other name: Collared Petrel
French name: Pétrel aux ailes blanches

IDENTIFICATION
Length 30 cm. A small dark and white gadfly-petrel with a white forehead and stubby bill. In flight shows a dark 'M' pattern across wings and lower back. Upperparts grey; head and nape darker, mantle medium-grey, rump lighter and tail sooty. Forehead is strongly freckled with white. Underparts variable, typically white with a diffuse grey breast band or mainly grey with white throat and undertail-coverts. The northernmost population from the Banks Islands is reported to have the greyest underparts. Lighter birds have mainly white underwing with dark leading and trailing edges but in darker birds the underwing is suffused grey with darker margins. Dark grey on head and nape extends to the side of the neck with clear demarcation diagonally and below the eye. The dark 'M' pattern seen in flight, indistinct in worn plumage, is formed by the grey back and inner part of the wings and the lighter grey secondaries contrasting with the sooty wing-coverts and primaries. Iris: brown. Bill: black, relatively short and stout with a short nasal tube. Legs and feet: flesh-coloured in nestlings, greyish-blue in adults with webs and toes distally black. It can be distinguished at sea from similar gadfly-petrels by the extensive black hood forming, or partly forming, a neck collar. It is smaller, with a stouter bill than the Fluttering and Audubon's Shearwaters which also lack the white forehead and dark 'M' markings.

DISTRIBUTION AND STATUS
This race *brevipes* breeds in Fiji, Vanuatu, New Caledonia and Tau, Samoa and disperses to the north and east into the central Pacific with records for Kiribati (Phoenix and Line Islands) the Cook Islands and the Tuamotu Archipelago. Known specimens from Vanuatu are one from Aneityum taken 28 February 1859 (Leiden Museum); one received at the British Museum (Natural History) in 1860 and 3 from Aneityum received there in 1888 which look as if they were collected at the same time; one from Efate on 4 June 1926, 6 collected at sea 48 km (30 miles) east of Mere Lava in the Banks group on 28 and 29 January 1927, and 4 from scattered burrows in woodland

above 300 m (1,000 ft) on the slopes of Mount Melon, Tanna on 1-2 April 1936 (one with an egg) are in the American Museum of Natural History, New York (Bourne pers. comm. 1990). There are other species and races within the Pacific region that resemble the White-winged Petrel. Mayr (1945) recognised two races, the nominate race *P.l.leucoptera* known as Gould's Petrel and the greyer race *P.l.brevipes* called variously White-winged or Collared Petrel. Harrison (1983) states that birds 'with characters intermediate between *leucoptera* and *brevipes* or forming undescribed races occur on the Solomons, New Caledonia and Vanuatu'. In Pratt *et al*, (1987) the Collared Petrel *Pterodroma brevipes* is given the other name of Gould's Petrel and they note: 'Sometimes considered conspecific with White-winged Petrel (*P.leucoptera*)'.

FIELD NOTES

They are swift and erratic flying birds, with their slender build giving the appearance of light, buoyant flight. Continuous, steeply banked arcs are interspersed by rapid wingbeats with wings slightly bending at the wrist.

VOICE

The most often heard call, uttered in flight and from the ground at the breeding sites, and often repeated, is a thin, high 'tee-tee-tee'. Also has various high-pitched squeaks and low sounds.

FOOD

It probably takes mainly squid, and crustaceans.

NEST AND BREEDING

In Vanuatu breeding has been reported in the Banks Islands from August to March and on Tanna in April, but few details are known. Nesting colonies are apparently established in certain valleys or steep slopes on coastal mountains. They may dig a burrow in the ground amongst dense vegetation or use rock crevices. The adult birds return to their colonies after dark and leave before first light.

Gould's Petrel   *Pterodroma leucoptera leucoptera*
French name: Pétrel de Gould

IDENTIFICATION AND FIELD NOTES

Otherwise similar, this petrel differs from *P.l.brevipes*, the White-winged Petrel, in having pure white underparts. Harrison (1983) states that '*brevipes* is usually regarded as a melanistic central Pacific race of Gould's Petrel'.

DISTRIBUTION AND STATUS

It breeds on the steep western slopes of Cabbage Tree Island off the Australian coast where it has been estimated that the total population is no more than 2,000 birds. This race is also thought to breed in New Caledonia. It has been recorded at sea off the Vanuatu coast which suggests that birds probably disperse towards the central Pacific frequenting subtropical and tropical waters.

6. White-necked Petrel *Pterodroma externa cervicalis*
Other name: White-naped Petrel
French name: Pétrel à nuque blanche

IDENTIFICATION AND FIELD NOTES

Length 43 cm. One of the larger dark and white gadfly-petrels, with long wings and short wedge-shaped tail. Upperparts mainly medium-grey with a darker grey 'M' pattern across the wings and back; forehead white; top of head black with a broad white nape. Underparts, including undertail-coverts white; underwing all white except for a thin but noticeable dark margin between the wrist and the leading primary. Iris: brown. Bill: short, heavy and black. Legs and feet: flesh-coloured with dark patches.

In flight it soars higher than most other gadfly-petrels, frequently well above the horizon and with wings bowed and angled. The steeply banked arcs and glides are interspersed occasionally with deep loose, fairly slow wingbeats.

DISTRIBUTION AND STATUS

This race breeds in the Kermadec Islands north of New Zealand while the race *P. e. externa* breeds in the Juan Fernandez Islands off Chile on the opposite side of the southern Pacific. This species commonly disperses northward into the west and central Pacific but little is known of its movements. The Kermadec population extends west to the Tasman Sea, to within 400 km of the Australian coast, during the breeding season. Six unusually small specimens with enlarged gonads (in breeding condition) were collected 48 km (30 miles) east of Mere Lava in the Banks group by the Whitney South Sea Expedition on 28 and 29 January 1927. These birds had all the plumage characteristics of *P. e. cervicalis* but their wing, tail, tarsus, bill and middle toe measurements were outside the range of the Kermadec Islands specimens collected over many years (Falla, 1976 and Bourne pers. comm. 1990). It is likely that they represented an unnamed race that breeds in the Vanuatu archipelago. King (1967) noted records for Vanuatu waters and that some observers believed it may breed here.

7. Antarctic Prion *Pachyptila desolata*
Other name: Dove Prion
French name: Prion Colombe

IDENTIFICATION AND FIELD NOTES

Length 25 cm. A small bluish-grey petrel with white underparts, characteristic high forehead and relatively broad bill. Upperparts blue-grey, darker on the head. Lores and eyebrows white with a dark mark through the eye; sides of neck are dusky, creating a partial collar. In flight shows a prominent dark 'M' pattern across back and wings, clearly visible at close quarters, wedge-shaped tail with a terminal black band across the central feathers and white underwing. Iris: brown. Bill: blue-black, broad and straight sided with a small black nasal tube. Legs and feet: blue, paler on webs.

At sea it may be seen singly, in groups or large flocks. Flight is erratic, rocking, twisting and banking with rapid, stiff wingbeats. A flock often suggests dry leaves whirling around in the wind. On sunny days the white underparts show even when they are far off but as they turn the blue-grey back merges with the sea. It is difficult to separate from the Broad-billed Prion *Pachyptila vittata* and the Lesser Broad-billed Prion *Pachyptila salvini*. Some authorities believe that they are races of the same species (Harrison, 1983).

DISTRIBUTION AND STATUS

Circumpolar, and essentially a bird of the cold antarctic and subantarctic regions, it breeds at islands in the Scotia Arc, South Georgia, Kerguelen, Heard, Macquarie, Auckland, and Scott Islands and at Cape Denison, Antarctica. *P. (v). salvini* breeds at Marion, Prince Edward and Crozet Islands. *P. v. vittata* breeds at Tristan da Cunha, Gough Island, St Paul, Amsterdam, Snares, Chatham and Stewart Islands and on certain mainland coasts of Southland, New Zealand. It has been recorded from the Kermadec Islands and at sea near Vanuatu.

8. Wedge-tailed Shearwater *Puffinus pacificus*
French name: Puffin à queue pointue
Local name: Koroliko on Tongoa

IDENTIFICATION

Length about 44 cm. An entirely dark, medium-sized shearwater with a slender slate-coloured bill, pale to whitish-flesh-coloured feet and a rather long wedge-shaped tail. Upperparts sooty-brown; primaries and tail black. Face, throat and rest of underparts greyish-brown; underwing dusky-brown. Birds in fresh plumage are almost black above, worn feathers becoming increasingly brown. There is a lighter colour phase occurring in some populations as in Shark Bay, western Australia and, generally, those breeding north of 10°N. This form has whitish grey underparts blending into the dark upper plumage and a whitish underwing with darker border and axillaries.

DISTRIBUTION, STATUS AND CONSERVATION

The breeding range of this abundant shearwater covers almost all the tropical and subtropical Pacific and Indian Oceans. In the Pacific it breeds on all island groups except Easter Island, the Cook Islands, Palau and Tuvalu. Tropical populations are probably non-migratory. The Wedge-tailed Shearwater, probably the commonest shearwater found in Vanuatu waters, breeds on Laika Island between Tongoa and Epi and possibly on Goat Island, off the coast of Erromango, and on several other small, uninhabited, offshore islands.

Large numbers of eggs, chicks and any adults found in burrows, are regularly collected for food by villagers from neighbouring islands throughout the breeding season. Due to the inaccessibility of many colonies there seems to have been no permanent damage in the past but it is feared that with the increasing human population and better means of transport, raiding parties may become more frequent, reducing the numbers of birds through over-collecting and developing eventually into a threat to the survival of the breeding colonies. In order to maintain the population, enough young birds must be allowed to grow to maturity to balance the normal mortality rate. Consideration should be given to having a biennial close season which should allow a sustainable yield of chicks. Adult birds and eggs should be fully protected as in Australia and New Zealand.

Adult Wedge-tailed Shearwater returning at night to feed the chick in a burrow on Laika Island

Apart from direct human predation and the threat of habitat destruction through development, these ground-nesting birds are particularly prone to predation by rodents, cats, pigs, dogs and in some Pacific islands, the mongoose. The natural vegetation may also be reduced or destroyed by stock animals like goats, pigs, sheep and cattle which trample the ground causing destruction of burrows and leading eventually to soil erosion. In order to preserve the natural equilibrium in some populations of petrels and other seabirds, the importance of establishing Island Reserves cannot be too highly stressed.

FIELD NOTES
It can be seen singly or in small parties. Flight is buoyant and graceful with the usual careening action of shearwaters. Occasional loose, shallow wingbeats are interspersed with long glides and the wings, characteristically bowed (wrists well forward) are held slightly above the body. The wings are broader and more rounded than those of other shearwaters. In moderate winds the birds remain fairly horizontal as they forage over the water. As the wind speed increases they arc and bank more steeply but seldom above the horizon. It can be distinguished from the Short-tailed Shearwater *Puffinus tenuirostris* by its larger build, longer tail, pale feet and less direct flight.

VOICE

It is usually silent at sea but has loud and discordant calls in the breeding colonies. On Laika Island continuous calling ebbs and flows over the breeding grounds from shortly after dark, abating somewhat in the early hours, and resuming in intensity just before dawn. Single mournful calls are most often given whilst in the air. The song on the ground has a wailing quality, 'ka-koooo-ahh, ka-koooo-ahh' with the first syllable soft, the second forced and the last long-drawn out. These caterwauling cries are often repeated in a doleful manner and with increasing frenzy until reaching an abrupt and hysterical climax. Songs have a common pattern but there is variation in rhythm, rate of delivery and length, and sometimes two or three birds call in unison, creating a rhythmically rising and falling wail. Calls decrease considerably after the early nesting period.

FOOD

Various kinds of squid and fish are taken, the birds catching their prey by flying close to the surface of the water and plunging head and neck down into the sea. Among shoals of fish they lunge for food while paddling on the surface with wings extended.

NEST AND BREEDING

They nest gregariously in burrows, usually in bare or grass covered earth or among low plants but sometimes, in Vanuatu, beneath forest canopies. On Laika Island several hundred birds are present during the breeding season. The sexually mature birds probably arrive during October or November. On light nights birds can be seen flying above the plateau and along its steep sides wheeling up and down in the air currents, calling and chasing, before coming in to land. Birds nesting in the open usually alight near their burrows and scramble towards the entrance. Those nesting beneath the trees tumble down with a fluttering flight to reach their nest sites. Like all petrels, they are awkward on the ground with a strange but effective gait. They rest on their thighs and belly, legs are held horizontally and then raised to a vertical position with each step. This movement is rather hurried and often accompanied with wing beating which assists balance. The nest chamber may be several feet from the entrance of the burrow and is often lined with some plant material or feathers. The burrow is prepared during nightly visits by first loosening the earth with the bill and then raking it out of the burrow with several, backward movements of one foot and then the other. Some colonies are closely packed and average one burrow per m^2. The single white egg (63 × 41 mm) is laid in December or later, with the chicks hatching in late January or early February and fledging from late April to June, with probably up to 70 days in the nest. The chick is covered with thick down, ash-grey above, lighter around the bill, throat and underparts, and is brooded by either or both adults for the first week or so before being left alone in the burrow during the day. The growth rate of the chicks is very rapid. Hatching weight is doubled in a week and the adult weight may be exceeded for a time; 20 specimens weighed from 330 to 410 g. Fed nightly at first by both parents, the intervals gradually become longer. Before leaving, the young emerge for several nights to beat their wings and then return to the burrow. They finally depart, unaided by the parents, under cover of darkness, working their way either to the precipitous side of the plateau where they simply drop into the air or, possibly, down to the shore and swimming out to sea.

9. Short-tailed Shearwater *Puffinus tenuirostris*
Other names: Tasmanian Muttonbird, Slender-billed Petrel/Shearwater
French name: Puffin à bec grêle

IDENTIFICATION AND FIELD NOTES

Length 40 cm. A medium-sized dark shearwater with a short, fan-shaped tail. Adult and immature similar, female is slightly smaller: mainly brownish-black above and below. Underwing is normally brownish-black, but is variable; some are all dark silvery-grey, some grey with a paler central streak and others, rarely, have an all white streak in the centre. Wing quills and tail are black. Iris: brown. Bill: slender, leaden-grey often tinged with olive. Legs and feet: outerside of tarsus blackish-grey-brown, innerside purplish-flesh, webs grey with darker edges.

It is usually seen in flocks, some immense, possibly not feeding whilst passing through Vanuatu waters on migration. Flight is generally level, fast and direct, a few rapid wingbeats alternating with stiff-winged glides. Differs from the Wedge-tailed Shearwater in its smaller size, short tail, dark feet and flight behaviour. It may be wrecked during cyclones. Sometimes follows ships.

DISTRIBUTION AND STATUS

It breeds on the southeast coast of Australia and islands in the Bass Strait and Spencer Gulf, migrating north to Alaska and western coasts of North America. It is said by Pizzey (1980), to be the most abundant Australian shearwater and possibly Australian bird. Maximum counts of 60,000 per hour have been made off the coast of New South Wales (Harrison, 1983). Large numbers occur throughout the central Pacific during October and November. A few records exist for Vanuatu. Possibly it was birds of this species that were seen by Richard Pickering, as they flew from west to east in tens of thousands, off Takara on the north coast of Efate, on 21-22 September 1985 (Naika 20:24).

10. Fluttering Shearwater *Puffinus gavia* PLATE 2
French name: Puffin volage

IDENTIFICATION AND FIELD NOTES

Length 32 cm. A stout, dark and light shearwater with a short, rounded tail. Upperparts dark brown extending well below the eye and merging into whitish-grey on chin, throat and breast. Underparts mainly white with dusky sides to the body and a noticeable browner patch on the thigh. Underwing mostly white with fairly thick dark margins. Iris: blackish. Bill: long and slender, dark, brownish-grey. Legs and feet: flesh-coloured with brown outerside to tarsus. Upperparts appear blackish-brown after moult, but fade and wear to rusty-brown for most of the year.

Flight is generally swift and low over the sea, short glides on outstretched wings being interspersed with rapid wingbeats. It is often seen in flocks and settles frequently on the surface of the sea. It differs from Audubon's Shearwater in being more brown than black above and more dusky below.

DISTRIBUTION AND STATUS

It breeds at many islands in northern New Zealand from Three Kings to Cook Strait

(Falla *et al*, 1981). Juveniles disperse to the southern and eastern coasts of Australia. Mayr (1945) and Harper and Kinsky (1978) note that this species breeds in 'the New Hebrides' but this has not been substantiated. It has been recorded as a vagrant in Vanuatu waters.

11. Audubon's Shearwater   *Puffinus lherminieri gunax*
Other name: Dusky-backed Shearwater
French name: Puffin d'Audubon

IDENTIFICATION
Length 30 to 32 cm. A small, stocky, dark and white shearwater with a long, thin bill. Upperparts: sooty-black extending to just below the eye and in a dark stripe on the outer side of the thigh. Underparts: white, sides of the neck and breast mottled grey; underwing white except for dark primaries and secondaries; undertail-coverts variable from dark to mottled white. Iris: brown. Bill: slate-black, paler on the lower mandible. Legs and feet: whitish-flesh to light bluish-grey with dark outer toes tipped black.

DISTRIBUTION AND STATUS
It is widespread in the tropical Pacific breeding on most island groups excluding Hawaii but with 9 or 10 races appears to be non-migratory throughout its range. The race *gunax* described by Mathews in 1930, has been recorded in Vanuatu along the coast of most islands. It does not disperse widely from the breeding grounds and is only seen within 160 km of the islands. Specimens have been collected on Mere Lava in the Banks group by Beck in 1926, near Malapoa on Efate and on ridges near Mount

Audubon's Shearwater, which breeds in the mountains, has been recorded along the coasts of most islands

Melon on Tanna (American Museum/New York), and on the beach near Port Vila, Efate by the author in 1975. The British Museum (Natural History) has one specimen collected on Aneityum on 18 January 1860 and Oslo Museum has one collected from Tongoa in 1897 (Bourne, pers. comm.). Dr Bourne also provided further information on the Tanna specimens in the AMNH: three were collected, at about 970 m (3,200 ft) on 11 March 1935 (one in a 6 ft (2 m) burrow, one with an egg); three on 1 December 1936 and one on 28 January 1937 with young in a slope at about 667 m (2,200 ft). It was established from villagers that in 1978 shearwaters bred in the mountains of Ambae but the species is not known (Robertson, pers. comm.). It is likely that Audubon's Shearwater still breeds in Vanuatu but colonies have yet to be located.

FIELD NOTES
Flight is generally level and fast with very rapid wingbeats on stiff wings interspersed with short glides close to the water. Returning at dusk, they perform sweeping display flights near their breeding grounds.

VOICE
It is usually silent at sea but raucous calls are heard at night during the courtship period while they circle in loose flocks. When breeding, a loud, high-pitched rapidly or irregularly delivered squealing or crooning call with variations may be heard from birds in or near the burrow.

FOOD
Squid, fish and marine invertebrates are taken. It can be seen in feeding flocks, resting or pattering on the surface and diving and swimming underwater.

NEST AND BREEDING
Reputed to breed in Vanuatu from September to April, it is strictly nocturnal on land and nests on high coastal mountains often far from the sea. The nest may be in a hole among rocks or in a long burrow excavated in the earth, most often on steep slopes. The egg (52 × 36 cm) is incubated by both adults. The chick has dark grey down above and is lighter below. It is fed frequently at first by both parents and thereafter is abandoned by day and visited irregularly by night until fully fledged.

Storm-Petrels *Oceanitidae*

Probably no other seabirds are subject to so much folklore and myths than the little storm-petrels, so called because of the sailors' superstition that their sudden appearance at sea presaged a storm. There are about 21 species in 8 genera ranging the seas of the world. Noted for their distinctive flight, they flutter erratically close to the surface or swoop and glide like diminutive gadfly-petrels. All are small delicate birds; none is over 25 cm long, the size of an Indian Mynah. They are all relatively dark above with paler wing-coverts, often with a white rump, and the colour below varies. They may be divided into two groups of genera, the Hydrobatinae and Oceanitinae, characteristic of different hemispheres but overlapping in range. The southern species (Oceanitinae) have short rounded wings, nearly square tails, long tarsi and short toes. They are adapted for skipping along or hovering close to the surface of the water and picking up small marine organisms, rarely alighting and dipping into the sea. They bounce over each undulation of the waves on fluttering wings, pattering the water with their feet, sometimes together but more often alternately, giving the illusion that they are walking on the water. Most are restricted to the southern hemisphere but the Polynesian Storm-Petrel Nesofregetta fuliginosa *is resident in the tropical Pacific and breeds in Vanuatu. Two others have been recorded as vagrants; both breed on antarctic and subantarctic islands. Wilson's Storm-Petrel is a transequatorial migrant wintering in the northern oceans and the Black-bellied Storm-Petrel migrates into the tropics during the southern winter.*

12. Wilson's Storm-Petrel *Oceanites oceanicus*
French name: Pétrel de Wilson

IDENTIFICATION AND FIELD NOTES
Length 18 cm. A dainty little petrel, all sooty-black except for the distinctive white rump and undertail-coverts, a pale diagonal bar across the upperwing-coverts and bright yellow webs to the feet. Iris: brown. Bill: black. Legs and feet: black with yellow webs, noticeable when pattering over the waves.

Flight is distinctive; it flutters erratically like a butterfly or bat with short glides interspersed with rapid shallow wingbeats. In level flight the feet project beyond the tail. When feeding, it can be seen darting to and fro picking food from the surface or hovering with the wings held vertically over the back and the legs dangling. A querulous, sparrow-like chattering can be heard from feeding flocks. It often follows ships to scavenge.

DISTRIBUTION AND STATUS
It breeds in the antarctic and subantarctic and scatters over most oceans in the winter. Rare in the tropical Pacific, it has been recorded from the Solomons, New Caledonia, the Marshall Islands, Kiribati and Vanuatu.

13. Black-bellied Storm-Petrel *Fregetta tropica*
French name: Pétrel tempête à ventre noir

IDENTIFICATION AND FIELD NOTES
Length 18 to 20 cm. Sooty-black above except for white rump and undertail-coverts; darker on the head, flight feathers and tail blackish; upperwing-coverts slightly paler. Throat and upper breast black; rest of underparts white except for a variable dark stripe down the centre of the belly to the undertail-coverts. Chin may be mottled with white; underwing white in the centre with broad, black edges. Iris: brown. Bill: black. Legs and feet: black.

It is slightly larger than Wilson's Storm-Petrel which also has a white rump but lacks white on the belly and underwing. It differs from the Polynesian Storm-Petrel by the more noticeable white rump and square tail. Direct flight is close to the surface, light and erratic with a butterfly-like appearance. It usually follows the contours of the waves with bill pointed downwards and legs dangling, patters on the surface when feeding and frequently splashes into the water. It is more often seen flying ahead of ships but occasionally follows, picking up marine organisms churned up by the propellers.

DISTRIBUTION AND STATUS

It breeds on antarctic and subantarctic islands including Kerguelen, Auckland and Antipodes Islands and migrates north into the tropics from May to September. The closely related White-bellied Storm-Petrel *Fregetta grallaria* which lacks the black central stripe, has a more northerly breeding distribution including Rapa. Both have been recorded from Samoa and the Marquesas and the Black-bellied Storm-Petrel in the Solomons and Vanuatu.

14. Polynesian Storm-Petrel   *Nesofregetta fuliginosa*
Other names: White-throated Storm-Petrel, Samoan Storm-Petrel
French name: Pétrel tempête à gorge blanche

IDENTIFICATION

Length 25 cm. A large storm-petrel with a long, deeply forked tail. Upperparts: sooty-black with a narrow white band across the rump. Underparts are variable, typically mostly white except for a broad, sooty band across the breast and undertail-coverts. Underwing-coverts white with sooty-black margins wider on the trailing edge. Darker phase birds, the Samoan form, are uniformly sooty-brown but intermediates have been observed, with continuous gradation from light to dark phase, in the Phoenix and McKean Island populations and with some dark flecking or streaks on white underparts in the Line Island and Kiritimati birds (Harrison, 1983). Bill: black. Legs and feet: black, the legs are long and laterally compressed and the feet are large. The deeply forked tail is diagnostic in flight.

DISTRIBUTION AND STATUS

Endemic to the tropical Pacific, it breeds in the Marquesas, Kiritimati, Samoa, Kiribati and Fiji and disperses throughout the island groups. Seven specimens were collected from Aneityum in 1860: four (11 January) are in the British Museum (Natural History); the Australian Museum has 2 (collected 15 and 16 January) and the Leiden Museum one (18 January). The American Museum of Natural History has a specimen found in a short burrow at about 424 m (1,400 ft) in a volcanic crater on Tanna 12 November 1935 (Bourne pers. comm.). It is widely thought that this storm-petrel is still breeding in Vanuatu but the present locations are not known.

FIELD NOTES

It bounds and skips in erratic zig-zags close to the surface of the sea. Pratt *et al* (1987) describe the characteristic kick and glide pattern: uses feet to push off, glides 20-30 seconds on outstretched wings, then kicks off again, changing direction. While feeding it patters the surface and picks up food without alighting.

VOICE

Soft whistling and monotonous piping notes have been heard at the nest site. It is said to be silent at sea.

FOOD

It probably takes small crustaceans, squid and fish.

NEST AND BREEDING
It nests in burrows on coastal mountains or atolls. Data from Kiritimati indicate that some nesting occurs throughout the year with peak numbers of eggs present in September to November and fewest eggs in March to June (Schreiber and Ashmole, 1970). In the Line Islands eggs have been found in January and in the Phoenix Islands in every month. It is said to breed in the Marquesas from July to December.

Order PELECANIFORMES
This order comprises six families of medium to large sized, aquatic, fish-eating birds: pelicans, boobies (and gannets), darters, cormorants, frigatebirds and tropicbirds. While each family is strongly distinctive all are linked by various characteristics of anatomy and behaviour, noticeably their foot structure. All four toes are connected by webs; the hind toe is turned partly forward and linked to the innermost front toe. On the inner edge of the third claw is a pecten or comb, for preening, but in the tropicbirds this is modified into a broad flange. All have short legs, sometimes extremely so, and long wings with 11 primaries. They are all strong fliers, most of them swim well but they are not good at walking. All have long beaks: the bill is hooked in pelicans, cormorants and frigatebirds but sharply pointed in boobies, darters and tropicbirds. Nostrils are very small or sealed externally in adaptation for diving. All have a distensible gular or throat pouch which, except in the tropicbirds and gannets, is unfeathered and is most developed in the pelican. In hot conditions the naked gular region is fluttered rapidly and the birds achieve cooling by evaporation. Gular fluttering also occurs in some groups of landbirds but in no other marine order.

There is usually a disparity in size between the sexes and in a few species also in plumage. Elaborate pair-forming rituals may be observed often involving nest material. Breeding biology is determined to a great extent by the availability of the food supply. Some lay only one egg but others a small clutch. Both sexes incubate; the period varying from 3 to 8 weeks, and the young spend 5 to 8 weeks in the nest, some remaining dependent on their parents for up to 6 months after fledging. Chicks are fed with regurgitated food; they insert their whole head into the open beak of the adult. A series of meals is usually given after the parents return to the nest.

Pelecaniformes are closely associated with water and their distribution is worldwide. Pelicans and cormorants migrate in North America and Eurasia to avoid the rigours of winter. Throughout tropical and temperate zones most species are relatively sedentary but the tropicbirds and gannets, particularly the immatures, wander considerable distances. In Vanuatu five of the families are represented: only the darters are missing.

Pelicans *Pelecanidae*
In the family Pelecanidae there is only one genus, Pelecanus, *which includes 7 or 8 species. Pelicans are very large, aquatic birds with a heavy body, long neck, large head and long straight bill, hooked at the tip; the lower mandible has an expandable pouch. The wings are long and broad and the tail is short and rounded. Apart from the Brown Pelican, plumage is mainly white with areas of black, grey or brown. Juveniles have varying amounts of brown in the plumage and maturity is reached in 3 to 4 years. Usually seen in flocks, they inhabit inland*

fresh and brackish lakes and coastal waters except for the Brown Pelican which is a marine species. They feed on fish and occasionally crustaceans; dipping the pouch in, they scoop up the fish, strain out the water and swallow the fish whole. They breed colonially in trees or on the ground and are very sensitive to disturbance. Their decline in range and numbers is thought to be due to the use of pesticides poisoning their food, to drainage of land for development and to encroaching human population.

Pelicans are found in most tropical and temperate regions of the world. The Australian Pelican occurs throughout Australia and in Tasmania. In seasons of drought it disperses widely and has been recorded in Vanuatu.

15. Australian Pelican *Pelecanus conspicillatus*
French name: Pélican australien

IDENTIFICATION AND FIELD NOTES
Length 160 to 180cm. A huge, heavy-bodied bird with a long pinkish bill and large pouch. The body is predominantly white with black shoulders, primaries, rump and tail; white undertail-coverts; large white patch in the centre of the upperwing. The head is sometimes a diffuse grey and immatures tend to show more brown than black. Iris: brown with a yellow orbital ring. Legs and feet; grey. In flight the head is tucked back against the body; wingbeats are slow, strong and loose and flocks fly in a spectacular V formation. It may glide motionless for long periods on updrafts. It frequents shallow, coastal and inland waters, islands and mudflats, and occasionally the open sea.

DISTRIBUTION AND STATUS
The Australian Pelican breeds in Australia and Tasmania where it is common in suitable habitat and nomadic according to seasonal variations in rainfall. In dry seasons it has reached New Zealand, Indonesia, the Solomons, New Caledonia, Fiji and Palau. It has appeared in New Guinea in large numbers in recent years, mostly around Port Moresby but occasionally wandering into the highlands or to the north coast (Beehler *et al*, 1986). In 1952 two flocks arrived on Aneityum in Vanuatu and a number of them survived there for over a year. They were gradually shot and eaten by the local people (Naika 19:2).

Boobies and Gannets *Sulidae*
The family Sulidae comprises 9 species in two natural groups; 6 species of boobies (genus, Sula), birds of the tropical seas and 3 species of gannets (genus, Morus), birds of temperate waters in the north and south. Some authorities prefer only one genus Sula for all species (Harrison, 1983). All are large seabirds with heavy, streamlined bodies, strong, conical bills, long necks, long pointed wings and long, wedge-shaped tails. There is no visible nasal opening. Feet are fully palmed with the outer and middle toes nearly equal in length. All have black and white or brown and white plumage and brightly coloured bill, gular pouch and feet. The sexes are similar in general appearance, and the plumage of the immature varies. They fly with the neck extended, a series of slow, powerful wingbeats alternating with short glides. At sea they float buoyantly and stand upright when on land. Food consists mainly of fish but squid are also taken. They catch fish by diving, often from a considerable height and pursue their prey under

PLATE I
1 Brown Booby   *Sula leucogaster*
2 Masked Booby   *Sula dactylatra*
3 Red-footed Booby   *Sula sula*
4 Royal Albatross   *Diomedea epomophora*
5 Least Frigatebird   *Fregata ariel* (male)
5a Least Frigatebird (male with gular pouch inflated)

PLATE 2
1. White Tern *Gygis alba*
2. Common Noddy *Anous stolidus*
3. Black-naped Tern *Sterna sumatrana*
4. Red-tailed Tropicbird *Phaethon rubricauda*
5. White-tailed Tropicbird *Phaethon lepturus*
6. Tahiti Petrel *Pseudobulweria rostrata*
7. Fluttering Shearwater *Puffinus gavia*

PLATE 3
1 Eastern Reef Heron   *Ardea sacra* (dark & light phases)
2 White-faced Heron   *Ardea novaehollandiae*
3 Little (Mangrove) Heron   *Butorides striatus*

PLATE 4
1. Australian Grebe *Tachybaptus novaehollandiae*
2. Little Pied Cormorant *Phalacrocorax melanoleucos*
3. Australian White-eyed Duck *Aythya australis*
4. Pacific Black (Australian Grey) Duck *Anas superciliosa*
5. Grey Teal *Anas gibberifrons*

PLATE 5
1   Barn Owl   *Tyto alba*
2   Brown (Australian) Goshawk   *Accipiter fasciatus* (adult)
2a Brown (Australian) Goshawk (immature)
3   Peregrine Falcon   *Falco peregrinus* (adult)
3a Peregrine Falcon (immature)
4   Swamp Harrier   *Circus approximans*

PLATE 6
1 Spotless Crake (Sooty Rail)   *Porzana tabuensis*
2 White-browed Crake   *Poliolimnas cinereus*
3 Purple Swamphen   *Porphyrio porphyrio*
4 Buff-banded (Banded) Rail   *Gallirallus philippensis*
5 Incubator Bird   *Megapodius freycinet*
6 Red Jungle Fowl   *Gallus gallus* (male & female)

PLATE 7
1   Pacific Golden Plover   *Pluvialis fulva*
    (breeding plumage)
1a Pacific Golden Plover (non-breeding
    plumage)
2   Ruddy Turnstone   *Arenaria interpres*
3   Beach Thick-knee   *Esacus magnirostris*
4   Whimbrel   *Numenius phaeopus*
5   Wandering Tattler   *Heteroscelus incanus*

PLATE 8
1. White-throated Pigeon *Columba vitiensis*
2. Vanuatu Mountain Pigeon *Ducula bakeri*
3. Pacific Imperial Pigeon *Ducula pacifica*
4. Vanuatu (Yellow-headed) Fruit Dove *Ptilinopus tannensis*
5. Red-bellied Fruit Dove *Ptilinopus greyii* (adult)
5a. Red-bellied Fruit Dove (immature)
6. Rufous-brown Pheasant-Dove *Macropygia mackinlayi*
7. Santa Cruz Ground Dove *Gallicolumba sanctaecrucis* (male)
7a. Santa Cruz Ground Dove (female)
8. Green-winged Ground (Emerald) Dove *Chalcophaps indica*

PLATE 9
1 Vanuatu (Yellow) White-eye *Zosterops flavifrons*
2 Grey-backed White-eye (Silvereye) *Zosterops lateralis*
3 Silver-eared Honeyeater *Lichmera incana*
4 Vanuatu Mountain (White-bellied) Honeyeater *Phylidonyris notabilis*
5 Cardinal Honeyeater *Myzomela cardinalis* (male)
5a Cardinal Honeyeater (female)
6 Green Palm (Vanuatu) Lorikeet *Charmosyna palmarum*
7 Rainbow Lorikeet *Trichoglossus haematodus*

PLATE 10
1. Long-tailed New Zealand Cuckoo *Eudynamis taitensis*
2. Shining Bronze-Cuckoo *Chrysococcyx lucidus* (adult)
3. Fan-tailed Cuckoo *Cacomantis pyrrhophanus*
4. Newly hatched cuckoo chick ejecting eggs of the foster-parent from the nest
5. Shining Bronze-Cuckoo *Chrysococcyx lucidus* fledgling being fed by foster-parent

PLATE 11
1 Uniform (Vanikoro) Swiftlet   *Aerodramus vanikorensis*
2 White-rumped Swiftlet   *Aerodramus spodiopygius*
3 White-bellied (Glossy) Swiftlet   *Collocalia esculenta*
4 Pacific Swallow   *Hirundo tahitica*

PLATE 12
1 Melanesian Cuckoo-shrike
  (Graybird)   *Coracina caledonica*
2 Long-tailed Triller   *Lalage leucopyga*
3 Polynesian Triller   *Lalage maculosa*
4 Vanuatu (Chestnut-bellied)
  Kingfisher   *Halcyon farquhari*
5 White-collared Kingfisher   *Halcyon chloris*
  (adult)
5a White-collared Kingfisher (immature)
6 Santo Mountain Starling   *Aplonis santovestris*
7 Rusty-winged Starling   *Aplonis zelandicus*
8 Indian Mynah   *Acridotheres tristis*

PLATE 13
1 Spotted Fantail   *Rhipidura spilodera*
2 Grey (Collared) Fantail   *Rhipidura fuliginosa*
3 Fantail Warbler   *Gerygone flavolateralis*
4 Thicket Warbler   *Cichlornis whitneyi*
5 Island Thrush   *Turdus poliocephalus* (three races illustrated)

PLATE 14
1 Scarlet Robin *Petroica multicolor* (male)
1a Scarlet Robin (female)
2 White-breasted Woodswallow *Artamus leucorhynchus*
3 Vanuatu (Buff-bellied) Flycatcher *Neolalage banksiana*
4 Golden Whistler *Pachycephala pectoralis* (male)
4a Golden Whistler (female)
5 Southern Shrikebill *Clytorhynchus pachycephaloides*
6 Broad-billed Flycatcher *Myiagra caledonica* (male)
6a Broad-billed Flycatcher (female)

PLATE 15

1 Chestnut-breasted Mannikin *Lonchura castaneothorax*
2 Common Waxbill *Estrilda astrild* (adult)
2a Common Waxbill (immature)
3 Black-headed Mannikin *Lonchura malacca* (adult)
3a Black-headed Mannikin (immature)
4 Red-throated Parrotfinch *Erythrura psittacea*
5 Royal Parrotfinch *Erythrura cyaneovirens* (adult)
5a Royal Parrotfinch (immature)
6 Blue-faced Parrotfinch *Erythrura trichroa*
7 Redpoll *Carduelis flammea* (male)
7a Redpoll (female)
8 House Sparrow *Passer domesticus* (male)
8a House Sparrow (female)

PLATE 16
1 Little Pied Cormorant *Phalacrocorax melanoleucos*
2 The dark morph of the Eastern Reef Heron *Ardea sacra* is the more common in Vanuatu
3 Pacific Black Duck *Anas superciliosa*
4 Common Waxbill *Estrilda astrild*

PLATE 17
1 The endemic Vanuatu Mountain Pigeon *Ducula bakeri* is found only in the highland forests on the larger islands of northern Vanuatu
2 Being wary and secretive the White-throated Pigeon *Columba vitiensis* sits or feeds silently in the trees
3 The melodious cooing of the Rufous-brown Pheasant-Dove *Macropygia mackinlayi* is one of the most pleasing sounds in the forests of Vanuatu
4 Green-winged Ground Dove *Chalcophaps indica* with two chicks
5 In Vanuatu the Santa Cruz Ground Dove *Gallicolumba sanctaecrucis* inhabits the mid-mountain forest on Santo
6 The gregarious Rainbow Lorikeet *Trichoglossus haematodus* is predominantly nomadic

1

2

3

4

5

6

PLATE 18
1 White-collared Kingfisher *Halcyon chloris* on the lookout for prey
2 The endemic Vanuatu Kingfisher *Halcyon farquhari*, a forest dweller, is restricted to some of the northern islands (H Schroeder-Born)

PLATE 19
1 Broad-billed Flycatcher *Myiagra caledonica*
2 The nest of the Fantail Warbler *Gerygone flavolateralis* is an oval dome suspended from leafy branches of vines
3 Thicket Warbler *Cichlornis whitneyi*

1

2

PLATE 20
1 Found mainly in the highlands on some of the northern islands, the endemic Vanuatu Mountain Honeyeater *Phylidonyris notabilis* is conspicuous as it darts noisily about the branches
2 The endemic Vanuatu White-eye *Zosterops flavifrons* is found throughout the islands and is probably the most numerous species

PLATE 21
1 The Buff-banded Rail *Gallirallus philippensis* though common is difficult to see as it is semi-nocturnal and a great skulker in thick vegetation

PLATE 22
1 The Blue-faced Parrotfinch *Erythrura trichroa*, which has almost completely switched to hole-nesting, is seen here in a limestone cliff
2 This brilliantly coloured Royal Parrotfinch *Erythrura cyaneovirens* is feeding on the seeds of wild figs

PLATE 23
1 There is less rainfall on the leeward side of the islands and the slopes of the mountains are covered with a mosaic of light forests and savannah

2 Mangroves form the main wetland vegetation in Vanuatu: the most extensive areas occur in the Maskelyne Islands and around the east and southeast coasts of Malakula (M Chambers)

PLATE 24

1 While the islands differ considerably in many ways, most have rugged and mountainous interiors covered with dense evergreen tropical rainforest, especially on the windward side

the water using their feet and half open wings to swim. Their bodies are highly adapted for plunge-diving having a network of air-sacs beneath the skin which cushion the impact. Feeding flocks wheel over the shoals of fish, dropping down into the water in a continuous stream and keeping the surface in constant agitation. Such flocks can be seen far away and help local fishermen in their search for fish.

All sulids except Abbott's Booby Sula abbotti from Christmas Island (Indian Ocean) breed colonially and on some cliffs and islands may cover every available space on the ground with crudely made nests of mud and vegetation. Two species, Abbott's Booby and the Red-footed Booby Sula sula make nests of twigs in trees or bushes. There are usually complex, ritual displays at the nest. Generally only one or two eggs are laid but if two eggs hatch one chick is favoured and the other usually dies. Conversely, the Peruvian Booby Sula variegata nesting near the rich fishing grounds of the Peruvian (Humboldt) current may raise up to four young. Incubation takes about 43 days and the eggs are carefully covered with the soles of the feet, the webs overlapping in the centre, before the body is lowered. Newly hatched chicks are brooded on the feet; they are blind at first and naked but soon grow a dense white down. Time in the nest varies considerably but, with the exception of one of the gannet species where the young are deserted at about 15 weeks old, all are fed as free-flying juveniles; the young Abbott's Booby for between 6 to 12 months. Immatures disperse widely and may not return to breed for 4 or more years.

The 3 species of Gannets breed around the north Atlantic coasts, on coastal islands off southern Africa and in the Australasian region off Tasmania and Victoria and in 12 colonies in New Zealand. Gannets derive their name from the same root as gander, a male goose, and they are much the same size: the old name 'sea goose' is still used in parts of Europe. Likewise the old Scandinavian name for this bird, 'Sula' has been appropriated for the scientific name of the family. Boobies are thought to be so called because seafarers long ago regarded them as dull-witted or 'boobies' in showing no fear. Boobies landing on ships would sit quietly and let the men catch them and nesting birds could be clubbed to death without attempting to escape. The 6 species of boobies are distributed over the tropical and subtropical regions but the ranges overlap. Two other species which may be seen at sea anywhere in the tropical Pacific are the Masked Booby Sula dactylatra, which is the largest (about 81 cm) of all the boobies and the Red-footed Booby which is the smallest (about 71 cm).

The Brown Booby and the Red-footed Booby breed in Vanuatu and the Masked Booby has occurred as a vagrant.

16. Brown Booby *Sula leucogaster* PLATE 1
French name: Fou à ventre blanc

IDENTIFICATION

Length 71 to 76 cm. Wingspan 132 to 150 cm. *Adult male:* plumage dark chocolate-brown except for white belly, white undertail-coverts and white centre of the underwing. The leading edge of the wing is darker brown above and below, primaries and secondaries are a lighter brown and the tail is brown and wedge-shaped. The clear-cut separation of the brown upperbreast and the belly is very noticeable. The bare face, eye-ring, base of the bill and gular skin are blue. Iris: light yellow to white. Bill: grey to light yellow. Legs and feet: olive-yellow. *Adult female:* larger than the male with similar plumage. Facial skin, eye-ring, base of bill, the gular skin and the feet are chrome-yellow. *Immature:* similar in pattern to the adult, dull brownish-grey above; head and neck mottled with light grey; uniformly brownish-grey white on the lower breast, belly and underwing-coverts. Face, base of the bill, gular skin and feet are pale olive-yellow. Bill is greyish to pale green with a blue tint towards the base.

The adult Brown Booby is separated from the Masked and Red-footed Boobies by the sharp demarcation between the chocolate-brown head and upper breast and the white lower breast and belly. The juvenile in mottled brown plumage could be confused with the juvenile Masked Booby, but is darker above, has no white collar and a different underwing pattern. Juvenile and immature are much darker than the brown phase Red-footed Booby and the underwing pattern is more clearly defined.

DISTRIBUTION AND STATUS
The Brown Booby is pantropical, breeding on islands in the tropical Atlantic and Indian Oceans and breeding on or visiting every island group in the tropical Pacific. In Vanuatu, the best known breeding and roosting site is Monument Rock in the centre of the group close to Mataso Island. About 30 to 50 breeding pairs are present there throughout the year, together with frigatebirds, tropicbirds and terns. Small numbers also occur around the coasts of other islands, especially in the north and may possibly nest on the Reef Islands and the cliffs of Ureparapara in the Banks group.

FIELD NOTES
It is apparently sedentary, as loose flocks range at sea mainly in the vicinity of their breeding or roosting sites. Adults are rarely found out of sight of land and only the young birds show a tendency to wander. In areas where it does not nest, it is usually encountered singly. Flight is fast and direct, deliberate wingbeats alternating with short glides. When foraging, the birds fly high, scanning the sea, until some prey is spotted then diving vertically, with head outstretched and wings partly folded, they hit the water with an impressive splash and catch their prey underwater. There is no more interesting spectacle than a feeding flock of boobies. They sometimes feed inshore as well as in deep water. Brown boobies are frequently harassed by frigatebirds being relentlessly chased until they disgorge their catch of fish. Although they nest on or near the ground they also perch on trees, bushes or rocks.

VOICE
The Brown Booby is not a vocal bird at sea. The calls of the sexes are different: the male uttering a high-pitched hissing and the female a louder low-pitched, harsh quacking. Breeding colonies are usually noisy with continuous squabbles between neighbouring birds.

FOOD
The diet consists mainly of fish and squid, caught most often by diving from some height and occasionally with shallow dives near the shore.

NEST AND BREEDING
The Brown Booby nests colonially in Vanuatu on inaccessible offshore islands and probably also on cliffs adjacent to deep water. The breeding season is apparently extended with most pairs breeding between August and March. There are elaborate displays by the mating birds; one is described from Australian nesting grounds in

which a piece of vegetation or stick is held by both birds and placed on the ground at their feet, the participants often entwining their necks in the process. The nest may be a hollow scraped in the ground, lined with some plants or a more substantial structure of twigs, grass, weeds and debris among or on bushes. The 2, rarely 3, chalky pale green eggs (61 × 40mm) are incubated by both birds for an average of 45 days. Only one chick is usually raised, probably the first to hatch. The chick supplicates for food by pointing the bill towards the parent and waving it from side to side, calling rhythmically. Older chicks mob the adult as it lands sometimes placing their wings around the parent as if to prevent escape. Studies of the Brown Booby on Ascension Island showed that the time from egg laying to the fledging of the chicks was 6 to 7 months (Dorward, 1962). The Brown Booby is said to be more timid and susceptible to disturbance when nesting than the Masked Booby or Red-footed Booby.

17. Red-footed Booby *Sula sula*   PLATE 1
French name: Fou à pattes rouges

IDENTIFICATION

Length 66 to 77 cm. Wingspan 91 to 101 cm. Slightly smaller than the Brown Booby, the adult is easily recognised by its red feet, but plumage is very variable. Four colour phases are described by Harrison (1983) and intermediate types are common. *Adult male and female:* can be distinguished from immature by the bright red feet and pale blue bill with a pink base and a black streak below; eye-ring and bare skin below the eye are blue. *White phase:* head and body white, often tinged gold on head; primaries and secondaries blackish; tail white; underwing-coverts white with a distinctive black patch at the carpal joint. *Intermediate phases:* head either white or brownish; underparts brownish with white belly and undertail-coverts; lower back, rump, uppertail-coverts and tail white; underwing patchy whitish and brown with black carpal area. *Brown phase:* completely grey or grey-brown, sometimes tinged golden on head and nape. *Juvenile:* in all phases plumage is brownish-grey, paler below. The bill is blackish, facial skin purple and legs and feet are yellowish-grey. The Red-footed Booby is separated from the Brown Booby by the red feet (if adult) and white tail in all but the brown phase. These brown phase birds are never as dark as the Brown Booby and the underwing pattern is much less distinct. It is noticeably smaller than the Masked Booby.

DISTRIBUTION AND STATUS

The Red-footed Booby is a pantropical pelagic species. Three races have been described; *S. s. rubripes* occurs in the Indian Ocean and the tropical Pacific. It breeds on many island groups, including Fiji, Samoa and on islands off the Queensland coast of Australia. There is strong circumstantial evidence of breeding on Hunter Island (22° 24′ S, 172° 05′ E), 260 km southeast of Aneityum. Barritt (1976) circled close to this volcanic island on board the survey ship HMS Hydra on 26 June 1974. He estimated about 2,000 at the island, either hovering over the bushy upper slopes or settled on the bushes. Red-footed Boobies were numerous up to about 24 km (15 miles) from Hunter Island and more appeared as the ship approached Matthew Island (22° 21′ S, 171° 21′ E), 66 km (41 miles) to the west. A booby that appeared to be immature was presented to the Cultural Centre at Port Vila, Efate on 16 August 1988 after it was found at the village of Ebau, East Efate. Plumage description and photographs taken at the time suggest that it was a second year Red-footed Booby (Euan Macdonald pers. comm. 1990). The Red-footed Booby is probably in offshore waters of Vanuatu throughout the year.

FIELD NOTES

This booby is gregarious on land when nesting and at sea when feeding. Groups tend to fly in lines, often close to the sea surface. In flight it appears slender with a fairly long tail. It is often attracted to ships and will perch on rigging or masts.

VOICE

At sea the Red-footed Booby is usually silent. In the breeding colonies the adults use loud croaking calls.

FOOD

Flying fish and squid are taken by plunge-diving, often at a great distance from the breeding grounds. This booby has been known to catch flying fish in the air as schools are driven to fly by predatory fish (Murphy 1936). Squid are probably taken at night when they rise to the upper layers of the ocean. The large eyes of this booby may be an adaptation for nocturnal hunting.

NEST AND BREEDING

This species nests almost exclusively on islands with trees or shrubs on which it builds large untidy platforms of twigs, sometimes lined with leaves. One tree may contain many nests, placed close together. Murphy (1936) comments on the importance of trees and shrubs for the continued existence of breeding colonies and notes that the same group of trees is often used repeatedly, year after year. Records from other parts of the range indicate that usually only one egg is laid, rarely two. Eggs are bluish with a rough chalky surface. Size and shape are very variable; Murphy (1936) quotes an average of 62.7 × 41.4 mm from a sample of 38 eggs. The main breeding season on islands off the coast of Australia is between June and November, exceptionally between May and December (Simpson and Day, 1989). In equatorial regions, egg-laying has been noted in all months of the year and breeding cycles can vary between different colonies on the same island (Schreiber and Ashmole, 1970).

18. Masked Booby *Sula dactylatra* PLATE 1
Other names: Blue-faced Booby, White Booby
French name: Fou masqué

IDENTIFICATION AND FIELD NOTES

Length 81 to 92 cm. Wingspan 152 cm. Much larger than the Brown and Red-footed Boobies. *Adult male and female* have similar plumage: head, neck and body white; upperwing-coverts white, primaries, secondaries, tips of longer scapulars and tail black; underwing-coverts white. In flight appears white with wingtips and trailing half of inner wings black. Iris: yellow. The bare skin around the base of the bill and the gular sac are bluish-black giving a masked appearance. Legs and feet: grey. Bill: all yellow in the male, yellow with a greenish base in the female. *Juvenile:* similar to

Brown Booby but upperparts are paler grey-brown; upper breast white, extending across the lower nape as a distinctive white collar; underwing-coverts white with central dark line of median coverts; rump brown with narrow white bar; tail blackish. *Second year immature:* nuchal collar white and more conspicuous; upperwing-coverts and rump mottled white; primaries, secondaries and tail blackish. Pratt *et al* (1987) note that the flight is strong and steady, usually 7-10m above the sea.

DISTRIBUTION AND STATUS

A pantropical species, breeding on many islands in the Pacific, Atlantic and Indian Oceans; the nearest known sites to Vanuatu of the race *S.d.personata* are on Fiji, Norfolk Island and islands near the Torres Strait off the northern coast of Australia. The Masked Booby may be seen almost anywhere at sea in the tropical western Pacific. There is one confirmed record in Vanuatu; a first-year bird banded at Phillip Island, off Norfolk Island on 5 December 1981 was found dead by Mark Kalo, a fisherman working off Devil's Point, Efate on 13 May 1982 (Naika 7:8).

Cormorants *Phalacrocoracidae*

Cormorants form the largest family among the Pelecaniformes with about 33 species in 5 genera, 2 of sea-cormorants or shags Leucocarbo *and 3 of the other cormorants* Phalacrocorax. *They are found around the coasts of the world except for Polynesia, north central Canada and Siberia. They are heavy-bodied with a long neck held in an S-shape when perched, long sharply hooked bill and long stiff tail. Most are uniformly dark in colour with a bronze to purplish gloss but some of the southern species have white bellies. The wings are relatively short and wide and the short legs are set far back on the body. The gular pouch may be bright yellow, orange or blue. Cormorants vary in size; some are as big as a large goose, others the size of a small duck. Their plumage is not water repellant and after fishing for some time, they must rest on land and dry out their feathers in the sun and breeze with wings halfspread. They are fairly strong fliers and the northern species migrate southward in winter. To escape danger they submerge rather than take flight and share with divers (Gaviidae) and grebes (Podicipedidae) the ability to sink under the surface and swim about with only the head visible. Their habitat is coastal waters, inland lakes and rivers; they are seldom seen on the open sea. All cormorants catch fish by diving from the surface and propelling themselves underwater with their feet using half-opened wings and tail to balance. Because of the quantities of fish they consume, fishermen usually regard cormorants as unwelcome competitors; studies have shown, however, that most of the species taken are of minor economic importance. At the same time, in some countries in the Far East, trained cormorants have been used to help fishermen. Teams of up to a dozen birds are tethered to the boat and perch on the bow. A thong is tied at the base of the neck and when the bird is tossed into the water it fills its throat with fish. The bird is then pulled aboard and the fisherman removes the fish.*

Most cormorants nest in colonies, often of many thousand pairs. Some species are ground nesters, others nest high in trees or on cliff ledges. On the coasts of Peru and offshore islands huge colonies of up to 6 million cormorants (Guanays) are known. 'Guano', rich in phosphates and nitrogen, the accumulated droppings at their roosts and rookeries over the centuries, up to 20m thick in places, has been excavated for fertiliser and shipped around the world.

The family Phalacrocoracidae is represented in Vanuatu by a single species, the Little Pied Cormorant.

19. Little Pied Cormorant   *Phalacrocorax melanoleucos*   PLATES 4, 16
Other name: Little Shag
French name: Cormoran pie   or locally: Canard japonais

IDENTIFICATION AND FIELD NOTES

Length 55 to 60 cm. A small black and white cormorant. *Adults* are similar in appearance, the male is slightly larger; glossy black above with all black wings; black, wedge-shaped tail and undertail-coverts. White throat, foreneck, breast and belly, the white on the foreneck extends around the eye to the base of the bill. The black feathers on the forehead form a short crest above the bill and in breeding plumage a short white crest develops either side of the crown. Iris: greyish-brown. Bill: stubby and hooked, olive-yellow with a dark brown ridge on the upper mandible. Legs and feet: black. *Immature:* much duller than the adult with black thighs. It generally looks more brown above and the black on the crown extends below the eye. When swimming the body is low in the water and the long neck with bill angled skywards is quite different from ducks. In flight the neck is outstretched. When perched the body is held in an upright position with the bill tilted slightly upwards.

These cormorants are often seen sitting quietly, with wings outstretched drying their plumage, on rocks, sandbars or on dead branches of trees near or in the water. They prefer calm inland lakes, freshwater lagoons and river estuaries, feeding on a variety of small fish, aquatic insects and their larvae, young frogs and crustaceans. They often find it difficult to rise from the surface of the water, beating their wings for some distance before becoming air-borne. They are usually found singly or in pairs though flocks are seen in good feeding localities. They do not usually fly in formation.

DISTRIBUTION AND STATUS

This species is resident from Australia and New Zealand to Malaysia, Indonesia, Palau, New Guinea the Solomons and New Caledonia. It is sedentary or locally nomadic. Little Pied Cormorants which have been observed in Vanuatu at the 'Little Duck Lake' on Efate and the Lolowai area on Ambae are probably visitors from New Caledonia or the Solomons. It is probable that small flocks regularly occur around isolated lakes on other islands. They are said to have bred in Vanuatu but this has not been confirmed.

Frigatebirds   *Fregatidae*
Frigatebirds are sometimes called 'Man of War' birds because of their piratical attacks on other birds forcing them to disgorge food. The most aerial of seabirds they soar magnificently in thermals, with no perceptible movement of the wings, just opening or closing the tail for balance and they can hover, twist and glide with apparent ease in updrafts along cliffs. Their distinguishing features are: a small body with very long pointed wings swept back from the wrist; long and deeply forked tail, often closed in flight; a short neck and long narrow bill hooked at the tip and extremely short feathered tarsi. All are large, slender birds and mainly black; the females are larger than the males and in most species have distinctive white patches on the underside. The males have a bright red throat patch which is inflated like a balloon during courtship. Frigatebirds nest on small islands often with other species of seabirds. The nests, made of sticks lined with softer materials, are usually in bushes or trees, infrequently on

the ground. Both parent birds share nest building, incubation and the care of the young. Usually only one white egg is laid. As the breeding cycle takes a year or more, successful breeders nest every other year. Juveniles of most species have a whitish head. Immatures of most species are usually marked heavily with rufous on the head and underparts and at first the distribution of white and black differs from that of their respective adults. The period to maturity is unknown, probably 4 to 6 years and identification at sea is perhaps 'the most difficult challenge in any seabird group' (Harrison, 1983).

Frigatebirds are known for their kleptoparasitic habits, mainly on boobies but also on shearwaters and terns. The unfortunate victim is chased and pecked until in an effort to get lighter and escape its tormentor it drops or regurgitates its food. Then the highly manoeuvrable pirate swoops down and catches most of the pieces in mid-air before they reach the water. However, frigatebirds are quite capable of catching their own prey. Flying fish form a major part of their diet and they also pick up with the bill almost anything small that swims near the surface: fish, squid, young turtles and other creatures. Frigatebirds also prey on the young of other seabirds, including the small frigate chicks in neighbouring nests. They are clumsy on land and usually roost at a height, where there is room to spread their wings and they can quickly gain speed in the air. They are most often seen near their breeding or roosting islands but individuals may be found any distance away from land.

There is a single genus Fregata in this family with 5 species and a number of races. One species, the Great Frigatebird, is probably a rare vagrant to Vanuatu and a second, the Least Frigatebird, breeds in the group.

20. Great Frigatebird   *Fregata minor*
Other names: Man of War bird, Sea Hawk
French name: Frégate du Pacifique

IDENTIFICATION AND FIELD NOTES

Length 86 to 100 cm. *Adult male:* mostly black with a metallic blue and green gloss on the upperparts and a diagonal buffish bar across the upperwing. The red throat pouch, inflated when courting, is reduced in non-breeding males and is only obvious at close quarters. Iris: dark brown, eye-ring is black or blue. Bill: blue-grey to black. Legs and feet: red or red-brown, webs come only half way down to the toes. *Adult female:* larger than the male, plumage mainly black except for a greyish-white throat and large white breast patch which extends a little either side of the abdomen. Iris: dark brown, eye-ring red. Bill: pink or bluish-grey. Legs and feet: pink to reddish-brown. *Immature:* upperparts dark brown with light brown wingbars. Head, neck and underparts mainly white, more or less tinged with rufous. The Great and Least Frigatebird are usually found fairly close to land and they have similar habits. The Great Frigatebird is larger, up to 20 cm more in individuals, and plumage differs slightly: the male appears all black and the female has the white/grey throat which is missing in the Least.

The apparent contradiction between 'Great' in the common name of this species and 'minor' in the scientific name comes about because it was originally called the Lesser Pelican, *Pelecanus minor*.

DISTRIBUTION AND STATUS
This species is found in most tropical areas of the world including the Indian, west Atlantic and Pacific Oceans. It breeds from the Marshall Islands and Fiji north to Hawaii and east throughout Polynesia and Palau. On Nauru, and on some other Pacific islands, hand-reared birds are often kept as free-flying pets. After breeding it disperses through the western Pacific to the west coast of Australia and has been recorded in New Zealand as a vagrant. Frigatebirds seen in the south of Vanuatu at Aneityum were apparently males of this species, but because of the similarity in appearance some sight records could refer to either species.

21. Least Frigatebird *Fregata ariel* PLATE I
Other names: Lesser Frigatebird, Man of War bird, Sea Hawk
French name: Petite Frégate

IDENTIFICATION
Length 71 to 81 cm: this is the smallest species in the family. *Adult male:* all black plumage except for triangular white patches on the flanks with spurs on the underwing and a bluish sheen on head and back. The red or bright orange pouch is only inflated when courting and at other times is hardly discernible. Iris: brown, eye-ring black. Bill: steel-grey or black. Legs and feet: black or reddish-brown, webs between the toes are deeply incised and come only half way down the toes. *Adult female:* averages distinctly larger than the male. Head is blackish-brown with nape and hindneck browner edged white forming a narrow collar; rest of plumage is mainly black with a brownish bar on the upperwing and the buffy-white of the breast extends either side of the abdomen. Iris: brown with pink, red or blue eye-ring. Bill: light purplish-grey to pink. Legs and feet: flesh-coloured to pink or red. *Immature:* head and throat white with varying amounts of rufous or brown and with black at some stage in the males; rest of plumage brownish-black with mantle and wing-coverts light brownish-grey, abdomen and flanks white; bill and feet tinged blue. It is difficult to separate Least and Great immatures. In adults the white flank patches of the male and black throat of the female are better distinguishing features than the size difference which is rarely apparent in the field.

DISTRIBUTION AND STATUS
Pantropical, less common than the Great Frigatebird in the tropical Pacific generally but locally abundant, the Least Frigatebird breeds on islands north and east of Australia, New Caledonia, the Caroline Islands, Kiribati, Fiji, Tonga, the Cook and Society Islands, the Tuamotu Archipelago and the Marquesas. Recoveries of nestlings banded on Howland and the Phoenix Islands in 1963 and 1964, suggest that dispersal is along a broad west-southwest front to the Solomons and New Guinea then northeast towards Japan, crossing wide expanses of open sea. Juveniles have been recovered over 6,000 km from their nesting sites. In much of their range they are hunted for food and in Kiribati, they are frequently kept as pets. In Vanuatu the best known roosting site is Monument Rock in the centre of the group close to Mataso Island. Birds are present there throughout the year but breeding has yet to be confirmed. The largest numbers recorded in Vanuatu are from Hunter Island which,

at 22°23.6'S, is the most southerly island of the group. On 26 June 1974, 200-300 were observed, hovering over the bushy upper slopes of the island, with about 2,000 Red-footed Boobies and a smaller number of Brown Boobies (Barritt, 1976). The same observer went on to Matthew Island (some 66 km from Hunter) and noted that a number of Frigatebirds and Boobies appeared as they approached within about 19 km of the island.

FIELD NOTES

The Least Frigatebird usually flies in small groups. They are superb aerial performers spending much of their time on the wing and they obtain some food by robbing other seabirds. They can be seen attacking boobies in particular as they return to their nests, the crop loaded with food for the young. In 1988 there were two reports of them flying close to the shore on Efate: the day after the cyclone Bola one was observed gliding over Port Vila harbour and on 12 April, as cyclone Dovi began moving away southwards, two, probably of this species, were seen in Mele Bay (Euan Macdonald, Naika 27 and 28).

VOICE

They rarely call when away from their breeding ground. At the nest a variety of grunts and a deep-sounding 'kukukuk' are uttered. The young make clopping or clicking noises with the bill and also call sharply with a drawn-out 'kikikikik'.

FOOD

Flying fish and baby turtles are picked from the surface and squid and fish are taken by piracy on other species.

NEST AND BREEDING

The time of breeding varies between island populations with most breeding from April to December. They usually nest colonially, on predator-free, off-shore islands often in association with boobies and other seabirds. The gular pouch of the male is inflated to great effect at the beginning of the breeding season but soon after the egg is laid it becomes less prominent. The nests, untidy platforms of twigs, stalks and other vegetation are often placed close together in trees, bushes or on the ground. The single chalky, white egg (64 × 43 mm) is incubated for about 40 days. The young remain dependent on their parents for food for some time after they have left the nest.

Tropicbirds *Phaethontidae*

They are aptly named for they rarely stray beyond the tropics ranging throughout the warmer regions of the Atlantic, Indian and Pacific Oceans. There are 3 species in a single genus, Phaethon, *the smallest of the Pelecaniformes. All are medium-sized white birds with a black bar across the eyes and black markings on some or all of the flight feathers. The plumage may however be suffused with delicate or richer rose-pink and in one race the plumage is apricot-yellow throughout. They have extremely long central tail feathers elongated into narrow streamers reaching 35 cm or more beyond the rest of the tail, but these may become damaged or broken in older birds. All have a stocky body, stout, pointed bill, rather long narrow wings and very short feet which cannot support the weight of the body on land and they shuffle forward awkwardly with the breast touching the ground.*

Tropicbirds are the most pelagic of their order and may be seen far from land, however, they are not gregarious and at sea seldom more than a single pair is encountered together. They are found in numbers only near the breeding grounds. They feed on fish and squid caught by diving. A foraging bird will hover a moment with rapid wingbeats then dive with half closed wings from a height of 6 or more metres. It remains underwater for up to 25 seconds then reappears with the prey in its bill and takes to the air again. They seldom rest on the water, being poor swimmers, but float buoyantly if they do alight. They may be attracted to ships and will circle over them once or twice, screaming loudly, before leaving.

They usually nest on steep cliffs where they can take-off easily but also on coral atolls. The nest is hidden in crevices or under overhanging rocks and the single egg is laid in just a scrape in the ground. The egg is oval, varying from pale buff to deep purple-brown in colour and it is incubated by both parents in watches of 2 to 5 days. Newly hatched chicks are covered with heavy grey or fawn down between one and 3 cm thick. They grow slowly and leave the nest fully fledged some 11 to 15 weeks after hatching. Like petrels the young are finally deserted by the parents and take their first flight unaided. When nesting, tropicbirds are amazingly indifferent to humans and will sit tight and allow themselves to be lifted from the nest. Some islanders value the long tail feathers, especially of the Red-tailed species, for ornamental use and gather them from the nesting birds. They also take eggs and in some areas, where the breeding season is extended, these birds are also subject to predation of nest sites and chicks by adults of the same or a related species.

Of the 3 species of tropicbirds, two occur in Vanuatu but are not common.

22. Red-tailed Tropicbird   *Phaethon rubricauda*   PLATE 2
Other name: (Red-tailed) Bosunbird
French name: Phaéthon à queue rouge

IDENTIFICATION AND FIELD NOTES

Length about 45 to 50 cm without 46 to 56 cm tail streamers: the largest of the tropicbirds. *Adult male and female* are similar: all silky white often tinted a delicate pink except for the following markings: a black eyestripe beginning at the base of the bill, curving upwards and passing through and behind the eye; black shafts to the primaries and broader black marks on the tertiary feathers. Tail is white except for the two central feathers which are red with a black shaft and extended as narrow, pointed streamers. Iris: blackish-brown. Bill: bright red. Legs and feet: blue-grey or light brown with the webs distally black. *Immature:* mainly white with heavy dark vermiculations and mottling on the upperparts giving a barred effect; the tail is tipped black, streamers are lacking or very short. The eyestripe is frequently only a patch in front of the eye and the bill is black.

Normal flight is rather direct consisting of glides alternating with rapid shallow wingbeats, but it also soars, hovers and dives. Mated pairs have a spectacular hovering display flight with a 'rowing' wingbeat, giving the appearance of flying in reverse, which identifies this species at some distance. When observed closely the red tail streamers and less black on the upperwing help to distinguish this species from the White-tailed Tropicbird.

DISTRIBUTION AND STATUS
It breeds on islands in the Indian Ocean and off the northern coast of Australia and in the Pacific in Hawaii, the Marianas, Kiribati, Rose Atoll, Fiji, Tonga, the Cook Islands, Tuamotu Archipelago, the Tubuai Islands and the Pitcairn group (Pratt *et al*, 1987). Non-breeding birds range throughout the tropical Pacific. The Red-tailed Tropicbird is uncommon in Vanuatu waters. Status is uncertain but it may be breeding on some of the offshore islets free from predators. One was disturbed from the water as the survey ship HMS Hydra approached Hunter Island, 26 June 1974 (Barritt, 1976). Known nesting attempts have been made at Laika Island and on a beach on Tongoa Island facing Laika.

23. White-tailed Tropicbird   *Phaethon lepturus*   PLATE 2
Other name: Golden or White-tailed Bosunbird
French name: Phaéthon à queue blanche

IDENTIFICATION
Length 30 to 40 cm excluding tail streamers which may be 33 to 40 cm long. A mainly white, slender bird with conspicuous long white, flexible tail streamers like narrow ribbons with rounded ends. *Adult male and female* are similar: all silky white except for a black crescent-shaped patch from the gape through the eye, a prominent, broad black diagonal wingbar (formed by the median wing-coverts and inner secondaries and their coverts) and the black leading edge of the outer primaries. White below with just the longer flank feathers tipped black but when soaring the shadow of the black

Graceful in flight, the slender White-tailed Tropicbird can only shuffle awkwardly on land

pattern on the upperwing shows through aiding identification. Iris: brown. Bill is variable, most are yellow but some orange-red. Legs and feet: light yellowish or bluish with black webs. *Immature:* has numerous dark vermiculations above from the crown to the rump and spreading on to the innerwing; has dark tips to the tail and lacks the tail streamers. The black bill of the chick soon becomes dull yellow with a blackish tip. Plumage may be tinged golden-yellow. There are 4 or 5 races. A race that breeds on Christmas Island (Indian Ocean), *P. l. fulvus* is suffused apricot-yellow throughout.

DISTRIBUTION AND STATUS
Pantropical except for the easternmost Pacific, it breeds on most island groups from Hawaii, Kiritimati and the Tuamotus to Vanuatu and New Caledonia but apparently not in the Solomons or the Bismarck Archipelago. In Vanuatu the earlier known breeding station is at Monument Rock in the Shepherd group. Robertson confirmed that a small colony was breeding on Malo in 1978 (pers. comm.) and an interesting description of the birds breeding in the village of Avunatari, west of Malo in 1989 is given by Voumaranda Bani (Naika 31:16-17).

FIELD NOTES
This is the smallest, most delicate tropicbird with narrow wings and it can be distinguished from the Red-tailed by the upperwing pattern, the white tail streamers and yellow or orange bill. Flight is strong and direct with deep, quick wingbeats interspersed with short glides but is less laboured and more graceful than the Red-tailed. It is often attracted to ships and hovers above before attempting to perch.

VOICE
Chattering screeches and sharp calls are made in flight, and loud defensive screaming calls at the nest.

FOOD
The diet consists mainly of fish and squid obtained by plunge-diving.

NEST AND BREEDING
In Bermuda, White-tailed Tropicbirds are known to breed seasonally and even leave the island altogether for part of the year. Elsewhere a non-seasonal breeding regime appears to be the norm (Prŷs-Jones and Peet, 1980) and breeding may occur whenever local conditions are suitable. They usually nest on rocky ledges on the windward side of high islands with exposed steep cliffs or further inland on crater walls. They also nest in hollows or in a stout fork of a tree. Only one egg is laid. On Malo they apparently nest in tree holes, banyan trees and in the top of coconut palms. Their interesting display flight has been described: small groups of courting birds fly in close formation over the nesting areas weaving up and down with dropped tails and uttering short chuckling sounds. This display often ends with a simultaneous swoop to the nests of the participants. Their breeding biology is described in the family *Phaethontidae* section.

Order CICONIIFORMES
This is rather a mixed order of 6 (or 7) families of medium to large birds with long legs and long bills adapted for wading in shallow water or marshes and living mostly on

fish or other aquatic animals. The flamingos, the Phoenicopteridae, are sometimes placed in their own order. Ardeidae, the herons and bitterns, is one family included though the Boat-billed Heron *Cochlearius cochlearius* is sometimes given its own family, Cochleariidae. The other families are storks (Ciconiidae), the ibis and spoonbill family (Threskiornithidae) and two stork-like species, the Hamerkop (Scopidae) and the Shoebill (Balaenicipitidae). Only the herons are represented in Vanuatu.

Herons *Ardeidae*

There are about 60 species of herons in 4 distinct groups: the bitterns (subfamily Botaurinae), not considered here, and the tiger herons (subfamily Tigrisomatinae), night herons and day herons. They are found throughout the world and range in size from the Zigzag Heron Zebrilus undulatus *which is barely 30 cm long to the great herons five times larger. The day herons have a slender body with long legs and long neck. The night herons are stouter with shorter necks. They all have a dagger-shaped bill and a comparatively short tail. They have 3 unwebbed forward toes and one hind toe; the middle toe has small serrations along the side like the teeth of a comb and is used for grooming. Plumage is variable, either white or coloured but mostly fairly muted shades of brown, blue and grey with black and white and the sexes are alike or closely similar.*

Powder-down patches, characteristic of herons, occur in pairs on the breast and rump with additional pairs on the back and thighs in some species. These short feathers, not usually visible as they are covered by normal feathers, are never moulted and continue to grow throughout the life of the bird. They fray continually at the tip into a powder that is used during preening. The grease, slime and dirt adhering to the feathers after a bird has struggled with a slimy eel or fish is absorbed by the powder which is applied either by the bill or by the bird rubbing its head through the powder patch. The powder is later vigorously scratched and combed out, mainly with the comb claw. Herons are found throughout the world with more species in the tropical regions and most of the temperate species are migratory. All of them fly with strong deliberate wingbeats; the feet may dangle on take-off but are soon held out straight beyond the tail and the neck is usually curved back against the body. The neck, which has vertebrae of unequal length, is also frequently retracted when at rest. Herons may assume an erect or semi-crouching posture when active and it is especially the S-shape of the retracted neck which enables the bird to dart its head forward at lightning speed to spear rapidly moving prey. Feeding in the shade of the wings is fairly common possibly attracting prey, reducing glare and enabling visibility. To forage successfully they may use a variety of 30 or more recognisable feeding techniques involving posture, body movements, wing and foot movements and aerial foraging which are aptly described in Hancock and Kushlan (1984). Herons are mainly carnivorous and most of their food is aquatic: fish, crabs, crustaceans and amphibians. They also take insects, reptiles and rodents depending partly on seasonal abundance. The night herons usually feed in the twilight or at night and rarely fly or fish during the day.

Some herons, like the tiger herons, are typically solitary while others are gregarious, feeding in large flocks and nesting colonially, sometimes in great numbers and often in company with other waterbirds. The nest is usually a substantial stick platform on trees, reeds or on the ground. The 2-7 eggs are pale blue, white or buff and are incubated by both parents. The newly hatched chicks are helpless at first and usually remain in the nest for several weeks before flying. In some species the young leave the nest after 10 days or so and roam in the vicinity, without being able to fly, returning to be fed. The beautiful delicate plumes which grow on the head, neck, breast or back of some species during the breeding season form another outstanding feature. At the turn of the century these plumes were in great demand for the millinery trade and led to mass capture and slaughter of these birds. Several species were in danger of extermination and it took a long campaign by conservationists to arouse public opinion enough to end the killing. Fortunately, protection is now nearly universal. The main threat to their existence today is the draining of swamps for land reclamation and the use of pesticides and related chemicals poisoning their food supply.

In Vanuatu the family Ardeidae is represented by 4 species: only the Reef Heron is widespread and well known; the Little (Mangrove) Heron occurs locally on several islands; the White-faced Heron breeds on New Caledonia and occasionally visits the southern-most islands of the group and the Rufous Night Heron is a vagrant.

24. White-faced Heron   *Ardea novaehollandiae*   PLATE 3
Other name: Blue Crane
French name: Héron à face blanche

IDENTIFICATION AND FIELD NOTES

Length about 58 cm. A medium-sized grey heron with a conspicuous white face: the forehead has a broad white bar extending behind the eyes to the white chin and throat. *Adult male and female:* all blue-grey above, primaries and tail a darker slate-grey; paler grey below tinged with chestnut-brown at the base of the neck and on the upper breast. Nuptial plumes are long and lanceolate, grey on the back and chestnut on the breast. Iris: yellow, the naked skin in front of the eye is olive-yellow. Bill: normally black but the lower mandible may be yellowish towards the base. Legs and feet: greenish to pale yellow. *Immature:* duller with grey rather than white on the head and has fewer dorsal plumes; underparts tinged brown but lack chestnut on neck and breast.

The White-faced Heron frequents a wide range of water habitats including marshes, the margins of inland waters, flooded grassland and the seashore. It may be seen singly in pairs or scattered groups, foraging on swampy land, wading in the shallows of ponds or rivers occasionally stirring the water or on beaches and estuaries hunting along the tide-line. It takes small fish, shrimps, crabs, lizards, and anything of a similar nature. When not feeding it is often perched on a post or tree with the neck tucked in between hunched shoulders. It flies with rather slow and deliberate wingbeats, and most of the time the neck is folded, the head is held close to the body and the long legs trail behind. In New Caledonia it breeds from September to January. The nest of bare twigs is normally constructed in trees and 2-3 pale blue eggs are laid. It may nest in loose groups and among colonies of other waterbirds. The White-faced Heron can, at close quarters, be distinguished from other species of herons known in Vanuatu by its conspicuous white facial pattern. In flight the contrasting darker flight feathers and lighter grey plumage separate this species.

DISTRIBUTION AND STATUS

The White-faced Heron occurs throughout Australia and Tasmania where there is suitable habitat. It is mainly sedentary but disperses at times and has become established in the Sunda Islands, Indonesia, the Louisiade Archipelago and Rossel Island and the smaller race *A. n. nana* is restricted to Lifou in the Loyalty Islands and New Caledonia. Breeding was first confirmed in New Zealand in 1941 where its appetite for the introduced Australian green frog *Hyla aurea* is thought to be one of the reasons for its rapid spread. It is now well established around the coasts and in some central areas up to 180 m above sea level and it is a vagrant in neighbouring islands. Immature birds observed and collected from Aneityum were probably vagrants from Lifou or New Caledonia where the species is common. There have been recent records of a White-faced Heron on Efate. One was observed at Duck Lake among a group of Pacific Black Duck *Anas superciliosa* on 18 September 1983 and there was a further sighting of a bird of this species in the pools of water near the road at Teouma in 1985 (Richard Pickering, Naika 11:10 and 18:11).

25. Eastern Reef Heron *Ardea (Egretta) sacra*   PLATES 3, 16
Other names: Reef Heron, Reef Egret
French name: Aigrette des récifs   or locally: Long cou
Bislama name: Longfala neck – Naūfa

IDENTIFICATION
Length about 50 cm. Two colour phases of this medium-sized heron are found in Vanuatu. The *white form* has pure white plumage with olive-yellow facial skin, a yellowish-brown bill and light olive-green legs and feet. The *dark form* is slate-grey to brownish-black with a thin white stripe on chin and throat which, according to Hancock and Kushlan (1984) is more pronounced in Indonesian birds and absent in some birds in the south and east of the range. In Vanuatu some may have the full stripe, some have just a line of pure white spots down the throat and others are all dark. Iris: light yellow. The facial skin appears dark. Bill: slate-brown, the upper mandible is usually darker than the lower. Legs and feet: olive-green with or without dark grey patches. *Male and female* look alike, the males are larger. *Immature* dark phase birds are much duller and browner and those of the white phase may be more or less mottled with grey, though some authorities give different plumage patterns for young birds. The proportion of dark to white birds varies according to locality but in most of Vanuatu the white herons are uncommon to rare. A third colour phase, a mottled dark grey and white form, is found in some areas of the tropical Pacific.

DISTRIBUTION AND STATUS
The widespread Eastern Reef Heron is a resident species along the shores from Japan to Burma, Malaysia, the Philippines, New Guinea, Australia, New Zealand and the Pacific islands as far as eastern Polynesia. It occurs throughout Vanuatu but is nowhere very common.

FIELD NOTES
The Eastern Reef Heron favours rocky coasts and reefs, sea cliffs, and mangroves and mudflats, but may also be found along river estuaries and creeks, and it was 'observed on several occasions along the course of the Apuna River (Santo) up to 12 km inland' (Medway and Marshall, 1975). Usually seen alone or in pairs it is strongly territorial, chasing other herons away from foraging areas and it may frequent a particular

The Reef Heron chicks in their nest are not the same size as incubation starts with the first egg

locality for years. It can be seen stalking gracefully through the shallows of the reef at low tide, occasionally walking briskly for a short distance or stopping suddenly to peer into the water, body horizontal with long neck and bill poised to strike. Sometimes it dashes forwards with long strides and wings flapping, stabbing repeatedly at a fish or crab until it is captured. A Reef Heron, possibly canopy feeding, was observed by John Edge at the southern end of Erakor Island: 'he presented a magically beautiful spectacle by spreading his wings repeatedly into a tight circular parasol, and fishing successfully into the shadow' (Naika 29:27). When resting, Reef Herons will spend many hours standing on outcrops of rock or perched in trees with head down and shoulders hunched. On most islands they are extremely wary, their vigilance making them difficult to approach closely, and when disturbed they fly to some more secluded spot, rising slowly, flapping the wings ponderously and giving a harsh croak of alarm.

In contrast, when found in remote regions they tend to be relatively tame. In flight the neck is folded back with the head close to the body and the legs, which are shorter than in comparable species of herons, trail only slightly beyond the tail.

VOICE

A hoarse croak is uttered when startled and various softer calls when feeding or with clopping of the bill when nesting.

FOOD

They feed mainly in the intertidal zone, and sometimes at night, taking small crabs, crustaceans, small fish and other marine animals. They also take frogs, lizards and insects.

NEST AND BREEDING

The Reef Heron most often nests in coastal trees at varying heights up to the canopy but also in the lower branches of bushes on the rocky shore, on the ground or on tiny offshore coral islets. Sometimes a few pairs will build in the same vicinity but hardly forming a tight breeding colony. The nest is of sticks, lined with twigs and if added to over a number of years becomes quite bulky. Two or 3 pale blue eggs are laid (45 × 37 mm). Incubation begins with the first egg; when the last chick hatches the first may be 6 days old. They are at first rather sparsely covered with down, longer and crest-like on the head; fledging takes about 5 and a half weeks. The nesting season is from February to July although this varies depending on local conditions; in Australia mostly September to January but also at other times throughout the year and in New Caledonia from September to December. When the dark and light phase birds interbreed the young are not intermediate phases but either pure grey or white and both white and dark birds can be found in the same brood.

26. Rufous Night Heron   *Nycticorax caledonicus*
Other names: Nankeen Crane, Nankeen Night Heron
French name: Héron de Nuit

IDENTIFICATION AND FIELD NOTES

Length 56 to 63 cm. A sturdy heron with a large head, thick neck and heavy bill. *Adult male and female:* upperparts and wings are various shades of rufous-chestnut. Crown and nape are black with two long white plumes in the breeding season. Underparts are white sometimes suffused pale rufous on the throat and upper breast. Bill: black with olive-green at the base of the lower mandible. Facial skin is olive-green. Iris: yellow. Legs and feet: greenish-yellow. *Immature:* heavily streaked buff, brown and white above and below but generally darker above with a rufous wash on the wings and tail and with conspicuous white spots on the back and wings. The bill is entirely black.

They may be seen singly or in small groups around ponds, in mangrove swamps, intertidal flats, estuaries, rivers and creeks. They roost in trees close to water by day and fly out at dusk to forage, sometimes in noisy flocks. The Rufous Night Heron breeds in New Caledonia from September to January. The nest of bare twigs may be placed at any height in trees or bushes and 2-3 light blue-green eggs are laid. They frequently nest in colonies.

DISTRIBUTION AND STATUS

The Rufous Night Heron breeds throughout mainland Australia in suitable habitat and young birds have dispersed widely, populating neighbouring islands. It is also found in the Philippines, New Guinea, Palau, Truk, the Solomons and other Melanesian islands. Beehler *et al*, (1986) note that a bird banded in South Australia was recovered in New Guinea. It is quite common in New Caledonia. This heron was recorded as a vagrant in Vanuatu by MacMillan and noted in Diamond and Marshall (1977b).

27. Little (Mangrove) Heron   *Butorides striatus solomonensis*   PLATE 3
Other names: Green-backed Heron, Striated Heron
French name: Blongios vert

IDENTIFICATION

Length about 40 cm. This is the smallest of all the herons in Vanuatu and it is dark with secretive habits. *Adult male and female:* crown and crest black glossed with green, back and wings dark greyish-brown with rufous spots and streaks and the long scapulars are glossy bronze-green; tail is short, grey with a bronze gloss. Neck and underparts are a dusky grey washed with ochre; middle of the upper throat is white with a blackish line along the centre. Facial skin: olive-yellow. Iris: light yellow. Bill: mainly black with the lower mandible dull olive-yellow with dark edges. Legs and feet: olive-green, sometimes with brown patches. *Immature:* heavily streaked and mottled and conspicuously different from the adult; brown above mottled with shades of buff and grey; paler below, spotted and streaked with buff and black.

DISTRIBUTION AND STATUS

This little heron is a cosmopolitan species with about 30 recognised races. They occur from North America to Argentina, south of the Sahara and around the Red Sea in Africa, in India, China, through Malaysia, Indonesia, Borneo and the Philippines to Japan. In Australasia they are found in south and west New Guinea, in the Melanesian chain to Fiji, Tahiti and the Society Islands and on the north, west and east coasts of Australia. In Vanuatu the race *solomonensis* is local and uncommon although it may be found in some numbers in the Torres group, Ureparapara, Vanua Lava, Gaua, along the Sarakata river on Santo, on Malakula, Erromango and Aniwa. The same race is found in the Solomons, Santa Cruz group and Fiji and *B. s. macrorhynchus* in New Caledonia.

FIELD NOTES

Coastal mangroves are the favourite haunts of the Little (Mangrove) Heron but it may also be seen, singly or in pairs on the adjoining mudflats at low tide, in marshy creeks, along river banks covered in dense undergrowth and in other swampy areas. It is not readily apparent unless looked for; this wary heron is usually only seen when it flies between stands, or is glimpsed as it stalks small aquatic animals amongst thick mangrove vegetation or shrubs along water courses. As the prey must be approached with care the bird often crouches low and almost slides over rocks or over the breathing roots of mangrove trees. Alternatively it may walk slowly for a few paces then stand motionless, sometimes for long periods at a time. It stares down into the shallow water then if prey comes within easy reach the long, snake-like neck and sharp bill shoot forward, generally succeeding in snapping it up. When disturbed in the open on mudflats it often freezes, crouching low, to avoid detection or alternatively runs over the mud for a distance before taking off with loud quacking calls. Flight is rather direct and usually close to the ground or water.

VOICE

It has been described as highly vocal with various harsh croaks repeated in series but it is silent at times. An explosive 'hoo' has also been recorded.

FOOD

The diet consists of small fish, often mudskippers, and crabs, prawns, frogs, insects and other small creatures.

NEST AND BREEDING

Very little is known about the breeding habits of this heron in Vanuatu. It breeds here probably from September to March at the latest. In Australia it may breed in any month of the year depending on the available food supply. The nest, a compact platform of sticks and twigs, is usually built fairly low in the mangroves but may be in trees and bushes standing in, or close to, water. Two to 4 pale bluish-green, sometimes mottled, eggs are laid ($38 \times 28\text{-}30$mm). Incubation takes about 21 days and the chicks are covered with light grey down above and white below. The young probably stay 4 weeks in or near the nest and at the age of a week or so begin to climb and jump around the branches nearby.

Order ANSERIFORMES

These medium-sized to large aquatic, marine and terrestrial birds are commonly known as Waterfowl. This order includes two families, the screamers (Anhimidae), with 3 species confined to South America and the ducks, geese and swans, family Anatidae, with over 150 species worldwide. They have some anatomical features and certain characteristics in common, they have unmarked eggs and the young may leave the nest immediately or soon after hatching, but there are great differences in their appearance and biology.

Ducks, Geese and Swans   *Anatidae*

These waterfowl were among the first birds to be domesticated and have been used by humans for food, sport and as a source of aesthetic pleasure. All members of this family are adept in the water; the 3 front toes are connected by a web for swimming and diving and the small hind toe is placed high. They have comparatively short legs, rather long necks and broad bills for dabbling and feeding on vegetable matter and aquatic animals. The bill has a nail-like tip and a row of lamellae, a fine comb-like structure lining the bill, enabling them to filter small particles of food. All waterfowl have dense, downy, waterproof plumage and, with a few notable exceptions, are strong fliers. In a fair number of species the male and female have the same or similar plumage but slightly duller in the female. In other species there is a strong contrast with the male being strikingly marked in the brightest of colours.

Though a few species are solitary, most are highly gregarious. Flocking is instinctive to them; they migrate in flocks, they feed in flocks and a few even breed colonially. Most build a simple nest on the ground, hidden in thick vegetation but some nest in hollow trees or holes in the banks of streams. The nest is copiously lined with down, which the female plucks from her breast, and a large clutch of white, sometimes tinged buff or bluish-green, eggs is laid. The young are covered in down and can walk and swim within hours of hatching. They take to the water where they are fairly safe from predators as soon as their down has dried.

The family Anatidae is divided into 3 subfamilies: Anseranatinae *with a single species, the Magpie Goose* A. semipalmata, Anserinae *which comprises the swans, geese and whistling ducks, and* Anatinae *which includes all the remaining species of ducks.*

The 4 species of ducks found in Vanuatu belong to the subfamily Anatinae *which is complex and includes 34 genera in 7 groups, commonly called tribes. Three of them are surface-feeding ducks of the genus* Anas *in the tribe* Anatini *(Dabbling Ducks). They are elongated in shape and keep the tail above the water line. They occasionally feed on land but typically forage in shallow water, reaching their food by dipping from the surface with the neck extended downwards, the body vertical and the tail pointing skywards. When surprised they take off with a loud splashing. Structurally the dabbling ducks differ from most members of the other tribes of Anatinae in having a simple claw for the hind toe without a flap or lobe. The three resident species have a patch of iridescent metallic feathers, the speculum, in the centre of the wing. One species, the introduced Mallard, may be present in small numbers; the Pacific Black Duck, is common and well known; the population of the Grey Teal fluctuates, sometimes large flocks are seen where before there were just a few birds or none.*

The fourth species belongs to the genus Aythya *in the tribe* Aythyini *(Pochards). This group of diving ducks dive for their food and also when in danger. They are characterised by a rather short, heavy body and by the strong lobe or flap on the hind toe. The pochards lack the metallic speculum of the dabbling ducks. The Australian White-eyed Duck is the only species of pochard known to occur in Vanuatu. Some other 'ducks' have been reported from Aore, Efate and Tanna but have not been identified.*

28. Mallard   *Anas platyrhynchos*
French name: Canard colvert

IDENTIFICATION AND FIELD NOTES

Length 52 to 68 cm, on New Caledonia 45 to 55 cm. A large dabbling duck with heavy body and a short tail. *Adult male* in breeding plumage has a glossy bottle-green head with white neck ring and ruddy-brown breast. Back and underparts pale grey with a white band in front of the black undertail-coverts; uppertail-coverts black; tail white with two central black feathers that curl upwards. Iris: brown. Bill: greenish-yellow. Legs and feet: orange-red. After breeding, as in all Anatidae, the flight feathers are moulted simultaneously and, for a time, it is unable to fly. In this *eclipse* plumage the male resembles the female but has a darker crown and breast and more yellow on the bill. *Adult female:* pale brown mottled and streaked darker brown above with a paler head and neck, dark crown and streak through the eye. Underparts are paler; tail whitish. The bill is dull orange with a blackish ridge and tip. *Immature:* resembles the female but is duller and the underparts are more streaked. *Ducklings:* black above with yellow wings and yellow markings on back and underparts. Face is yellow with a black line through the eye and extending to the nape.

Flight is rapid; the pale underwing and whitish tail show clearly and birds of all ages are recognised by the bright purplish-blue speculum on the secondaries edged both sides with white. In Australia the Mallard interbreeds with the Pacific Black Duck and hybrids usually resemble the latter.

The Mallard is gregarious and usually congregates with other species of ducks on any form of still water, freshwater lakes and ponds, sheltered coastal bays and estuaries. It feeds mainly by dabbling while swimming but also wades in the shallows and grazes on land.

DISTRIBUTION AND STATUS

The Mallard is very common throughout the northern hemisphere and well-known because of its adaptability to almost any shallow aquatic environment with fringing vegetation and by its readiness to take artificially supplied food. Most domestic ducks are descendants of wild Mallards. It is migratory throughout most of its range. It was introduced to Australia in the 1860s and is found in the south-west and south-east and in Tasmania on park lakes and reservoirs but not often in the wild. A small number of Mallard were introduced to New Caledonia some 20 years ago and are now found throughout the island. From the conservation point of view, the spread of the Mallard presents a danger to the Pacific Black Duck as it has similar food and habitat needs and apparently competes successfully. In addition, the Mallard interbreeds with the indigenous species. Mallards have been introduced to New Zealand from Britain and the United States and they are now feral and widespread. Research on migration there has shown that the Mallard is rather more sedentary than the Pacific Black Duck. However, movements of up to 1,300 km have been recorded and a Mallard banded at Lake Tuakitoto in South Otago was shot near Adelaide in 1962 (Falla *et al*, 1981). Studies show that in New Zealand the Mallard is gradually replacing the Pacific Black Duck and some authorities say that Mallards in the wild should be shot. In Vanuatu there is a single record by Harriet Fowler of a Mallard duck, rescued as an orphaned duckling from Lake Siwi and taken to Lowiakamak, in Middle Bush, Tanna as a pet (Naika 11:5).

29. Pacific Black Duck   *Anas superciliosa pelewensis*   PLATES 4, 16
Other names: Australian Grey Duck, Black Duck
French name: Canard à sourcils
Bislama names: Big fala dak dak, Wael dak dak

IDENTIFICATION

Length 50 to 61 cm. A large, dark brown duck with conspicuous facial markings and glossy green wingbars. All plumages are similar: uniform greyish-brown above with the edges of many feathers tipped pale buff giving the body a scaly appearance; crown dark; sides of the face and throat light buff marked by two horizontal broad blackish-brown lines, one from the top of the bill through the eye and another from the gape crossing the cheek. The sides of the head, neck, breast and underparts are finely mottled with buff and brown. Wings are dark brown above with a bright metallic green speculum bordered by narrow bands of black; underwing is white with darker flight feathers. Iris: brown. Bill: lead-grey with a lighter tip and black nail. Legs and feet: yellowish-olive with dark patches. Ageing and sexing is difficult in the field, the male is slightly larger than the female. The *ducklings* are dark grey on head, neck and back and the face and underparts are yellow. There is a conspicuous black line through the eye. This duck always appears much darker than the Mallard which has no pattern of light and dark on the head. It is much larger than the Grey Teal which also lacks the facial markings and has red eyes and the Pacific Black Duck does not habitually perch on dead trees in the water like the Grey Teal.

DISTRIBUTION, STATUS AND CONSERVATION

Widespread throughout the Australasian region and western Pacific islands, this is a particularly interesting species with three races recognised. The race *superciliosa* breeds in New Zealand and islands to the south, and is not so dark as the race described. The race *rogersi* which tends to be duller, with facial pattern less bright, breeds throughout Australia, southern New Guinea and several Indonesian islands. The race *pelewensis*, described above, is a collection of many former races with subtle differences in size and plumage populating the various groups of islands in the western Pacific including the Society and Cook Islands, Tonga, Samoa, Fiji, New Caledonia, the Loyalty Islands, Santa Cruz, the Solomons, Bismarck Archipelago, Palau and northern lowland New Guinea. They are smaller, darker and have narrower pale fringes to the body feathers, a broader black eyestripe and darker side to the head (Madge and Burn, 1988). In Vanuatu *pelewensis* is known to breed on Gaua, Santo, Ambae, Malakula, Efate, Erromango, Tanna and Aneityum. This is a popular game-bird in Vanuatu and could perhaps survive controlled hunting. It is protected by a close season and may only be killed in the 3-month period 1 April to 30 June. Of much more concern is the destruction of habitat by the draining of swamps and the pollution of lakes and water courses. There have been several unconfirmed reports from the interior of Efate of ducks perishing in considerable numbers. This may be due to bacterial poisoning, perhaps botulism, caused when the water-level in the lake falls and conditions are right for the growth of such organisms. Some ducks that have perished have had lead shot in their stomachs and it can be presumed that these ducks have been foraging in lake-mud containing lead shot. Steel shot should now be used as lead may also cause accidental poisoning to many animals.

FIELD NOTES

The Pacific Black Duck is the best known and most likely to be seen duck in Vanuatu, frequenting swamps, rivers, lakes, creeks, mangroves, estuaries and even the mountains and the outer reefs. It can be found singly, more often in pairs or small flocks on almost any stretch of fresh or saltwater and may sometimes be flushed from surprisingly small pools. Where they are common they congregate out of the breeding season in fair numbers, often with other species, and prefer the shallows of inland lakes. They are very wary and, when disturbed, gain height rapidly, form a compact flock, circle a few times and generally leave the area. Flight is strong and direct, the silhouette typically duck-like with head and neck extended, pointed wings and short tail.

VOICE

Call-notes consist of the drawn-out quack of one or two syllables known from domesticated ducks. Males are reported to have a loud 'peep' and hiss when courting and the females a raucous quack.

FOOD

Seeds and leaves are stripped from plants growing in shallow water by up-ending and dabbling. They also take other vegetable matter, insects, worms, slugs, shellfish, tadpoles and other aquatic organisms. Australian studies have shown that about three-quarters of their food consists of plants and seeds.

NEST AND BREEDING

The nest is usually built on the ground in the shelter of thick vegetation, in a hole between the roots of a tree or even in a hollow branch of a tree and it may be some distance from water. It is lined with leaves, grasses, feathers and down and 6-12 creamy or greenish eggs (averaging 57 × 40mm) are laid. As with other dabbling ducks, when the clutch is complete the male leaves and the female looks after the eggs and ducklings alone. The incubation period is 3 to 4 weeks and the mortality rate of ducklings is high, with 1 to 3 surviving from a clutch. They normally breed from July to December or January.

30. Grey Teal *Anas gibberifrons gracilis* PLATE 4
French name: Sarcelle grise
Bislama name: Smole fala dak dak

IDENTIFICATION

Length 37 to 44cm, the male is larger. This medium-sized dull-coloured duck is distinctly smaller than the other three species. *Adult male and female* have similar plumage: more or less dark grey-brown above with paler edges to the back feathers; crown and back of the neck are blackish-brown, speckled with lighter brown; rump, tail and uppertail-coverts very dark brown. Sides of the head are light buff finely mottled with brown; chin and throat are very pale buff, almost whitish-grey: underparts light brownish-grey, with a dark brown centre to each feather giving a scaly appearance. Wings are dark brown above: the broad metallic black speculum has a conspicuous glossy, emerald-green patch in the centre and a white band either side which extends in a prominent triangular wedge to the centre of the wing above and is narrow below. Underwing is mainly dark with a white band in the centre and white axillaries. Iris: bright red, duller in the female. Bill: slender, upper mandible lead-blue, lower mandible grey with a broad orange patch. Legs and feet: greyish-black. *Immature* is paler especially on the head and neck. Ducklings are grey-brown on the back and head with two dark stripes on the side of the head, one through and one below the eye. Wings and back are spotted white and the underparts are light grey-brown. In the field, the Grey Teal looks similar to the Pacific Black Duck but differs from the latter by its much smaller size, by the complete absence of any facial pattern and the red (not brown) eye.

DISTRIBUTION AND STATUS

According to Madge and Burn (1988) four races are recognised, one of which, *remissa*, from Rennell Island in the Solomons has recently become extinct because of the introduction of large fish, *Tilapia*, into its only lagoon. A second race *albogularis*, which occurs on the Andaman Islands in the Indian Ocean, has white markings on the head and neck. The nominate race *A. g. gibberifrons* is a little smaller and darker than *gracilis* with a noticeably bulging forehead and is found throughout Indonesia. Only the race *gracilis*, described above, has a wide distribution. In Australia it is abundant in the Murray-Darling basin and highly nomadic in other areas relying on erratic rainfall to produce suitable wetland habitat. The range extends to Papua New Guinea and to New Zealand where it was uncommon until 1957 and 1958 when prolonged drought in Australia led to huge invasions and it is now a widespread breeding species. It also occurs on New Caledonia, Macquarie Island and the Aru and Kai islands off New Guinea, where it may be a resident or temporary breeder following irruptions, and it has occurred in the Chatham Islands (Madge and Burn, 1988). In Vanuatu the Grey Teal *A. g. gracilis* was first recorded by the author in 1970 on the Great Duck Lake, Efate. It appears to be established locally and undergoes periodic fluctuations being fairly common at times and then more or less absent for some years. It is protected by a close season from 1 July to 31 March. It has been recorded as breeding on the inland lakes of Efate occasionally and it is thought to breed on Tanna.

FIELD NOTES
This elegant little duck is a great wanderer and may turn up, singly, in pairs or flocks on any island with suitable habitat, mainly freshwater lakes, swamps and marshes. Partly a nocturnal feeder, it frequently rests during the day concealed in the dense fringing vegetation of lakes, ponds or rivers, or often perched on dead trees or branches overhanging or in the water. In the cooler hours of the afternoon several ducks begin to collect on the open water, emerging in pairs from their hiding places, and usually feed about the lake all night long. They are shy birds and quick to fly, circling overhead several times and then settling on the other side of the lake or swamp. Flight is fast with rapid wingbeats and flocks wheel and turn with great agility.

VOICE
The male has a soft whistle and the female a loud quack, often repeated rapidly. Chuckling sounds may be heard at night.

FOOD
They feed by dabbling, up-ending and dredging or by stripping seeds from plants growing in or overhanging the water. Their diet consists mainly of vegetable matter but also insects, mussels, crustaceans and other small aquatic animals.

NEST AND BREEDING
The nest, made of grass lined with soft down, may be concealed almost anywhere, in a clump of vegetation, a crevice between rocks, or in a hollow branch or fork of a tree. The 6-12 eggs are creamy-white and average 54×39 mm. In Vanuatu it probably breeds from June to December or even February. In Australia it may breed in any month provided the conditions are favourable.

31. Australian White-eyed Duck   *Aythya australis extima*   PLATE 4
Other name: Hardhead
French name: Nyroca austral   or locally: Col marron

IDENTIFICATION
Length 42 to 47 cm. This handsome brown and white duck is more compactly built than the dabbling ducks. *Adult male:* head, neck and breast rich chestnut-brown and slightly glossy; back and tail duller brown; lower breast and belly white with the sides mottled brown; undertail-coverts white. Upperwing mainly brown with a broad, white wingbar across the secondaries, diagnostic in flight; outer primaries light brown, inner primaries greyish-white with brown tips; underwing white with brown borders. Iris: milky-white. Bill: black with a light slate-blue bar at the tip and a black nail. Legs and feet: grey with slate-grey webs. *Adult female* is paler and duller with a brown iris. *Immature* is similar to the female but more buffish-brown and the white on the belly is mottled brown. The ducklings are light, yellowish-brown above and pale yellow below. Iris: pale ochre. Bill: blue-grey and pale pink. The Australian White-eyed Duck differs from the other ducks found in the group by the uniformly rufous-brown head, neck and upper breast, the white belly, the whitish band on the tip of the bill, the white eye in the male and the white (not metallic) speculum.

DISTRIBUTION AND STATUS
The Australian White-eyed Duck is common in southeast Australia and smaller numbers are found in the southwest and north to Queensland. It disperses in times of drought and the range extends to Java and Sulawesi, New Guinea, the Solomons and New Caledonia. It was formerly abundant in parts of New Zealand but is now a rare vagrant. A smaller race *extima* (Mayr, 1940), described above, is resident in Vanuatu though Madge and Burn (1988) state that as 'its measurements fall within the range of the Australian form; this may prove to be another example of islands temporarily colonised by the somewhat nomadic Australian Hardhead'. In Vanuatu it has been recorded on Gaua in the Banks Islands, on Santo, Aore, Malo, Ambae, Efate, Erromango and Tanna but is not numerous on any island of the group. It is well established on the crater-lake on Gaua, in swamp areas on Aore and Ambae, the two inland lakes of Efate and the big Lake Siwi on Tanna. On 18 September 1983 'between 40 and 50' were seen at Duck Lake to the north of Teouma Bay, Efate (Richard Pickering, Naika 11:10). This moderately common duck is fully protected by law and should not be hunted at any time of the year; nevertheless, shooting is still the main threat to its survival in Vanuatu.

FIELD NOTES
Restricted to freshwater habitats, the Australian White-eyed Duck apparently favours quiet inland lakes, and swamps and streams in the lowland. It is probably more mobile than the Pacific Black Duck. Normally shy and wary it is certain to spot an observer first and usually stays well out on open water preferring to dive to escape danger. If surprised it reacts quickly by rising vertically into the air and gaining height rapidly. Typically it swims with the body sloping down at the tail but the white undertail is sometimes clearly seen. Being a good diver it can stay underwater for up to 30

seconds, gathering food from the mud at the bottom of the lake. It is sociable and is usually seen in pairs or small flocks, sometimes congregating with other waterfowl.

VOICE
It is rather a silent bird, infrequently uttering a soft quacking murmur.

FOOD
It feeds mostly on a variety of plants and seeds but also takes molluscs, insects, shrimps and probably small fish.

NEST AND BREEDING
The nest, a deep cup of grass and other soft vegetation, thickly lined with down is well-hidden under some kind of dense cover. It may be in a shallow depression on the ground between the partly exposed roots of a tree, in a thick bush growing in or near the water or in a tree-hollow. The eggs (57×41 mm), usually between 6-14, are creamy-white and incubation takes about 25 days. The breeding season in Vanuatu appears to be from September to January. Rainfall determines the breeding season in Australia; October to November in the southwest but between September and December in New South Wales. When there is no flooding there is little breeding but when flooding is extensive the breeding season is extended.

Order ACCIPITRIFORMES
This order, the diurnal birds of prey or raptors comprises 5 families with about 280 species: Cathartidae, the American or New World vultures; Pandionidae, ospreys; Accipitridae, the Old World vultures, hawks, buzzards, eagles, kites and harriers; and Sagittariidae with a single species, the Secretary Bird. Some ornithologists regard the Accipitridae as a family of the Falconiformes. Relationships between these diverse families are uncertain, authorities differ and further study is needed.

Kites, Harriers, Hawks and allies   *Accipitridae*
These birds of prey ranging in size from the small sparrowhawks to the large and powerful eagles are found throughout the world except in Antarctica. Like all predatory birds they are comparatively scarce and generally solitary. Excluding the vultures, which are not in any case found in Australasia, they are easily recognised by the sharply downcurved and hooked bill with a cere, a fleshy membrane, across the base of the upper mandible through which the nostrils open and by the powerful feet with strong toes and long curved claws or talons; the bill is used for ripping and tearing and the sharp talons for grasping the prey. All are strong winged, capable of powerful flight and superb soaring. Some species are migratory. The female is usually larger and slightly duller than the male and plumage generally is dull with blended grey, brown or black and barred or streaked underparts; only a few have bright colours or white in the plumage. They are almost entirely carnivorous, hunting live prey or scavenging. Most species nest in trees or on rocky crags or in crevices, occasionally on tall buildings or on the ground and the nest is made of sticks and lined with leaves or grass; some are large structures added to in successive years. Small clutches of 1-2 eggs are typical of the larger species and up to 6 in the smaller ones; eggs may be white to yellow, pale brown or blue and are all spotted or blotched with red to red-brown. The female incubates and, until the young are able to be left,

looks after the young while the male brings the food. At first this is torn into small pieces for them but before fledging the young tear up prey for themselves.

Simpson and Day (1989) list 12 Australian genera and 19 species of which 3 are known in Vanuatu. There is one record of the Brahminy Kite, genus Haliastur. *The Brown Goshawk, genus* Accipiter, *is only known to breed on one island but may be extending its range northwards. The Swamp Harrier, which belongs to the genus* Circus, *breeds throughout Vanuatu.*

32. Brahminy Kite   *Haliastur indus*
Other names: Red-backed Kite, Sea Eagle
French names: Milan brahmane, Aigle de mer à dos rouge

IDENTIFICATION AND FIELD NOTES

Length 43 to 49 cm (male), 48 to 51 cm (female). Wingspan up to 125 cm. The Brahminy Kite has a distinctive slow, wheeling flight with broad, rounded wings outspread as it searches for prey. *Adult:* head, neck and breast are white and the rest of the plumage is mainly a rich chestnut with black wingtips and a rounded, white tip to the tail. The *immature*, streaked buff and brown above and below with paler buff on the belly, has a more uniform underwing pattern and a shorter tail than the similar Whistling Kite *Haliastur sphenurus* which occurs in New Guinea and New Caledonia.

The Brahminy Kite inhabits coastal or swampy areas and offshore islands and is usually seen singly or in pairs. It feeds on carrion of all kinds and sometimes fish, frogs and reptiles.

DISTRIBUTION AND STATUS

It occurs in coastal northern Australia and islands and in coastal habitats from India, where it is sacred, to the Philippines, Indonesia, Papua New Guinea and the Solomon Islands and in some areas it is very common. An adult Brahminy Kite was observed by Peter Kaestner in the Santo Mountains during the weekend of 14-17 June 1985. It was seen 'for several minutes at a distance of 100 m ... soaring over an area of forest with numerous clearings at about 300 m, 10 km north of Ipayato' (Naika 19:7). In 1988, John Edge reported seeing a 'large raptor' on Efate, 'dark in colour and heavily built, with wide not pointed wings' which he thought might be an immature Brahminy Kite. He had four sightings 'two over the Lagoon and two over the plateau south of Havana Harbour' but was not close enough for identification (Naika 29:28).

Goshawks and sparrowhawks, genus *Accipiter*, are dashing fliers with broad, rounded wings, long tails, rather long thin legs and powerful feet and talons. They are bold and aggressive and all inhabit woodlands or forests being adept at catching prey in thick vegetation.

33. Brown Goshawk   *Accipiter fasciatus vigilax*   PLATE 5
Other name: Australian Goshawk
French name: Autour australien

IDENTIFICATION
Length 38 to 45 cm (male), 45 to 55 cm (female). Wingspan up to 1 m. *Adults* have similar plumage but the female is much more powerful. Upperparts dull grey-brown with an indistinct rufous collar across the nape; head grey, lighter on the face; throat pale grey. Flight feathers and tail are dark grey-brown above and pale silver-grey with dark barring below. Underparts and underwing-coverts pale rufous with white bars which are narrow on the breast and become progressively broader towards the tail; thighs lighter rufous with finer barring. The eye is yellow and looks fierce. Bill: blue-grey with a black tip and the cere is pale to olive-yellow. Legs and feet: pale yellow. *Immature:* distinctly different from adult, dark brown above with inconspicuous rufous barring and shadow of the rufous band on the nape. Underparts greyish-white with narrow dark brown streaking on the face and throat, large dark brown spots on the breast and with irregular bars across the rest of the underparts, which are more rufous-brown on the belly and thighs and darker blackish-brown on the tail. Iris is brown and the bill and feet lighter than in the adult.

DISTRIBUTION AND STATUS
The race *fasciatus* is widespread and common in suitable habitat in Australia and New Zealand and the smaller and paler *didimus* is restricted to northern Australia. The Brown Goshawk is also found in the Lesser Sundas, Buru Island in Indonesia and New Guinea. The race *vigilax* occurs in New Caledonia, the Loyalty Islands and in Vanuatu (Wattel, 1973). The only definite records are from Aneityum where it is not numerous. Several recent sightings of a 'goshawk' on Efate could refer to this species and if so indicate an extension of its range (Euan Macdonald pers. comm. 1990).

FIELD NOTES
The Brown Goshawk frequents a variety of wooded habitats in the lowlands and the mountains but apparently prefers the edge of the forest, wooded grassland or secondary growth. It may be seen perched on the outer limb of a tree or scurrying through the trees in search of prey or pairs may be seen soaring on outstretched wings over the tree-tops. When hidden, its presence is sometimes betrayed by the loud alarm calls of small birds and in flight it may be mobbed by woodswallows, honeyeaters and others. This aggressive hunter preys mainly on small birds, taken in mid-air, often after a dashing pursuit, twisting and turning through the tree-tops. It will also wait in ambush darting suddenly from its hiding place to swoop down on its prey. Lizards, rodents and large insects such as beetles and grasshoppers are attacked on the ground and Goshawks occasionally take domestic chickens. Normal flight may be direct with rapid wingbeats or rather leisurely with slow wingbeats interspersed with glides. When hunting, flight is fast and manoeuvrable; the broad wings and long tail give the speed and control for it to fly swiftly through woodland, to check its movements quickly and to make abrupt turns in pursuit of prey.

VOICE
Normally it is rather silent but it can be noisy in the vicinity of the nest during courtship. It has a strident, high-pitched 'kek-kek-kek-kek', also shrill chatter, a drawn-out plaintive 'swee-eet' and short high-pitched sounds.

FOOD
The diet consists of a wide variety of animals as described in the field notes. Prey other than birds may form a large part of its diet.

NEST AND BREEDING
The nest is a rough platform of twigs lined with leaves, usually high up in the trees, and may be used in successive years. The 2-4 whitish eggs (38 × 30 mm), sparingly blotched with reddish-brown or lavender, are incubated by the female. The male hunts and brings food to a nearby roost several times a day and the female leaves the eggs and flies out to eat it there. After hatching the young are closely guarded by the female who feeds them with pieces of food brought to the nest by the male. The chicks are later fed by both parents until they are about 24 days old. The breeding season is from September to December/January.

Harriers, genus *Circus*, are raptors with long square tails, long slightly rounded wings and fairly long legs. In some species male and female differ considerably in plumage. They prey on small rodents, waterfowl and amphibians and derive their name from their habit of coursing low over open country in search of prey. Most harriers are ground-nesters.

34. Swamp Harrier   *Circus approximans*   PLATE 5
Other names: Marsh Hawk/Harrier, Australasian Harrier
French name: Busard australien
Bislama names: Big fala hawk, Mala

IDENTIFICATION
Length 49 to 55 cm (male), 55 to 61 cm (female). Wingspan 115 to 130 cm. This is the largest raptor in the region. *Adult male and female* generally have similar plumage: back and mantle all dark brown; wings greyish-brown; tail grey, barred with brown and with a prominent white rump; neck and sides of the head whitish streaked buff and brown, sometimes with facial disc apparent; underwing-coverts and undertail pale buff and underparts pale buff to whitish with narrow reddish-brown streaks. The colour varies between individuals and with age, some being very dark and some older birds having much lighter underparts. Iris: yellow. Bill: black with a greenish-yellow cere. Legs and feet: yellow. *Immature* is much darker than adult: blackish-brown above and rufous-brown below. The plumage becomes lighter with each moult; the rump, which is buff in younger birds, becoming paler with age. Iris: brown. The Swamp Harrier is best identified by the typical flight silhouette: the bird glides with the long, pointed wings held up above the back in a wide open V-shape and the long tail projecting; the white band above the tail is usually visible as the bird tilts from side to side.

DISTRIBUTION AND STATUS
Harriers are found in open country throughout the world except in the polar regions and some islands. This species has a wide distribution: Australia and Tasmania, New Zealand, New Guinea and the Sunda Islands and islands in the south Pacific. The race

The Swamp Harrier builds a platform nest on the ground hidden in dense vegetation

approximans has been recorded from Fiji, Tonga, the Loyalty Islands, New Caledonia and Vanuatu (Brown and Amadon, 1968). It is fairly common in suitable habitats on most of the islands of Vanuatu; there are no records for Gaua, Mota Lava, Mere Lava or Tongariki.

FIELD NOTES

The Swamp Harrier spends most of the day on the wing being seen singly or in pairs, usually in open country but also frequently over the forest. Normal flight is slow but vigorous and buoyant, a few pronounced wingbeats followed by a long glide; soaring high in thermals, round and round, may also be observed in most months of the year. They are active hunters and forage by quartering low over grassland, plantations, marshes, lakes and other open habitats. Harriers usually surprise their prey, mostly small birds, before they can fly or run for cover; sometimes they are pursued on the wing for a considerable distance. The prey is secured by gripping it with the talons, sometimes bearing it off but generally devouring it on the spot. Harriers rarely perch high preferring to rest on the ground or on a stone or fallen tree. When waterfowl have young, these harriers may be seen skimming low along the edges of lagoons or lakes in pursuit of ducklings; every now and then they swoop down on a swimming brood, often without success. Most harriers have no interest in domestic birds but when very hungry may raid poultry yards and snatch a chicken. Some individuals become addicted to this behaviour and can make inroads into poultry stocks.

VOICE

Generally quiet, it is very vocal during courtship display-flights and high-pitched, peevish whistles are uttered while soaring and circling.

FOOD

It takes a varied range of food; mainly small birds, especially the young, sick or injured; rats, mice, lizards, frogs, large insects, snakes and probably fish and it also devours carrion.

NEST AND BREEDING

At the beginning of the breeding season, which is from September to January, they engage in acrobatic display-flights in pairs, or occasionally several birds at a time. They circle and glide, often at great height and their aerial manoeuvres consist of side-slipping, and plummeting with half-closed wings, often uttering loud mewing, whistling calls.

The Swamp Harrier nests on the ground, among dense cane-grass, reed beds, bushes or high grass. The nest is a platform of reeds, vegetation and sticks lined with finer grass and the same site may be used in successive years. The 3-6 eggs (50×39 mm) are rounded, dull white to pale ochre and incubated for about 5 weeks by the female. The nestlings are thickly covered in whitish down and are fed by the female with pieces of the food brought by the male. They can fly at about 6 weeks but often leave the nest earlier, scattering and being fed by the parents separately.

Order FALCONIFORMES

The family Falconidae was originally included in the Accipitriformes but further study of the anatomical features, in particular of the species in South America, has led to them being placed in an order of their own.

Falcons *Falconidae*
There are about 60 species of falcons, divided among 4 subfamilies: the forest falcons, restricted to the New World tropics; the laughing falcon, with just one species inhabiting the forests of tropical America; the caracaras, very common in South and Central America in open country; and the true falcons, subfamily Falconinae *with 4 genera including the genus* Falco *with 37 species found throughout the world. This genus contains the small to medium-sized typical falcons with thick-set body, long, broadbased, swept-back wings and relatively short, tapering tail. A moustachial stripe and strongly toothed bill are present in many species. These falcons are known for the speed and agility of their flight; they attack their prey, which is mainly small birds, in full flight by gripping them in the talons or striking them with a blow of the feet so that they are killed or stunned and fall to the ground.*

The only widespread falcon in the Pacific is the Peregrine Falcon which, although found in many island groups including Vanuatu, is uncommon.

35. Peregrine Falcon *Falco peregrinus nesiotes* PLATE 5
French name: Faucon pélerin

IDENTIFICATION
Length 36 to 42 cm (male), 45 to 50 cm (female). This powerful flier with broad, pointed wings and tapering tail is almost black above, whitish with black barring below and has characteristic facial markings. *Adult male:* black above, variously barred with slate-grey and with paler edges to the flight feathers; head and nape all sooty-black which extends below the eyes like a helmet. The throat, side of the neck and upper breast appear white from a distance and are whitish to pale rufous; lower breast and abdomen are creamy-white to rufous with a few black streaks and spots on the lower breast and narrow black bars densely covering the rest of the underparts, which look dark grey from a distance. Underwing-coverts are light with numerous black bars and the tail has dark bars and a pale tip. Iris: brown, the skin around the eye and the cere are yellow. Bill: black with a bluish base. Legs and feet: yellow. *Adult female:* much larger than the male, otherwise similar except for richer chestnut on the breast. *Immature:* dark brown above with rufous edges to some feathers; greyish to rufous below, paler on the throat and breast and heavily streaked blackish-brown. Legs, feet and cere are grey-blue.

DISTRIBUTION AND STATUS
This almost cosmopolitan species breeds from Eurasia to Africa, the Americas, Australia and many oceanic islands though it is absent from New Zealand. It is uncommon and considered to be an endangered species worldwide. Some 16 geographical races are recognised which differ slightly in size and colouration; those in Australia being blue-grey above and generally paler below. The darker race *nesiotes*, described above, has been recorded on Gaua, Santo, Malo, Malakula, Tongoa, Efate, Erromango, Aniwa, Tanna, Futuna and Aneityum but probably occurs on other islands. In Vanuatu it is most often encountered in the vicinity of suitable nest sites and around lakes like Lake Siwi on Tanna. This race is also found on New Caledonia, the Loyalty Islands and Fiji (Brown and Amadon, 1968).

One of the swiftest birds of prey, the Peregrine Falcon, with a Rainbow Lorikeet

FIELD NOTES
Usually solitary or in pairs, it is found hunting over a variety of habitats: the seashore, plantations or even suburban gardens, open and lightly wooded country, forests and rugged mountains but its preference seems to be near cliffs. The Peregrine Falcon is highly adapted for killing birds in flight with its streamlined shape, large round head and wide chest tapering back to the narrow tail and with long, pointed wings. Legs are thick and muscular with long and powerful talons. The strongly hooked bill has a tomial tooth fitting into a notch in the lower mandible: if the prey is not killed instantly it is brought to ground and finished off with a bite to the neck. The Peregrine may be seen perched quietly, in an upright position, on some vantage point, a cliff top or tree on the look-out for prey. It is wary and usually flies at low to medium altitudes with powerful, fast wingbeats interrupted occasionally by glides. The appearance of a Peregrine causes panic among potential victims; birds that are in the open rush for cover and honeyeaters, parrots and other birds utter continuous cries of alarm. The Peregrine Falcon captures its prey in direct pursuit or by striking it from above, stooping from a height with partly folded wings, when it can reach a speed estimated to be about 280 km per hour.

VOICE
It is usually only vocal in the vicinity of nesting and roosting cliffs. A variety of mewing and harsh calls have been noted. Most often heard is a loud, fairly high-pitched and repetitive 'hek-hek-hek' or 'kew-kew-kew'.

FOOD
The diet consists mainly of small birds which are carried to a sheltered place, plucked and devoured. In Vanuatu it commonly takes doves, pigeons, starlings, waders and Rainbow Lories and less often ducks or seabirds. One was 'observed chasing swiftlets' at Devil's Point on Efate (John Edge, Naika 29:28). It may occasionally take rodents and flying-foxes and sometimes raids poultry yards.

NEST AND BREEDING
It breeds from August to January. At the start of the breeding season pairs may be seen in courtship display above their breeding ground and also soaring to great heights. They do not build nests and eggs may be laid on inaccessible cliff-ledges in rock crevices or in large hollows in trees; sometimes the abandoned nests of other birds may be used. The 2-4 eggs (51 × 41 mm) are pale buff thickly marked with reddish-brown lines and blotches. They are incubated chiefly by the female for about 4 weeks. Nestlings are covered with creamy-white down at first. The male brings food for the female to give to the chicks and fledging takes about 5 weeks. After leaving the nest the young are fed by both parents until they develop their own hunting skills.

Order GALLIFORMES
This is a large order with about 225 species in 4 families: Megapodiidae, the megapodes (this word meaning literally 'great feet'); Cracidae, the curassows; Phasianidae with most species including pheasants, quails, fowls and turkeys, and Opisthocomidae with just one species, the Hoatzin. All members of this order, sometimes called gallinaceous birds, share some of the characteristics of the domestic

fowl and many of them are game-birds. Most of them are ground-living birds, typically good runners, and some only take to the trees to roost. They have developed strong legs and feet for scratching and digging; some are armed with spurs; the feet have three toes in front and a shorter one at the back and strong claws. The bill is short and stout. The wings are short, rounded and curved and 'fit' the body; most species can fly well but for short distances only.

Several species were among the earliest wild birds to be domesticated (their breeding and maintenance being controlled by humans) because of their succulent meat and production of eggs. Some have been kept in captivity as ornamental birds because of the attractiveness of their plumage. Through domestication the ranges of the more adaptable species have been considerably extended. The order Galliformes is almost cosmopolitan, absent only from Antarctica, and although most Polynesian islands lack indigenous species feral domestic fowl are found on many islands. There are two representatives of this order in Vanuatu, the Incubator Bird in the family Megapodiidae and the Red Jungle Fowl, family Phasianidae.

Megapodes *Megapodiidae*
This family has 6 genera which can be divided into 3 ecological groups: the scrubfowl, with 2 genera; the brush-turkeys, 3 genera; and the Malleefowl. They are best known for their aberrant breeding behaviour. They do not incubate their eggs with their own body heat but use other natural sources of heat to provide the necessary temperature. On some islands megapodes use solar energy, depositing their eggs along certain beaches in black volcanic sand which absorbs the heat from the sun. Some species lay their eggs in burrows dug into the ash on the flanks of active volcanoes or near a geothermal source where the heated soil incubates the eggs, as on Savo Island in the Solomons (Roper, 1983). Others scratch and scrape earth and decaying vegetation together into a large mound where the combination of heat from the sun and fermentation maintains the temperature required for the development of the embryo. These mound-builders are perhaps the best known of the Megapodiidae and their roughly conical mounds, which in some densely forested areas may be up to 12 m across and 3 m high, are probably the largest structures built by birds. Some species like the Australian Brush-turkey Alectura lathami *of the dense forests and the Malleefowl* Leipoa ocellata *of dry areas in Australia show still more complex behaviour. They do not abandon their eggs and leave the incubation to chance but maintain temperature control (at about 34°C) by visiting the mound regularly and shifting the material of the mound with their powerful feet, covering over cooler sections and opening up parts that are becoming too hot (Campbell and Lack, 1985).*

The Megapodiidae are birds of the Australasian region: the 10-12 species vary in size, appearance and behaviour and are widely distributed from Australia, the Andaman Islands in the Indian Ocean, Indonesia, New Guinea, the Philippines, the Marianas and the south western Pacific islands to Tonga. The Incubator Bird, a scrubfowl, is the only species in this family found in Vanuatu.

36. Incubator Bird *Megapodius freycinet layardi* PLATE 6
Other name: Scrubfowl
French name: Mégapode
Bislama names: Skraptak or Sikraptak, Namalau

IDENTIFICATION

Length about 32.5 cm. A uniformly dark ground-bird with a strong bill, short tail and distinctively sturdy legs, it is the same size and has some behaviour in common with the domestic fowl. *Adult male* is blackish-brown above, only slightly tinged with brown, and sooty-grey below. The crown has a short crest and the forehead is bare with red skin which also shows through the sparsely feathered cheeks and neck. Iris: brown. Bill: horn-colour to brown. Legs and feet: yellow with black patches on the toes; the claws are long and broad, like a shovel. *Female:* similar to the male but slightly smaller with paler legs and plumage. *Immature:* resembles adult but all colours are duller and the legs brownish. Chicks are cryptically coloured, mostly buff-brown with numerous dark brown bands across the body, especially on the wings and back, and pale buff on the abdomen. Iris: light brown. Bill: dark olive-brown. Legs and feet: yellowish-ochre with blackish-brown patches especially on the toes. The average weight of newly hatched chicks is 60 g.

DISTRIBUTION, STATUS AND CONSERVATION

This species, *Megapodius freycinet* has been re-classified as *M. reinwardt* in Australia but no taxonomic evidence is given in Pizzey (1980) or Simpson and Day (1989). In Campbell and Lack (1985) reference is made to the 9 species of *Megapodius* recognised by Peters (1937), which included 28 races, and the work of E Mayr in reviewing the genus and recognising just 3 species: *M. freycinet*, *M. laperouse*, and *M. pritchardii*. Authorities obviously differ and further study is needed. This species with many races is found from the Nicobar Islands through Indonesia, Borneo, the Philippines, Papua New Guinea, coastal northern Australia and islands and the Solomons. The race *layardi* occurs on virtually all islands in central and northern Vanuatu. It is mainly a bird of the lowland forest but can also be found at moderate altitudes. Though still common in suitable habitat, on some islands, for example Efate, its nesting sites and forest environment are threatened by encroaching agricultural and other development. Eggs of this species have been collected as food for centuries and are a valued source of protein for village people. Only the more accessible sites were visited and this harvesting of eggs has had little detrimental effect in the past on the megapode population. With development, and an increase in the human population and their mobility, it is by no means certain that these unusual birds will survive without some measure of official protection. The establishment of Lowland Forest Reserves around important egg-burying grounds, more efficient control of illegal shooting and a limit on egg-collecting should be urgently considered. The Incubator Bird is a game-bird in Vanuatu but it is partly protected and should only be hunted from 1 April to 30 June.

FIELD NOTES

It is usually seen singly or in pairs on the forest or thicket floor, behaving much like a domestic fowl, scratching among the damp vegetation-litter for food. It is wary, and

On hatching, the precocious Megapode chick is independent. It digs upward through the mound and from the moment it emerges, fends for itself and is even able to fly

tends to run quickly into the undergrowth at the slightest disturbance. It will fly if surprised but often just to the lower branches of a nearby tree. It is able to fly well, with deliberate wingbeats and intermittent glides, and may visit offshore islands to roost. Some concentrations of these birds may occur around the larger laying sites but they disperse after the laying period. They roost at night in high thick scrub or trees, pairs usually on the same branch together.

VOICE

It is quite vocal at times, usually a subdued or loud hoarse clucking. A loud call can be heard particularly at dawn and dusk and even at intervals through the night. Pairs may call in duet or several birds in concert for long periods possibly advertising their territories. A loud, two-syllabled, somewhat slurred and far-carrying call 'took-tooorrr' may be repeated for long periods; first syllable short, second drawn-out and decreasing in volume near the end. Feeding pairs emit soft, short notes at irregular intervals.

FOOD

Insects, grubs, worms, snails and other invertebrates are taken. They also eat fruit, seeds and other vegetable matter.

NEST AND BREEDING

In Vanuatu two methods of incubation are apparently used. On islands with active volcanoes, according to the village people, the hens bury their eggs in a number of communal sites scattered in the vicinity of the craters; volcanic heat vents and the availability of loose soil determine these areas. Most of their egg-laying sites are however, scattered throughout the lowland forest often near the coast. Sites vary considerably in size, commonly a few metres in diameter but they may be up to 10m wide. The smallest measured was less than half a metre and visited by only one hen. The Incubator Bird may use the same site year after year and some mounds, which are frequented by a number of hens and are excavated repeatedly, have served countless generations and become larger and deeper with time.

The majority of birds bury their eggs around the base of large decaying, forest trees where the heat generated by the fermenting vegetable matter mixed with earth and/or sand, incubates the eggs. It is not clear which factors determine the locality of the laying site, perhaps the soil is not so compacted between the roots and more suitable for burrowing or perhaps they do not have to dig so deep to reach an adequate temperature for incubation. Eggs are laid at different depths and it has not been established yet if the female Incubator Bird can detect the temperature of the soil. A laying site typically consists of a series of discrete excavations scattered over the area. The period of greatest activity is the morning with birds arriving early to dig their burrows but some may also visit the site later in the day. They usually walk round for a while and scratch in a few places first before beginning to dig in earnest. Pairs may visit the site together but the female digs the burrow, using both feet alternately, scratching into the material of the mound and pushing it backwards with shovel-like claws. As the burrow deepens the hen reappears at the entrance at intervals and looks around and when the excavation is complete remains inside for about 30 or more minutes while she lays a single egg which may be positioned vertically or almost horizontally. The burrow is then filled with small roots, rotting leaves, other forest litter and soil scratched from the burrow and the surrounding forest floor. These burrows may be 0.3 to 1.2 m deep, up to 2 m long and have an entrance of about 0.4 m in diameter. The bird returns a few days later to deposit another egg which is laid in a separate burrow. In the cases observed the time taken for the whole process involved varied considerably and took between 2 and 4 hours.

The long oval eggs are pale to pinkish-brown when newly laid but may soon become stained with rotting vegetation. They are very large in relation to the adult bird and contain a high proportion of yolk. Twenty eggs examined were found to be 77 to 85 mm long with a diameter of 43 to 47 mm and weighed from 50 to 70 g. The exact length of incubation is not known, probably varying with slight differences in temperature, but it is over 45 days. It was not possible to measure temperatures in the mounds. Studies of the Niuafo'ou Megapode *Megapodius pritchardii* which is endemic to Niuafo'ou (Tonga) give incubation periods from 47 to 51 days and records show that the soil temperature in the immediate vicinity of the eggs varied between 29°C and 38°C (Todd, 1982-83). Data for other *Megapodius* spp are generally in the same range (Crome and Brown, 1979 and Campbell and Lack 1985).

The chicks are independent on hatching and use their powerful feet and long claws to dig their way upwards to the air through the mound. Even so the process may take hours and once on the surface they often rest for a while before taking to the shelter of the undergrowth. From the moment they emerge the precocious chicks are able to fend for themselves and to fly if the need arises but they usually remain hidden, resting for the first day or so before becoming active and feeding. There are often a few chicks that die naturally at different stages of development in the egg-shell. The thickness of the layer and density of the nest material probably has a bearing on this and the frequent digging and shifting of material in the mound as new burrows are made may be in part responsible.

In Vanuatu, according to the village people, freshly laid eggs of the Incubator Bird can be found in every month of the year suggesting that the breeding cycles of the individual females are asynchronous and similar in this respect to the Orange-footed Scrubfowl *Megapodius freycinet (reinwardt)*. The number of eggs laid by one female and the intervals between successive eggs is not known in Vanuatu but an Orange-footed Scrubfowl in northern Queensland has been recorded as laying 12 or possibly 13 eggs at intervals ranging from 9 to 20 days (Crome and Brown, 1979).

Pheasants, Fowls and allies *Phasianidae*
Jungle fowl are included in the family Phasianidae *which has about 48 species in 16 genera but they constitute a very special genus* Gallus *and are not closely related to any other. One common characteristic is that the plumage of the male and female is distinct; the male is often brilliantly coloured and gives spectacular strutting displays, fanning the tail and whirring the wings. The jungle fowl differ in having a comb, wattles and an arched tail, curved in the cock. There are 4 species of jungle fowl, one of which the Red Jungle Fowl is thought to be the ancestor of all domestic breeds. This species was introduced to Vanuatu. Anthropologists believe that wild fowl were first domesticated in the Bronze Age about 4000 BC and they have been by far the most important birds in human settlement since that time. Many varieties, also called*

breeds, have been developed through breeding in captivity and some of the modern types bear little resemblance to their wild ancestors. They have been used for religious purposes, for food, as ornamental birds and for sport as fighting cocks and game-birds.

37. Red Jungle Fowl   *Gallus gallus*   PLATE 6
Other names: Wild Fowl, Jungle Fowl
French name: Coq Bankiva   or locally: Coq sauvage

IDENTIFICATION
Length about 70 cm (male), about 45 cm (female). This species could only be confused with the more slender breeds of domestic fowls. *Adult male* has bright iridescent, multicoloured plumage resembling the black and red domestic rooster. Head is mostly bare red skin with crimson comb and wattles; elongated neck feathers glossy reddish-brown; mantle maroon; back chestnut-red; wing-coverts glossy blue; rump hackles glossy red-orange and the long arching tail feathers are black with a green gloss. The underparts are black. Iris: orange-red. Bill: upper mandible is dark brown and the lower mandible light brown. Legs and feet: lead-grey or brownish to yellow in mixed-blooded birds. *Adult female* is inconspicuously brown with buff and black vermiculations; neck feathers blackish-brown with golden-yellow margins. Iris is light red, bill is horny-brown, legs and feet are like the male. *Chick* is brownish-yellow all over with a dark band behind the eye and a characteristic broad rich-brown band edged narrowly with black and white extending down the back from the crown. In mixed-blooded chicks these markings are absent or not so extensive. In the wild these striking patterns serve as a protective device; when alarmed the chicks scatter and bury themselves in the dense vegetation or crannies where they are partly concealed and the back plumage blends so completely that only a very sharp eye can penetrate the camouflage.

DISTRIBUTION AND STATUS
Originating in southeast Asia the Red Jungle Fowl now has a much wider distribution. In the Pacific they were introduced to most islands by the earliest settlers and have been reported from Samoa, Tonga, all the Fijian islands that are free from the mongoose, New Caledonia and Micronesia. It is found on almost all the islands in Vanuatu usually in lowland forests, occasionally at moderate altitude and only rarely on high mountains. They have freely interbred with feral domestic birds and many show strong traces of various modern breeds in their plumage; pure-blooded birds have become rare in some areas. A much appreciated game-bird, the Red Jungle Fowl is still quite common where hunting is not excessive.

FIELD NOTES
They are birds of the forest and scrub but frequently show themselves early in the morning and late afternoon in clearings, cultivated patches, even near isolated huts and small villages. Medway and Marshall (1975) found them in closed forest on several islands and up to 485 m on Malakula. They can also sometimes be seen as they cross a road, path or stream. Clever at hiding in thickets during the day they are usually difficult to detect unless the unmistakable crowing of the cocks gives their presence away. At Narabut on Efate, Medway and Marshall (1975) found 5 cocks maintaining

adjacent territories in and around their 2 ha study area. The cocks are quite vocal at times but though one can hear them calling frequently, and they appear to be close, it requires much patient observation to actually see them. Reluctant to fly, they will do so if surprised, rising abruptly with a burst of wingbeats then gliding away on outstretched wings, the long tail of the cock trailing. After a short distance they drop back into cover.

VOICE

The territorial crow of the wild cock is shrill, short and is usually repeated frequently. All other calls resemble those of the domestic fowl.

FOOD

The Red Jungle Fowl is omnivorous feeding on insects, seeds, fruits, bulbs, shoots, worms, small molluscs and even small vertebrates like lizards.

NEST AND BREEDING

The hens usually nest on the ground in the shelter of bushes, tree roots, ferns or high grass. Most clutches have 8 eggs and the average weight of the eggs is 30 g. The nest is a shallow hollow scraped in the ground by the female and lined with grass and leaves. Breeding may take place at any time of the year but most birds breed during September to December/February.

Order GRUIFORMES

This order contains 11 families of ground-living birds, feeding and nesting on the ground, some rarely if ever flying, which include: the Turnicidae, the button (bustard) quails; Rallidae, the rails, crakes and allies; Gruidae, cranes, a cosmopolitan family with several endangered species; and Otididae, bustards. Members of these 4 families occur in the Australasian region but in Vanuatu only the Rallidae family is represented.

Rails, Crakes, Swamphen and Coots *Rallidae*

Commonly known as rails, this family has about 130 species in 18 genera and is found throughout the world, except in polar regions. They have established themselves on almost all the major oceanic islands and on an astonishing number of the minor ones. A number of these island populations have been isolated for so long that they have developed into monotypic genera, many of them flightless.

Rails are small to medium-sized, running, wading or swimming birds. The typical rails are distinguished by the narrowness of their bodies, which are compressed as an adaptation for running through thick swamp vegetation or dense undergrowth. They all have strong, medium to long legs and several species have extremely long toes to facilitate walking over marshes and floating vegetation; in the coots the toes are lobed for swimming. Their wings are short and rounded and the tail is usually short. Though rails are relatively weak fliers, and some even flightless, some species make long migratory flights by night over water as well as land. However most rails do not resort to flight if they can help it, and when in the air appear out of their element. The tail is often flicked as they walk or swim and when agitated. The bill varies in size being long in the typical rails and shorter and thicker in the crakes. It is heavier and almost conical in the coots and swamphen, which also have a frontal shield, a horny plate, extending from the base of the upper mandible to the forehead and in some species to the top of the head. Their plumage is rather sober in colour, blending well with their surroundings. Most are brownish, greyish or reddish; some are attractively banded or marked with contrasting colours and only a few are brightly coloured. All rails are omnivorous and able to sustain themselves on a wide range of both vegetable and animal food. This partly explains their success in establishing and maintaining themselves in so many parts of the world.

Rails build coarse nests of vegetable matter, well hidden in grass, reeds or on the ground. The clutch size varies from 3 to 15 or more eggs. Usually both adults share incubation duties and the care of the young. The downy chicks of all species are black and leave the nest shortly after hatching. Most rails are rather solitary and typically shy, but some of the more sociable species like coots are seen in parks and gardens. Some rails are nocturnal, most of them are secretive birds and, being great skulkers, keep out of sight of even the most skilful observer. Their presence is usually only revealed by their calls which are uttered frequently and are specific, aiding identification. Marshes, swamps or thick stands of reeds along the edges of ponds and streams are favoured habitats for most rails. Some of the species in the Pacific islands however are forest birds and others frequent the dense secondary growth of abandoned gardens or impenetrable cane-grass thickets. Many have a restricted distribution and a number lead a precarious existence today. In the past, with no terrestrial enemies, they had no need to fly and lost the power of flight but flightless species are seldom able to survive changes in their environment, particularly the appearance of new predators. When the Europeans came and brought with them rats, cats, dogs and mongooses these specialised rail populations were unable, in most cases, to cope with the new enemies and have become extinct. At least 15 distinctive species have been lost during the past century including rails from the islands of New Zealand, from New Caledonia, Fiji, Wake, Laysan, Kosrae, Hawaii, Tahiti and Samoa. A number of additional species have been seriously depleted and are rare or endangered.

Four species of rail are found in Vanuatu; they are all widespread species and easy to distinguish. No endemic species are known in Vanuatu.

38. Buff-banded Rail *Gallirallus philippensis sethsmithi* PLATES 6, 21
Other name: Banded Rail
French name: Râle à bandes
Bislama name: Nambilak

IDENTIFICATION

Length about 30cm. A medium-sized, slender, long-legged rail with prominent whitish and rufous facial markings and black and white barring on breast and belly. *Adult male and female* are similar: crown streaked black on brown; back, rump and tail feathers blackish-brown with ochre margins and scattered black and white spots; wings blackish-brown with broad white and chestnut bars. There is a broad rufous stripe through the eye beginning on the lores and extending to the nape contrasting strongly with a whitish-grey eyebrow. Chin is whitish; throat olive-grey; the rest of the underparts are heavily barred black and white except for a buffish-white centre to the lower belly and thighs. Some individuals have a conspicuous rufous-buff band across the upper breast. Iris: red. Bill: pale red, tips and ridge of the upper mandible brownish. Legs and feet: olive-grey. *Immature:* much duller, iris ochre and bill brownish. The downy chicks are all black.

Nest of the Buff-banded Rail; the black downy chicks still show the egg-tooth on the bill, used for chipping the shell

DISTRIBUTION AND STATUS

The Buff-banded Rail is widely distributed on islands in the eastern Indian Ocean through the Lesser Sundas, Sulawesi, and New Guinea to the Philippines. Also on islands in the southwest Pacific Ocean to Samoa and Tonga and in Australia and New Zealand. This species is sometimes placed in the genus *Rallus* (Olson, 1973). There are about 9 races in the southwest Pacific but the differences between them are insufficient to distinguish them in the field. The race *sethsmithi* occurs in Fiji and probably throughout Vanuatu but has so far only been recorded in Vanua Lava, Santo, Malo, Maewo, Ambae, Pentecost, Malakula, Ambrym, Epi, Tongoa, Emae, Efate, Nguna, Emau, Erromango, Tanna and Aneityum. This rail is found from sea-level to the mountains and is fairly common in suitable habitats on most islands.

FIELD NOTES

The Buff-banded Rail may be found singly, in pairs or family parties in almost any kind of habitat where abundant vegetation provides cover, plantations, gardens and forest, often far away from water. It is more common in places where grassland, marshy areas and small groves of trees intermingle, or in swamps, lagoons and along watercourses and lakes. These rails frequently live close to human settlement in back yards and house gardens but are seldom seen as they are semi-nocturnal and spend much of the day concealed in thick vegetation. Being secretive rather than actually shy they will venture from cover, especially at dawn or late in the afternoon, if they think they are not being observed. They may often be seen on the road-side or as they run across the road with neck outstretched and after or during heavy rain they frequently take a bath in the water accumulated in the potholes. Like other rails they flick the tail nervously up and down when alarmed and often when walking. Though they can fly, they usually seek safety by running away quickly and hiding among the tall grass and bushes. If flushed they rise abruptly and fly somewhat ponderously, with legs dangling, but not far; after several wingbeats they glide and soon drop back to the ground.

VOICE

The call heard most is a loud piercing 'prueet-prueet', which can be repeated several times. A muffled sound which resembles a fast drum beat and squeaks and croaks have also been noted. They may call at any time of the day or night but are more often heard at dusk. The warning call is a short and sharp 'krek' and calls at the nest are soft. The chicks maintain contact with moderately loud but penetrating 'chipping' calls at intervals as they walk along.

FOOD

Like most rails they stalk about foraging for a wide range of insects, worms, snails and even small vertebrates like lizards. Seeds and shoots of various plants are also taken.

NEST AND BREEDING

The nest can be a grass-lined scrape in the earth or a more substantial structure of grass, leaves and a few twigs, or reeds pulled down and woven into a cup. It is generally well hidden among dense vegetation which is sometimes drawn together from above to form a slight canopy. The 4-6 slightly pointed eggs (39-40 × 28-30mm) are pale ochre and blotched with purplish-red, brown and grey, mainly on the rounded end. Both parents share incubation of the eggs for 18 to 19 days. The newly hatched chicks leave the nest as soon as their down is dry to follow the adults and they stay with them for several weeks before becoming fully independent. John Edge in 1988 noted that a family of 2 adults and 2 juveniles was 'seen at the bottom of the [forest] track regularly in August, but not since' (Naika 29:27). The Buff-banded Rail has an extended breeding season but probably nests mostly from October to February/March. There is probably more than one brood in a season.

39. Spotless Crake *Porzana tabuensis tabuensis* PLATE 6
Other name: Sooty Rail
French name: Marouette fuligineuse

IDENTIFICATION

Length 15 to 16cm. A small dark rail with conspicuous red eye and red legs. *Adult male and female:* crown slate-grey suffused with brown; hind neck, back, wings and tail dark walnut-brown, blackish on the rump and tail. The sides of the head, neck and underparts are sooty slate-grey, paler on the throat; undertail-coverts are mottled and barred with white. Iris: ruby-red with a thin red eye-ring. Bill: short, dark olive-green.

Legs and feet: deep pink to red. *Immature:* lighter and duller than adult, underparts more or less marked with white. Iris: ochre. The black downy chicks have a white stripe along the chin and throat.

DISTRIBUTION, STATUS AND CONSERVATION

The Spotless Crake is widely distributed in the Pacific from the Philippines and New Guinea through many islands in Melanesia and Polynesia to New Zealand, Tasmania and Australia. The smaller race *tabuensis*, described above, occurs in Vanuatu but its distribution is not fully understood as this secretive little rail is so difficult to see in its preferred habitat. It is local and uncommon and has been recorded from Erromango, Tanna and Aneityum. There is a single record from John Edge of one 'seen on the roadside in the north of Efate' (Naika 29:27) and it could occur on other islands. This race is also found in Polynesia, Fiji, New Caledonia, the Solomons, New Guinea and the Philippines (Olson, 1973). In Vanuatu the minute population of the Spotless Crake, restricted to some small swamps, is extremely prone to extinction. It is fully protected by law but further conservation measures may be necessary in future to prevent pollution or destruction of its habitat.

FIELD NOTES

This is the smallest of the rails in Vanuatu. It is elusive and shy and more likely to be heard than actually seen as it calls sporadically from thick cover during the day. Records are largely from coastal areas, the comparatively large swamps round Lake Siwi on Tanna and smaller areas of swamp in the Anelghowat district on Aneityum. It frequents areas of dense vegetation in freshwater swamps or surrounding marshy lake-edges and marshy grasslands near water and occasionally saltmarshes and mangroves. Seen singly or in pairs in fairly well-defined territories, they are most active at dawn and dusk but are generally overlooked as they merge so closely with their surroundings. They seldom fly, seeking safety by running away, and will only take flight when seriously threatened. They swim well and may dive to escape danger.

VOICE

A variety of calls may be heard during the day or night including a peculiar, low purring note. The main call-note is a sharp, often repeated 'creek-creek', starting slowly and becoming rapid as the call trails off. Both these calls betray its presence but the bird itself is difficult to find.

FOOD

Small water snails, worms and insects are taken and the seeds and shoots of various aquatic plants.

NEST AND BREEDING

The Spotless Crake builds a saucer-shaped nest of grasses and stems in a clump of grass or aquatic plants, well camouflaged by a canopy of surrounding vegetation. The 4-6 eggs (30 × 23 mm) are glossy pale buff, marked faintly all over with chestnut-brown. The breeding season is apparently from September to January/February.

40. White-browed Crake *Poliolimnas cinereus tannensis* PLATE 6
Other name: White-browed Rail
French name: Râle à sourcils blancs

IDENTIFICATION
Length about 18 cm. A small grey-brown rail, about the size of a thrush with a distinct facial pattern and long legs. *Adult male and female:* generally brown above, rather greyish on the head; mantle, back, wing-coverts and tail have feathers with dark brown centres, giving the impression of stripes. There is a broad, dark grey-brown line through the eye to the crown bordered by a whitish-grey eyebrow stretching from the base of the upper mandible to above the eye and a longer whitish-grey line extending from the chin to the nape. Throat whitish, sides of head, neck and most of the underparts light grey; thighs, lower belly and undertail-coverts pale to deep ochre. Iris: red. Bill: dull red with a lighter red base and yellowish tip. Legs and feet: olive-green with long slender toes, the middle toe being about 35 mm in length. *Immature:* similar to the adult but paler with an indistinct facial pattern. Younger birds are mottled rufous all over and the downy young are all black.

DISTRIBUTION, STATUS AND CONSERVATION
The White-browed Crake ranges from the Malay Peninsula to the Philippines, Sulawesi, New Guinea, Micronesia, Polynesia and islands in the southwest Pacific to Australia. In Vanuatu the race *tannensis* is local and uncommon with records from Gaua, Erromango and Tanna only although it may occur on other islands in suitable habitat. It has mainly been observed on Tanna where it is apparently confined to a belt of floating vegetation on the edge of Lake Siwi and small swampy areas in the vicinity. The same race occurs in New Caledonia, the Loyalty Islands, Fiji and Samoa (Olson, 1973). The White-browed Crake is fully protected by law but the small population in Vanuatu is limited by its restricted habitat preference and therefore prone to extinction if swamps are drained for development or rivers and lakes become polluted. Lake Reserves and protected swamp areas are essential for its long-term survival.

FIELD NOTES
It may be seen singly or in pairs in similar habitats to the Spotless Crake, the edges of lakes, swamps and watercourses. The White-browed Crake seems to prefer to forage in the shallows, its extremely long toes enabling it to walk about on the leaves of plants and floating vegetation. It is shy and secretive staying in thick cover and rarely coming into the open. When disturbed it runs for cover and only flies as a last resort and then in an awkward fashion with long legs dangling and just for a short distance. It is consequently rarely seen and its presence is revealed only by the characteristic calls which can be heard at close range. It seems to be most active in the early morning or evening though it also moves about during the day. On Tanna these rails can best be seen as they feed in the open along the edge of Lake Siwi in the late afternoon.

VOICE
The most common call is a rapid, loud, clattering series of short notes which can be imitated by running a peg down a washboard. Pairs often call in duet and a number of birds may call simultaneously when alarmed. They also have other short, sharp or softer calls.

FOOD
Insects, freshwater molluscs and other aquatic invertebrates are taken and the seeds and shoots of various plants.

NEST AND BREEDING
The nest, a slightly cupped platform of grasses, rushes and other plants is lined with finer grass and is well hidden among swampy vegetation usually surrounded by water. The 3-6 eggs (29 × 22 mm) are pale grey or olive covered with light markings of reddish or yellowish-brown. It may breed from September to March but probably, mostly November to February.

41. Purple Swamphen *Porphyrio porphyrio samoensis* PLATE 6
Other name: Purple Gallinule
French name: Poule sultane
Bislama name: Nambiru

IDENTIFICATION
Length 35 to 37 cm. The large size, bright purple-blue plumage, heavy red bill and frontal shield, long red legs and conspicuous white undertail make this rail unmistakable. *Male and female* are alike but the female is smaller. Head sooty-black; lower back, mantle, wings and tail blackish olive-brown. Cheeks, neck, upper shoulders, breast, belly and flanks glossy purplish-blue; throat and shoulder glossy light blue, abdomen and thighs blackish; undertail-coverts pure white. Iris: red. Bill and frontal shield: bright red. Legs and feet: pale red with brownish patches on the joints of legs and toes. *Immature:* duller than adult, brownish above, paler blue below with feathers edged with buff; abdomen ochre. Bill, frontal shield and feet are pale red and the iris ochre. The downy young are black with a greyish-white bill and pale red feet and are readily distinguished by the bulky bill and small frontal shield.

DISTRIBUTION AND STATUS
In Neotropical regions the Purple Swamphen is highly migratory. In the Old World it is distributed from the Mediterranean region, Africa south of the Sahara to southern Asia, with 16 races from India and Australia east to the Philippines, Pacific islands and New Zealand. The race *samoensis* probably occurs throughout Vanuatu and has been recorded on Santo, Malo, Maewo, Ambae, Pentecost, Malakula, Ambrym, Epi, Tongoa, Tongariki, Emae, Makura, Efate, Nguna, Emau, Erromango, Tanna, Futuna and Aneityum. It is common on most islands from sea-level to about, 1,000 m. The same race is also found in New Guinea, the Solomons, the Loyalty Islands, New Caledonia, Fiji (on islands without the mongoose), Tonga and Samoa (Olson, 1973).

FIELD NOTES
The Purple Swamphen is not restricted to swamps being found in or on the edge of the true forest, even more often in secondary growth and overgrown village gardens. It is more numerous, however, in or near stretches of permanent water, lakes, swamps and rivers, which are fringed with reed beds or other vegetation in which it can nest and hide. These swamphens appear to be sedentary in more protected areas and live in permanent territories in pairs or small family groups. They usually remain hidden

during the brighter parts of the day coming out on to the adjoining open areas at dusk. Where they are not molested, small loose parties accompanied by their young may be seen searching for food on pasture land or in shallow marshy areas. When walking, and especially when alarmed, the short tail is usually cocked and flicked up and down in a jerky manner displaying the white undertail. When disturbed they almost always run fast into the undergrowth and only fly if really frightened. Then they rise from the ground rather clumsily, neck outstretched, long legs raised level with the body and protruding behind the tail. Generally they fly just a short distance dropping into the nearest shelter but they are capable of sustained flight and when necessary swim well. They also climb trees readily and may roost in them.

Curious bathing behaviour has been observed among Purple Swamphens held in captivity in Port Vila. Frequently, as light rain was falling, the two birds pranced about in their large aviary, walking round with quick steps and with wings half open, alternately leaping high in the air. These fairly spectacular antics, which were continued until the plumage was sufficiently dampened by the raindrops, were reminiscent of the dancing display of cranes.

VOICE

The usual call is a series of typical, harsh screeching notes 'kee-owww' with a resounding and sometimes explosive quality. As the species is semi-nocturnal this call may be heard during the day and at intervals all through the night and is often taken up by other swamphens in the vicinity. Cacklings, grunts and squawks may also be heard.

FOOD

The Purple Swamphen is largely vegetarian, eating the roots, soft shoots and fruit of various plants but insects, molluscs, fish, frogs, lizards and the eggs of other birds are also taken. These rails may cause some damage to crops as they visit gardens to feed on banana fruits and to dig out and eat batatas or kumalas (sweet potatoes) and taro. They have an interesting feeding technique, holding large pieces of food firmly between the toes, like some of the parrot species.

NEST AND BREEDING

The nest, a large, untidy platform of reeds or leaves and stalks of various plants is usually in thick reed beds, grass or bushes but may be on the ground. The nest materials vary according to location but are always long and coarse and the nest is generally in marshy surroundings. The 3-7 eggs (50 × 35 mm) are pale creamy-brown, speckled and blotched with brown and purple. The adults remain together but apparently the male does most of the incubation. After hatching the black downy chicks remain in the nest for just a few hours before running to follow the adults. The usual breeding season is from August to January but eggs may be laid as late as March or as early as July, when conditions are favourable. There may be more than one brood in a season.

Order CHARADRIIFORMES

This diverse order, found practically everywhere in the world including the polar regions, comprises 18 families roughly divided into three suborders: Charadrii, the plovers, curlews and sandpipers and allies commonly known as waders or shorebirds; Lari, the skuas, gulls, terns and skimmers; and Alcae which contains the auks, guillemots and puffins. There are about 300 species in this order and although they look physically different they share a number of structural peculiarities and behaviour patterns.

The *Charadrii* are small to medium-sized birds, mostly inhabiting coastal waters, beaches, marshes and meadows. Most species are gregarious and all feed and nest on the ground. A few are pelagic, some stay well inland and never come near the sea but most spend their time along the seashore, river estuaries or salt marshes. In open situations they rely for safety on cryptically coloured plumage, mottled patterns of dull browns, buffs, greys and white. They can run quickly for short distances and fly strongly and many species undertake long migrations. The bill is extremely variable and in some species diagnostic. It may be moderately to extremely long and mainly straight for picking up small invertebrates along the tideline or in some species curved down or up in adaptation for probing in soft mud. The legs may be short or long and though some species have webs the toes are generally free and the hind toe is usually small or absent. The plumage of the sexes is generally alike. At the beginning of the breeding season the plumage of some species becomes quite spectacular with black, white and russet contrasting strongly. Several colourful species never acquire a drab winter or eclipse plumage. Two peculiar examples of behaviour have been observed in many species: the birds raise their wings aloft momentarily on alighting and there is a seemingly nervous jerking of the head and tail at intervals when the bird is resting.

Most waders nest once a year, some in colonies. The nest is usually a depression in the ground, lined with soft plants, twigs or shells but some species build floating nests of vegetation or nest on cliffs. The eggs are strongly pigmented, varying from fine spotting to heavy blotches. Incubation lasts from 18 to 28 days or longer. The chicks on hatching are covered with barred and patterned grey or brown down which provides excellent camouflage. Observers are usually right upon the chicks before becoming aware of their presence. The young of most species leave the nest almost immediately after hatching but some remain in or near it until nearly fledged. In most species both adults share the nesting duties but in some, like the snipes (Scolopacidae), the female does most of the work. In the phalaropes (Phalaropodidae) the female is larger and more colourful in breeding plumage than the male and courtship and nesting roles are reversed. In the painted snipes (Rostratulidae) the females, similarly larger and more colourful are polyandrous, regularly mating with 2 or more males in a season, leaving the males to incubate and rear the young.

The *Lari* include the terns, gulls and skuas. They may be fairly small to relatively large in size and most species have predominantly white plumage. They have webbed feet. They are birds of the sea coasts, inland lakes and marshes and are highly gregarious, breeding colonially. Some species are trans-equatorial migrants.

The *Alcae* are highly specialised birds, adapted to swimming underwater. They are restricted to the northern hemisphere and are predominantly pelagic coming ashore only to breed on their nesting cliffs.

Twenty-five species in 5 families are represented in Vanuatu. Many species of waders and terns undertake long migrations and regularly visit Vanuatu on their annual migration from their breeding grounds in the northern hemisphere to their wintering grounds in the southern hemisphere. They begin to arrive about September and depart again in March to April/May. However, a few individuals of all species may stay on throughout the year. Other species which breed in Australia and New Zealand may occur in Vanuatu as vagrants or non-breeding regular visitors. Although they have been studied on many occasions, actual counts of the numbers of different species have rarely been made. As occasional papers in *Naika* show, any observer can make a valuable contribution by keeping exact records of all relevant data on the number, the seasonal movements and behaviour of these birds and intensive field work will undoubtedly add further species to the Vanuatu list.

Thick-knees *Burhinidae*
There are 9 species of thick-knees in 2 genera: Burhinus, *with 7 species and* Esacus *with 2 species. Relationships within this family are not yet clearly understood. Common names used variously include 'plovers' and 'curlews'. The Beach (Reef) Thick-knee* Esacus magnirostris, *the only representative occurring in Vanuatu, is the* same *species that is given the name Beach Stone-curlew* Burhinus neglectus *in Pizzey (1980). This confusion in the scientific name is also noted in Beehler et al (1986). Birds in the genus* Esacus *tend to be larger and have a much heavier, longer bill. The legs are long and the name 'thick-knee' comes from the obvious thickness of the upper joint on the leg; the feet are partly webbed at the base and the hind toe is absent. Plumage blends well with their background and they are very difficult to detect as they spend most of the day hidden in the undergrowth. They have relatively large, yellow eyes as an adaptation to their mainly crepuscular or nocturnal existence and they feed on a variety of prey including insects, small reptiles, rodents and small amphibians.*

42. Beach Thick-knee *Esacus magnirostris* PLATE 7
Other names: Reef Thick-knee, Large-billed Shore Plover, Beach Stone-curlew
French name: Oedicnème des récifs

IDENTIFICATION
Length 53 to 57 cm. A large plump, long-legged, shorebird that looks more like a small heron than a wader. The heavy bill, large head and conspicuously black and white patterned face are diagnostic. *Adult male and female* are alike: all greyish-brown above; wings pale grey with one broad blackish-grey band and two narrower white stripes. A broad black band through the eye is bordered with white bands above and below and there is a black patch at the base of the lower mandible, either side of the white chin and upper throat. The lower throat and breast are pale grey becoming white on the belly and undertail. Iris: yellow. Bill: black with a yellowish base, long and heavy. Legs and feet: olive-yellow with a swollen 'knee' joint. *Immature:* like adult but paler with buff fringes to feathers. Iris and base of the bill are duller yellow.

DISTRIBUTION AND STATUS
This species is widely distributed in coastal habitats from the Andaman Islands through the Malay Peninsula, Indonesia, the Philippines, New Guinea, the Solomon Islands and New Caledonia. It is found in coastal northern and eastern Australia where it is uncommon. It is very rare and unevenly distributed in Vanuatu.

FIELD NOTES

The Beach Thick-knee frequents reefs, beaches, estuaries and open ground with low vegetation or grassland near the coast and is usually seen in pairs. Little is known about the species in Vanuatu though two birds have been observed along Santo's west coast in pebbly areas between the village of Kerepua and Vusi. These silent birds seem to be shy and wary and they are hard to see as they are so well camouflaged. They have a peculiar upright stance with the head and neck pulled down into the shoulders. They may also stand very erect with the long neck stretched, when the characteristic head and bill shape, large eye and patterns on the face and wing are prominent features. When they remain still in the shelter of vegetation or squat on the ground they can easily be overlooked. If approached the birds will move away slowly or run in a crouched position like the Little (Mangrove) Heron. If disturbed they will fly away, usually low over the ground, with deliberate wing-beats and legs trailing. The prominent white patches on the wing are distinctive in flight. During the day the birds seem to do very little and at high tide roost in the shade of trees along the foreshore or occasionally forage for small animals stabbing them with the stout bill.

VOICE

The main call is a loud, harsh, mournful 'wee-loo' usually repeated and uttered often at night, particularly just before the breeding season. It also has a soft 'peet-peet' call when alarmed.

FOOD

The feeding habits have not been recorded in Vanuatu. Elsewhere *E. magnirostris* is known to eat crabs, crustaceans and other marine invertebrates. It probably also takes insects and lizards.

NEST AND BREEDING

In Australia this species breeds from October to February. The nest is a hollow scraped in the ground on or near to the shore, often among the flotsam washed up on the beach. There is usually one egg (64 × 46 mm), infrequently 2, creamy-coloured and irregularly streaked, spotted and blotched with brown, black and underlying grey.

Oystercatchers *Haematopodidae*

Oystercatchers are a distinctive group of large, black and white or black waders with long red bills specially adapted for opening shellfish and probing sand. They fly rapidly and their piercing calls are used frequently in flight and are often heard at night. There is a single genus and, complicated by the existence of some melanistic populations, the number of species and races has yet to be determined. Possibly 11 species inhabit the shores of most continents except tropical Africa, southern Asia and the polar regions. They are occasional visitors to the tropical Pacific.

The South Island Pied Oystercatcher Haematopus longirostris finschi *has been recorded once in Vanuatu. The species is restricted to Australasia (Marchant et al, 1986) though it is treated as a local race of the Eurasian Oystercatcher* H. ostralegus *by Simpson and Day (1989).*

43. South Island Pied Oystercatcher *Haematopus longirostris finschi*
French name: Huîtrier de Finsch

IDENTIFICATION AND FIELD NOTES

Length 46cm. A large, conspicuous, black and white wader with bright red eye and eye-ring and long, orange-red bill paler at the tip. The *male and female* are indistinguishable by colour but the female is slightly larger and has a longer bill. Head, upper breast and back are shiny black sharply divided from the white lower back, rump and belly; wings are black with a prominent white wingbar and the tail is black. Legs and feet are medium pink to orange. *Immature:* bill is dull yellowish-pink at the base with a brown tip; legs are greyish becoming brighter with age. Attention may be drawn to this bird by the plaintive, musical, piping call 'keeeeep' used in flight or on the ground.

It breeds inland in South Island, New Zealand, even as high as 1,800m (Falla *et al*, 1981). It feeds in pasture or arable land near the breeding grounds and after breeding quickly migrates northwards to winter in coastal regions where it forages mainly in the intertidal zone.

DISTRIBUTION AND STATUS

The larger, nominate Australian race *H. longirostris* is mainly sedentary. It prefers coastal habitats for breeding and in winter gathers in large flocks in estuaries. The South Island Pied Oystercatcher *H. l. finschi*, described above, appears to be highly successful and the numbers in wintering flocks in the North Island have increased remarkably over the last fifty years. Juveniles may move further north than adults and flocks of non-breeding birds remain in the north for the summer. Marchant *et al* (1986) note a breeding record for North Island and record its occurrence northwards to Lord Howe Island and Vanuatu. They also note a record from Norfolk Island of an oystercatcher that was probably of this race. A South Island Pied Oystercatcher *H. l. finschi* was seen by J R Hay on 29 September 1983 at Vila on Efate. It first landed on the grassed area by the sea wall then later 'circled several times and settled very briefly on the flat roof of one of the waterfront buildings before flying across the harbour towards Iririki Island' (Naika 13:12).

Plovers, Lapwings and Dotterels   *Charadriidae*

Plovers are small to medium-sized birds with a round head, large eyes and rather short bill. They run quickly and flight is swift and graceful. There are about 65 species in this cosmopolitan family. The 37 small plovers (and 2 dotterels), genus Charadrius *include birds that occupy a great variety of habitats from the Arctic to tropical deserts. Lapwings, 24 species in the genus* Vanellus, *are mainly found in the tropics and most are sedentary. The genus* Pluvialis *contains 4 species of the rather large, grey and golden plovers which are all highly migratory. The remaining species differ in several ways and most are classed as single species genera.*

Of the 16 species occurring in the Australasian region 8 are resident and 8 are migrants. Three species have so far been recorded in Vanuatu and additional species may probably be encountered, like the Grey Plover Pluvialis squatarola *which has been recorded in New Caledonia though it is rare in the southwest Pacific. There are also undated records of vagrant Double-banded Plover* Charadrius bicinctus *on New Caledonia, Vanuatu and Fiji (Marchant* et al, *1986).*

44. Pacific Golden Plover *Pluvialis fulva*

PLATE 7

Other names: Lesser Golden Plover, Eastern Golden Plover
French name: Pluvier doré

IDENTIFICATION AND FIELD NOTES

Length 23 to 25 cm. A medium-sized plover with a rounded head, short and straight bill, short neck and long legs. *Adult male and female* are alike in *non-breeding plumage* as usually seen in Vanuatu: upperparts all strongly mottled brown and golden-buff; eyestripe, face and sides of neck pale buff; breast lightly mottled grey-brown and suffused golden-buff; belly pale buff to cream; underwings and axillaries grey. *Breeding plumage* is quite spectacular; darker above and more conspicuously spangled golden; all black below from face and chin with white splashes on the undertail-coverts separated from the upperparts by a broad white stripe from the forehead over the eyes and along the neck and flanks. The male is slightly blacker on average than the female and has less white flecking. Iris: dark brown. Bill: blackish-brown. Legs and feet: slate-grey. *Immature:* similar to non-breeding adult but the breast is more buff-brown and the flanks and belly are finely barred dark brown.

The Pacific Golden Plover is seen in Vanuatu in non-breeding or intermediate plumage. On arrival during the southern spring, mostly in September though occasionally at the end of August, the birds are moulting and some have traces of breeding plumage with black feathers below. Most birds are in winter plumage from November to February but before they leave in April or May for their breeding grounds in the northern hemisphere, some birds are variably marked with black and a few may be in complete breeding plumage.

The Grey Plover *Pluvialis squatarola* with which it may be confused has conspicuous and unique black axillaries that contrast with the white underwing-coverts, a heavier bill, a white rump, a broad white wingbar and is spangled grey-brown on white, lacking the golden-buff. Only the immature has any yellowish tinge in the plumage. The Grey Plover has not yet been recorded in Vanuatu but it is a regular migrant to coastal New Guinea and Australia and reaches New Zealand in small numbers.

The Pacific Golden Plover is fairly common around the coasts of Vanuatu; reefs, debris-strewn beaches and estuaries are the preferred feeding grounds and rocky areas and partly exposed reefs the favourite roosts. It also frequents areas of short grass, pastures, sports grounds or airfields near the coast. Sometimes just a few, or flocks of up to 30 birds, may leave the reefs and tidal flats between low tides to rest in short-cropped pastures several kilometres inland. They mainly feed on small invertebrates: crabs, shrimps, worms, snails and insects and a small amount of vegetable matter. The birds move about quickly while feeding, running a few paces then stopping abruptly to pick up some item of food before moving on again. Standing birds have a typical alert upright posture and bob the head frequently. Flight is fast and straight with strong, regular wingbeats and the feet project beyond the tail. When disturbed, flocks gather in close formation in the air, gain height quickly and fly to another feeding locality. The usual call-note is a two or three syllable whistle, a mournful 'too-wheet' given once or twice at rest or in flight.

DISTRIBUTION AND STATUS

A migrant from northeastern Siberia and western Alaska it disperses widely during the northern winter to southeast Asia, the western and central Pacific islands, Australia and New Zealand. It was earlier thought to be conspecific with the American Golden Plover *Pluvialis dominica* but recent studies in Alaska have found no evidence of interbreeding where both occur together (Marchant *et al*, 1986). Fairly large numbers may be seen throughout Vanuatu, often with other species of waders. Flocks may be seen regularly between October and April feeding on the short grass at Bauerfield Airport (Naika 19:5) and Euan Macdonald notes that it is among the more common waders, with Bar-tailed Godwit *Limosa lapponica*, Whimbrel *Numenius phaeopus* and Common Sandpiper *Actitis hypoleucos*, wintering in Efate; 'all of which can be seen within a mile or two of Port Vila' (Naika 32:30).

45 Mongolian Plover   *Charadrius mongolus*
Other name: Lesser Sand Plover
French names: Gravelot de Mongolie, Pluvier mongol

IDENTIFICATION AND FIELD NOTES

Length 19 to 21 cm. A small, round-headed, plain brown and white plover with noticeable brown patches either side of the breast in non-breeding plumage and dark grey legs. *Adult male breeding:* forehead white with thin vertical black line and narrow black border behind; crown light brown; lores, around eye and ear-coverts black, forming a prominent dark face patch; sides of nape and neck chestnut, extending as a broad chestnut band across the breast and fading onto the flanks; back and wings grey-brown with darker flight feathers showing a narrow white wingbar in flight; rump grey-brown edged white; tail brown with narrow white edge. Chin and throat white; lower breast and belly white. *Adult female breeding:* similar to male but head pattern less marked, with little black; chestnut on breast less extensive. *Adult non-breeding:* has no black or chestnut colour; forehead white, extending over the eye as a narrow streak; crown and upperparts grey-brown, thinly fringed with white; underparts white with large grey-brown patches at side of breast. Iris: dark brown. Bill: black and fairly thick. Legs and feet: dark grey, appearing black at a distance. *Immature:* similar to non-breeding adult but breast patches are more buff and the upperparts fringed buff.

It occurs regularly on mudflats, sandbeaches and marshes, less often on rocky shores and reefs and rarely inland. The usual call-notes, often used when taking flight, are a short, clear 'trik' or 'chitik'.

This species is easily confused with the Greater Sand Plover *C. leschenaultii*, which has not yet been recorded in Vanuatu. The Greater Sand Plover has a more angular head, heavier and longer bill and longer, paler legs with toes projecting beyond the tail in flight. Call-notes are similar but usually a longer, trilling 'treep-treep-treep'. Identification is difficult in non-breeding plumage, but note that adult Mongolian Plover reach wintering areas in August before starting to moult into non-breeding plumage while the Greater Sand Plover moults before flying south.

The Double-banded Plover *Charadrius bicinctus*, which breeds in New Zealand and migrates to Australia, Lord Howe Island, Norfolk Island and Fiji, also shows a close resemblance to both species in non-breeding plumage; the bill is smaller, legs paler greenish and the plumage above more buff than the Mongolian Plover. Pratt *et al* (1987) suggest that it may be present in Fiji between January and July.

DISTRIBUTION AND STATUS

The Mongolian Plover breeds in eastern Siberia, mainly in mountainous areas, and winters (August to April) from the Philippines through Melanesia to all coasts of Australia, rarely in New Zealand. It is a common non-breeding visitor to New Guinea. It has occurred as 'a straggler to Vanuatu' (Robertson pers. comm. 1989).

46. Oriental Plover *Charadrius veredus*
Other names: Eastern or Oriental Dotterel, Eastern Sand Plover
French names: Pluvier oriental, Gravelot oriental

IDENTIFICATION AND FIELD NOTES

Length 22 to 25 cm. Slightly smaller than the Pacific Golden Plover it has a similar upright stance and bobbing head action but has longer wings and legs. *Adult non-breeding:* appears uniform grey-brown above with a darker grey-brown cap, a creamy forehead and eyestripe and a dark line through the eye curving on to the cheek; the tail is broad and rounded with a dark brown sub-terminal band and is narrowly fringed at the sides and tip with white. The throat is buffish-white and it has a brownish-grey breast band and white underparts. The axillaries are brown and the underwing mainly brown. Iris: brown. Bill: black. Legs and feet: yellowish-olive or sometimes with a fleshy tinge. It is unlikely to be seen in Vanuatu in breeding plumage when it has a white head with a grey-brown cap and stripe through the eye and a brilliant chestnut breast band separated by a black line from the white belly. Flight is strong and powerful with erratic turns.

It prefers areas of dry grassland but single birds or migrating flocks may be found on coastal mudflats and beaches, often with Pacific Golden Plover.

DISTRIBUTION AND STATUS

The Oriental Plover breeds in northern China and winters in Indonesia, New Guinea, Australia and very rarely in New Zealand. There is a single record of this species in Vanuatu, a bird seen in October on Efate by John Edge: 'On two mornings there was a very tame medium-sized wader with diffuse soft brown colouring across the breast and striking head markings' which he was satisfied was an Oriental Plover (Naika 29:27).

Curlews, Godwits, Sandpipers and allies *Scolopacidae*
A large family of about 88 species in 27 genera, the Scolopacidae vary from very tiny (12 cm) to medium large (60 cm) in body-length. Most species breed in moorland or tundra habitats in the northern hemisphere and many are highly migratory, wintering far into the southern hemisphere. Generally they have long slender bills with flexible tips for probing in soft mud or shallow water and for picking insects from low vegetation. Most species have long legs, long and pointed wings, long necks and short tails. Their plumage is usually patterned grey, brown or reddish above and streaked on white below when breeding; winter plumage is more uniform.

Flight is rapid and flocks perform aerial evolutions, particularly over their feeding grounds.

Over 40 species have occurred in the Australasian region and almost any of these could occur in Vanuatu as regular visitors or as vagrants wandering from their traditional routes or being blown off course by cyclones. Some species are rather difficult to identify without careful observation. Ten species are known to have occurred in Vanuatu.

47. Ruddy Turnstone   *Arenaria interpres*   PLATE 7
French name: Tourne-pierre

IDENTIFICATION AND FIELD NOTES

Length 23 to 25 cm. A distinctively marked, robust shorebird with a short neck, short pointed bill and short, orange legs. *Adult male and female* in *non-breeding plumage:* upperparts dark brown with paler fringes to the feathers except for white wingbars and a white strip along the centre of the back separated from the white rump by a V-shaped black bar; tail is white with a broad, dark subterminal bar; face is grey-white with a dark grey-brown line across the forehead through the eye and down the side of the neck; underparts including the axillaries and underwing-coverts pure white contrasting with the well-defined, blackish-brown breast band. *Breeding plumage* is very attractive: upperparts are variegated with patches of black and rust-brown giving a tortoiseshell effect, lower back and tail identical to winter plumage; crown and nape white; facial patterns and breast band similar to winter plumage but glossy black on white. Iris: dark brown. Bill is black, wide at the base, short and sharply pointed. Legs and feet: orange, brighter in the breeding season. *Immature:* similar to adult in winter plumage but browner above with buffish-white fringes to the feathers and yellow-brown legs. Most turnstones arriving in Vanuatu or leaving at the end of the season are in intermediate plumage stages and some may be in complete breeding plumage.

Turnstones apparently prefer pebbly or rocky beaches and fringing reefs but they also frequent mudflats and sandy beaches. There are a few inland records for Efate, on open ground with sparse low vegetation and in short-grassed paddocks. Turnstones are among the most restless waders when feeding: walking or dashing about from one feeding spot to another; flipping over the stones, seashells, pieces of wood, seaweed, and other beach debris in search of the small animals concealed beneath, then snatching at them as they become exposed. This species is not particularly shy and will often allow a close approach before flying off, alighting further along the beach and starting to feed again. Though groups of turnstones may be overlooked when they are resting among the seashore litter they become conspicuous in flight, forming a flock which flies swiftly in unison, showing their distinctive dark and white pattern on wings, back and tail.

DISTRIBUTION AND STATUS

A circumpolar breeder in arctic and subarctic areas during the northern summer, the Ruddy Turnstone may be found wintering on coasts almost worldwide and reaching southern South America, southern Africa, the Pacific islands, Australia and New Zealand. Turnstones are found along the coasts of Vanuatu, often with other small waders, but not in large numbers. They begin to arrive in September and start to leave for their breeding grounds in March; most have left by May though some individuals may remain throughout the year.

48. Far Eastern Curlew *Numenius madagascariensis*
Other names: Australian Curlew, Eastern Curlew
French name: Courlis de Sibérie

IDENTIFICATION AND FIELD NOTES

Length 53 to 66 cm, the female is slightly larger. This is the largest curlew likely to be seen in Australasia with a very long downcurved bill nearly half the length of the body and a distinctive call. *Adult male and female:* pale greyish-buff heavily streaked and barred dark brown above including the rump; slightly paler below and lighter on the lower belly and undertail contrasting with the underwing which is heavily barred brown. Breeding plumage is similar but tinged rufous above and on the tail. Iris: dark brown. Bill: black, pink at the base; the female has a longer bill (average 184 mm) than the male (155 mm). Legs and feet: blue-grey. *Immature* is similar to adult. Flight is strong, the wings slightly swept back and tapering, the bill is prominent and the toes protrude beyond the tip of the tail.

The Far Eastern Curlew is found in coastal habitats, mangroves, estuaries, mudflats, and occasionally grassland close to the coast. It usually feeds singly, picking from the surface or probing in mud for small invertebrates but gathers to roost in mangroves or in trees on offshore islands. Its distinctive melancholy call-notes are a high-pitched, ringing 'cour-lee cour-lee' often heard in flight and a strident 'ker ker-ee ker-ee' when disturbed. It also has a bubbling trill. It occasionally associates with other shorebirds and can be distinguished from the Whimbrel which has a similar shape and plumage by its much greater size, darker rump and different head markings; plain brown crown lacking the light head-stripe of the former.

DISTRIBUTION AND STATUS

The Far Eastern Curlew breeds in Siberia and is a migrant in southeast Asia, the Philippines, New Guinea, the Solomons, Australia and New Zealand. It has been recorded occasionally in Vanuatu and may be a regular visitor in small numbers. A record of 'a party of a dozen large waders' thought to be of this species appears in *Naika* (29:26). Marchant *et al* (1986) note recent evidence of a decline in the numbers of this species reaching Australia and they give an estimated world population of 10,000 to 15,000 individuals.

49. Whimbrel *Numenius phaeopus variegatus* PLATE 7
Other name: Asiatic Whimbrel
French name: Courlis courlieu

IDENTIFICATION AND FIELD NOTES

Length 40 to 45 cm. A medium-sized curlew with long legs and neck and a distinctly downcurved bill. *Adult male, female and immature:* crown dark brown with a light grey central stripe and light grey eyebrow; back and wings mottled buff and dark brown; rump whitish with brown bars; tail buff, barred with dark brown; underparts pale grey, throat and neck finely streaked with brown, breast heavily streaked with brown, flanks and undertail-coverts with narrow light brown bars; thighs and belly are nearly white. Axillaries white with brown bars. Iris: dark brown. Bill: brown with a reddish base to the lower mandible, long and downcurved. Legs and feet: olive-grey. The race *N. p. hudsonicus* differs in having an all dark rump.

It apparently prefers coastal habitats: sandy shores, mangroves, tidal mudflats, reefs and pebbly beaches but also visits grassland near the coast and there are a few inland-lake records. At low tide whimbrels can be seen foraging far out on the mudflats, singly or in scattered flocks, and heard calling to each other. They use their long bills to probe in mud or soft sand for worms and molluscs or to pick up small invertebrates among stones, coral, seaweed and beach litter. The call-note is a distinctive shrill rippling 'tee-tee-tee-tee-tee' or 'tetty-tetty-tetty-tet', the same note repeated about 7 times. They may often be seen in association with other shorebirds.

The Whimbrel flies quickly with faster wingbeats than the larger curlews and can also be distinguished by the light stripe down the centre of the crown.

DISTRIBUTION AND STATUS

The four races of whimbrels breed in the far north of Europe, Asia and North America and winter almost worldwide. The race *N.p.variegatus* breeds in northern USSR and migrates to southeast Asia, Indonesia, New Guinea, Micronesia, the Solomon Islands, New Caledonia and Fiji to Australia and New Zealand. Whimbrels begin to arrive in Vanuatu in September and leave again in March/April though some, probably immatures, may be present throughout the year. Most whimbrels in the tropical Pacific are likely to be of this race although *N.p.hudsonicus* which breeds in northern Canada and Alaska also occurs (Pratt *et al*, 1987) and regularly reaches New Zealand in small numbers and rarely, Australia.

50. Siberian Tattler   *Heteroscelus brevipes*
Other names: Grey-tailed or Polynesian Tattler, Grey-rumped Sandpiper
French names: Chevalier cendré, Chevalier à pieds courts

IDENTIFICATION AND FIELD NOTES

Length 25 to 26cm. Only slightly smaller, with similar but lighter plumage than the Wandering Tattler and with the same behaviour, they are extremely difficult to separate though their call-notes are distinctive. *Adult male and female* in *non-breeding plumage:* light grey above, including the wings and tail, with a distinct white eyebrow, extending almost the full length of the head and meeting across the forehead at the base of the bill; mainly white below suffused pale grey on the sides of the neck and breast forming a wide breast band. In Vanuatu birds may be seen in intermediate plumage stages. In *breeding plumage*, throat, breast and flanks are finely barred dark grey, belly and undertail-coverts are white (Wandering Tattler is all barred below); axillaries and underwing-coverts dark grey with whitish tips. Iris: dark brown. Bill: straight and slaty-grey with a yellowish base to the lower mandible and at close range, or when the bird is in the hand, it can be seen that the nasal groove extends only half the length of the bill (two-thirds in the Wandering Tattler). Legs and feet; dull greenish-yellow. *Immature* is like the non-breeding adult but may show fine grey bars on the breast.

It may be seen singly or in small flocks with other shorebirds in coastal areas, beaches, mangroves and mudflats and sometimes inland (the Wandering Tattler prefers rocky coastal habitats). The Siberian Tattler has a distinct high-pitched fluty double whistle 'troo-eet' or 'ter-whee' but occasionally a soft trill. Flight is fast, direct and low over the water with rapid wingbeats.

DISTRIBUTION AND STATUS

The tattlers were previously placed in the genus *Tringa*. The Siberian Tattler breeds in northeastern Siberia and moves south in August to winter on continental coasts, Indonesia, the Philippines, New Guinea, Micronesia, the Solomons and western Pacific islands, reaching Australia, where it is a fairly common regular migrant on all coasts and islands, and New Zealand. It has been recorded on the coast of Efate on occasions. It is likely to be seen in Vanuatu between September and March though some individuals may overwinter.

51. Wandering Tattler *Heteroscelus incanus*   PLATE 7
French names: Chevalier voyageur, Chevalier à croupion gris

IDENTIFICATION AND FIELD NOTES

Length 27 to 29 cm. A medium-sized, slender, rather plain coloured shorebird. *Adult male and female* in *non-breeding plumage:* uniform dark slaty-grey above (darker than the Siberian) and pale grey, almost white below, often with some fine dark grey barring; has an indistinct, short white eyebrow with dark eyestripe below. In *breeding plumage* the entire underparts are conspicuously barred dark brown and the superciliary stripe, which does not meet across the forehead, is distinct. Iris: brown. Bill: blackish-brown; at close range it can be seen that the nasal groove extends to about two-thirds of the length of the bill (only half-way in the Siberian). Legs and feet: olive-yellow. *Immature* is similar to adult in non-breeding plumage.

Solitary birds or pairs may be seen along the coast wherever there are rocky shores and coral reefs, or mudflats and sandbanks exposed at low tide. At high tide they rest on beaches or in mangroves and tattlers are occasionally also found up the larger rivers, on lake edges or short coastal grassland. They are active feeders running with bobbing action and digging under pebbles or among seaweed for small crustaceans, molluscs, worms and other aquatic invertebrates. They may also catch flying or resting insects with a rapid thrust of the bill. Tattlers can be difficult to see at a distance when resting among the stones as their plumage blends almost perfectly with their surroundings. In the field they are distinguished from most other shorebirds by their peculiar, fast and direct flight, low over the water, holding the wings bowed downwards, giving a few rapid beats as they fly between perches. On landing the tail is usually, gently bobbed up and down as is the head when the bird is alarmed. They are said to swim well. The call which is diagnostic is a series of up to 10 short notes uttered in rapid succession 'whee-wee-wee ...', each note shorter than the last but at the same pitch and decreasing in volume. It also has shorter calls.

DISTRIBUTION AND STATUS

The Wandering Tattler breeds in Alaska, northern Canada and at Anadyrland in northeastern Siberia (Campbell and Lack, 1985) and migrates to Central and South America and throughout the tropical Pacific, though it is less common in the west (Pratt *et al*, 1987). It is scarce in New Guinea occurring mainly on rocky reefs along the coast and on offshore islands (Beehler *et al*, 1986). It is a rare but probably regular migrant to New Zealand and eastern Australia. Most birds apparently arrive in Vanuatu during September and leave again in February/March but some individuals stay in the group throughout the year.

52. Common Sandpiper   *Actitis hypoleucos*
French name: Chevalier guignette

IDENTIFICATION AND FIELD NOTES

Length 20 cm. A small, slender sandpiper with short legs, and characteristic 'teetering', nervous bobbing of the head and body and tail wagging. The tail extends well beyond the tip of the folded wing. *Adult male and female* in *non-breeding plumage:* olive-brown above with a shadow of barring apparent at close range and on the tail which has white margins; wings darker brown with a prominent white wingbar; head grey-brown with a white eyestripe and a thin dark brown line from the bill through the eye; sides of the neck and breast suffused pale brown, almost forming a breast band; rest of underparts all white extending to the sides of the rump. In *breeding plumage* upperparts are faintly streaked darker and the sides of the breast are streaked brown. Iris: brown. Bill: short and straight, dark brown with a yellowish base. Legs and feet: pale grey-green sometimes tinged yellow. *Immature* is similar to adult, though dark feathers are edged with buff.

Usually seen singly or in small parties, the Common Sandpiper frequents mangroves, reefs, sandy beaches and estuaries but may also be seen on riverbanks or the edges of inland lakes. It feeds mainly on insects caught when stationary or low-flying, and other small invertebrates, crustaceans, worms, and spiders, picked from crevices in rocks or under stones. The call often heard in flight, is a plaintive whistling 'twee-wee-wee'. Typically flies close to the water, with rapid shallow 'flickering' wingbeats and glides, showing the white wingbar.

DISTRIBUTION AND STATUS

It appears to be highly adaptable breeding throughout a wide range of climatic regions, and from sea level up to 4,000 m, across central and northern Europe and northern Asia to Japan. It winters through temperate and tropical regions to South Africa, India, southeast Asia, Indonesia, New Guinea, Micronesia and southwest Pacific islands to Australia. There are 8 records for New Zealand (Falla *et al*, 1981). It is a regular visitor to Vanuatu where a few are likely to be seen on Efate at Bauerfield with other shorebirds between October and April (Richard Pickering, Naika 19:5) or on Mele Beach, often among Golden Plover (Naika 29:26). Euan Macdonald notes that it is 'among the more common waders wintering in Efate' with Golden Plover, Bar-tailed Godwits and Whimbrel and 'can be seen within a mile or two of Port Vila' (Naika 32:30).

53. Bar-tailed Godwit   *Limosa lapponica baueri*
Other name: Eastern Bar-tailed Godwit
French name: Barge rousse

IDENTIFICATION AND FIELD NOTES

Length 37 to 45 cm, the female is larger with a longer bill. A fairly large, mottled, pale brown wader with a long, pointed, slightly upcurved bill. *Adult non-breeding:* pale brownish-grey above with dark brown centres to the feathers giving a streaked and mottled appearance; rump and tail are barred dark brown and white. Crown is grey-brown; a pale fawn eyebrow contrasts with dark lores and eyestripe; neck and breast are washed grey-brown and finely streaked brown; rest of underparts whitish; underwing white, finely barred brown. In *breeding plumage* the head and underparts of the male are rich, chestnut-red flecked paler on the flanks and the upperparts are patterned with black and buff; female is much paler. Iris: dark brown. Bill: distal half blackish, base yellowish-pink. Legs and feet: dark grey, tinged greenish. *Immature* is more heavily streaked buff and brown and the breast and neck are buffish streaked brown.

The Bar-tailed Godwit is seen in coastal habitats, usually mudflats or estuaries, probing along the tide edge in soft sand or mud for small invertebrates. Food is chiefly insects, molluscs, crustaceans and marine worms. It is also to be seen on grassland near the coast or on airfields, singly or in small parties with other shorebirds or roosting in mangroves. Generally not very vocal except when breeding, the flight note is a harsh 'kirrik'.

DISTRIBUTION AND STATUS

It breeds in Siberia and northwestern Alaska and the eastern race *baueri* winters from southeast Asia to Australasia and western Polynesia. A regular visitor throughout Micronesia and Fiji (Pratt *et al*, 1987) and a common widespread migrant to Australia and Tasmania (Pizzey, 1980), it also reaches New Zealand. It occurs in Vanuatu in small numbers. Most recent records are from Efate and the mudflats at the mouth of the Sarakata river at Luganville, Santo, are also a favoured feeding area (Naika 19:9).

54. Sharp-tailed Sandpiper *Calidris acuminata*
French name: Bécasseau à queue pointue

IDENTIFICATION AND FIELD NOTES

Length 17 to 20cm. Smaller than the similar Pectoral Sandpiper this species has a shorter straight bill, longer legs and does not have a clearly defined pectoral band. *Adult non-breeding* has a chestnut crown with dark streaks, white eyebrow which is broader behind the eye, dark eyestripe and white eye-ring and is streaked buff, brown and white on sides of head and neck; rest of upperparts scaly with dark brown centres to the feathers and buff tips; rump and tail blackish with white sides and dark tip and slightly longer central tail feathers (not a useful field-mark). Throat whitish, breast greyish-buff, finely streaked and spotted dark brown becoming whitish on the belly. *Breeding plumage:* prominent chestnut cap and chestnut tinge to the plumage above; more buff below, heavily spotted with dark brown crescents on the breast and flanks. Iris: dark brown. Bill: pale grey-brown, darker at the tip. Legs and feet: olive-green. *Immature* has rufous cap and golden-buff neck and breast, with fewer dark markings.

It is usually seen feeding with other waders in coastal grassland areas, estuaries, mudflats or mangroves, but may be seen inland in marshes and swamps. Call-note in flight is a typical 'wheep' or 'trit-trit' often in a short sequence. In flight there is no obvious wingbar and the tips of the toes project beyond the tail, otherwise similar pattern to the Pectoral Sandpiper.

DISTRIBUTION AND STATUS

It breeds in arctic Siberia and winters from India through New Guinea, Micronesia and the southwest Pacific islands to Australia, New Zealand and subantarctic islands.

Pizzey (1980) rates this species as one of the commonest, most widespread wader migrants to coastal and inland Australia and Tasmania from August to April. It is a regular passage migrant through Vanuatu and may be encountered in coastal habitats.

55. Pectoral Sandpiper   *Calidris melanotos*
French name: Bécasseau tacheté

IDENTIFICATION AND FIELD NOTES

Length 19 to 23 cm. Larger than the Sharp-tailed Sandpiper, with similar non-breeding plumage, this wader has an erect stance, small head, slightly downcurved bill and clearly marked pectoral band. *Adult non-breeding:* head is buff-brown, streaked dark brown on the crown, with a white eyebrow and eye-ring and a dark line through the eye; back feathers have black centres and buff edges appearing scaly; rump and tail blackish with white sides and dark tip and the central tail feathers are slightly longer; sides of the head, neck and breast are grey-buff streaked dark brown, paler on the throat, forming a wide V-shape on the breast and giving a diagnostic, bibbed effect against the pure white of the lower breast and belly. *Breeding plumage* is much brighter and fringed rust-brown on the head and back. Iris: dark brown. Bill: dark brown with a black tip, yellowish at the base. Legs and feet: yellow-ochre. *Immature* is difficult to separate.

The Pectoral Sandpiper prefers shallow, freshwater habitats, swamps or flooded pastures but also occurs in coastal grasslands, estuaries or saltmarsh. It often feeds among vegetation away from water picking up small invertebrates. In flight the wings look dark with a thin pale wingbar and whitish trailing edge to the inner secondaries.

DISTRIBUTION AND STATUS

It breeds on the arctic coasts of North America and eastern Siberia and both populations apparently migrate mainly to southern South America. It has been recorded in fewer numbers in southeast Asia, Micronesia, New Guinea and Kiribati and is a regular but rare migrant in Australia and New Zealand. There is one record for Vanuatu of a single bird seen among Pacific Golden Plover at the eastern end of Mele Bay on Efate in 1988 (Naika 29:25).

56. Red-necked Stint   *Calidris ruficollis*
Other name: Rufous-necked Stint
French name: Bécasseau à col rouge

IDENTIFICATION AND FIELD NOTES

Length 12 to 15 cm. The smallest of the arctic shorebirds to visit Vanuatu, it is difficult to see when not actively feeding. *Adult non-breeding:* grey-brown above extending to the side of the neck, faintly streaked and mottled darker; the forehead is white, a dark line from the base of the bill through the eye contrasts with the white eyebrow and face; all white below with greyish streaks on the side of the breast. In flight there is a prominent white wingbar; rump and tail are edged white with a dark central stripe, broader on the rump; the tail has a grey tip. In *breeding plumage* the head, neck and breast are rich pinkish-chestnut and the mantle and scapulars are deeper brownish-grey with darker centres and chestnut fringes. Iris: dark brown. Bill: black, stubby and straight. Legs and feet: grey-black. *Immature* is browner above and has fine dark streaks on the side of the breast.

The Red-necked Stint is found in fresh or saltwater habitats, often with other much larger waders. When feeding it is constantly running about, twittering and picking up small invertebrates and has been described as voracious with a sewing machine action (Falla *et al*, 1981). It is highly gregarious and in other areas migrating flocks of several hundreds may be seen on beaches, mudflats, marshes or airfields.

DISTRIBUTION AND STATUS

It breeds in northern Siberia and northern Alaska and both populations apparently winter in southeast Asia from Burma to southern China and through Indonesia, New Guinea, the Philippines, western Micronesia (common), the Marshall Islands and Fiji (less common) to Australia where it is numerous. It regularly reaches New Zealand in small numbers. There is only one definite record 'a minute wader seen resting on one of the floating platforms' in the lagoon at Port Vila on Efate (John Edge, Naika 29:26). It is probably a regular visitor to Vanuatu, a view supported by Euan Macdonald (pers. comm. 1990).

Gulls, Terns and Noddies   *Laridae*
Gulls are coastal birds with pointed wings and slow, flapping flight. They have a fairly stout, slightly hooked bill and are generally white below and darker, grey or black, above: some take several years to achieve full adult plumage. About 45 species occur throughout the world though few are found in the tropics and as gulls are coastal rather than oceanic birds they are unlikely to breed on Pacific islands far from the continental shelves. However, some species have been recorded in the tropical Pacific, usually solitary wanderers that remain on an island for several months. One species has been a regular visitor to Vanuatu for a number of years.

57. Silver Gull   *Larus novaehollandiae*
Other names: Red-billed Gull, Seagull
French name: Mouette australienne

IDENTIFICATION AND FIELD NOTES

Length 38 to 43 cm, the male is larger than the female. *Adult non-breeding:* the mantle, back and wing-coverts are a uniform pale silver-grey; rump and tail white; the primaries are mainly black, tipped white in fresh plumage and the outermost primaries have broad, white subterminal bands ('mirrors'); the outerwing shows a white leading edge; head neck and underparts are white with pale silver-grey underwing-coverts. Iris: white with bright red eye-ring. Bill, legs and feet: bright red. *Juvenile* is mottled grey-brown on mantle and secondaries, feathers have darker tips edged buff and the primaries are mainly black. All white below and on the rump; tail is white with a narrow brown subterminal band. Iris: brown. Bill: dark brownish-black. Legs and feet are black at first, becoming yellow-brown. *Second winter immature* resembles adult but the eye looks dark and the bill, legs and feet are dull reddish-brown.

The Silver Gull is a scavenger usually found in coastal waters, seldom far from land but is sometimes seen inland on rivers or recently ploughed land. It has adapted to urban areas and is commonly found on rubbish tips. It often follows ships to scavenge. Call-notes are a harsh 'kwarr' sometimes repeated or 'kek-kek-kek' and several calling together can be rather noisy.

DISTRIBUTION AND STATUS

According to Harrison (1983) this is a southern hemisphere species with 3 races in Australasia, *L.n.fosteri* breeding in New Caledonia and northern Australia; *L.n. novaehollandiae* in southern Australia and Tasmania and *L.n.scopulinus* in New Zealand. All populations disperse after breeding (egg dates vary – April to December). The first recent record of this species in Vanuatu is a note from Euan Macdonald of 'two gulls, possibly three, believed to be Silver Gulls in the bays around Port Vila' (Naika 28, written on 14 June 1988). Another 'gull' record for Efate was 'a party of nine very pale gulls' off the southern end of Erakor Island which John Edge thought 'could have been Silver Gulls' but 'they were too far off for certain identification' (Naika 29:27). In November 1988 'at least one Silver Gull' often accompanied Crested Terns 'at Mele Bay and Hidaway Island' (Naika 29:25) and a couple were present for several weeks 'in the harbour area of Port Vila in 1989' (Naika 32:30).

Terns and noddies *are the graceful relatives of gulls differing in their more slender build and longer, narrower wings. Most have forked tails and jerky flight. The bill is long and pointed; the horny covering undivided. The short feet are webbed, but may be incised to varying degrees, and have a small hind toe. There are about 42 species, cosmopolitan in distribution, and there is some disagreement about the number of genera. Most terns, about 30 species, are included in the genus* Sterna *with white bodies, grey upperparts and black crown feathers which in some species are extended into a crest. A few terns are almost black and the lovely White Tern, with its own genus* Gygis *has pure white plumage but has some characteristics of the noddies. The plumage of the sexes is alike in all species but in some differs in the breeding and non-breeding seasons and most immature birds are mottled or barred with darker colours. Some species that have been recorded in Vanuatu, the Common, Roseate and Black-naped Terns, are so alike that they are difficult to distinguish at a distance and a combination of features including: size and shape; plumage; length of bill and leg; and the amount of translucency in the underwing has to be taken into account.*

The noddies, almost wholly dark with a grey or white crown, are pelagic terns of tropical and subtropical seas with 2 species in the genus Anous *and one species, the Grey (Ternlet) Noddy* Procelsterna cerulea, *with its own genus. The noddies are regarded, on behavioural grounds as the most primitive of the terns having many gull-like features. They have broader wings and glide like gulls; their legs and feet are stronger than other terns and their tails are broad, rounded and deeply notched. Noddies like gulls regurgitate their food; the only other terns that do this are the Sooty* Sterna fuscata *and the Bridled Tern* Sterna anaethetus.

Terns are typical birds of the seashore and coastal waters though a few species are found far inland wherever there are large rivers, lakes or marshes. They are the most conspicuous seabirds in tropical waters; whenever a shoal of fish agitates the surface a wheeling flock of terns gathers above them diving for small fish or picking up floating titbits. They hover momentarily before plunging, seldom immersing themselves but rather splashing the surface as they grab their prey with the bill. Inland terns also take insects, which they hawk on the wing, or feed on grubs or other small creatures in newly ploughed fields. Even though they are web-footed and float buoyantly most terns, unlike the noddies, rarely swim or rest on the surface but prefer to perch on fixed or floating objects including buoys, pieces of driftwood, coconuts and even turtles. Most species seldom soar but fly gracefully with steady rhythmic wingbeats: the body appears to rise and fall with each beat; head and bill are often pointed downwards rather than forwards. All have similar sharp, rasping calls but there are distinctive differences between species.

They breed colonially on low sandy islets in estuaries and bays, sand spits and island beaches. The nest of most terns is a simple depression on the ground decorated with small pebbles, shells or grass. It may be situated almost anywhere, often just above the high water mark. Only a few species construct real nests; some noddies build a firm platform of sticks and seaweed on bushes or low trees. The most curious nesting habit is that of the smallest of all terns, the dainty White Tern, perching its single egg precariously on a bare branch which often is scarcely larger than the egg. Depending on the species, terns lay 1-3 relatively large eggs which vary considerably in ground colour and markings; some are quite plain while others are spotted or blotched with darker colours. Incubation is shared by both adults alternately and may take from 21 to 35 days. The newly hatched chicks are fluffy balls of dense down and they remain in the nest for a few days at the most and then seek cover in surrounding vegetation or run about the breeding ground. Both adults feed the young, frequently with fish that are longer than the chick itself; the young bird waits with the tail protruding from its bill for the lower half to be digested and to make room for the rest of the fish. The young can fly after 3 to 5 weeks but the adults continue to feed them for several weeks until they develop sufficient skill to catch their own food. Most breed for the first time when they are 3 to 5 years old and they may live for thirty or more years. On the breeding ground various species react differently to the presence of humans; while some may sit tightly and allow themselves to be touched others are shy and desert their eggs or young readily when intruders walk over the site. The mortality rate of terns, especially the young, is so high that some species have difficulty in maintaining their numbers. On the breeding grounds gulls, rails, rats, lizards and crabs all take unattended eggs or chicks. Adults and young are taken by birds of prey, commonly owls and frigatebirds, and great quantities of eggs have been taken by people, destroying some colonies entirely. Some of the famous rookeries in the Abrolhos group of islands off western Australia, which were calculated in 1889 to hold over one million birds including terns and noddies, were destroyed in the past by egg collecting. This group is the present stronghold of the Roseate Tern where colonies with more than 2,500 nests have been recorded (Pizzey, 1980).

Though several species are apparently more sedentary most terns disperse widely, after breeding, across the oceans of the world. A young Arctic tern Sterna paradisaea banded in Murmansk in northwestern USSR was found alive ten months later, overwintering near Fremantle on the western coast of Australia.

Nine species of terns and noddies have been recorded in Vanuatu. Two species breed and several more may breed although actual records are lacking. While terns and noddies are not abundant in Vanuatu, they appear to be more numerous around the Banks Islands in the north, in the waters around the Maskelynes, (a group of small islands with extensive mangroves off the southeastern point of Malakula) and in the far south where Matthew Island appears to be the home of about 10,000 Sooty Terns Sterna fuscata.

58. Common Tern *Sterna hirundo*
Other name: Eastern Common Tern
French name: Sterne pierregarin

IDENTIFICATION AND FIELD NOTES

Length 31 to 37 cm. The Common Tern is difficult to separate at a distance from the other *Sterna* terns. *Adult non-breeding* has a white forehead; black cap from behind the eye to the nape; blackish bill, sometimes with traces of red at the base and all white underparts. Wings pale grey above with a variable dark wedge on the tips of the outer primaries, showing most clearly in poor light; white below with diffuse blackish trailing edge to the primaries and only the inner primaries appear translucent against the light. Tail streamers are shorter. It is unlikely to be seen in Vanuatu in breeding plumage when the adult has a red bill with a black tip and a complete black cap; belly and upperparts are grey and the rest white. Tail streamers are longer but do not protrude beyond the folded wings. Iris: blackish. Legs and feet: scarlet, legs are mid-length. (The race *S. h. longipennis*, common in Australia, has brown legs). *Immature* first year: wings above have a dark carpal bar, blackish primaries and grey secondaries with a noticeable broad pale grey patch on the secondary coverts; tail is greyish and lacks streamers.

The usual habitat is offshore waters, beaches and reefs, tidal mudflats and estuaries and occasionally freshwater or brackish swamps near the coast. Call-notes are a long drawn-out 'kee-aah' and a rapid 'kik-kik-kik'.

DISTRIBUTION AND STATUS

Four races: all breed in the northern hemisphere and migrate southwards. *S. h. longipennis* breeds in northeast Asia and disperses through southeast Asia and the southwest Pacific to Australia. It is abundant seasonally along the coasts of New Guinea between October and April and many non-breeding birds stay throughout the year (Beehler *et al*, 1986). In Australia most records are from the east coast and though generally uncommon, there is a record of about 1,500 at Newcastle Bight in New South Wales in 1972 (Pizzey, 1980). It is uncommon in Micronesia and Fiji (Pratt *et al*, 1987) but has been recorded in Vanuatu.

59. Roseate Tern *Sterna dougallii*
Other name: Graceful Tern
French name: Sterne de Dougall

IDENTIFICATION AND FIELD NOTES

Length 32 to 40 cm. A slender looking tern with a longer bill than the Common Tern and, when breeding, very long tail streamers. *Adult in breeding plumage:* very pale, silver-grey above and white often suffused rose-pink below; the glossy black cap is complete; rump is white and the all-white tail streamers, when developed, are longer than in other 'commic' terns and extend about 100 mm beyond the wingtips when perched. Iris: blackish-brown. Bill: black, dull red at the base. Legs and feet: dark red. *Adult non-breeding* is usually all-white below, possibly with traces of pink on the belly; forehead is white and the crown is blacker on the rear and nape; upperwing has a blackish leading edge and a narrow white trailing edge; bill is black and legs and feet orange-brown. *Immature:* has a black spot before the eye; crown is black, streaked paler, forehead is white freckled brown; upperwing mostly pale grey with noticeable white trailing edge; shoulder and mantle variably mottled dark buff-brown; otherwise as non-breeding adult.

In northern temperate regions the Roseate Tern breeds in the summer but in the tropics eggs have been found in all months of the year and birds may be observed in all stages of plumage. An oceanic species, this tern may be seen in offshore waters or around islands and reefs. Flight is graceful with shallow wingbeats. Call-notes are a soft 'chew-ick', a rasping 'aach' and a noisy 'kekekekek'.

DISTRIBUTION AND STATUS

The Roseate Tern with 5 races breeds in coastal northern temperate and tropical regions and numbers are apparently decreasing. Some populations are migratory while the tropical populations are probably sedentary. Harrison (1983) notes that *S.d.gracilis*, described above, breeds in the Moluccas and northern Australia and *S.d.bangsi* breeds in the Ryukyu Islands, the Philippines and the Solomons. Pizzey (1980) notes isolated colonies from Malaysia to New Guinea, the Solomons and New Caledonia. This species has been recorded in Vanuatu but the race has not been identified.

60. Black-naped Tern *Sterna sumatrana* PLATE 2
French name: Sterne à nuque noire

IDENTIFICATION

Length 30 to 35 cm. A medium-sized tern with a long, deeply forked tail, it appears all white from a distance apart from a distinctive black band across the nape. *Adult male and female:* crown and most of head white; a black crescent starts almost at the base of the bill, continues through the eye and broadens to form the black nape; upperparts mostly pale grey, outermost primaries edged black; tail lighter grey, deeply forked with long streamers; underparts white with a pink hue in some individuals. Iris: brown. Bill: black, sometimes tipped yellowish. Legs and feet: black. *Immature* has a pale and incomplete band on the nape; back and wing feathers are edged buff-brown and the flight feathers are grey; tail lacks long streamers. The downy chicks are pale grey with black flecks; bill is red with a dark tip and the feet are pale red.

DISTRIBUTION AND STATUS

The Black-naped Tern is common around islands in the tropical Indian and western Pacific Ocean. *S.s.mathewsi* breeds on islands in the western Indian Ocean and *S.s.sumatrana*, described above, from Malaysia, the Philippines, Indonesia, New Guinea, and Micronesia to Australia, New Caledonia, Tuvalu, Fiji and Tonga. It is a rare visitor to the central Pacific. It breeds on most islands in the southwestern Pacific but is not common off the coasts of Vanuatu and can only be seen in numbers in the waters around the Maskelyne Islands off Malakula. Breeding has been confirmed on islets off the north coast of Efate.

FIELD NOTES

It is usually seen singly or in small flocks along the coastline and in estuaries but can also be found well out at sea. It flies gracefully with fairly slow, deliberate wingbeats, appearing to be all white in flight. It is easily distinguished from similar terns by its white crown and black nape and from the White Tern (immature often has a dark shoulder mark) also by its larger, more slender shape and different flight pattern. Flocks may be found feeding over a shoal of fish with other seabirds such as noddies, boobies and petrels. Black-naped Terns fish by skimming over the surface of the sea, rather than by diving, often hovering while looking for prey. They often perch on buoys or other floating objects.

VOICE
A noisy bird especially when feeding in flocks. The best known calls are a series of short, sharp high-pitched notes 'tru-chee-chi-chip' persistently repeated and when alarmed 'chit-chit-chit-cher'.

FOOD
The diet consists mainly of small fish, molluscs and other marine animals.

NEST AND BREEDING
The Black-naped Tern generally nests in colonies, mainly on inshore coral islets, but lone nests have also been found. The eggs, usually 2 but sometimes one or 3, are laid almost anywhere the birds can find room: on coral fragments, bare sand or rock just above the high water mark. The eggs (39×29 mm) are oval in shape, pale buffy-grey-white, blotched with reddish-brown and underlying markings of lavender or grey, particularly at the larger end. Off north Efate nests containing eggs have been found in May. In New Caledonia it breeds from October to January and in Australia from September to January.

61. Sooty Tern *Sterna fuscata*
Other name: Wideawake Tern
French name: Sterne fuligineuse

IDENTIFICATION
Length 40 to 46 cm. A tern with strongly contrasting, sooty-black and white plumage and deeply forked tail. *Adult male and female in breeding plumage:* crown, nape and rest of upperparts blackish-brown; tail blackish-brown above with elongated outer tail-feathers edged white; forehead white extending as a band to just above the eye and separated from white chin, ear-coverts and side of the neck by a blackish-brown stripe from the base of the upper mandible through the eye; underparts mostly white, pale grey on the belly when breeding; undertail white; underwing white with dark grey on the quills. *Non-breeding plumage* is generally dull and faded especially on the nape. Iris: brown. Bill, legs and feet: black. *Immature:* sooty-brown above with whitish edges to feathers on back, wings and tail-coverts; greyish-brown below, lighter on the abdomen; underwing-coverts pale grey; forked tail lacks the long streamers. *Downy chicks* are difficult to see on a beach: upperparts speckled black and buff; throat and underparts are grey with white margins to the wings; bill is brown and legs and feet are pale red.

The Sooty Tern may be confused with the Bridled Tern but is darker above with a much shorter white eyebrow ending just above the eye, which is diagnostic in flight.

DISTRIBUTION AND STATUS

This tern is widespread and abundant with 7 races in tropical and subtropical seas throughout the world. In the Pacific it has been recorded as breeding in nearly every island group. The race *S. f. serrata* breeds in Australia, New Guinea, New Caledonia, Norfolk Island and Lord Howe Island. The largest number recorded in Vanuatu is from Matthew Island on 26 June 1974 during the visit of the surveying ship HMS *Hydra*. About 10,000 were concentrated on crags to the northwest of the main part of the island (Barritt, 1976). The Sooty Tern may be encountered in Vanuatu waters throughout the group.

FIELD NOTES

The Sooty Tern is a pelagic species and in normal conditions comes to islands only to breed. It flies with slow, deliberate wingbeats, the body appears to move lightly and buoyantly up and down on each beat. It is believed to sleep on the wing and rarely to land on the water though some 'Sooties' off Matthew Island were seen 'sitting on the water for short periods riding like Tropicbirds' (Barritt, 1976). Large flocks may congregate over shoals of fish and fishermen in the Pacific often locate shoals by observing these feeding flocks.

VOICE

It has a distinctive, plaintive call 'wack-a-wack', from which the name 'Wideawake' is derived (quite unlike the barking call of the Bridled Tern). It also has explosive screams, drawn-out growls and other harsh notes used as alarm or threat calls and during displays.

FOOD

The Sooty Tern swoops down to snatch its food, mainly small fish, cephalopods and crustaceans, from the surface and apparently also feeds at night.

NEST AND BREEDING

It breeds in colonies, some of immense size. The nest is just a scrape in the ground with or without nest material and under low vegetation if available. Eggs have been found in every month of the year. On Matthew Island the 10,000 terns of this species were concentrated on crags to the northwest of the main island. The island was described as 'two peaks separated by an isthmus. The large peak is punctured by a huge crater filled with sulphurous vapours and marked with yellow deposits. The sea at this point is also covered with floating sulphur. The only vegetation is some scant scrub on rubbly slopes, particularly on the west of the island' (Barrritt, 1976). Adults are thought to remain in adjacent seas after breeding but immatures disperse widely over tropical seas; young birds banded at Lord Howe Island have been recovered on the east coast of Australia, some 644 km distant. Another banded there in 1962 was recovered in the Philippines, 5,860 km to the northwest, four years later (Serventy *et al*, 1971).

62. Bridled Tern   *Sterna anaethetus*
Other name: Brown-winged Tern
French name: Sterne bridée

IDENTIFICATION AND FIELD NOTES

Length 36 to 42 cm. *Adult male and female* have similar plumage and there is no marked seasonal variation although the underparts are slightly darker grey when breeding. This tern is smaller, and more slender than the Sooty Tern with which it might be confused: the white patch on the forehead is narrower but extends backwards as an eyebrow above and well beyond the eye; the black eyestripe, crown and nape are separated from the grey-brown back and wings by a variable pale collar; the white underparts are lightly clouded with grey; the underwing is like the Sooty Tern but the primary bases are silver-grey, shading into black; the tail is longer with more white on the streamers and inner feathers. Iris: dark brown. Bill, legs and feet black. *Immature:* crown is grey strongly streaked white; eyestripe blackish, continues to nape; upperparts grey-brown patterned with buff tips to feathers; underparts white, underwing as adult; the tail is shorter, less deeply forked.

The Bridled Tern may be seen well offshore foraging with noddies, dipping to the surface occasionally plunging, and sometimes resting on the surface. It also frequents inshore waters and usually returns to land to roost. Call-notes are a high, barking 'yapp' often heard when roosting and harsher calls when feeding.

DISTRIBUTION AND STATUS

Widely distributed with 7 races breeding mainly in the tropics, the Bridled Tern is absent from most of the tropical Pacific (Pratt *et al*, 1987). Two Australian races: *S. a. rogersi* breeds in western Australia and *S. a. novaehollandiae* in Queensland. A further eastern race *S. a. anaethetus* breeds in the Philippines and Formosa. All are migratory and dispersive (Harrison, 1983) and widespread in the Indian and western Pacific Oceans. Beehler *et al* (1986) note that it is apparently common along most of the coasts of New Guinea. It has been recorded as a vagrant in Vanuatu waters. A good description of some 'unusual' terns off Matthew Island (Barritt, 1976) could refer to this species but numbers are not given.

63. Great Crested Tern   *Sterna bergii*
French name: Sterne huppée

IDENTIFICATION AND FIELD NOTES

Length 43 to 48 cm. A large whitish-looking tern with a long yellow bill, black cap, grey upperparts and deeply forked tail. *Adult male and female in breeding plumage:* forehead white; crown and nape black, frequently with some white speckling; hind crown and nape feathers are elongated and erected as a shaggy crest when the bird is excited or alarmed; neck and underparts white; back grey, upperwing pale grey with dark grey inner webs to primaries; tail pale grey. In *non-breeding plumage* the crown and nape are strongly streaked white; outermost primaries are darker grey. Iris: dark brown, Bill: yellow tinged green. Legs and feet: brownish-black. *Immature:* similar to non-breeding adult, the bill is greener and the wing-coverts are edged buff. Younger birds have a whitish crown mottled with brownish-black and pale-buff extending as a collar on the sides and back of the neck and dark flight feathers. Chicks are pale yellow to yellowish-brown densely spotted blackish above.

This large and handsome tern is usually seen near the coast. It fishes singly or in small groups over shallow water along the coastline, lagoon or estuaries; diving from aloft to the sea to capture prey on or near the surface but usually without immersing itself much. Diet is almost exclusively fish though it occasionally takes turtle eggs, young turtles or the chicks of smaller seabirds. Flight is more powerful and heavier than in the smaller terns, but nevertheless graceful with steady, deep and deliberate wingbeats. Calls are various short disyllabic notes: alarm call 'wep-wep'; also has harsh notes in flocks 'kirrick' and carrying notes during courtship display. The Great Crested Tern nests on offshore islands where it prefers areas with some vegetation. It usually nests in densely packed colonies. Pizzey (1980) notes about 8,000 pairs at North Solitary Island, New South Wales. The nest is a depression in the ground often with shell or coral fragments. Egg dates vary: September to December and March to June in Australia and January to March in New Caledonia. Banding in Australia has shown that young and adults disperse widely from the breeding colonies mostly within 400 km but movements of 900 km and 1,800 km have also been recorded.

DISTRIBUTION AND STATUS

This widespread species with 6 races occurs throughout the Indian Ocean, in southeast Asia and in the southwestern Pacific. There are 2 races in Australia, *S. b. gwendolenae* in northern and western Australia, and *S. b. cristatus* in southeast Australia which also breeds in the Pacific islands north to Japan and east to Fiji. The Great Crested Tern was reported as a vagrant in Vanuatu in the past; breeding was suspected but not confirmed. More recent records, mostly from Efate, are of birds seen in different plumages and at various times of year. Euan Macdonald notes that these terns are 'normally always to be seen' at Mele Bay and Hidaway Island, Efate (Naika 29:25) and 'if not flying are almost always to be seen in the lee side of one of the coral/shingle banks off Hidaway Island, except at high water' (pers. comm.).

64. Common Noddy *Anous stolidus* PLATE 2
Other names: Noddy Tern, Brown Noddy
French name: Noddi niais

IDENTIFICATION AND FIELD NOTES

Length 38 to 40 cm. A dark tern with a prominent whitish-grey cap, long, slender wings and wedge-shaped tail. *Adult male and female:* mostly uniform dull, blackish-brown above and below, upperwing and tail darker; forehead and crown white sharply demarcated from the black lores but shading gradually into the grey of nape and neck; a narrow black eye-ring is broken above the eye by a short white arc and by a longer arc below; throat grey; underwing grey-brown with darker edges; tail is long and spatulated with a shallow central notch. Iris: dark brown. Bill: black, shorter and thicker than in other noddies. Legs and feet: brownish-black with long hind toes. *Immature:* similar to adult but cap is less extensive and less well defined; forehead is white with only a little grey or none on the crown.

During the breeding season the Common Noddy is usually numerous only within a relatively short distance of land. Flying in loose, extended flocks they generally leave their nesting and roosting grounds in the early morning and return just before dark. After breeding they disperse widely and flocks have been seen feeding far out to sea.

Their flight is less graceful and buoyant than in other terns; wingbeats are strong and steady with only occasional soaring. They also fly closer to the water than most terns, with glides reminiscent of shearwaters. They usually pick up food from the surface of the sea, predominantly small fish but cuttlefish, small molluscs and plankton have been recorded. At times, however, they fish by landing abruptly with tail and wings elevated, then take off quickly with the captured fish; apparently they occasionally dive. They swim well, roost on the sea for long periods and may also perch on floating objects. They have a variety of calls including a loud 'kraa-kraa-kraa' uttered whenever disturbed or alarmed; also loud purring noises and short violent, threatening noises. The Common Noddy usually breeds colonially on offshore islands and pairs perform aerial display flights and bow and nod to each other or present nest material. The nest of seaweed and leaves, often interwoven with sticks or even coral and shells, may be in a low shrub on the ground. A single egg (53 × 36mm) is laid and the incubation period is 32 to 35 days (Watson 1908).

DISTRIBUTION AND STATUS

The Common Noddy breeds on tropical and subtropical islands worldwide. It is widespread in the tropical Pacific and common in Hawaii, Micronesia, Fiji and Polynesia. In Australia it breeds in huge colonies (of up to 50,000 birds in recent years) in the Abrolhos Islands and is fairly common along the northern coasts and islands. The race *A. s. pileatus* ranges throughout the southwest Pacific and breeds as far south as Norfolk and Lord Howe Islands; it has not been recorded in the Kermadecs and is not present in New Zealand. The Common Noddy may breed in Vanuatu though it is not seen frequently in the group.

65. Black Noddy   *Anous minutus (tenuirostris)*
Other names: White-capped Noddy, (Lesser Noddy)
French name: Noddi à cape blanche

IDENTIFICATION AND FIELD NOTES

Length 30 to 36cm. The Black Noddy is smaller, darker and has a longer, more slender bill than the Common Noddy. These characteristics are hardly distinguishable at a distance but they also have different flight patterns: the wings of the Black Noddy are narrower and flight is more fluttery with faster wingbeats. *Adult male and female* are alike in plumage and there is no seasonal variation: mostly dark grey-brown except for whitish forehead and crown extending well below the eye and gradually shading to darker grey at the nape; underparts greyer; tail is almost square with a central notch. Iris: dark brown; black eye-ring is interrupted by a small arc of white above the eye and a longer arc below. Bill: black. Legs and feet: brown. *Immature:* resembles adult; white on the head is usually restricted to the forehead but some show white caps (Serventy *et al*, 1971). This noddy is described by Beehler *et al* (1986) as 'uniformly blackish-brown with neatly contrasting white cap'. It is common in New Guinea waters and nesting is 'restricted to tree-covered islands'.

The Black Noddy inhabits coastal and offshore waters and is generally only seen in numbers near its nesting and roosting areas, leaving in the morning to fly out to the open sea to feed and returning in the afternoon. It flies close to the water while fishing and picks food, mainly small fish, plankton or molluscs, from the sea or catches it by shallow dives or dipping from the surface. Calls are a nasal rattling 'chrrr' also a croaking 'krik-krik-krik' or soft purring. It is very noisy at breeding colonies. Fairly substantial nests are generally built close together in mangroves or coastal trees. A single egg (45 × 30 mm) is laid and both adults share incubation and the care of the young.

DISTRIBUTION AND STATUS

Some authorities consider the Black Noddy (7 races) to be conspecific with the Lesser Noddy *Anous tenuirostris* of the Indian Ocean and western Australia (Harrison, 1983). The Black Noddy breeds on islands, cays and atolls in the tropical and subtropical Pacific and Atlantic Oceans and some colonies number tens of thousands. Although non-migratory, the birds are said to vacate some nesting islands for a short time during the non-breeding period. In the southwest Pacific the Black Noddy breeds from the Tuamotu Archipelago, to Samoa, New Caledonia, New Guinea, the Kermadec Islands and Norfolk Island and Queensland, Australia. It has been recorded in Vanuatu and may breed but this has yet to be confirmed. The most recent record is of a bird identified by Richard Pickering. It was found in an exhausted state on Efate on 13 January 1985 after Cyclone Odette and later released (Naika 17:12).

66. White Tern   *Gygis alba*   PLATE 2
Other names: White Noddy, Fairy Tern
French name: Sterne blanche

IDENTIFICATION AND FIELD NOTES

Length 28 to 33 cm. This delicate, snowy-white tern with a narrow ring of black feathers around the eye is unlikely to be confused with any other species in the region. *Adult male and female* are alike and there is no seasonal variation in plumage: some individuals have dusky shafts to the primaries and tail feathers; tail is slightly forked with sharply pointed feathers. When folded the wings reach beyond the tail. In flight, against a clear sky, the wings and tail appear almost translucent. Iris: dark brown; appears large and black at sea, the black eye-ring giving this impression. Bill: black with a deep blue, broad base and is very slightly uptilted. Legs and feet: blue-grey to black with yellowish webs. *Immature:* head mainly white except for a black spot behind the eye and brown mottling on the nape and mantle; back and wings greyish-white with variable brownish tips and black shafts to the outer primaries; rump white, tail grey; all white below.

The dainty White 'fairy' Tern is not very sociable and is usually seen singly or in small numbers. It is common near the breeding colonies and less numerous further out at sea but individuals may be encountered any distance from land. This tern has a buoyant and erratically fluttering flight; wingbeats are slow and effortless, with the body moving up and down on each beat. When foraging it flies close to the surface taking food, mainly small fish but also squid, crustaceans and plankton, from the surface. Earlier observers, quoted in Murphy (1936) have described these terns fluttering and hovering over the water to catch flying fish as they jump into the air, sometimes collecting two or three across the bill. Also noted is their curiosity and that they show little fear of humans 'fluttering just in front of one's face in a manner that soon becomes disagreeable – not attacking but merely staring, hovering like overgrown mosquitoes, and wheezing'. A variety of call-notes includes a low guttural 'heech-heech' and a pleasing high-pitched flight call.

They may breed in single pairs or loose colonies on the coast or often inland where there is better shelter. They make no nest of any kind but lay a single egg (44 × 33 mm) on a high, horizontal bare branch, wherever there is a shallow, natural pit in the branch, damaged bark with a slightly raised rim or any other irregularity that will keep the egg from rolling off. After hatching, the chick clings tenaciously to its branch, grows very quickly and is said to fly while still largely covered with down (Bell, 1912).

DISTRIBUTION AND STATUS

The White Tern (7 races) breeds on islands in the tropical and subtropical Atlantic, Indian and Pacific Oceans. *G. a. royana* breeds at Norfolk and Kermadec Islands; they return early in September and most have left by April. It is a vagrant on the east coast of Australia and in New Zealand. *G. a. candida* breeds throughout the southwest Pacific but not apparently in the Bismarck Archipelago and the Solomons where it is a common migrant. It is seen infrequently in Vanuatu, though it may occur more regularly in some parts of the group and may even breed.

Order COLUMBIFORMES

This order of pigeons and doves, family Columbidae, also included the Dodo, family Raphidae, and the two Solitaires, family Pezophapidae now extinct. Sandgrouse, family Pteroclididae, were formerly considered to belong to a suborder of Columbiformes but many authorities consider they are best placed in their own order, Pteroclidiformes (Cramp ed. *et al*, 1985). Further study of the relationships of these groups is obviously required.

The Dodo is one of the most widely known symbols of extinction. The Dodo from Mauritius and the Solitaire from Rodriguez and Réunion were gigantic, aberrant flightless pigeons which roamed the forests. They were the size of a turkey or larger and weighed up to 50 pounds. These birds were first discovered in their peaceful, faraway, island sanctuaries by sailors in the 16th century and from that time were killed in great numbers for food by the crews of sailing ships. The Dodo became very rare by 1640 and the last substantiated report was in 1662 on offshore islets of Mauritius. The Dodo was possibly finally exterminated by predatory cats, pigs and monkeys introduced to the islands. A few Solitaire were reported from Rodriguez in 1755 and 1761 and these are thought to be the last, feral cats being blamed for their extinction though dry-season fires may have been a contributory factor (Campbell and Lack, 1985). All that remains are a few skeletons in European museums.

Pigeons were probably among the first birds to be domesticated. The common Rock Pigeon or Rock Dove *Columba livia* of temperate Europe and western Asia, is the ancestor of all the many breeds of domestic pigeons. Nowadays large numbers are raised not only for food, their meat being considered a delicacy, but also for their beauty. Hundreds of varieties, often far removed from their ancestral stock in colour, shape and feathering have been developed. Pigeons have also been used for hundreds of years to carry messages and while modern communications have displaced them, carrier pigeons are nevertheless still raised, trained and raced by thousands of pigeon-fanciers.

The general terms 'pigeon' and 'dove' have no taxonomic significance and are used interchangeably throughout the family. In practice the larger, more heavily built birds, with square or rounded tails tend to be called pigeons and the term dove is applied to the smaller, more graceful species with long pointed tails. The single family Columbidae in the order Columbiformes has about 295 species of pigeons and doves divided into about 43 genera. They are found throughout the world in both temperate and tropical regions but they have their greatest development in the Oriental and Australasian regions where almost two-thirds of the species occur.

Pigeons and Doves *Columbidae*
In spite of the diversity of species and differences in habits all share distinctive characteristics. Most are stout-bodied with rather short necks and small heads and short, straight bills, hard at the tip but rather soft at the base, with a bare cere. Their plumage is thick and heavy and their feathers are loosely attached to the skin. All live predominantly on vegetable matter such as fruit, grain and leaves but some species also take small invertebrates and all have large crops and feed their young by regurgitation. Pigeons and doves are among the few species of birds (with sandgrouse and some species of estrildid finches) possessing the ability to drink by sucking. They immerse the beak and drink their fill of water without raising the head as practically all other birds have to do. Their calls are either a soft plaintive cooing or booming which can become, and often is, monotonous.

Many species build flimsy nest-platforms and lay small clutches of 1-3 pure white (in a few species yellow to buff) eggs. The male usually shares the incubation duties during the day and the incubation period varies from 12 days for the tiny (14 cm) Scaly Ground Dove Columbina passerina *from South America to almost 4 weeks for the (90 cm) crowned pigeons* Goura spp *from New Guinea. On hatching the young are practically naked and their eyes are closed and they are fed at first on a cheesy curd known as 'pigeon's milk' produced by the lining of the crop of both adults. To obtain this the young bird pokes its soft bill into the mouth of the adult. The young mature rapidly and leave the nest at any time from 2 to 3 weeks after hatching. Most species compensate for their small clutches by rearing two or more broods each year.*

The fruit doves and fruit pigeons are among the most brilliantly coloured birds in the world. Their plumage is of bold and contrasting colours, often astonishingly gaudy at close range but in spite of this the birds are often difficult to see as their bright colours are extremely concealing in the canopy of the forest. They are highly adapted to arboreal life. They have short feathered tarsi (legs) and rather wide soles on the toes. They feed on fruits picked directly from the trees and because of their wide gape can swallow large fruits whole. The Imperial fruit pigeons, especially, live on big fruits and nuts, often larger than their heads, and can stretch the flexible maxilla to accommodate them. Once the succulent parts of the fruit have been digested the hard pits of the larger fruits are regurgitated and the smaller seeds pass unharmed through the alimentary canal. The birds therefore play an important part in the dissemination of these plants. All other species have thinner bills and feet, smaller heads and the tarsi are not feathered. They are not strictly arboreal, often feeding close to the ground or on the ground, and their diet is mainly berries and seeds.

Eight species of pigeons and doves in 6 genera occur in Vanuatu. Two are predominantly green, fruit doves, genus Ptilinopus, *two large Imperial pigeons, genus* Ducula, *one true pigeon,* Columba, *two ground doves,* Chalcophaps *and* Gallicolumba *and a small long-tailed dove,* Macropygia. *At least half of these wander from island to island in their search for the ripe fruits and seeds of their favourite food plants. Identification may not be easy for some species, particularly the fruit doves and pigeons. They often occur in mixed flocks and are generally well concealed in the luxuriant foliage of tall forest trees. However, nearly all the species are distinct or restricted in range, each species has a unique call by which it can be identified and they may be seen in flight. The feral domestic pigeon* Columba livia *has not been recorded in Vanuatu though Pratt et al (1987) note that it can be expected almost anywhere in the Pacific. It has been reported from Fiji and Samoa in the southwest, Hawaii, French Polynesia and Micronesia. As pigeons and doves are favoured game-birds, they are likely to be rare in localities where they are overhunted, but they are capable of increasing in numbers when they are effectively protected. Their survival therefore depends largely on compliance with hunting regulations.*

67. Red-bellied Fruit Dove   *Ptilinopus greyii*   PLATE 8
French name: Ptilope de Grey   or locally: Pigeon vert à tête rouge
Bislama name: Smole fala green Pijin

IDENTIFICATION

Length 21 to 24 cm. A small compact dove which, although multi-coloured, blends perfectly with the foliage. In flight or when foraging it appears to be greyish-green. *Adult male:* plumage generally is pale grey-green; crown purplish-red, fringed with yellow at the sides and rear; mantle, wings and tail bright green; throat yellowish; patch on lower breast purplish-red; undertail-coverts pinkish-orange; wing-coverts and secondaries fringed with yellow; primaries dark; tertials may have some large pinkish-vinaceous spots; terminal tail-band greyish; underside of wing and tail grey; breast feathers, as in other fruit doves, are bifid: divided by a deep cleft into two parts, giving an indented appearance. Iris: orange-red. Bill: olive-green. Legs and feet: wine-red. The *adult female* is similar to the male but red on the breast is less extensive. *Immature:* smaller in size, all dull green with pale yellow edges to the feathers and with only a few or no red feathers on the crown and belly. Iris is light ochre. Bill has a brownish wash. Legs and feet are red tinged with black or brown. The Red-bellied Fruit Dove is smaller than the Vanuatu Fruit Dove with which it could be confused and the latter has no red in the plumage.

DISTRIBUTION AND STATUS

The fruit doves of the large and widespread genus *Ptilinopus* are found mainly in the South Pacific. Their range extends even to small and remote islands throughout Micronesia, Polynesia and Fiji. The Red-bellied Fruit Dove has been recorded from New Caledonia, the Loyalty, Santa Cruz, and Reef Islands and Gower Island in the Solomons (Ripley and Birckhead, 1942, Cain, 1954 and Goodwin, 1970). This species is the most common fruit dove throughout Vanuatu and is partly protected by law with a close season from 1 July to 31 March. The Red-bellied Fruit Dove co-exists with the Vanuatu Fruit Dove. Although these possibly competing species occupy the

The common Red-bellied Fruit Dove is primarily a forest bird but may be seen in other habitats when tree fruits ripen

The nest of the Red-bellied Fruit Dove looks flimsy but it is securely built with interlocking twigs

same habitat they are separated by an obvious size difference and a presumed differing feeding strategy.

FIELD NOTES
These attractively coloured doves may be seen singly, as pairs or in flocks. At times, especially out of the breeding season, they may be found in feeding flocks of up to 30 birds, often in fruiting trees with other species, particularly the Vanuatu Fruit Dove and Pacific Imperial Pigeon. They frequent a wide variety of habitats, mainly in the lowlands and at moderate heights. The Red-bellied Fruit Dove is primarily a forest bird, occupying the denser parts of the canopy but it can also be found in secondary growth and on low shrubs if these bear fruit, or in savannah woodlands and it will emerge from the forest to feed in isolated fruit trees in open country. Flight is swift and direct with rapid wingbeats, usually close to the canopy, and over wide open areas often fairly low over the ground. It also feeds near human settlements like villages or in suburban gardens. Some of these doves are present in most forests almost all the time but their numbers can increase suddenly when favoured feeding trees bear ripe fruit. They are active, aggressive feeders, crawling with agility between and over the foliage, often along very thin twigs and at times even hanging upsidedown to reach a fully ripe fruit. They are locally nomadic as different fruits ripen and probably also make longer journeys from island to island, but it is not known how far an individual

may travel. Although the Red-bellied Fruit Dove is brightly coloured it is inconspicuous in dense foliage. The best way to see it, or any other fruit dove, is to wait under or close by a tree bearing ripe fruit. The doves may be seen feeding or, more often, their presence is revealed by the sound of dislodged fruits striking the undergrowth.

VOICE
These birds are most vocal early in the morning and at sundown when often whole choruses can be heard, but they may call at any time of the day and even during the night. The identifying call is a loud resonant cooing which is usually repeated several times 'Coo-coo-coo-coocoocococoo', the first 2 or 3 notes loud and short and the rest, increasing in speed and trailing off. Other calls include short, soft or sharp 'coo' notes.

FOOD
Fruits and berries. Their favourite foods include the strangling-fig (*Ficus obliqua*, *F. proxila*, and *F. virgata*), fleshy fruits like those of the *Drysoxylum* spp, and the introduced panama cherry tree *Mutingia kallabura* but also the rather dry fruits of the prickly solanum shrub *Solanum torvum*.

NEST AND BREEDING
The nest consists merely of an insubstantial layer of a few twigs, so loosely put together, that the single, elliptical white egg (32 × 21 mm) is visible from beneath. Nests have been found mainly at the edge of the forest, also in secondary growth and park-like savannah country. The nest is placed in the thinner branches of a tree, often only a few metres from the ground. The breeding pair stay near the nest and share incubation (about 18 days) and care of the young. The breeding season is from September to February.

68. Vanuatu Fruit Dove *Ptilinopus tannensis* PLATE 8
Other name: Yellow-headed Fruit Dove
French name: Ptilope de Vanuatu   or locally: Pigeon vert à tête jaune
Bislama name: Big fala green Pijin

IDENTIFICATION
Length 28 to 30 cm. A larger, plumper bird than the Red-bellied Fruit Dove. *Adult male:* mainly grass-green except for the olive head, some greyish-white spots on the edge of the shoulder, a bright yellow patch at the tip of some tertial and secondary feathers, pale yellow abdomen with some green, light yellow undertail-coverts with green centres, a terminal greyish tail band and grey underwing and tail. Iris: milky-white. Bill: light bluish-green. Legs and feet: wine-red. *Adult female:* similar to male but slightly smaller with fewer greyish-white spots or none on the wing bands, and much more pale yellow on the lower abdomen. *Immature:* smaller in size, lacks the olive-yellow on the head and the greyish-white spots on the shoulder edge. Most feathers, especially on the back, wings and underparts are edged with yellow and the abdomen is light yellow. Iris: ochre. Bill: olive greyish-brown. Legs and feet: very pale red.

DISTRIBUTION, STATUS AND CONSERVATION

The Vanuatu Fruit Dove is widely distributed throughout Vanuatu but is rare on Aneityum and there are no records from the Torres group, Ureparapara, Makura, Aniwa and Futuna (Amadon, 1943, Cain, 1954 and Goodwin 1970). This interesting, endemic fruit dove is only moderately common and although it is partly protected by law the doves may breed or still have young in the nest during the open season from

The endemic Vanuatu Fruit Dove depends on the availability of tall fruiting trees and could become an endangered species

1 April to 30 June. This species could soon become endangered and most probably deserves the status of being fully protected.

FIELD NOTES

The wary Vanuatu Fruit Dove may be seen singly, in pairs or in small flocks, although it sometimes gathers in a favourite feeding tree in larger groups with other species. Favourite habitats are the true forests and open woodland of trees which normally grow in the forests but it can be found in a wide range of wooded habitat, provided there are some tall fruit-bearing trees growing in the area. It will also visit isolated fruit trees in plantations and gardens. It is found particularly in the lowland, sometimes at moderate heights and only rarely higher. Medway and Marshall (1975) found it only in the forest and not above 500 m. The Vanuatu Fruit Dove, like the Red-bellied, spends most of the time in the dense foliage of large trees, rarely descending much lower and unless it moves it is very difficult to see. As with other fruit doves, its presence is often only revealed by the sound of fruits, dislodged by the feeding birds, rattling through the undergrowth. It is known to be locally nomadic following the fruiting of different trees and probably also travels between islands.

VOICE

It is usually silent except for a moderately loud, deep 'woo'. This brief call may be repeated a number of times but can only be heard over a relatively short distance. It is also uttered when the doves chase each other while feeding in the same tree.

FOOD

It has similar feeding habits to the Red-bellied Fruit Dove. Medway and Marshall (1975) noticed both species 'feeding in the same trees (notably figs) on several occasions'. However, although there is overlap, the Vanuatu Fruit Dove is predominantly a canopy feeder and is not as gregarious. Common food trees include various *Ficus* and *Drysoxylum* species but also fruits of vines and probably palms are taken.

NEST AND BREEDING

The nest is a typically flimsy platform of thin, loosely interwoven twigs built in a horizontal fork, mostly high up in a tree in forest or parkland country. A single white oval egg is laid. Both adults incubate and brood and feed the young. Nests containing eggs have been found in April and fully feathered nestlings at the end of May. There is probably more than one brood in the season.

69. Pacific Imperial Pigeon   *Ducula pacifica pacifica*   PLATE 8
Other name: Pacific Pigeon
French name: Carpophage pacifique   or locally: Nautou des îles
Bislama name: Nawemba

IDENTIFICATION

Length about 40 cm. A large, grey pigeon with a black knob at the base of the upper mandible and shiny greenish wings and tail. *Adult male:* head, neck and upper back light grey; remaining upperparts dark, greenish-grey with a variably intensive metallic blue-green sheen, especially on the mantle and wings. Underparts light grey, more or less washed with pinkish-vinaceous, strongest on the breast; chin is paler and face and

The young Pacific Imperial Pigeon has remnants of down and shows the fold of skin on the bill which develops into a knob

flanks greyer; undertail-coverts rich chestnut; underwings dark slate. The characteristic, enlarged black cere or 'knob' is bordered by a narrow white band around the base of the bill. Iris: red. Bill and knob: black. Legs and feet: red. *Adult female* is similar to the male but slightly smaller and with a smaller knob: all colours are paler and the pinkish area around the breast is less pronounced. *Immature:* has no knob; all colours are dull and lack gloss on wings and back. The iris is pale ochre and the legs and feet very pale red. This species differs from the Vanuatu Mountain Pigeon and the White-throated Pigeon in having a black knob on the bill and lighter coloured plumage and from the former in its less restricted range.

DISTRIBUTION STATUS AND CONSERVATION
The 4 races of the Pacific Imperial Pigeon are widely distributed throughout the tropical central and western Pacific, from the Cook Islands to Kiribati, the Bismarck Archipelago and Louisiade Islands. In Vanuatu the race *pacifica* is found on almost all islands (there are no records for Paama, Lopevi, Tongariki and Makura). The same race occurs in the Loyalty Islands (from which it is an occasional straggler to New Caledonia), the Santa Cruz Islands, the Solomons, Fiji (where it is absent from the larger islands), Tonga and Samoa and even on some isolated islands like Wallis and Futuna. The Pacific Imperial Pigeon is fairly common in Vanuatu wherever sufficient forest exists but is much less numerous than it was and persecution has driven this handsome pigeon to the more remote parts on most islands. In recent years its

numbers have declined alarmingly on several islands (Santo, Efate and Tanna for example) partly due to the clearing of forest for plantations, gardens and other development but mainly because of the widespread use of firearms and excessive shooting. The populations are nowhere near the size of those in about 1960 when on Efate one person alone could shoot more than 30 birds in a day. This pigeon's loud call, gregarious nature and habit of staying in or close to one tree as long as it bears fruit make it an easy target. The Pacific Imperial Pigeon is now protected by a close season which has been gradually extended to nine months of the year. It should only be shot from 1 April to 30 June yet it continues to suffer a good deal at the hands of poachers in remote forest areas. It is important for conservationists in Vanuatu to actively promote the protection of this species.

FIELD NOTES

This species tolerates a wide range of wooded habitats; forest, parkland and any other localities with fruit trees, mainly in the lowlands but it has been found in fruiting trees at 800 to 1,000 m, and it is said to have been seen, though only rarely, higher up in the mountains. Medway and Marshall (1975) did not find it above 400 m on Santo. It was present in tall forest up to 450 m on Malakula but not at their netting plot at Amok (485 m). These pigeons can be found singly and during the breeding cycle the pairs seem to keep to themselves, but they are gregarious by nature and may form flocks of up to 50 or more birds. They often congregate in considerable numbers in favourite feeding-trees. They are highly adapted to arboreal life usually keeping to the forest canopy and are not easy to observe until they come down to feed in the lower storey; they do not normally descend to the ground. In dense forest their presence is usually revealed by their calls or by the sound of fruit falling and striking the undergrowth or the forest floor. The first hint of their presence may be the loud clap of wings and the crash of bodies hurtling through the trees as the pigeons leave, frequently not to fly far but to perch in nearby trees and motionlessly eye the intruder.

The Pacific Imperial Pigeon is strongly nomadic and often undertakes long journeys between islands in search of food. It flies at high speed in a straight path over the forest canopy, with deep steady wingbeats. These movements and flock concentrations have an appearance of regularity where the tree species fruit seasonally.

VOICE

The main calls are resounding and have great carrying power. The identity call is a deep, loud raucous 'roooo-prrroooooo' and is often followed, after a short pause, by a soft, low drawn-out 'hoooooooo'. During the first call the bird keeps its body and head in normal perching position with throat and breast inflated, whereas during the second call the body is held erect with tail pointing downwards and with head and bill pressed against the inflated throat. The second call may be the response of the male or female to its partner. Also has a harsh, short, barking 'prroo' or 'rooo-prooo' and subdued 'coos'.

FOOD

The bulk of its food consists of fruits of several species of fig trees and other large trees such as *Cananga odorata*, *Guettarda* spp. *Drysoxylum* spp. *Myristica* spp. and *Endospermum* spp. It most probably also takes young, still tender leaves of some forest trees and vines. Like *P. greyii* and *P. tannensis*, the *Ducula* pigeons obtain most of their water by sipping it from leaves or where it has accumulated in a hollow in the canopy of large trees but in dry weather they drink at creeks, perching on rocks or clinging to low overhanging branches.

NEST AND BREEDING

The nest is a substantial platform of good-sized twigs and some leaves, usually on a leafy, horizontal branch. Normally only one white, long-oval, egg (40 × 29 mm) is laid although it is said sometimes there are 2. Most nests have been found between September and January but a few also in July and August. Both adults incubate the egg and brood and feed the young.

70. Vanuatu Mountain Pigeon *Ducula bakeri* PLATES 8, 17
Other name: Baker's Imperial Pigeon
French name: Carpophage de Baker   or locally: Nautou des montagnes
Bislama name: Nawemba blong hill
Local name: Manutu, from the village of Nokovula at the foot of Mount Tabwemasana on Santo

IDENTIFICATION

Length about 40 cm. *Adult male:* head light slate-grey; mantle, wings and tail dark slate-grey; collar, back and breast dark chestnut with a slight gloss; abdomen rufous-brown; undertail-coverts cinnamon. The iris is of two colours, the inner ring is yellow and the outer ring red or orange-red. Bill: black. Legs and feet: bright red. *Adult female* is similar to the male but slightly smaller and less brightly coloured. *Immature:* probably like the adult but much duller and without any gloss. Differs mainly from the Pacific Imperial Pigeon in having dark underparts and no knob on the bill.

DISTRIBUTION, STATUS AND CONSERVATION

The rather uncommon, endemic Vanuatu Mountain Pigeon is found only on the larger islands of northern Vanuatu: Ureparapara, Vanua Lava and Gaua in the Banks group, Santo, Maewo, Ambae, Pentecost and Ambrym where it is confined to the highland forest (Amadon, 1943, and Goodwin, 1960 and 1970).

The way in which related species with similar habitat and food requirements can live on the same island is well demonstrated by the Vanuatu Mountain Pigeon and the Pacific Imperial Pigeon. Their ranges overlap considerably in the northern islands, both live in forest habitat and their food comes essentially from the same sources, yet they are not in competition with one another. Direct competition is avoided by the Vanuatu Mountain Pigeon living in highland forests and rarely descending to lower regions whereas the Pacific Pigeon apparently prefers the lowland and intermediate forests so that these species could only overlap in the mid-mountain forest. They could also be confined to these ranges by specific ecological needs which are so far unknown. At present, the Vanuatu Mountain Pigeon is partly protected by law and may be hunted from 1 April to 30 June. Because of its limited range, however, this endemic species is potentially endangered and therefore should be fully protected.

FIELD NOTES

These beautiful pigeons live in the primaeval mountain forest being found from 600 m to the tops of the mountains. They are usually seen singly or in pairs except when feeding, when a group of about 6 may be seen together on the same tree. They are less sociable than other species. They feed primarily in the canopy and the lower storeys of the rainforest but are said to feed close to the ground when certain shrubs fruit. Little is known of their movements except that they are locally nomadic throughout the year, following the ripening of various fruits, and may fly considerable distances on some islands. These pigeons are among the wariest birds in the mountain rainforest and are more likely to be heard than seen. It is only in the early morning that they display themselves prominently, sitting quietly in the treetops on bare branches to be warmed by the first rays of the sun after a particularly cool night on the high mountain.

VOICE

The call of the Vanuatu Mountain Pigeon is typical of the high mountain rainforest. It is a succession of deep notes of great carrying power. A booming, powerful 'twoo-too-too-too-too', is repeated frequently at short intervals. The first note is long and the following notes are delivered with a staccato-like rapidity at the same pitch. This call is one of the most characteristic sounds of the mountainous interiors on the northern islands and is similar to that of the Giant Imperial Pigeon *Ducula goliath* from New Caledonia.

FOOD

Ducula bakeri, like the Pacific Imperial Pigeon is a true frugivore, feeding especially on fleshy fruits. The detailed composition of the diet is not known but it takes fruits and berries of various native trees, shrubs, vines and possibly also palms.

NEST AND BREEDING

Very little is known of the breeding habits of the Vanuatu Mountain Pigeon. They are thought to be similar to those of the Pacific Imperial Pigeon.

71. White-throated Pigeon *Columba vitiensis leopoldii*   PLATES 8, 17
Other name: Metallic Wood Pigeon
French name: Pigeon à gorge blanche   or locally: Collier blanc
Bislama name: Natarua

IDENTIFICATION

Length 37 to 40 cm. A large dark pigeon with diagnostic, conspicuous pure white on chin and upper-throat extending to the cheeks and the side of the neck. *Adult male:* upperparts mainly dark slate-grey with a more or less pronounced metallic purplish-green sheen; wings and tail blackish-grey. Underparts slightly lighter grey with a chestnut wash, which is strongest on the breast. Iris: orange-red, with a ring of naked red skin around the eye. Bill: cherry-red with a yellowish-white tip. Legs and feet: bright red. *Adult female:* similar to male but with a less distinct dull white or greyish throat and little or no chestnut on the breast. *Immature:* resembles adult but all colours are dull with no metallic gloss and little or no chestnut; throat is an inconspicuous brownish-grey. The White-throated Pigeon is more slender in build than the *Ducula* pigeons with a smaller head, thinner neck and rather long, square-ended tail. In adults the white throat is distinctive.

DISTRIBUTION AND STATUS

The White-throated Pigeon, with about 8 races, is widespread in the western Pacific from western Samoa, Fiji, the Solomons, western Papuan Islands and New Guinea, the Lesser Sundas and the Philippines to the smaller islands north of Borneo (Amadon, 1943 and Goodwin, 1970). This is the only pigeon in Vanuatu belonging to the genus *Columba* (wood pigeons) which indicates that it is a 'true' pigeon and of the basic pigeon stock from which all other species of pigeons and doves have evolved. The race *leopoldii* is peculiar to Vanuatu and is found on all islands with suitable habitat; there are no records from Gaua. It is common but much less numerous than the Pacific Imperial Pigeon. It is partly protected by law and may only be hunted from 1 April to 30 June.

FIELD NOTES

The White-throated Pigeon usually lives singly, in pairs or small groups except when feeding in favoured areas, when small flocks of about 30 birds may be encountered. It frequents all suitable habitats from the coast to the high mountain peaks; forests and forest-edge, secondary growth, grazing land with groups of trees and bushes, village gardens and even scrub-like bush close to dwellings but it is of somewhat irregular distribution. Less arboreal than the preceding species, often feeding in the lower storeys of the forest and close to or even on the ground, it is rarely found with other species of doves or pigeons. It is nomadic, the local movements being governed by the ripening of indigenous berries and fruits, and it even flies between islands. Being wary and secretive it sits or feeds silently in the trees and often the first sign of its presence is the clapping of wings from only a few metres away as it leaves. In open country and when travelling long distances it flies straight, at high speed, with deep, deliberate wingbeats but when flying in the lower storeys it weaves its way through the vegetation. Like many other species of pigeons and doves, if alarmed it will stretch out the neck and slowly, or rapidly, bob the head often at the same time uttering a scarcely audible 'coo'.

VOICE

It is normally rather quiet but has two main calls; either a deep booming 'whoo-woowoowoo' with the second note softer and trailing off gradually or a moderately loud 'whoo-whoo' with constant pitch. Both calls may be repeated a number of times. Also has other soft 'coo' notes.

FOOD

The White-throated Pigeon feeds on a wide variety of berries and other small fruits, small nuts, seeds and tender shoots. It has adapted to feeding on the introduced solanum shrub *Solanum torvum* and especially the introduced chilli bush *Capsicum fretescens*. Medway and Marshall (1975) noted that at Narabut on Efate in July many were feeding on fruit in *Olea paniculata* trees but later, when most fruit had fallen, fed on the ground. In some areas chilli-fruits in season form the main bulk of their diet.

NEST AND BREEDING
The nest is a small platform which is more substantial than that of the fruit doves. It is built of twigs and vine tendrils and may be at any height in the trees or bushes or even on the ground, close to the tree trunk between the roots or under shrubs and ferns on a bed of twigs and leaves. Generally only a single, white long-oval egg is laid. Breeding usually takes place during the period September to January/February but a few nests have been found in July and August.

72. Rufous-brown Pheasant-Dove *Macropygia mackinlayi mackinlayi* PLATES 8, 17
Other name: Rufous-brown Cuckoo-Dove
French name: Colombe à longue queue   or locally: Longue queue
Bislama names: Long fala tel, Longtel

IDENTIFICATION
Length 28 to 31 cm. A slender, brown dove with a long, graduated tail which is the same length as the body, a small head and short legs. *Adult male:* upperparts rufous-brown, darker on the wings and tail. Underparts pale cinnamon; throat often speckled with black; undertail-coverts bright cinnamon; underside of tail feathers dark brown with rufous edges. A peculiar colour phase, brownish-grey above and pale grey below occurs rarely on several islands but is found more often on Tanna. Iris: red. Bill: black. Legs and feet: red. *Adult female:* like the male but all plumage is slightly duller and the throat is more strongly mottled with black. *Immature:* whole plumage is much duller and scalloped with dark brown and ochre. Iris: brownish-ochre. Legs and feet: brownish-red. No other pigeon in Vanuatu is uniformly brown and has the very long graduated tail.

DISTRIBUTION AND STATUS
The Rufous-brown Pheasant-Dove ranges in 4 races from the Santa Cruz Islands to the Solomons and the Bismarck Archipelago. Allied species are found on the east coast of Australia, Malaysia and the Philippines. The race *mackinlayi* occurs throughout Vanuatu although there are no records from the Torres Islands and Aniwa. (Amadon, 1943 and Goodwin, 1970). It is fairly common on most islands but not numerous and it is rare on Aneityum. It is partly protected by law and the open season is from 1 April to 30 June.

FIELD NOTES
These doves frequent a wide range of forest habitats at all altitudes but seem to prefer the understorey and the more open parts of the primary forest, clearings and village gardens overgrown with low vegetation, scrub, berry-bearing bushes and weeds. They generally announce their presence by their melodious cooing which is one of the most pleasing sounds in the Vanuatu forest. They are usually found in the vicinity of small fruit-bearing trees, bushes or vines. They are not gregarious and are usually seen singly or in pairs. Several pheasant-doves may be observed feeding together in the same tree but they arrive from different directions and leave separately. When foraging on low vegetation they can be approached fairly closely. They have not been recorded as feeding on the ground in the wild but they do land to drink from creeks or

water-holes. Apparently they seldom travel far but move from one tree or clump of bushes to another nearby. They usually fly among the tree-tops in the substage of the forest, low over the forest canopy or in the open, low over the scrub. They can fly swiftly and with agility but appear to be weak fliers somewhat handicapped by the long tail.

VOICE

The identity call is a quiet series of pleasing, melodious, two-syllabled 'coo-coooo's', slightly rising then dropping in pitch and trailing off but with no change in tempo. The call is not loud but can nevertheless be heard over a fair distance. Pheasant-doves call more frequently in the late afternoon and also, some people believe, before rain.

FOOD

They feed on a wide variety of small berries, fruits and seeds usually beneath the canopy in small trees, shrubs and vines. They also take the fruits of the introduced chilli bush *Capsicum fretescens* and the lantana-shrub *Lantana* spp.

NEST AND BREEDING

The nest is a solid platform of twigs, vines and a few leaves, somewhat saucer-shaped. It may be placed in a variety of sites, on a forked leafy branch in a tree fern or epiphytic bird-nest fern, or tucked into a tangle of vines, usually in the lower storeys of the forest, within 3 to 6 m from the ground. The clutch consists of 1-2 white eggs. The breeding season is from September to February. Display flights may be seen mainly at the beginning of the reproductive cycle; the doves fly up high then glide down, often spiralling, with wings and tail spread wide.

73. Green-winged Ground Dove   *Chalcophaps indica sandwichenis*   PLATES 8, 17
Other names: Green-winged Emerald Dove, Emerald Ground Dove
French name: Colombe turvert   or locally: Tourterelle
Bislama name: Sot leg

IDENTIFICATION

Length 24 to 26 cm. A medium-sized ground dove with brown body, green wings and a rather short tail. *Adult male:* head, neck and upper back purplish-rufous; lower back blackish-brown crossed by two broad, light grey bands; rump grey; tail mainly brown with a dark subterminal band, outermost tail feathers light grey with a black subterminal band. Mantle and wing-coverts bright, metallic emerald green; top edge of shoulder (bend in the wing) white; primaries brown; underwings reddish-brown; underparts vinaceous-brown, paler and more greyish on the abdomen; undertail-coverts grey; undertail brown. Iris: brown. Bill: bright orange-red, cere dark vinaceous-red. Legs and feet: bright red. *Adult female:* like the male but duller and generally lacking the vinaceous tint; the white patch on the shoulder is less extensive and more greyish; bill is yellowish, noticeably paler than the male. *Immature:* usually smaller, brown above, paler below, scalloped all over with dark brown; wing feathers edged with rufous-cinnamon. Bill, legs and feet: brownish. No other ground dove has the combination of rich brown body and green wings. The Santa Cruz Ground Dove lacks the emerald green wings and in Vanuatu is only found in the higher regions on Santo.

The Green-winged Ground Dove, a solitary feeder, has benefited from all types of agricultural developments

DISTRIBUTION AND STATUS

This species is very widespread with about 9 races found in India, southeast Asia, Malaysia, Indonesia, the Philippines, the Lesser Sundas and Australia, eastern New Guinea, the Solomons and New Caledonia. The race *sandwichensis* has been reported from the Loyalty Islands, the Santa Cruz group and throughout Vanuatu (Goodwin, 1970). It is common on most islands but may be overlooked as it is quiet and somewhat shy and stays in the undergrowth most of the time. The Green-winged Ground Dove is partly protected by law. The open season is from 1 April to 30 June.

FIELD NOTES

Although this dove is primarily a bird of the forest floor it frequents all types of disturbed habitat and is more common in the lowland. Apart from its natural haunts it has also colonised coconut and cacao plantations, orchards and other agricultural land and may be seen near villages or suburban gardens, in overgrown clearings and scrub. It is solitary and usually found alone or in pairs though several may congregate at an abundant food source, where figs, other fruit or seeds have fallen from the trees. It forages on the ground but perches readily and roosts in trees. When not disturbed it becomes fairly tame tolerating a close approach before darting off. When flushed it rises from the ground with a loud clapping of wings and flies with great agility through the tangled undergrowth to alight on a low, thick branch at a relatively short distance or to drop to the ground and disappear amongst the vegetation. It does not appear to be nomadic though it has irregular local seasonal movements. Pairs defend small territories when breeding and attack other doves that come into their area. The Green-winged Ground Dove may be seen foraging along a country road or jungle track or flying across open areas at high speed beating the wings continuously and keeping low.

VOICE
It is a moderately vocal bird. The main call is a penetrating, low drawn-out mournful cooing, 'too-hoowooot', repeated a number of times or for long periods, and often getting quicker at the end. It is more vocal at noon. The call could be confused with that of the Red-bellied Fruit Dove, especially when heard at a distance. The Green-winged Ground Dove, however, usually calls when sitting on a low, thick, horizontal branch in the undergrowth or on the ground whereas fruit doves perch in the canopy.

FOOD
The diet consists mainly of various seeds, kernels, pits of fruits and small berries which have fallen to the ground. The blue berries of the introduced Lantana-bush are also taken. It sometimes picks fruit and seeds direct from the branches, but generally feeds on the ground and will also take some insects and worms. It also gathers at the copra-dryers to feed on the left-over small pieces of coconut when the coconuts are being shelled-out.

NEST AND BREEDING
The nest may be built in a tangle of horizontal branches, a junction of branches with a mass of vines, on the top of a bird-nest fern growing on trees or between the leaves of pandanus palms. It can be a scanty or more substantial platform of interlaced thin twigs and leaves about 17 cm in diameter and is generally from one to 5 m above the ground. Two oval, pale cream to light ochre eggs (18 × 24 mm) form the clutch. Incubation takes 14 to 16 days and the young fledge after about 12 to 13 days. Both adults share the incubation and rearing duties. The main breeding season is probably from September to February but nests have also been found between May and July.

74. Santa Cruz Ground Dove   *Gallicolumba sanctaecrucis*   PLATES 8, 17
French name: Tourterelle de Santa-Cruz
Local name: Pimo – at Nokovula, the mountain village in the Tabwemasana Massif (the same name is probably given to the Green-winged Ground Dove)

IDENTIFICATION
Length 22 to 25 cm. A medium-sized brown, dimorphic ground dove with a short tail. *Adult male:* crown, nape, upper neck and upper back brown; rest of the upperparts chocolate-brown tinged with glossy purple and with a large, strongly metallic violet-purple patch at the bend of the wing; forehead, side of the head and neck light grey; throat and breast shield form a large white patch tinged pinkish-buff, greyer on the side; abdomen chocolate-brown; primaries and tail-feathers dark brown. Iris: brown. Bill: black. Legs and feet: bright purplish-red. *Adult female:* lighter, more brownish than the male. Head, neck and breast shield tawny-chestnut. Back, tail and

wings have a uniformly dull greenish gloss; abdomen grey-brown. *Immature* is uniformly brown, lacking the distinguishing characters of the adult. It has similar habits to the Green-winged Ground Dove but differs in plumage with a completely brown back, metallic purple shoulder patch and black bill.

DISTRIBUTION AND STATUS

Seven species in this genus, *Gallicolumba*, occur in the southwest Pacific. All differ in colouration but their habits seem to be essentially the same, except for the Guam species *Gallicolumba xanthonura* which is reported to have adapted to living in trees probably to escape persecution from cats brought to the island by whaling ships and settlers (Goodwin, 1970). *Columba (Gallicolumba) ferruginea* supposedly collected by Forster on Tanna in 1774 is generally assumed to be based on an error, though it might imply an extinct race of *Gallicolumba sanctaecrucis* on Tanna (Peters 1937, Stresemann 1950, Greenway 1967 and Diamond and Marshall, 1976). The Santa Cruz Ground Dove is known only from the islands of Tinakula and Utupua in the Santa Cruz group and from Espiritu Santo in Vanuatu. In 1972 this species was recorded by the author in the primordial rainforest of the Santo highlands at around 1,000 m but has not been found higher despite apparently suitable habitat. It was mainly seen lower, in the forests surrounding the abandoned village of Punampioni and the village of Latuba at the foot of Mount Kotamtam. During a visit by Peter Kaestner to Santo in June 1985 a female bird of this species was flushed 'from inside a stand of forest at about 300 m where the forest was broken by grazed land' (Naika 19:7). This uncommon dove of the mountain rainforest, apparently scattered in suitable habitat, may be rarely seen rather than actually rare.

FIELD NOTES

The Santa Cruz Ground Dove inhabits the mid-mountain forest and does not venture far beyond the forest edge. It is mainly terrestrial and spends most of the time on the forest floor though it frequently perches on low branches and roosts in trees. These doves can run fast and prefer to escape from an intruder by running off to hide in the undergrowth, with the tail held erect above the back, rather than fly. When startled they take off, often accompanied by a loud clap of the wings, fly a short distance then land on the ground out of sight. Found singly or in pairs these timid, wary birds are usually seen only in fleeting glimpses, a brown bird running to hide or in swift and agile flight through the tangled forest vegetation.

VOICE

The Santa Cruz Ground Dove is only moderately vocal but may call at any time of the day from the forest floor or at night when roosting on low branches. The low, moderately loud 'woot' is monotonously repeated (it has been heard over 15 times in succession) and often increases in rapidity at the end.

FOOD

It forages on the floor of the true forest for the basic diet of seeds, berries and plant shoots and also takes insects and worms.

NEST AND BREEDING

There are no definite records but village people of the Santo highlands say that the nest and eggs of this species resemble those of the Green-winged Ground Dove, though a single white egg may be the norm.

Order PSITTACIFORMES
In this order the identifying characteristics are the large head, short neck, hooked bill with cere at the base, the strongly downcurved upper mandible fitting over the shorter lower mandible and the zygodactyl foot which is strong and grasping, with two toes directed forwards and two backwards. These with other physiological features and behaviour patterns combine to make the Psittaciformes one of the most natural groups of birds. This order of mainly vegetarian birds, generally known as parrots, has about 82 genera and 330 species in the single family Psittacidae. Distribution is nearly worldwide in the tropics, being plentiful in the lowland forests, and extends to higher latitudes mainly in the southern hemisphere. In Australia about 52 species are known (Simpson and Day, 1989) and there are 7 native and 3 introduced species in New Zealand (Falla et al, 1981). While parrots have never been domesticated in the sense that poultry have, their rich colourful plumage and amusing mannerisms, their ability to imitate the human voice and the ease with which many species are tamed and maintained has meant that parrots have been kept as pets for centuries. In recent times the parrot populations of the world have been decimated by their exploitation for trade and by the destruction of their tropical forest habitats and about 100 species are now at risk of extinction. Over 200,000 parrots arrive in the European Economic Community every year and at least 40 of the threatened species can still be imported there legally. In 1989 the International Council for Bird Preservation proposed urgent conservation measures and launched a campaign for the protection of parrots (World Birdwatch Vol.11 No.4). The Vanuatu government joined CITES, the Convention on International Trade in Endangered Species of Wild Fauna and Flora, in 1989. The two parrots in Vanuatu are both listed in Appendix II of CITES and export is now strictly controlled. Permits should be given exceptionally, mainly for research purposes. It is essential that the identity of species for which applications are made is verified before permits are issued and that export licences for parrots, or any other species, are only issued if the authorities are satisfied that such exports will not be detrimental to the wildlife heritage of Vanuatu.

Parrots *Psittacidae*
Parrots vary in size from the tiny pygmy-parrots (9 cm) of New Guinea to the long-tailed macaws (100 cm) of South America. Most are brightly coloured, predominantly green marked with yellow, red or blue, although some are black or white, and in most species the sexes are alike in plumage. Many species are gregarious and mostly arboreal with shrill or squeaky voices. Almost all are cavity nesters; most nest in tree-holes, some in rock crevices or burrows in the ground, two Australian species dig a chamber in termite mounds and one species builds colonial nests out of sticks and twigs. They lay 2 to 5 white eggs, depending on the species, the female incubates but the male later shares the care of the young. Characteristically the young are fed by the adult holding the bill of the chick in its own. Family parties usually stay together until the following breeding season.

Some authorities have recognised up to 8 subfamilies in the family Psittacidae which include the *Cockatoos* Cacatuinae, *Lorikeets or Lories* Loriinae *and the 'true' Parrots* Psittacinae which includes 58 of the 82 genera.

The 2 species of parrots occurring in *Vanuatu* are classified in the subfamily Loriinae. Both species are highly gregarious and are usually seen in feeding flocks but breeding birds are encountered in pairs. They feed mainly on nectar and pollen and have anatomical modifications related to this method of feeding. The bill is relatively elongated and narrow and the tongue is tipped with papillae, forming a horseshoe-shaped brush-like appendage. The papillae are shortened and compressed when the bird is eating seeds or at rest and are expanded, when the tongue protrudes, for licking pollen and nectar from flowers or the flesh from soft juicy fruits.

75. Rainbow Lorikeet   *Trichoglossus haematodus*   PLATES 9, 17
Other names: Coconut Lory, Rainbow Lory
French name: Perruche des cocotiers
Bislama name: Nasiviru

IDENTIFICATION

Length 25 to 27 cm including the 10 cm tail, the female on average is probably slightly smaller. These strikingly coloured lories, mainly green with a red breast, usually draw attention to themselves by their penetrating screeches. *Adult male and female:* forehead, forecrown, lores and chin bluish-mauve; remainder of head dark brownish-purple; collar across hind-neck yellow-green; rest of upperparts, including the pointed tail, bright green. Throat purplish-black; breast red, feathers narrowly edged with black giving a scaly appearance; belly green; lower belly, thighs and undertail-coverts green strongly marked with yellow. Tail is graduated, comprising rather narrow, pointed feathers, green above and olive-yellow below. Underwing-coverts red; underside of flight feathers broadly banded yellow. Some individuals, as in the Australian race, are variably marked with deep violet-blue on the flanks and lower belly. Iris: bright red. Bill: orange-red to red, cere dark grey. Legs and feet: lead-grey. *Immature:* duller than adult with a shorter tail. The iris is dull brown at first and the bill dark horn-coloured. In central Vanuatu, Efate and Emae, individuals with light yellow partly replacing the green plumage have been observed on 2 occasions. In one of these birds, an immature, this colour reverted to the normal green after the first moult.

DISTRIBUTION, STATUS AND CONSERVATION

The Rainbow Lorikeet occurs in about 21 races (Cain, 1955) from Indonesia and the Lesser Sundas to New Guinea, the Solomon Islands and New Caledonia and in coastal eastern and southeastern Australia. The race *massena* is found in the Bismarck Archipelago, the Solomon Islands and throughout Vanuatu though there are no records from Lopevi and Futuna. It is numerous wherever there are flowering trees and movements are usually erratic as it travels widely in search of food, even between islands. The Rainbow Lorikeet is listed in Appendix II of CITES, and at some time in the future it may be necessary to review measures for its protection in Vanuatu.

FIELD NOTES

It may be encountered in most types of wooded habitat, primarily in the lowland although it is not uncommon in the mountains when favourite trees or shrubs are flowering. These lories are more often seen in disturbed habitat than in the true forest or mangroves; savannah-woodland, trees bordering watercourses or surrounding paddocks, suburban gardens and in nearly every coconut plantation. The gregarious lories are predominantly nomadic, their presence or number in any area being governed by the availability of favourite food and flocks may gather on concentrated sources of flowers or fruit. They are generally seen in pairs or small flocks while feeding in the canopy of a flowering tree, calling attention to themselves with their shrill chatter. A feeding flock of 30 or more lories is a fascinating sight. The birds move with agility from one flowering spray to another, cling acrobatically in all possible positions to the twigs on which the blooms grow, also hanging upside down, and at the same time chase away honeyeaters or any other birds that may approach too closely. Like most other parrot species, they commonly use the bill to hold on to branches. Lories passing overhead will respond quickly to the chatter of feeding flocks and wheel and circle before swooping down to alight in the feeding trees. When alarmed, these generally noisy and active feeders will remain motionless and then, despite the red breast they are difficult to see in the canopy as they often turn their backs to the intruder, watch warily over one shoulder, and eventually fly off screeching loudly. During the heat of the day the lories become inactive and sit quietly among the dense foliage in the treetops, often mutually preening or idly investigating leaves or twigs with their brush-tongues. In the afternoon the entire flock returns to the feeding area but may fly off to a common roost in the evening. On short flights they twist and turn with great agility through the branches of the canopy but fly high when travelling longer distances. Over open country, when flying from one group of trees to another they often fly fairly low over the ground but soar upwards and away widely at the sight of an unusual object. Flight is swift and direct with rapid wingbeats and the whirring sound of the wings can be heard as they pass overhead. The flight silhouette is distinctive; slim body, tapering wings and long pointed tail and the bright red breast and yellow bands on the underwings are often conspicuous.

VOICE

The Rainbow Lorikeet is usually extremely noisy and attracts attention by its loud, harsh shrieks. The contact call, generally given in flight, is a sharp rolling screech, repeated at intervals. Feeding flocks keep up a shrill chattering but they twitter softly while resting and are usually silent when raiding maize or sorghum fields.

FOOD

Nectar and pollen form the staple diet taken from flowers of a variety of native and introduced trees, particularly coconut palms, Indian coral-tree *Erytrina variegata*, African tulip-tree *Spathodea campanulata* and sago palm *Metroxylon rumphii*. They are important pollinators of coconut palms. They also take soft juicy fruit and berries including the introduced panama cherry tree *Mutingia kallabura* and such cultivated fruits as oranges, mandarins, mangoes and papayas causing some damage in orchards with ripening fruit. They may raid maize and sorghum crops to feed on the unripe milky grains. Half-ripe seeds of *Casuarina* trees are occasionally taken and insects and their larvae are probably taken unintentionally together with nectar and fruit. They drink water trapped in leaves or reach surface water from half-submerged logs and bathe in the rain or by fluttering among foilage soaked by dew or rain.

NEST AND BREEDING

The Rainbow Lorikeet breeds mainly between August and January but some nesting has also been recorded earlier or later. The nest is built in a hollow limb or hole in a tree, usually high above the ground, with a layer of wood dust at the bottom. The clutch is two, oval white eggs (28 × 23 mm) and observations on captive birds show that only the female incubates for about 26 days. The nestlings remain in the nest for 60 days and after fledging are fed by both parents for up to 8 weeks. The young become sexually mature in the second year. Further details on breeding biology and ethology are given in Ulrich, Ziswiler and Bregulla (1972).

76. Green Palm Lorikeet *Charmosyna palmarum* PLATE 9
Other name: Vanuatu Lorikeet
French name: Loriquet des palmiers
Local names: Denga, Dedenga or Maramarei – Nokovula village, Santo; Vini on Tongoa Island in the Shepherd Group

IDENTIFICATION

Length 15 to 16.5 cm including about 8 cm tail. *Adult male:* almost entirely green, lighter and more yellowish on the underparts; chin, around the base of the bill and some feathers on the cheeks pale red; mantle slightly washed with olive; tail long and graduated, central tail feathers broadly tipped and lateral feathers narrowly tipped with yellow; underwing greyish-green. Iris: orange-red. Bill: coral-red, cere orange. Legs and feet: orange-yellow. *Adult female:* similar to male but with only a few pale red feathers or none on the chin or around the base of the bill. *Immature:* similar to female but all colours are duller. Iris is ochre and the bill yellow-brown.

DISTRIBUTION, STATUS AND CONSERVATION

Formerly the 14 *Charmosyna* species were grouped together in the genus *Vini* with the 5 species of lorikeet occurring mainly on Polynesian islands. They have now, on reasonable grounds, been placed by most authors in the genus *Charmosyna*. This species is not endemic to Vanuatu but is found elsewhere only in the Santa Cruz Islands (Treasurers, Taumoko in the Duff Group, Tinakula and Vanikoro). See Amadon (1942b). The Green Palm Lorikeet perhaps exemplifies Vanuatu species that go through fluctuations in their distribution which could be related either to cyclones (Diamond, 1975) or to colonisation cycles during periods of population 'blooms' (Diamond and Marshall, 1976). In 1879 observers and collectors reported that this lorikeet had appeared on Efate, in central Vanuatu, for the first time in 30 years. By the 1930s MacMillan found it on several islands of southern Vanuatu, including Aneityum. By the 1960s the Green Palm Lorikeet had disappeared again from Efate and the southern islands and was confined to islands from Emae and Tongoa northwards: Epi, Lopevi, Paama, Ambrym, Malakula, Pentecost, Ambae, Maewo, Santo, and most of the Banks Islands. There are no records from the Torres Islands. Mainly a bird of the uninhabited mountain forest, not uncommon above 1,000 m on larger islands, this species is fully protected by law. The Green Palm Lorikeet is listed in Appendix II of CITES, and it is likely that further measures, including the designation of Forest Reserves may be necessary for its long term survival.

FIELD NOTES

These lories can be found regularly only at the higher altitudes of their range, where they inhabit all types of mountain forest and may be encountered anywhere there is suitable food. Predominantly nomadic, they travel widely between feeding areas; the flowering of favourite species of trees, palms and vines largely determines their movements and in a given area numbers may decrease or build up in accordance with the supply of food. They may be seen singly or in pairs but are generally found in small flocks and larger groups may congregate on profusions of some preferred blossoms, often in the company of honeyeaters and white-eyes. Although the presence of Green Palm Lorikeets is usually betrayed by their constant chatter, the birds are difficult to see because of their small size and their predominantly green plumage which blends with the foliage and an observer beneath a tree where they are feeding may take some time to spot the birds high in the canopy. Being agile and acrobatic feeders, they move quickly among the twigs, often hanging upside down to investigate blossoms and they seem intent on getting to as many blossoms as possible. While resting during the middle of the day or towards evening, before they settle down to roost, pairs may be observed sidling up to each other and allopreening suggesting that the pair bond is maintained in a flock. Observations on captive birds show that pairs may spend the night in nesting hollows. Flocks are usually seen climbing amongst branches covered with flowers or flying high overhead. Their flight is similar to that of the Rainbow Lorikeet, swift with rapid wingbeats, which are clearly audible as they fly overhead. When travelling some distance flight is high and direct but when flushed from a tree they weave their way through the treetops. The Green Palm Lorikeet is an irregular and unpredictable visitor to the coastal lowlands, suddenly appearing in large flocks in some years while in others it is not seen at all. Sporadically, large numbers have been reported on the coasts of Santo and Malo when Indian coral-trees are flowering and generally a few can be seen on flowering sago palms along the coasts of islands in the Banks group.

VOICE

The contact call, always repeated at intervals during flight is a short, high-pitched screech 'tswit-tswit', or a more quickly delivered series 'tswitswitswit', somewhat similar to that of the Rainbow Lorikeet but not so loud or discordant. Feeding is accompanied by continuous shrill twittering but while resting during the day they utter softer notes. On taking flight a soft 'tswit' with a melodic inflection is normally heard as they depart but when disturbed the birds fly off screeching loudly.

FOOD

Nectar and pollen form the staple diet, taken from flowers of a variety of trees, palms, lianes, and shrub species. Flowering sago palms *Metroxylon rumphii* are one of their favourite feeding sites. They have been observed feeding at fruit of some native figs and on berries, taking juice from soft flesh surrounding the seeds. Small insects and larvae are most probably taken together with nectar from flowers and tiny larvae may be swallowed when eating the flesh of soft fruits. They drink water from leaves and bathe in soft rain or by fluttering amongst foliage soaked by clouds or rain.

NEST AND BREEDING
Little is known about their breeding biology. In early December 1961 a nest containing 2 half-feathered chicks was found in cloud forest above the mountain village of Nokovula at approximately 1,600m on Santo. It was in a hollow limb of a tree about 6m above the ground.

Order CUCULIFORMES
This order comprises 2 families, Musophagidae, the turacos, endemic to the Afrotropical region and the closely related Cuculidae, cuckoos, koels and coucals. These are rather solitary birds, mostly arboreal with short legs and rounded wings and the largest number occur in the tropics. Those living in temperate and colder regions tend to be migratory and have long, pointed wings. They generally have a slender body, long tail and a narrow downcurved bill. The fourth toe can move sideways in turacos and the first and fourth backwards in cuckoos (zygodactylous). The family Cuculidae is represented in Vanuatu.

Cuckoos, Koels and Coucals *Cuculidae*
There are about 130 species in 34 genera in this family found throughout the world. They range in size from about 12 cm to 60 cm and most are attractively but rather plainly coloured with grey, brown, chestnut and black being predominant or more often a combination of these colours. However a few have striking, bold patterns of glossy violet, green or yellow. Many species have a characteristic call, which may be melodious whistling, a simple moderately loud 'chuck' or raucous noises. Several species call so often during the mating season that their monotony becomes tiresome and this has given rise to the epithet of 'brain-fever bird'. The well known call 'cuck-oo' of the common european Cuckoo Cuculus canorus is not heard in the Pacific islands but it is this springtime mating call from which the family name comes. Insects form the main diet of most cuckoos and they are among the few bird-species that regularly take hairy caterpillars.

The Cuculidae are best known for their practice of nest parasitism, duping other species into assuming the chores of incubation and of feeding their young. However, this practice is by no means limited to the Cuculidae nor is it the regular practice of all species in the family. The coucals build open cup-shaped nests and lay a clutch of 3-5 eggs and both adults incubate and raise the young. The parasitic breeding behaviour has been studied intensively and proved to be incredibly complex. Each female normally lays 4-5 eggs, sometimes many more, at about 48 hour intervals and the eggs are smaller in relation to body size than in the nesting cuckoos. Each one is deposited in a different nest of one species whose eggs most resemble her own. These are often insect eaters, usually songbirds, and are almost always smaller in size than the cuckoo. The female cuckoo watches prospective foster-parents building their nest and when the eggs are laid and the nest unguarded she takes one of the eggs in her bill, lays her own egg in the nest and flies off with the stolen egg which may be swallowed or dropped. As the incubation period of the cuckoo egg is only 12 to 13 days it may hatch before or simultaneously with those in the nest. Soon after hatching the naked, sightless, cuckoo fledgling ejects anything that it touches from the nest. It is structurally adapted, having a shallow hollow on its back, and wriggles beneath the egg or nestling and hoists it with some effort, legs braced and wings outspread, backwards over the edge of the nest. Disposing of all competition is of vital importance to the young cuckoo for it soon grows larger than its foster parents and needs all the food that would normally be brought to their own brood of 2 to 5 young. It is an amazing sight to see a tiny warbler or fantail feeding a huge baby cuckoo yet the instinct to rear the young in their nest is so strong that it overpowers any possible realisation that this young bird is not of their own kind. They faithfully feed and care for the imposter for the 20 to 23 days it takes for the young cuckoo to fly off and fend for itself.

There are only three species of cuckoos found in Vanuatu; two of them are resident and one a non-breeding regular visitor from New Zealand. All are so different that they cannot be mistaken for each other and none of them builds a nest or rears its own young.

77. Fan-tailed Cuckoo *Cacomantis pyrrhophanus schistaceigularis* PLATE 10
French name: Coucou à éventail

IDENTIFICATION
Length 24 to 25 cm, including 13 to 14 cm tail. A medium-sized cuckoo, the slender body, blackish above and rufous below, and conspicuous white markings on the long, but not obviously fan-shaped, tail are diagnostic. *Adult male:* head slate-grey; rest of upperparts dark slate-grey with or without slight gloss and tail feathers rippled with white along the edges. Throat grey; breast and belly rufous, undertail-coverts rufous to buff. Underside of tail heavily barred black and white. Iris: reddish-brown to bright red, eye-ring yellow. Bill: maxilla black, mandible pale brown, tip black. Legs and feet: pale yellow to yellow-brown. *Adult female:* similar to male but greyer above and paler below. *Immature:* very different to adult; upperparts dark grey-brown with ochre edges to feathers; underparts mottled pale grey and dark brown; throat and upper breast darker; tail shorter than in adult. Iris is reddish-ochre, bill and feet are brownish. There are intermediate phases in the changes to adult plumage.

DISTRIBUTION AND STATUS
Some authorities classify this species in the genus *Cuculus*. Several races of the Fan-tailed Cuckoo are found in Australia, New Guinea, New Caledonia, the Loyalty Islands, the Solomon Islands where, according to Mayr (1945), it is apparently a rare visitor from New Caledonia and Fiji where a less common sooty-black form occurs (Amadon, 1942b). The race *schistaceigularis* was found to be widespread in Vanuatu by Layard in the 1870s and it was still widespread and common when the Whitney and the Oxford University Expeditions were active in the 1920s and 1930s. It was recorded on Ureparapara, Vanua Lava, Gaua, Santo, Malo, Malakula, Ambrym, Paama, Lopevi, Epi, Emae, Nguna, Efate, Erromango, Aniwa, Tanna and Futuna. Diamond and Marshall (1976) note that it had also been recorded on Valua (Mota Lava). Medway and Marshall (1975) suggest that this species might be at least partly migratory within Vanuatu. Its range seems now to have contracted down to islands in the north where it is uncommon and it has been recorded by the author on Ureparapara, Vanua Lava, Santo, Ambae, Malakula and Ambrym.

FIELD NOTES
The Fan-tailed Cuckoo is mainly a bird of the lowland forest, secondary growth and open park-like country. It is solitary and leads a secluded and inconspicuous life, but attention is usually drawn to its presence by the whistling calls. This cuckoo is

characteristically seen sitting motionless on a low perch or turning its head to scan the surrounding country. It flies from time to time, either down to the ground to pick up some insect or to grab a caterpillar from a nearby leaf, often without landing. It generally flies just short distances through the foliage of the substage with strong fast wingbeats and short glides. On alighting the long tail is usually held slightly upwards and bobbed or fanned a little. The Fan-tailed Cuckoo is frequently mobbed by smaller birds and sometimes is even forced to fly from too aggressive an attack.

VOICE

Though generally not a vocal bird, its distinctive song is more often heard through the night and at dawn but it may also be delivered at any time of the day. The usual call is a shrill series of identical 2 or 3 syllabic whistles, somewhat mournful and sounding like 'torwee'. The first note is slow but each successive note increases in tempo and volume and is higher in pitch. This song is frequently monotonously repeated from a high tree or low perch. Also single whistling calls and strident short screams are uttered and a series of whistles descending the scale has been reported.

FOOD

Insects and their larvae are taken, including hairy caterpillars.

BREEDING

The host species of the Fan-tailed Cuckoo are usually small insectivorous birds like the Scarlet Robin *Petroica multicolor*, Fantails *Rhipidura* spp, Broad-billed Flycatcher *Myiagra caledonica*, Trillers *Lalage* spp and other songbird species. The dull white eggs marked with brown are laid from August to December/January; the clutch size is unknown.

78. Shining Bronze-Cuckoo   *Chrysococcyx lucidus layardi*   PLATE 10
Other name: Shining Cuckoo
French name: Coucou cuivré

IDENTIFICATION

Length about 16 cm. The smallest of the Vanuatu cuckoos, iridescent green above, barred below. *Adult male:* crown to mantle dull copper-bronze; back and wings bright bronze-green; primaries dark bronze; tail-feathers dark bronze-green with a dark subterminal band, lateral tail-feathers broadly banded black and white. Underparts white finely barred with glossy green; barring of throat is inconspicuous. The metallic-greenish sheen above is less pronounced in this race *(layardi)* than in others. Iris: light brown, eye-ring pale grey to whitish. Bill: black. Legs and feet: dark grey. *Adult female:* similar to male, but is duller above and the barring on the underparts is fainter. *Immature:* upperparts brownish to bronze with little green gloss or none and grey underparts practically without barring.

DISTRIBUTION AND STATUS

Formerly placed in the genus *Chalcites* this species is now classed as *Chrysococcyx* (Friedmann, 1968). Several different races of the Shining Bronze-Cuckoo occur in the Solomons (2 endemic races on Rennell and Bellona), the southwestern Pacific islands and in Australia and New Zealand (Mayr, 1932b). The Australian race *C. l. plagosus* is a regular migrant to mainland New Guinea and the Bismarck Is. (Beehler *et al*, 1986). The nominate race breeds in New Zealand and migrates northwards in the southern winter, from March to September, through Lord Howe and Norfolk Islands to the Bismarck Archipelago and the Solomons and irregularly to the east coast of Australia. This is one of the most remarkable flights of all migratory cuckoo species; a considerable journey, over about 3,000 km of the trackless Pacific Ocean, to be undertaken twice a year by a bird about 16 cm long. The race *layardi*, described above, ranges from New Caledonia, through the Loyalty Islands and Vanuatu to the Santa Cruz group. Its distribution has changed considerably since the last century. It was recorded as widespread in Vanuatu in the 1870s by Layard and in the 1920s and 1930s by the Whitney and the Oxford University expeditions (listed on Vanua Lava, Gaua, Santo, Malakula, Ambrym, Lopevi, Epi, Nguna, Emau, Erromango, Aniwa, and Futuna, though the birds observed on Futuna and Erromango may have been visitors, [Mayr, 1945]). By the 1960s it was apparently confined to the larger and species-rich islands of Santo, Malakula and Ambrym and uncommon there. A bird of this species was recorded for the first time on Efate on 21 May 1983 by Richard Pickering. It was observed in the grounds of the Manuro Club on the east coast. In this individual the 'barring was absent from the throat and the centre of the breast but dark elsewhere' perhaps indicating that 'it was an immature'. He suggests that *layardi* was now confined to Santo and that this bird was possibly on migration from New Zealand though 'May seems rather late for a bird of passage' (Naika 10:13). In the southwest Pacific islands the distribution of the Shining Bronze-Cuckoo seems to be closely related to that of the Fantail Warbler *Gerygone flavolateralis*, its favourite host-species.

FIELD NOTES

This handsome cuckoo frequents the true forest, secondary growth, open park-like country and also gardens in the lowlands and mountains but seems to be more numerous at lower or moderate altitudes. These inconspicuous birds are generally hard to observe, as they keep to the leafy parts of trees or shrubs, and are only discovered by their calling. Pairs or sometimes small courting groups, generally of one female and two or three males have been seen between November and January following each other and engaging in courtship display, repeating their high-pitched whistles frequently. Their flight is swift and undulating.

VOICE

The Shining Bronze-Cuckoo is normally rather quiet except during the mating season when the rich, full whistling series, different from that of any other bird in Vanuatu, is heard frequently. The call is described as a 'series of double notes, upward slurs, often repeated, followed by fewer downward slurs, the whole in a musical whistle with ventriloquistic effects' (Oliver in Mayr, 1945). The elements are a high-pitched whistle ending in a long note, 'toeee' or 'toweee' and generally repeated 4 to 7 times. The birds may call from the dense foliage of treetops or from an exposed branch.

FOOD

They mainly take insects and their larvae, including hairy caterpillars.

BREEDING

This cuckoo is parasitic on a considerable number of species including fantails, white-eyes and other small birds. In Vanuatu the Shining Bronze-Cuckoo usually chooses the domed nests of the Fantail Warbler. There is some doubt about the method of placing the egg in the nest which has only a small entrance hole. It was believed for years that the cuckoo laid the egg on the ground and put it in the nest with her bill but careful observation has shown that when a cuckoo is seen with an egg in its bill it is carrying off one of the eggs of the host species. Cuckoos may lay their eggs in a matter of seconds and it could be possible that the cuckoo props herself against the small nest entrance with wings and tail spread for support and ejects her egg into the nest. New Zealand birds of this species, laying in the domed nests of wrens or warblers have been observed to force their way into the nest, putting the head through the opposite wall, lay the egg and then fly off through the hole they have made. The owner of the nest returns and unconcernedly repairs the damage. The cuckoo egg is pale olive-brown to bronze-brown and the clutch size is unknown. Eggs are laid during September to December/January.

79. Long-tailed New Zealand Cuckoo *Eudynamis taitensis* PLATE 10
French name: Koel à longue queue

IDENTIFICATION AND FIELD NOTES
Length 40 cm, including tail of about 24 cm. A fairly large, slender, long-tailed cuckoo which could perhaps be confused with an immature goshawk but it is of less sturdy build. *Adult male:* upperparts dark brown barred with rufous; wings and back spotted with white; head streaked rufous with conspicuous white stripes above and below the eye, a dark line through the eye and a dark moustachial stripe. Underparts white to buff variably marked with longitudinal blackish streaks, particularly on the breast; thigh feathers are long, undertail-coverts whitish barred dark brown. The long tail is graduated with outer feathers much shorter than the central ones, all feathers are barred blackish-brown and rufous and tipped white. Iris: pale yellow. Bill: stout and strongly arched; maxilla blackish-brown; mandible pale horn-colour. Legs and feet: olive-green, soles yellowish. *Adult female:* similar to male but slightly smaller and more rufous. *Immature:* conspicuously marked with larger white spots on head, back and wings; underparts buffish-rufous with variable dark streaks.

These migratory cuckoos may be encountered on any island and in any wooded habitat or scrubland. They keep to the seclusion of leafy trees and shrubs, and as they are generally silent in their winter quarters, the birds are often hard to observe. Falla *et al* (1981) describe the call as a harsh, piercing screech 'zzwheesht' and state that it is used at night on migration, but this has not been noted in Vanuatu. Usually solitary, the Long-tailed Cuckoo is frequently mobbed and put to flight by smaller songbirds, in a similar way to raptors. Insects are probably the main food but it also eats lizards, young birds and their eggs and has even been known to kill adult birds, as large as a thrush. Flight is fairly rapid and straight with continuous wingbeats interspersed by occasional short glides; the long tail is conspicuous.

DISTRIBUTION AND STATUS
New Zealand is the only country in which the Long-tailed Cuckoo is known to breed. It returns in October and is parasitic on a number of native and introduced species in

North, South and Stewart Islands. It begins to move north in February/March and ranges over much of the Pacific and has been recorded in the Cook Islands, the Tuamotu Archipelago and the Marquesas in the east, the Marshall and Caroline Islands in the north and Tonga, Fiji, Samoa, New Caledonia, the Solomons and Bismarck Archipelago in the west. It is a rather rare visitor to Vanuatu and there are no records from the Banks Islands. The birds may arrive about April and depart in September, though some individuals could remain longer. Richard Pickering noted that a Long-tailed Cuckoo was seen at the end of July 1985 'between Eton and Rentapao on the south coast of Efate' by a visiting birdwatcher from Australia (Naika 19:10).

Order STRIGIFORMES
This order comprises about 134 species divided between 25 genera in 2 worldwide families, the typical owls and hawk owls in the family Strigidae, with about 124 species, and 10 species of barn owls in the family Tytonidae, which includes the only representative found in Vanuatu. Owls, the nocturnal birds of prey, form one of the most distinctive orders of birds. Their obvious characteristics are the large head, short hooked bill directed downwards with a soft cere at the base, the large eyes set in some form of facial disc, soft plumage and short tail. Some species have conspicuous ear tufts. The legs are usually long, typically feathered or partly feathered, the feet are powerful with large talons for catching and tearing prey and the outer toe is reversible but directed laterally at rest. The eyes are directed forwards giving the birds binocular vision but the owl has to turn its head to look sideways and some species have the ability to rotate the head through a maximum of about 270°. Like most nocturnal birds the owls are cryptically coloured, usually with a soft, disruptive pattern of grey, brown, black and white. They are therefore difficult to detect and identify as they normally stay well concealed in tree hollows or thick foliage during the daytime.

Owls vary considerably in size from 60 to 75 cm in the Eagle Owls, genus *Bubo*, to only 12 to 14 cm in the Least Pygmy Owl *Glaucidium minutissimum*, the smallest of the family. Whatever the size, the hooked bill together with the powerful grasping feet identify owls as predators and everything about them seems to be designed for hunting at night; the eyes and ears operating as an incredibly efficient prey detecting system. The eyes, actually far larger than they appear from the outside, collect dim light and resolve it into a relatively bright image on the highly sensitive retina. Even though owls cannot see in absolute darkness, they can still see well in conditions of extremely low illumination that would leave a human helpless. Contrary to popular belief, owls are not blind during the daytime and a few species, like the big, white Snowy Owl *Nyctea scandiaca* of the northern tundra which perforce hunts in the continuous daylight north of the Arctic Circle in summer, are partly or entirely diurnal. The hearing of owls is also acute and some species appear to hunt more by sound than sight, their ears, though hidden under their feathers, being highly perceptive to the small noises, rustles and squeaks made by their prey. The characteristic facial disc gathers and concentrates sound-waves, much like the parabolic reflector used by a sound technician, which increases their binaural efficiency in locating prey. The noiseless flight of most owls, which supposedly helps them to pounce on unsuspecting prey is more likely a refinement to increase their hearing power. The flight and contour feathers are covered with fine filaments, which deaden the noise as the wings beat through the air. The few diurnal and fishing species of owls lack this adaptation and their facial discs are not so well developed.

Most owls feed on small mammals, birds (including smaller owls), reptiles, amphibians and insects but there are some impressive owls in Africa and southern Asia which catch mainly fish and crabs. Like other birds of prey, owls do not chew their food but tear off big pieces or swallow it whole. The acid, gastric juice can dissolve the softer parts but is unable to liquefy larger bones, fur and feathers and these indigestible remains are compacted into a firm 'pellet' in the stomach and regurgitated. Owls usually bring their prey back to a favourite roost, often used for long periods, and large quantities of pellets may accumulate at these roosts and at nest sites. The bones, skulls, beetle-elytra, legs and other remains in the pellets can often be identified, yielding interesting information about the owl's diet, even occasionally leading to the discovery of some animal, hitherto unknown, within the locality. Owls are mainly cavity nesters using hollow trees, holes in cliffs or buildings or they may dig a burrow. A few species appropriate abandoned nests of other species or nest on the ground in the open on top of a slight rise. Little nest material is used, if any, and the clutch varies from 1-7 or more light coloured eggs. The call-notes of owls are diagnostic. In some species the male and female have different notes. Their cries, which vary from a soft, pleasing trilling to strange, eerie hooting or wailing are possibly responsible for their unsavoury reputation. Owls are often regarded with a mixture of fear and to some people with superstitious beliefs, they are birds of sorcery and ill omen.

Barn Owls and allies   *Tytonidae*

Barn owls differ from the typical owls in having a heart-shaped facial disc with a dark edge and long legs which are usually completely feathered down to the feet. In grassland species the feathers are shorter and sparser near the lower tarsus and in some reduced to bristles or almost bare. The eyes are dark and relatively small; wings are long with a rounded tip and the tail rather short. Another peculiar feature is the comb, serrations on the claw of the middle toe, which probably assists grooming and is found elsewhere only in herons Ardeidae *and goatsuckers* Camprimulgidae. *Eight of the 10 species in the family Tytonidae belong to the genus* Tyto *which includes the cosmopolitan Barn Owl found throughout Vanuatu.*

80. Barn Owl   *Tyto alba*   PLATE 5
French name: Effraie des clochers   or locally: Chouette
Bislama name: Hoknaet

IDENTIFICATION
Length 31 to 34cm, the female is slightly larger. A very light coloured owl with distinct, heart-shaped facial disc, slender legs and upright stance. *Adult male and female:* upperparts ash-grey mottled with buff and with numerous fine dark lines near the tips of the feathers and white and blackish spots immediately below; tail pale grey with brownish-grey bars and fine flecking. Underparts silky-white, more or less

spotted with dark brown; undertail white. The prominent white facial disc is edged buff on the upper half and blackish-brown on the lower half and has dark streaks from the inner corners of the eyes, commonly called 'tears'. Iris: blackish-brown. Bill: horn-colour to pale brown. Legs are covered with short, fur-like white feathers, usually reduced to sparse bristles on the lower parts; feet are dusky-grey to pale brown. *Immature:* similar to adult, may have heavier spotting on the breast. The Barn Owl on the wing appears to be all white, especially when seen at dusk.

DISTRIBUTION AND STATUS

The Barn Owl is cosmopolitan and about 36 races have been described. There are numerous races in the Australasian region. *T.a.lulu* is common in Fiji and *T.a.delicatula* is found throughout Australia. The race *interposita*, described above, is found in the Santa Cruz group and on almost all islands in Vanuatu though there are no records from the Torres group, Vanua Lava, Gaua, Paama, Lopevi, Tongariki and Makura. Birds from southern Vanuatu (Erromango, Tanna and Aneityum) have whiter plumage and may belong to the race *lifuensis* (Amadon, 1942b), which occurs in the Loyalty Islands and New Caledonia. A common species, particularly in open park-like country.

FIELD NOTES

They may be found at all altitudes and in almost any habitat from the forest to suburban gardens but are more numerous in open, lightly wooded or cultivated country, along the forest edge, in pasture land, plantations, and around villages. They are normally active only at night. In the daytime they are seldom seen abroad, remaining well hidden in leafy trees, tree hollows, caves or any other dark roosting spot, no doubt to avoid the bright light and to avoid being found and mobbed by smaller birds. Barn Owls are not often seen at night though sometimes car headlights will reveal a white bird sitting on a post along a country road or flying away from the roadside. When hunting they fly low over the ground or listen from low perches, paddock-posts or trees, waiting for prey to cross an open space, then they glide or drop silently on to the victim. Because of their occasional attacks on young domestic chickens and other poultry, Barn Owls are generally regarded with suspicion by village people but their damaging role is over emphasised. Actually owls do a great deal more good than harm in Vanuatu for they are one of the few predators able to kill rats and mice. These rodents take a far higher toll of poultry than owls and cause considerable damage to crops in plantations and gardens.

Barn Owls may be seen singly but pairs occupy territories all year round, use the same roosts by day and may return year after year to the same nest site. When disturbed, they react by standing bolt upright looking very long and slender but when escape is impossible, like other species in the genus *Tyto*, they crouch, fluff their feathers, spread their wings and swaying slowly from side to side, snap their bills and hiss.

VOICE

The Barn Owl calls infrequently, the typical call being a shrill, long drawn-out, weird screech. It also has a variety of chuckling notes and one like a snore. Anger or irritation is expressed by clacking the bill and hissing.

FOOD
Around plantations and gardens it feeds mainly on rats and mice. The diet also includes beetles, moths and other night-flying insects, nocturnal reptiles like geckos, and small birds. Any prey that is too big to be swallowed whole is torn up and eaten piece by piece. The Barn Owl hunts more by sound than sight and can locate prey in total darkness.

NEST AND BREEDING
The Barn Owl usually nests in tree-holes, in hollows formed by the tangled aerial roots of large strangling-fig trees and also in caves. The clutch of 3-5 chalky-white eggs (43 × 32 mm) are laid on fine wood-debris or directly on the floor, sometimes with a few leaves for lining. Incubation begins with the first egg and the female incubates for about 28 to 32 days. The eggs usually hatch at intervals of a few days resulting in young of different ages and sizes in the nest. The young remain in the nest for about 7 weeks and are cared for and fed by both parents. They become independent after a further 3 to 5 weeks and scatter widely. If threatened, young birds in the nest clap their bills and if that is not sufficient to repel a possible attack the nestlings may lie on their backs and point their claws towards the intruder. The breeding season is generally from April to October but a nest with fully feathered young has been found on Efate in January. It breeds in New Caledonia from May to August but in Australia it may breed in any month depending on food supply.

Order APODIFORMES
The family of swifts and swiftlets, Apodidae is grouped with the crested swifts, family Hemiprocnidae, and the tiny hummingbirds, family Trochilidae, in the order Apodiformes. Although the 3 families are so different in appearance and aerial skills, the structural characteristics which they share have led most ornithologists to believe that they are more closely related to each other than to any other group of birds. Swifts and hummingbirds have short legs, small feet, similar wing structure and rapid wing movements and all are among the most accomplished of fliers. They have 10 rectrices, the large quill feathers of the tail, whereas most other birds have 12. Swifts are cosmopolitan but hummingbirds are restricted to the Americas with the greater number, about 235 species, in South America. Only swiftlets, part of the family Apodidae are represented in Vanuatu though some of the larger migratory swifts could occur as vagrants on their journeys to and from northern Asia and Australia.

Swifts and Swiftlets   *Apodidae*
About 83 species of swifts and swiftlets in 18 genera are scattered throughout the world mostly in tropical and subtropical regions. The few species that breed in the temperate northern hemisphere migrate to warmer regions in late summer. Swifts and swiftlets as the name implies are exceptionally fast fliers, though naturally not all species reach the estimated 150 km/h of the large spine-tailed swifts from eastern Asia. Swifts and swiftlets are the most aerial of birds, feeding, drinking and gathering nest material on the wing, and are presumed never to land except at their nest or roost. As some cave-swiftlets are frequently encountered far from caves in the twilight hours they may even sleep on the wing. The swifts and swiftlets vary

in size from 9.5 to 25 cm in length with extremes in weight being represented by the White-bellied Swiftlet Collocalia esculenta at 7.5 g to the Purple Needletail Hirundapus celebensis at 180 g (Campbell and Lack, 1985). Most species are dark coloured in greys, browns and black sometimes glossed with metallic blues and greens with lighter or white rumps and underparts. The sexes are alike; they have a streamlined body, long, narrow wings which are curved back into a graceful crescent and usually a short tail, though in some species it is forked and in others the shafts of the feathers are extended as spines. The flattened, slightly downcurved bill appears tiny but an enormous gape opens back to behind the eye, for catching insects in flight. All species have deep-set eyes with a ridge of feathers just in front.

As their short legs and small feet do not allow them to perch on branches or settle on the ground they may roost clinging upright to vertical surfaces propped up by their stiff tails. With their strong, sharp claws they can cling to the most unlikely of surfaces; vertical cliffs, cave walls, trunks of trees, house walls, and chimneys. They nest in similar places. All species have one peculiarity, they glue their nests into place with sticky saliva and the salivary glands of both sexes are greatly enlarged during the breeding season. The nests are built of moss, lichen, plant fibres and other light materials which are glued together and against the nest support with varying amounts of hardened saliva. Swifts have a grasping foot with the first 2 toes opposing 3 and 4 but the grasping motion is lateral inward allowing them to collect nest material and hold it while it is being glued. Campbell and Lack (1985) note that when the toes are not grasping they lie together, as they do in museum specimens, giving rise to the common misconception that in swifts all the toes point forwards. The composition of the nesting material is diagnostic for most species. Some of the Malaysian and Indonesian swiftlets make their nests entirely of saliva and these are the nests collected and used for the famous 'bird's nest soup' of the orient. Most species lay one or 2 elongated eggs, only a few 4-6. Depending on the species, the young hatch after 16 to 20 days of incubation, but do not leave the nest for a further 4 to 6 weeks until their flight feathers are fully developed and they are capable of sure, sustained flight. Swifts live entirely on insects which they catch in flight and they drink by skimming low over the surface of rivers, reservoirs, lakes and ponds.

The 3 species occurring in Vanuatu are all cave-swiftlets. They were formerly all classed as Collocalia but a review of echolocation and systematics in swiftlets by Medway and Pye (1977) led to alterations in generic and specific names. One is now the single species in the genus Collocalia and 2 are in the largest group of 12 species in the genus Aerodramus. Their flight has not the breath-taking rapidity of the larger swifts but is much slower and when feeding it is more erratic and bat-like. Swiftlets are often mistaken for swallows but though resembling them superficially, they are not closely related and the different flight patterns are diagnostic; between series of rapid, shallow wingbeats, they glide intermittently on outstretched narrow, sickle-shaped wings and do not fold the wings against the body like swallows. At rest the folded wings extend beyond the tip of the tail. They have short weak legs and if grounded they can just shuffle forwards slowly but a few wingbeats will generally lift them into the air again. They most often nest in colonies, sometimes by the hundreds and all 3 species glue their scoop-shaped nests to a vertical surface in caves. The Uniform (Vanikoro) Swiftlet and the White-rumped Swiftlet are echolocating species and nest generally in the darker parts of caves. The ecological separation of the 3 species is not fully understood. The 2 common species, the Uniform Swiftlet and the White-bellied (Glossy) Swiftlet, have a similar range and there seems also to be a habitat overlap but altitude could be involved to some degree and the larger Uniform Swiftlet apparently feeds at a greater height above the ground.

81. White-bellied Swiftlet *Collocalia esculenta uropygialis* PLATE 11
Other name: Glossy Swiftlet
French name: Martinet soyeux

IDENTIFICATION
Length about 9.5 cm. This is the smallest of the Vanuatu swiftlets, a delicate species, glossy blue-black and pure white. *Adult male and female:* upperparts black with bluish-green gloss, rump pure white; tail black, almost square with a shallow notch. Chin, throat and upper breast dark grey; lower breast and abdomen white; undertail-coverts black, some feathers fringed with white. Iris: dark brown. Bill, legs and feet: black. *Immature:* similar plumage pattern to adult with greyish-white and less gloss. It differs from the White-rumped Swiftlet in the slightly smaller size, more glossy appearance and distinctive white belly.

DISTRIBUTION AND STATUS
The White-bellied Swiftlet is very widespread and common from Malaysia to the Philippines, Indonesia, New Guinea, and the Solomons and it has been recorded as a vagrant and 'possibly a regular summer visitor in small numbers' in northeastern Australia (Pizzey, 1980). The various races differ in plumage mainly by the extent of white on the underparts or the lack of the white rump. The race *uropygialis*, described above, ranges from Vanikoro and Utupua in the Santa Cruz group to New Caledonia and the Loyalty Islands and is common in Vanuatu. It has been recorded throughout the group but there are no records from Makura and Tongariki (Medway, 1966).

FIELD NOTES
The ubiquitous 'glossy' swiftlets may be found hawking in a variety of habitats and at any altitude. They mostly feed fairly low down among trees in open patches of the forest and along the forest edge but also over open country, in gardens, villages and plantations and even river gorges and the shore. They flit about lightly in the most erratic manner and at times in flocks they utter excited, high-pitched twitters. They are highly gregarious and flocks of up to 30 or more individuals spend most of the daylight hours together hawking for insects. The birds can circle slowly or glide almost continuously, interrupted by brief bursts of shallow wingbeats. The flocks may feed in loose open order but at times, especially in the evening and close to the nest sites, the birds gather together into a careering group. Like other swiftlet species, the birds often congregate in areas where the maximum movements of insects occur in warm, humid rising air just before rain. Almost entirely aerial, the swiftlets apparently alight only on cave walls or at their nests.

VOICE
They call most often in feeding flocks when an intermittent or continuous jumbled series of high-pitched, twittering notes may be heard.

FOOD
They feed in flight on flying insects, including flies, winged ants and termites, small butterflies, moths and beetles which are caught in the wide-open mouth.

NEST AND BREEDING
They usually breed in colonies, sometimes in large numbers. The nests are built in the

204 SWIFTS AND SWIFTLETS

Nests of the White-bellied Swiftlet are glued with saliva to vertical surfaces in caves, in tree holes or even amid the aerial roots of giant fig trees

lighter entrances of caves, hollow trees, among the roots of large banyan trees, on overhanging cliffs or other more open locations and even in abandoned buildings. In some instances bats have been found at the same site and a single overhang may contain colonies of birds at one side and of mammals at the other. The nests are tiny, deep cups made of plant fibres, moss and some feathers cemented together but not covered with the bird's saliva, which are glued to the nest-site walls either singly or in clusters of 3 or more. Usually only one white egg is laid (16 × 12 mm). These swiftlets seem to have an irregular or an extended breeding season. Eggs are apparently laid from the middle of June onwards but all stages from eggs to chicks have been found in large colonies from July to February. Both parents share nesting duties.

82. White-rumped Swiftlet   *Aerodramus spodiopygius*   PLATE 11
Other names: Grey-rumped Swiftlet, Grey Swiftlet
French name: Martinet à croupion blanc

IDENTIFICATION
Length about 10.5 cm. A dull-coloured swiftlet with whitish rump, slightly smaller than the Uniform (Vanikoro) Swiftlet. *Adult male and female:* dull black above with a pale greyish-white band on the rump. Greyish below, darker on the breast and abdomen. Tail has a slight central notch. Iris: dark brown. Bill: black. Legs and feet: blackish. *Immature:* similar but paler than adult. This species differs from the

White-bellied (Glossy) Swiftlet by the dull colour and the absence of white on the underparts and from the Uniform (Vanikoro) Swiftlet by the whitish bar on the rump.

DISTRIBUTION AND STATUS

The White-rumped Swiftlet occurs in a number of races and from sea-level to 1,000m or more in northeastern Australia, the Solomons and on islands with caves through Melanesia east to Samoa, Tonga and Fiji. The race *leucopygia*, described above, is found in the Santa Cruz Islands, the Loyalty Islands, New Caledonia and Vanuatu. In the past century the range of the White-rumped Swiftlet has contracted down to islands in the north of the archipelago. It was found to be widespread by Layard in 1870 when it was recorded on Ureparapara, Santo, Malo, Malakula, Ambrym, Epi, Emae, Efate, Erromango, Tanna and Aneityum. In the 1920s and 1930s (Whitney and Oxford Expeditions) its range had been reduced to 5 islands and by the 1960s it was found only on Malo and on the west coast of Santo where it was uncommon. Richard Pickering writing in 1983 noted that he had not seen this species in Vanuatu (Naika 3:4). A note by John Edge of 'up to a dozen White-rumped Swiftlets *(Collocalia spodiopygia)* at any time' during 3 months on Efate in 1988 may refer to the White-bellied (Glossy) Swiftlet which also has a white rump but is common on all islands and is not mentioned in the article (Naika 29:27).

FIELD NOTES

These swiftlets may be found in feeding flocks in almost any habitat; over the forest canopy, along the seashore, scrubland, cultivated land, villages and also under and between trees. They fly from low over the ground to the forest canopy or higher and, like other swiftlets, apparently alight only at their roosts or nest sites. Flight is rapid with intermittent glides, but more erratic when hawking insects. When not feeding and in a steady wind, long curving glides are interrupted only by brief bursts of shallow wingbeats.

VOICE

In flight various high-pitched squealing and short twittering notes are uttered, and a pleasant warble 'tooweet-tooweet-ziweet'. In dark breeding caves, sharp short clicking sounds are used for echolocation; the echoes received from the walls and any obstacles and the sound of wingbeats allowing the birds to orientate themselves accurately in the nesting colonies.

FOOD

They feed and drink only while on the wing. Flying insects are captured in the enormous gape.

NEST AND BREEDING

The White-rumped Swiftlet normally nests in the darkest parts of caves where it navigates by echolocation but the nest may also be built under an overhanging cliff or in an abandoned house or cellar. The nests are small cups of plant fibres, moss and lichen or other fine plant material all cemented together and glued to the support, singly or in small groups, with congealed saliva. One or 2 white eggs are laid (16 × 10mm). Probably both parents incubate the eggs, feed and guard the young. This swiftlet sometimes associates with the White-bellied Swiftlet in the same cave. The breeding season is probably from October to January/February.

83. Uniform Swiftlet   *Aerodramus vanikorensis vanikorensis*   PLATE 11
Other names: Vanikoro Swiftlet, Island Swiftlet, Lowland Swiftlet
French name: Martinet de Vanikoro

IDENTIFICATION
Length 12.4 to 13 cm. The largest swiftlet in Vanuatu, a nondescript species slightly darker above than below. *Adult male and female:* upperparts uniformly sooty-black with a faint greenish gloss; tail slightly notched. Throat silvery-grey; rest of underparts dark grey. Iris: blackish-brown. Bill: blackish-brown. Legs and feet: light brown, toes dark brown. *Immature:* similar to adult.

DISTRIBUTION AND STATUS
The Uniform Swiftlet is also found in the Philippines, Sulawesi, New Guinea and Micronesia, where it is abundant on most islands though the Mariana Islands population is endangered (Pratt *et al*, 1987). In Melanesia, the race *vanikorensis*, described above, is found throughout the Santa Cruz group, on certain of the Solomon Islands and in Vanuatu where it is fairly common on all islands (Mayr, 1937b, Medway, 1966 and 1975).

FIELD NOTES
The Uniform Swiftlet may occur anywhere in the islands from beaches and mangroves inland though it is seen more in open habitats than the other swiftlets and is common only in the lowland and at moderate altitudes. It is regularly seen near suitable nesting sites. The birds may forage low over the ground but generally fly much higher than the smaller swiftlets, up to 30 m or more above the ground. The feeding flocks usually fly in loose open order, their erratic flight and alternating intermittent glides with short bursts of flapping being typical of swiftlets. They may also be seen circling slowly or rising in thermals.

VOICE
Calls in flight may be shrill twittering notes or a long warble and inside the dark caves, a series of sharp echolocating clicks, help the swiftlets to orientate themselves accurately and avoid obstacles.

FOOD
Flying insects including winged ants and termites, flies, small moths and beetles are caught in the wide open gape. Like all swifts they drink by skimming low over the water surface.

NEST AND BREEDING
The Uniform Swiftlet nests in the dark parts of true caves. Pratt *et al* (1987) note that in Micronesia it also nests in abandoned gun emplacements. The nest, which may be on its own or in a group, is a small, shallow bracket-shaped cup composed of congealed saliva reinforced with plant fibres and other fine particles of plants, moss and flecks of bark bound together and generally completely covered with saliva. (For further details please refer to Medway, 1975). Usually 2 white eggs are laid and both adults probably incubate and feed the young. The breeding season is from August to December/February.

Order CORACIIFORMES
The kingfishers, family Alcedinidae, together with the bee-eaters, family Meropidae, the rollers, Coracidae and 7 other families including the hoopoes and hornbills are grouped in the order Coraciiformes. One of their structural peculiarities, clearly evident in the kingfishers and bee-eaters is for the 3rd and 4th toes to be joined together for much of their length, a condition known as syndactyl. Many of the birds in this order have strikingly beautiful plumage, crests and large bills and some have long tails. Most are partly arboreal and they generally nest in holes, some excavating long burrows. Only the kingfisher family, Alcedinidae, occurs in Vanuatu.

Kingfishers *Alcedinidae*
Kingfishers are a well marked family of cosmopolitan distribution, only absent from the polar regions and some oceanic islands. Classification of kingfishers has caused much controversy in the past but about 86 living species are now recognised in 14 genera. The majority, about 60 species, are found from central and eastern Asia to Australia in the south and the Pacific islands in the east. Kingfishers occur in the New Guinea region in a greater variety of forms than anywhere else in the world. The two best known representatives of the Alcedinidae family are without doubt the small jewel-like, and most widespread, Kingfisher Alcedo atthis *and the giant of the family the Laughing Kookaburra* Dacelo novaeguineae *of Australia. Kingfishers are notable for their upright posture and habit of sitting motionless on an exposed lookout. They are thickset birds with large heads, short necks, and comparatively short tails. A few have elongated tail feathers or erectile crests. The distinctive bill is long, heavy and pointed, the legs short and the feet small and relatively weak. When moving on the ground the kingfishers do not walk but hop stiffly. Most kingfishers are brightly coloured, mainly in blues and greens but also orange-rufous and chestnut with contrasting patches, bars or spots of red and white and some have a conspicuous red or yellow bill. The sexes are usually alike or similar but the females are somewhat duller in colour.*

Kingfishers vary considerably in size; the range in Australia varying from the Little Kingfisher Alcedo pusilla *at only 11 cm to the Laughing Kookaburra (45 cm). Their calls are loud and harsh and in some species even disturbing. There may be a succession of harsh rattles, a wild crazy laughter or in the small species a sharp, shrill whistling. The flight of kingfishers is swift, strong and direct; wings are rather short and rounded and a succession of rapid wingbeats may be followed by a short glide and then another series of wingbeats, especially fast in the smaller species. The flight is seldom long-sustained, except in the migratory species. All kingfishers are solitary feeders, watching from an exposed perch or hovering then diving for fish or pouncing on reptiles, amphibians, small mammals and birds or darting out to catch flying insects. They stun or kill their prey by beating it against a perch with their long bill before swallowing it whole, usually beginning with the head. A few also feed on worms and snails. The indigestible parts of their food including bones of animals, fish scales, fur or feathers and insect remains are regurgitated in the form of neat pellets. All kingfishers are cavity nesters, digging holes in banks, rotten trees or termite nests. They excavate their burrows by chiselling with their beaks and scraping out the loose pieces with their feet.*

Though all kingfishers are alike in most of their essential features they may be broadly divided into 3 subfamilies: the smallest group, 9 species of wholly aquatic-feeding kingfishers Cerylinae; the mainly aquatic-feeding kingfishers Alcedininae *(22 species); and the more primitive tree-kingfishers* Daceloninae *(55 species), many of which are terrestrial feeders.*

Of the fishing-kingfishers, the Cerylinae have generally duller or pied plumage with the primaries barred or spotted with white and in all species the colour of the underparts differs between sexes. The Alcedininae, which include the European Kingfisher and the Little Kingfisher, are rather small, very bright, often brilliantly, coloured, with a strong dagger-shaped bill which is compressed laterally, and a very short tail. Almost all species dwell along the banks of freshwater or brackish rivers, small forest streams or lakes. Their food consists of fish, crustaceans and water insects, obtained by plunging from a perch which might be a stick projecting from the water or a bare overhanging branch. The nest is excavated in a river bank or steep slope and the tunnel extends back horizontally from a few centimetres to 3 m and ends in an oval nesting chamber where 3-6 mostly white eggs are laid on the bare floor. A few kingfishers lay as many as 8 eggs. No nest-lining material is used and as they do not practise nest-sanitation in the burrows, the young are raised on a putrefying layer of droppings, food scraps, the remains of fish and insects and the carapaces of crabs. Both parents incubate and feed the young, the incubation period varying from 18 to 24 days, and the young remain in the nest for 3 to 4 weeks after hatching. They are blind and naked at hatching but after only a few days start growing feathers. Each feather is protected from exrement and other foul material in the nest-chamber by a waxy sheath which is retained until just before the young leave the nest. These plastic-like envelopes give the nestlings a strange bristly appearance as if they were covered with spines. Usually the adults remain with the young for some time after they leave the nest, feeding them until they have acquired enough skill to catch prey for themselves. None of the aquatic-feeding 'fishing-kingfishers' occurs in Vanuatu; the nearest is found in the Solomons and 2 species occur in Australia.

The forest or tree-kingfishers (Daceloninae) are a large and varied group. Most species are much larger in size than the fishing-kingfishers and have a broader more flattened bill. Many of the species live far from water, hunting in the forest and savannah for their prey. When hunting they may dart out in pursuit of flying insects like flycatchers or pounce on their prey like shrikes. Others frequent streams and feed in part at least on aquatic prey. Their nest is always in a hollow, either in a decaying tree-trunk or dug out of a tree-termite nest or in some species in steep banks usually along water courses. Their call-notes are loud, harsh, even weird and distressing and are often repeated. The largest group of tree-kingfishers (about 35 species) are in the genus Halcyon *and are primarily woodland birds not associated with aquatic habits.*

Two species are represented in Vanuatu: the White-collared Kingfisher is widespread and common; the Chestnut-bellied Kingfisher is more local and less numerous. Both species exist together on many of the northern islands but there is only a slight habitat overlap. It is apparent that the White-collared Kingfisher is the more generalised species with a broad habitat tolerance found mainly in more open and modified habitats, whilst the Chestnut-bellied Kingfisher is primarily a forest dweller, rarely encountered away from large tracts of forest or thick secondary growth, and does not penetrate agricultural areas.

84. White-collared Kingfisher   *Halcyon chloris*   PLATES 12, 18
French name: L'Alcyon à collier   or locally: Martin-pêcheur
Bislama name: Nasiko

IDENTIFICATION
Length 22.5 to 23 cm. A medium-sized kingfisher, blue and green above and white

below, variably washed with rufous or buff. *Adult male:* head markings are distinctive; crown greenish-blue, superciliary stripe (above the eye) white or washed ochre, a black band from the base of the bill through the eye encircles the crown and is separated from the greenish-blue mantle by a broad white or cinnamonish collar extending from the throat and breast; wings and tail bright blue. The nape frequently has a white or buffish spot which may or may not be visible. Underparts entirely white or washed ochre on flanks and belly. Iris: brown. Bill: black, base of the lower mandible light horn-coloured. Legs and feet: dark greyish-brown. *Adult female:* like male but more greenish (bottle-green) above. In populations with buff or rufous in the plumage males tend to have more on the eyestripe, nuchal-collar and the flanks, than the females. *Immature:* slightly smaller and much duller in colour than the adults, the breast feathers are edged with dark grey and wing feathers edged ochre giving a scaly or mottled appearance. Adult plumage is achieved during the second year. The bill is shorter than in the adult with a whitish tip. According to Mayr (1945) 5 races are recognisable in Vanuatu. They differ mainly in the amount of rufous-ochre in the plumage. For example, in the Torres race the belly is pure white whereas the race from Tanna has a more or less reddish-brown belly. The races, from the whitest and lightest, are described as follows:

H. c. torresiana (Mayr, 1931a), Torres Islands, – very bright bluish or greenish above and pure white below.

H. c. santoensis (Mayr, 1931a), northern Vanuatu including the Banks Islands and

H. c. juliae (Heine), central Vanuatu, Ambae, to Malakula and Efate, – intermediate, the flanks more or less washed with ochre but otherwise white below.

H. c. erromangae (Mayr, 1938), Erromango, Aneityum, – flanks and abdomen in the male washed with pale ochre.

H. c. tannensis (Sharpe), Tanna, – male deep ochre below. (Mayr, 1931a).

DISTRIBUTION AND STATUS

The White-collared Kingfisher is one of the most widely distributed kingfishers in the world. Its range extends from the Red Sea along the coast of India and through Indonesia to Australia and the southwest Pacific islands to Samoa. About 45 races have been described, though there is uncertainty about some which show only minor variations in size and colour. The White-collared Kingfisher is the more conspicuous and common of the 2 Vanuatu kingfishers. It has been recorded from all islands, even the smallest.

FIELD NOTES

This striking blue and white kingfisher occurs singly or in pairs from the coasts to the mountains. It may be found close to water or in dry areas, in almost any type of savannah-like country and more rarely in the deep forest. It can be seen perching, often conspicuously, on a bare branch, post or telephone wire but usually reveals its presence by its penetrating calls. The White-collared Kingfisher frequents the sea-shore, mangrove swamps, rivers, and creeks, forest clearings and the forest edge, plantations and trees in villages and gardens. During the breeding season at least, each pair occupies a loosely defined territory which varies in size in the different types of habitat. In suitable habitats there tends to be a high population density and a favoured stretch of coast will often have a pair of kingfishers every few hundred metres. In

Plastic-like sheaths, which protect the feathers from excrement and the rotting remains of food that foul the nesting burrow, give the young White-collared Kingfishers a bristly appearance

Vanuatu the White-collared Kingfisher feeds mainly on large insects and lizards caught in typical tree-kingfisher manner. Only birds living near the coast, rivers or lakes also take crabs and other aquatic prey. The kingfisher spends much of its time perching and waiting for prey and a number of favourite lookout perches are used by an individual. Along the coast whenever mudflats and reefs become uncovered at low tide these kingfishers can be regularly observed sitting on a projecting stick, coral rock, or branch overhanging the shore waiting for crabs and small fish. The bird will sit for hours staring down, head occasionally bobbing. When suitable prey appears the bird dives down in a flash, seizes and carries it back to the perch in the bill and if large or active, it is dashed a few times against the perch before being swallowed. The White-collared Kingfisher occasionally preys on the still-naked nestlings of small songbirds and is then often harassed by such birds as flycatchers, whistlers, fantails and others. It has also been known to kill the baby chicks of poultry. During the breeding season these kingfishers often become especially aggressive and poultry, other birds, cats and even dogs may be subjected to indiscriminate screaming, 'dive-bombing' attacks whenever they venture too close to the nest site. When not persecuted they can become comparatively tame and allow a close approach, provided one is cautious. If alarmed or excited, like most other kingfisher species they bob the head and flick the tail. Occasionally, after heavy rain, kingfishers can be seen taking a bath in the shallow pools of water accumulated in the pot-holes of country roads. Flight is fast and direct with rapid wingbeats; the long, strong bill is conspicuous.

VOICE

The White-collared Kingfisher has a variety of calls, either crescendo-like or monotonous, mostly loud and discordant. They are often the first birds to be heard just before first light and the last to be heard at dusk. During the day they are much quieter, calling only infrequently and they may sometimes be heard calling at night, especially if disturbed. The following calls are most frequently heard:

a wild crescendo or laughing-like scream uttered either when perched or when darting away from an observer 'tchae-tchae-tchaeea-tchaeeaea', the first 2 or 3 notes in fairly rapid succession, the remainder slower and drawn-out

a short, loud and monotonously repeated 'tchaek-tchaek-tchaek

a more pleasing call, only moderately loud, 'tchae-riiiiii', first note short, second higher and drawn-out.

All calls may be repeated a number of times.

FOOD

It will feed on practically any animal which can be overpowered; large insects, small reptiles, nestlings, crabs, fish and probably on occasions, mice. However, the bulk of its diet in most areas consists of beetles, large grasshoppers and lizards. On Efate at least, in the coconut plantations, the young are raised predominantly on a diet of large elephant beetles *Xylotrupes* spp.

NEST AND BREEDING

The nest-hole of the White-collared Kingfisher may be found in a variety of sites and at any height from as low as half a metre up to 12 m. The birds excavate a new nest chamber for every clutch; arboreal termite nests are commonly used, more rarely rotten tree trunks or tree-fern stumps. They are said also to burrow into earth banks. The birds usually drill a tunnel of only a few centimetres leading into a nest chamber about 15 cm long and 9 cm high. Both sexes work on the burrow using the bill as a digging tool and the feet as scoops. No nest material is used and the 3-5 almost spherical eggs (25×31 mm) are laid on rubble or the chamber floor. Both adults incubate the eggs and feed the young which probably fledge after about 3 weeks. After hatching the young kingfishers grow remarkably quickly and soon bunch together as apparently they are unable to rest unless they are pushing up against their nestmates. They huddle in the darkest corner of their nest-hole, with their heads pointing towards the light. The mandible of each black bill extends beyond the maxilla for 2 mm or more and the bill has a distinctly white tip, presumably to guide the parents in the semi-darkness of the chamber. The growing chicks keep up a continuous squeaking while awake and the racket intensifies if one adult approaches thee nest entrance. There is some behaviour which helps to keep the nest clean; the parent birds as well as the growing young drop indigestible food remains outside the nest and void more or less accurately through the nest tunnel. Even so, the nest chamber and especially the entrance-tunnel soon become littered with the regurgitated, indigestible parts of their food and fouled by their own excrement. The breeding season is from October to December/January or later and there is possibly more than one brood in a season.

85. Vanuatu Kingfisher *Halcyon farquhari*   PLATES 12, 18
Other name: Chestnut-bellied Kingfisher
French name: L'Alcyon à ventre roux   or locally: Martin-pêcheur rouge
or Martin-pêcheur des îles du nord
Bislama name: Red Nasiko
Local name: Hiomatokara in Nokovula village, Santo

IDENTIFICATION
Length 19 cm. A small richly purplish-blue and chestnut coloured kingfisher. *Adult male:* head black with a white spot on both sides of the forehead and a dark purplish-blue eyestripe continuing behind the eye; back, wings and tail rich glossy dark purplish-blue; rump brighter. Throat and nuchal collar white, breast and abdomen deep glossy chestnut. Iris: brown. Bill: black above, light horn-colour below. Legs and feet: blackish-grey. *Adult female:* otherwise similar, it can be distinguished from the male by a white patch on the lower abdomen. *Immature:* similar to adult but all colours are duller and the bill is shorter with a white tip.

DISTRIBUTION AND STATUS
The endemic Vanuatu Kingfisher is found only in the northern Vanuatu islands of Santo, Malo and Malakula. It is less common than the White-collared Kingfisher and their range overlaps in these islands. Both species have similar feeding and nesting requirements but they apparently avoid competition by occupying different habitats. The Vanuatu Kingfisher is strictly a bird of the forests whereas the White-collared Kingfisher prefers more open habitats. The Vanuatu Kingfisher is fully protected by law.

FIELD NOTES
This strikingly coloured kingfisher frequents the substage of the true forest or secondary growth mostly far away from water. It can be found in the lowland but seems to prefer the hill forest and is more numerous there. It is apparently absent at higher altitudes. It spends much of its time perched motionless on a branch but also has a characteristic jerking of head and tail, especially if excited or alarmed. It sits so well concealed in some tree that it could be overlooked if it was not for its loud calling. When hunting the Vanuatu Kingfisher perches on a low branch, usually only a few metres above the ground watching for movements of prey. It then makes wheeling flights in pursuit of flying insects or more often dives down to grab a crawling beetle or unwary lizard from a tree trunk or the forest floor. After feeding it reverts to its watching position and waits for more prey. Flight is fast and direct with rapid wingbeats; the long strong bill is conspicuous.

VOICE
The loud and shrill call of the Vanuatu Kingfisher is uttered monotonously many times throughout the day. The single call-note 'teek' or 'tweet' may be repeated as much as 20 or more times, most often starting off slowly but getting progressively faster towards the end.

FOOD
The Vanuatu Kingfisher feeds predominantly on large insects and small lizards but

probably also takes small land crabs and possibly, still-naked nestlings of songbirds.

NEST AND BREEDING

The Vanuatu Kingfisher usually nests in an arboreal termite nest and has similar nesting habits to those of the White-collared Kingfisher (but presumably it is a different termite species). Most of these termite mounds are hemispherical to oval shaped, dark to light brown lumps attached to tree trunks, either high up or close to the ground. The birds select a large enough mound (about 35 cm or more in radius) and make the initial hole for a burrow by clinging to the side of the mound. They tunnel a short entrance in the side of the mound and then hollow a nesting chamber where the 3-4 white, almost spherical, eggs are laid. The long bill is used as a pick to dig out the burrow and the feet for clearing out the debris, the joined toes making an efficient scoop, and the whole process apparently takes both adults about 15 days. After the burrow has been completed the termites seal off all the sections of their mound that have been encroached upon by the kingfishers. The breeding season is probably mostly from November to January/February but also from September.

Order PASSERIFORMES

Members of this world-wide order are found on all major land areas except Antarctica, and on most oceanic islands. The Passeriformes or passerines, also known as perching birds or songbirds (oscines) is by far the largest, most complex and highly developed order of birds with development still in progress. This order contains approximately 5,400 species, roughly three-fifths of all the known living birds, in about 80 families.

Although it is an extremely diverse order containing such widely differing species as the birds of paradise and the parrotfinches there are a number of characteristics which inalienably link them together. The primary common feature is the anisodactyl foot with 3 similar unwebbed toes pointing forwards and a hind toe, the hallux, directed backwards. The hallux is often as long or longer than the middle toe and the claws are a similar length. This foot which is highly suited for perching by gripping is able to curl around a thin branch, stem or wire and grip tightly. The tendons of the leg are so arranged that if the bird relaxes, squatting lower, the toes are pulled into a tighter grip so that the passerine is safe upon its perch even while sleeping. The wings of passerines are variable in form with 10 primaries, though the outermost is frequently rudimentary, and the tail, also variable in form has 12 rectrices. One other particular characteristic is the syrinx or voice organ which is more specialised in structure and musculature than in other birds and enables the birds to sing. More than a century ago the German anatomist Muller showed that the order could be divided on the basis of differences in the number and attachment of syringeal muscles. More recent work noted in Campbell and Lack (1985) has shown that the extent and type of variation must also be determined before the structure of the syrinx is used for taxonomic decisions. On hatching, all passerines are naked or nearly so, blind and helpless, though they grow quickly. They are reared in the nest, and do not leave it until their feathers are well developed. On leaving the nest they are fed for some time by their parents. All passerines are landbirds of small to medium size. The largest are the ravens and the Australian lyrebirds and the smallest some species of the flowerpecker or sunbird family.

The passerines have developed and multiplied into so many successful species that the exact relationship between these species and the clear definition of them into families and genera is a vexed question and a great deal of disagreement exists on their classification. Therefore the sequence in which they are listed is still a matter of contention depending largely on the characteristics considered most important by the individual systematist. The American ornithologists tend to place the seedeaters and related 'nine-primaried' oscines in the top position (listed terminally in the literature). These Old World and New World finches and weaverfinches closely followed by the white-eyes and honeyeaters are generally considered to be the most successful of all bird groups. They show the greatest and most recent adaptive radiation and development and therefore represent the main stream of songbird evolution. In other regions ornithologists have placed crows and the related bowerbirds and birds of paradise at the apex; crows because of their supposed higher intelligence and bowerbirds and birds of paradise for their very complex display pattern and plumage development. Campbell and Lack (1985) note the recent work of Sibley in biochemical and DNA research which has added a new and scientifically based dimension to classification. It is his view that similarities between many of the Australian songbird families and those in other continents are due to convergent or parallel evolution rather than adaptive radiation from a common stock.

Simpson and Day (1989) note the traditional 4 sub-orders in the Passeriformes and, at present, 35 families of passerines in Australia. Fourteen families are represented in Vanuatu and the important characteristic features are given for each family. In the interests of regional uniformity the present listing of families within the order follows the Australian pattern.

Swallows and Martins *Hirundinidae*
The 80 or so species of swallows and martins are almost cosmopolitan in distribution, only absent from the polar regions and some oceanic islands. Most species are migratory or nomadic and those that breed in the temperate northern hemisphere migrate to the tropics or even further south early in autumn. The term 'swallow' and 'martin' are used somewhat interchangeably among the species of this family, the name swallow being more widely used. The simplest and generally accepted difference between the two is that the swallows have a long deeply forked tail whereas in martins the tail is shorter, almost square and only slightly forked. Birds of this family are often confused with swifts but though there is some superficial resemblance they are not closely related and differ widely in anatomy. Their similar appearance is the result of convergent evolution in two separate bird groups that have become adapted to the same way of living. Swallows and martins are small birds from about 10 to 22.5 cm long with slender bodies, short necks, long pointed wings and often deeply forked tails. They have only a tiny bill but their wide gape, surrounded by bristles, acts as an effective aerial fly-scoop which enables them to feed on a variety of flying insects.

Their feet are short and poorly adapted for walking but unlike swifts, they readily perch on twigs, branches, telegraph wires and roofs. However, they can walk a short distance, with some difficulty, and are normally only seen on the ground when they are collecting nest material. Their plumage often has a metallic sheen and is usually darker above than below. Though not as thoroughly aerial as swifts, swallows and martins are very graceful fliers and spend much of their waking hours on the wing, hawking back and forth for insects. Most species either build mud-nests or nest in holes in trees, sometimes those made by woodpeckers, and they usually line the nest with mud. Builders of mud-nests may attach their nests to cliffs, branches, walls or beams of houses or place them in cave entrances. Some build open cups of mud strengthened with plant fibres while others, like some martins, build bottle-shaped nests. A few species tunnel into clay and sand banks or dig burrows in sandy shoals exposed when rivers are low during the dry season. The 2-6 eggs are white and incubation takes 14 to 16 days. The fledging period is comparatively long, from 18 to 24 days. Several species frequently rear more than one brood in a season. Many are gregarious and nest in colonies, often in unbelievably high numbers. Swallows and martins show strong faithfulness to their nesting territory and if not disturbed will return year after year to the same site. Some species nest in close association with humans and plaster their mud-cups to the eaves of houses or barns. Farmers often encourage the birds by nailing small shelves under the roofs and ceilings of sheds, barns and stables.

Only one species, the Pacific Swallow, is known to occur in Vanuatu.

86. Pacific Swallow   *Hirundo tahitica subfusca*   PLATE 11
Other names: House Swallow, Coast Swallow, Welcome Swallow
French name: Hirondelle du Pacifique

IDENTIFICATION

Length about 13 cm. A small swallow with moderately forked tail. *Adult male and female:* upperparts glossy blue-black with metallic sheen, flight feathers and tail blackish-brown. Forehead, cheeks, chin and throat rufous-chestnut, a blue-black stripe from the bill through the eye separates the rufous on forehead and throat; breast and remaining underparts dull brownish-grey. The wings are long and pointed and the tail has a shallow fork; the outer tail feathers are not elongated. Iris: brown. Bill: black, small and flat with a wide gape. Legs and feet: black. *Immature:* similar to adult but duller with less rufous or none. In Vanuatu the Pacific Swallow could be confused with the swiftlets but differs in the rufous markings and the forked tail. It can also be distinguished by its more direct, fast sweeping flight with wings frequently pressed close to the body (swiftlets have erratic flight and hold their wings rather stiffly outstretched). The Pacific Swallow also, unlike the swiftlets, perches readily and frequently. A similar species, the Australian or Welcome Swallow *Hirundo neoxena*, sometimes treated as a race of the Pacific Swallow, has elongated outer tail feathers and conspicuous white subterminal spots on the inner tail feathers. The Welcome Swallow has not yet been recorded in Vanuatu but it is undergoing a spectacular increase in New Zealand (Falla *et al*, 1981) and has been recorded in New Caledonia and New Guinea.

DISTRIBUTION AND STATUS

Various races of the Pacific Swallow occur from southern India through Indonesia and New Guinea to Tonga and the Society Islands in Polynesia and also in Melanesia. The race *subfusca*, described above, is found in Fiji, the Bismarck Archipelago, the Solomons, Santa Cruz Islands, Loyalty Islands and New Caledonia and it is widespread but somewhat local and irregular in distribution throughout Vanuatu. It has been recorded on Hiu, Loh and Toga in the Torres group, Mere Lava, Santo,

Malo, Maewo, Ambae, Pentecost, Malakula, Ambrym, Paama, Lopevi, Epi, Tongoa, Tongariki, Emae, Nguna, Efate, Erromango, Aniwa, Tanna, and Aneityum. It is nowhere abundant but locally common though on most islands it is somewhat elusive. The Pacific Swallow is one of the few bird species in Vanuatu that has benefited from changes in the natural environment. The clearance of forests for agricultural and other developments has created more of the open country favoured by swallows and the building of sheds and houses has provided additional suitable nest-sites. The better known permanent colonies may be seen around Lake Siwi on Tanna; around Vila, at Bauerfield Airport, at the municipal rubbish tip at Tagabe and at Mele abbatoir on Efate, on Santo at the wharf and on Ambae near the Presbyterian mission school. Richard Pickering noted an apparent recent increase at Tagabe from one or two pairs regularly seen perched on the power lines opposite the Co-operative Federation building from May 1979 onwards to over a dozen birds in 1983 (Naika 10:6).

FIELD NOTES

The Pacific Swallow is essentially a resident bird of the coastal regions but in some areas it is more nomadic and may also be encountered in open countryside over grasslands, swamps, lakes, along rivers, in agricultural areas and near human habitations. Pairs or small parties spend many daylight hours on the wing, flying backwards and forwards, hawking low over the ground or water for small insects or soaring and circling high. Their flight is graceful and swooping and they are more likely to be seen in the vicinity of their roosting or nesting sites though hawking birds may be found some distance away. They also spend much time perched on bare tree branches, on reeds, fence posts, telephone wires and buildings but rarely alight on the ground where they could be vulnerable to predators.

VOICE

The Pacific Swallow has various moderately loud, short notes. The song is a musical mixture of rapid twittering and warbling notes strung together and is most often delivered from a perch.

FOOD

It feeds on a variety of flying insects and often drinks on the wing, skimming low over the surface of lakes, rivers or ponds with bill open.

NEST AND BREEDING

The nest is a deep cup made of grass, stems, rootlets, and other plant fibres cemented together with mud which the birds collect from the edges of lakes, streams and ponds. The cup is lined thickly with softer vegetation, downy feathers and animal hair. The nest may be substantial, particularly if it is built on the remains of nests used over several years. It usually has some support through being attached to the side of the mouth of a cave, under a cliff overhang, attached to a bough of a tree, placed in tree-holes or under the eaves of or in all sorts of buildings, usually on beams. The normal clutch is 2-3 eggs (about 18×13 mm), white and flecked with greyish-purple; incubation takes about 14 to 16 days. Both adults take part in nest building and rearing the young but the female probably incubates most and at night the male usually sleeps beside the nest. The young depend on the parents for food for about

3 weeks after fledging. The breeding season is from August to December, possibly even earlier. The birds nest alone or in a small colony and pairs may raise more than one brood in a season.

Cuckoo-shrikes *Campephagidae*

The 70 species of this family include the colourful minivets, genus Pericrocotus, *and the somewhat drab coloured cuckoo-shrikes in 8 other genera. They are found from Africa eastwards through India and the warmer parts of Asia to Samoa in the Pacific Islands and southwards to Australia. The northern species and 3 Australian species are wholly or partly migratory. Cuckoo-shrikes is a misleading name for this group of Old World birds for although the shape, barred plumage and undulating flight are reminiscent of a cuckoo and the notched bill resembles that of a shrike, they are not close relatives of either. Although they may be related to the Old World flycatchers, the family name, Campephagidae, which literally means 'caterpillar-eater' seems to be more suitable than cuckoo-shrikes for this group of primitive insect-eaters with uncertain antecedents and relationships. They are a group of small to medium-sized birds about 12 to 35 cm long, with soft fluffy plumage, stout bill which is hooked at the tip, long legs, relatively short feet and long graduated or rounded tail. Several species have strongly coloured wattles on the base of the bill. Most are rather plain grey, black or white, some have barred underparts or bright shoulder patches but a few (the Asian minivets) are generally strikingly coloured in red, yellow and orange. A notable characteristic is that most species have thickly matted, spine-like feathers (with rigid, pointed shafts) on the lower back and rump which are partly erectile and easily shed possibly serving as a defence mechanism (Campbell and Lack, 1985). Most are strictly arboreal though a few sometimes feed on the ground and the somewhat aberrant Australian Ground Cuckoo-shrike* Coracina (Pteropodocys) maxima *is frequently seen on the ground in social or foraging groups. All eat insects or other small animals and a few add berries to their diet. Some species are fairly conspicuous and gregarious birds and except when breeding, wander in noisy flocks. Their call-notes are often loud, either harsh or whistling. A habit of settling the wings after alighting is common to a number of species. Typically, cuckoo-shrike nests are shallow cups bound together with bark and cobwebs and placed on a horizontal branch or fork of a tree. Most species lay 2-5 eggs which are whitish-green or pale blue-green and usually blotched and speckled with grey, brown or purple.*

Cuckoo-shrikes are represented in Vanuatu by 3 species. The large crow-like Melanesian Cuckoo-shrike is found only in several of the northern islands and on Erromango and two, small, black and white Trillers are found throughout the islands.

87. Melanesian Cuckoo-shrike *Coracina caledonica*   PLATE 12
Other name: Melanesian Graybird
French name: Echenilleur de Mélanésie

IDENTIFICATION
Length about 37 cm. A dark bird, the size of a crow, with relatively long and heavy bill. *Adult male and female:* dark slate-grey above and below with black wings and long, black tail. Iris: light yellow. Bill: black. Legs and feet: black. *Immature:* instead of

being plain grey, the feathers are faintly edged light grey and the iris is brown. Two races are known to occur in Vanuatu:

C. c. thilenii, described above, is found on Santo, Malo and Malakula

C. c. seiuncta which is a somewhat lighter, pale grey on Erromango.

DISTRIBUTION AND STATUS

Restricted to islands in the southwest Pacific, different races of the Melanesian Cuckoo-shrike occur in New Caledonia, the Loyalty Islands and the Solomons. In Vanuatu it has been recorded on Santo, Malo, Malakula and Erromango where it is moderately common.

FIELD NOTES

It frequents forests and well wooded open country at any altitude but appears to be more numerous in the lowland and hill forest. It is commonly seen in pairs or small parties as they wander through the forest canopy in search of food, gleaning insects from twigs and leaves. It is partial to tall trees and infrequently descends to lower levels. Flight is direct but undulating with alternate flapping and gliding. After alighting the birds always shuffle and settle their wings with typical exaggerated motions, rapidly flicking one then another into place, a performance that could well serve some other purpose than just display. The Melanesian Cuckoo-shrike is a conspicuous bird with a loud, piercing call and distinctive shape that make it easy to recognise from a long distance. When perched it mostly has a characteristic upright stance and the wings are usually rapidly flicked when calling.

VOICE

Most often uttered is a piercing, often repeated single note contact call 'zweeee', given from the top of a tall tree. Pairs or groups of 3 to 5 birds will often fly together from tree to tree calling to each other in sequence from the forest canopy. The nasal, moderately loud song 'qua quawa quawa' is delivered in a monotonous series without changing pitch. It also has various loud, harsh notes when disputing territory. Both the far-carrying contact call and the song are unlike those of any other bird in Vanuatu and once heard are not easily forgotten.

FOOD

Primarily an insect eater, it probably also takes berries and other small fruits.

NEST AND BREEDING

The nest is a shallow but massive cup of fine twigs, plant stems and rootlets covered with cobwebs and studded with lichens, resembling the branch on which it is built. It is usually placed at a great height on a fork near the end of a branch and is almost invisible from below. Male and female share the task of nest building but the female probably incubates most. Two eggs are laid; olive-green marked with brown. The nestlings are covered with greyish-white down. After fledging the young remain with their parents and wander around in small flocks until these scatter to breed. The breeding season is from September to January/February.

88. Polynesian Triller *Lalage maculosa*   PLATE 12
French name: Echenilleur de Polynésie

IDENTIFICATION

Length 15 to 16cm. A small active bird, mainly of the forest and forest edge, with contrasting black and white plumage. *Adult male:* upperparts dull black or brownish-black, crown with some white streaks and back finely barred white; lower back and rump greyish-white; a broad white eyestripe continues to the nape; the wing has an extensive white or rusty-white shoulder patch, and wing feathers are edged white; the dark tail feathers are tipped white. Underparts and cheeks greyish-white, sometimes with a buff wash or slight black barring. Iris: brown. Bill: black, lower mandible yellowish-brown. Legs and feet: black. *Adult female:* similar to male but duller and more brownish. *Immature:* rather pale brownish above with feathers tipped white; dull greyish below.

There are 2 races in Vanuatu which differ in the amount of white mottling on the back and black barring and buffy wash on the underparts:

L. m. modesta has more barring on the sides of the breast and sometimes a buffy wash on the underparts. It is found on Santo, Malo, Malakula, Paama, Epi, Tongoa and Emae

L. m. ultima has more mottling above, more extensive light area on the rump and almost pure white underparts. It is found on Efate, Nguna and Emau.

This species may be confused with the Long-tailed Triller for although they prefer different habitats they can live side by side in central and northern Vanuatu (from Efate northwards) where the two species overlap. The Polynesian Triller can be distinguished by its duller colours, distinct eyebrow and much shorter tail (only about half the length).

DISTRIBUTION AND STATUS

Numerous races varying slightly in plumage occur in Fiji, Tonga, Futuna, Niue, western Samoa and the Santa Cruz islands (Mayr and Ripley, 1941). Pratt *et al* (1987) note that it is widespread and common and 'one of central Polynesia's most characteristic and conspicuous birds'. In Vanuatu it frequents the lowland and mountain forest but it is only moderately common on most islands.

FIELD NOTES

It may be seen singly or in pairs and occasionally in small parties in the forest and secondary growth, in open woodland and in gardens. The birds are not particularly shy and can be located by their trilling calls uttered frequently as they search for food. In the tall forest they usually stay in the upper and middle layer of the canopy but in more open country may forage on low bushes or sometimes even on the ground. When feeding they move relentlessly through the foliage of the outer branches, searching carefully for insects, their larvae, pupae and eggs on the top and underside of the leaves, twigs and branches. Occasionally they sail out to catch a passing flying insect. They are mainly sedentary, but make small-scale movements during the non-breeding season. They fly quickly and directly with rather fluttering wingbeats; the pale shoulder patches are prominent in flight.

VOICE

The most frequent call is a moderately loud, flute-like 'zwee', or a high-pitched rasping whistle, both repeated at intervals. It also has a high-pitched, melodious, short advertising song 'zee-tzee-tzee'.

FOOD
The Polynesian Triller takes various insects in all stages of their development and also some small fruits which are swallowed whole.

NEST AND BREEDING
The small, compact cup-shaped nest is made of fine grass stems interwoven with vine tendrils and rootlets and the exterior is lightly covered with cobwebs, lichens and pieces of bark. It is generally placed in a horizontal fork, high up in a tree. The 1-2 eggs are pale olive-green marked with red-brown splotches. The breeding season is probably from September to January/February.

89. Long-tailed Triller   *Lalage leucopyga*   PLATE 12
French name: Echenilleur Pie

IDENTIFICATION
Length 17 to 18cm. A small black and white bird with a rather long tail. *Adult male:* all black, slightly glossy above except for greyish-white rump, white shoulder patch on the wing and white tips to the lateral tail feathers. Underparts pure white or buffy-white. Iris: brown. Bill, legs and feet: black. *Adult female:* similar to male but is blackish-brown where the male is glossy-black and the shoulder patch is buffy-white. *Immature:* resembles female but all dark feathers are tipped with light grey, some white feathers are tipped dark grey and the shoulder patch is ochre.

Three races have been separated in Vanuatu. They differ in the colour of the lores and rump and in the presence, extent or absence of a white eyebrow:

L. l. deficiens from the Torres and Banks Islands: little or no white on the lores, no eyestripe and a grey rump

L. l. albiloris in central and northern Vanuatu from Efate northward: with white lores, variable eyestripe and more greyish rump

L. l. simillima from Erromango, Tanna and Aneityum: with black lores, no eyestripe and whitish-grey rump. This race is also found in the Loyalty Islands.

Birds in the north are much greyer below than those in the southern islands which have almost pure white underparts. This species may be confused with the Polynesian Triller but has brighter, more glossy plumage, a less distinct or no eyestripe and a much longer tail (almost twice the length).

DISTRIBUTION AND STATUS
Several different races of the Long-tailed Triller are found from San Cristobal and Ugi in the Solomon Islands, the Loyalty Islands and New Caledonia to Norfolk Island (Mayr and Ripley, 1941). In Vanuatu this species occurs on almost all islands. It has not yet been recorded from Tongariki, Makura and Futuna. It is common, but not numerous on most islands.

FIELD NOTES
It frequents lowland and mountain forest but prefers open park-like country and is more common on the edge of the forest, in secondary growth, plantations, gardens in villages and towns and in coastal vegetation. The birds are usually seen in pairs or small parties in trees or bushes, foraging quietly among the outer branches, carefully

examining the foliage for insects. The search is continued from bough to bough until all have been thoroughly inspected when they fly off to another tree or bush. They also come to feed on insects on the ground and can be seen hopping across suburban lawns. These trillers are not very vocal but are nevertheless relatively easy to detect as they do not hide among the leaves or under the canopy of treetops but usually perch in full view. During the breeding period pairs hold fairly well-defined territories which are usually vigorously defended by the male.

VOICE

The Long-tailed Triller has a characteristic short, moderately loud and somewhat rasping call-note 'goo' or 'gee', repeated at intervals. It also has a loud melodious, often repeated song 'tee-zeeia--tee-zeeia--tee-zeeia'.

FOOD

It feeds mainly on insects and their larvae but also eats berries.

NEST AND BREEDING

The nest, a shallow cup of fine twigs, rootlets, rather coarse weed stalks, casuarina needles and plant wool is bound together with cobwebs and ornamented with pieces of bark and some lichen. It is placed in a horizontal fork, usually high up in a tree, from 8 to 20m above the ground. Two eggs are laid; pale blue-green marked with red-brown. The breeding season is probably from September to January/February.

Thrushes *Turdidae*

This family is often treated as a subfamily (Turdinae) of the larger group, Muscicapidae, as in Simpson and Day (1989) and Pratt et al (1987) but is considered separately in Beehler et al (1986). The thrush family with about 300 species in about 45 genera is almost cosmopolitan, absent from Antarctica and some Polynesian islands and represented in New Zealand by 2 introduced species. The northern species are migratory. Several small, specialised island populations have become victims of rapid environmental changes and have vanished within the last century. Thrushes are small to medium-sized songbirds, 12 to 30cm in length. Most are plain coloured birds, often brown, but some are attractively marked with contrasting colours, mainly black and white. The bill is variable in length, usually short, straight and slender with the culmen slightly downcurved at the tip. The wings are long and pointed and the tail is usually shorter than the wings and square to slightly rounded. The legs are booted, the scales being fused to form a continuous outer layer, and are fairly long with strong feet. Most are ground feeding birds eating invertebrates and fruit, commonly insects, worms, grubs, snails and berries. The majority of species build well-formed, cup-shaped nests of twigs, grasses and leaves sometimes strengthened with mud, though some are cavity nesters. Thrushes often maintain pair bonds throughout the year, and in sedentary species from year to year, keeping their own breeding and feeding territories and advertising them by song.

Some of the finest songbirds in the world belong to this large and extremely varied family which is represented in Vanuatu by 2 species, the widespread and variable resident Island Thrush and the vagrant Song Thrush.

90. Island Thrush *Turdus poliocephalus* PLATE 13
French name: Merle des îles

IDENTIFICATION
Length about 23 cm. A medium-sized plump bird with bright yellow bill and legs and distinctive habits. The considerable geographical variation in colour of the numerous races makes a general description impossible. The most widely occurring colour type is all black but in others the body may be greyish or brownish, head and throat white and the belly black, white or chestnut. Iris: brown, eye-ring yellow. Bill, legs and feet: yellow. At least 8 races have been separated in Vanuatu:

T. p. vanikorensis from Santo and Malo (and the Santa Cruz Islands),

T. p. whitneyi from Gaua and

T. p. efatensis from Efate: the male at least is all sooty-black with variable amounts of chestnut in the centre of the lower belly or none.

T. p. placens from Vanua Lava and Bligh,

T. p. malekulae from Pentecost, Malakula and Ambrym and

T. p. becki from Paama, Lopevi, Epi and Emae: all are more brownish or greyish in varying degrees.

T. p. albifrons from Erromango: like *pritzbueri* but has a whiter head and some white on the lower belly.

T. p. pritzbueri from Tanna and formerly also Lifou in the Loyalty Islands but it is probably now extinct there: head, neck, throat and upper breast creamy-white; rest of plumage sooty-black. In the female, head and throat are brownish-grey.

In all races, females and young males are generally lighter and more brownish with paler yellow bill and brownish legs and feet. *Immature:* much paler than adult, streaked rusty-buff above and mottled with tawny, white and black below. Bill, legs and feet are brownish to pale yellow (Mayr 1941a).

DISTRIBUTION AND STATUS
The Island Thrush is widespread with 22 races distributed on islands in southeast Asia from Taiwan to New Guinea and in the central and southwest Pacific to Lord Howe Island. It is not found on all islands and in some parts of its range as in the Solomons it is confined to the highest mountains. In New Guinea it occurs from 2,700 to 4,100 m, rarely as low as 2,200 m (Beehler *et al*, 1986). In Vanuatu the Island Thrush can also be found in forests near the coast though it is more numerous in the montane forest. It is fairly common on most islands. On some islands it occurs in heavy forest at all levels. The absence of this species at lower altitudes on other islands may be due to the modification of its forest habitat for agriculture and other development. In addition to those islands listed above it has also been recorded on Ureparapara, Maewo and Ambae.

FIELD NOTES
The Island Thrush is essentially a forest-haunting bird that prefers the mature, most humid and shady parts of the forest with a fairly open substage, but may visit adjoining secondary growth or overgrown gardens. In such places it feeds singly or in pairs on the ground. A number of thrushes may gather where food is plentiful but they do not move about in flocks. They forage energetically amongst the fallen debris, actively

Nest of the Island Thrush, thickly covered with green moss, built here in the centre of a pandanus palm

hopping around, turning over leaves for insects, worms, snails and fallen fruit or digging with the beak in places where the soil is soft. When disturbed they take cover in a series of swift hops, or more often fly swiftly and low through the undergrowth to another clearing uttering a penetrating alarm call in flight. On alighting the tail is often flicked up and down. At any time of the day in the breeding season, but more often in the evening, the males may be heard singing, usually from a tree or other prominent perch. The thrushes are otherwise rather quiet, shy and difficult to see and most observers, even after a careful approach, must be content with a fleeting glimpse of a dark shape dashing through the undergrowth, calling as it flies away. A male banded on Efate was netted again in the same area after 5 months.

VOICE

It is normally silent when feeding. Among a number of other call-notes, the short contact call, 'tchook' or 'tchaak-tchaak' is more often uttered and becomes a rapid, high-pitched chatter 'tchook-tchook-toaweetoweet-toaweetoweet' when the bird is excited or alarmed; also a persistent 'ptink' and a drawn-out, somewhat plaintive 'chweeeeee', descending in pitch. Less often heard is the subdued, melodious fluting song, of varied quality, made up of several parts divided by pauses.

FOOD

All kinds of small invertebrates are taken including worms, small molluscs, beetles, moths and other insects and their larvae. It also takes small lizards and berries and small fruits.

NEST AND BREEDING

The nest is rather substantial (155×75 mm outside and 85×40 mm inside), a deep, well-built cup made of rootlets, plant stems, fibres and leaves usually liberally coated externally with green moss and thickly lined with softer plant materials. It is usually fairly low down in the forest undergrowth, one to 2 m above ground or higher in a fork of a tree, on branches close to the trunk, in a large shallow tree-hole or between the leaves of pandanus palms. Normally the clutch consists of one or 2 eggs but sometimes 3 are laid. The olive-green eggs (about 21×28 mm) are flecked reddish-brown, especially at the larger end, sometimes concentrated to form a zone. The breeding season is known to be from September to January on Efate.

91. Song Thrush *Turdus philomelos*
Other name: English Thrush
French name: Grive musicienne

IDENTIFICATION AND FIELD NOTES

Length 23 cm. A slender, light brown bird, the same size as the Island Thrush, with a beautifully spotted breast. *Adult male and female:* uniform brown above with a thin buff eyebrow and buff cheeks, streaked brown. Chin white, throat, breast and flanks buff heavily spotted dark brown; abdomen creamy-white, lightly spotted; underwing-coverts buff, noticeable in flight. Iris: dark brown. Bill: mainly dark brown, lower mandible yellow at the base with a brown tip. Legs and feet: pale flesh. *Immature:* like adult but is streaked buff above and is more buff with smaller dark spots below.

In New Zealand it occurs in all types of country including dense bush up to about 1,300 m (Falla *et al*, 1981). Usually seen singly or in pairs the Song Thrush feeds mainly on open ground, with short runs or bouncing hops between pauses. It has an upright stance when standing still, often with head on one side listening for movements of worms or insects. It commonly feeds on snails, using a stone, rock, wall or thick stem as an anvil on which to smash the shell. It resorts to cover if disturbed.

Flight is direct and slightly undulating with flaps and glides. It has a variety of short calls, usually a thin 'sipp' when flushed or in flight, and a loud 'tchook' when alarmed. The song is flute-like, clear and vigorous with often repeated phrases and it may sing for very long periods, especially at dawn and dusk, during the breeding season (June to January in New Zealand).

DISTRIBUTION AND STATUS

The Song Thrush breeds in Europe and in western parts of Asia and winters as far south as north Africa. It was introduced to Melbourne, Australia in 1860 and later to Sydney but it is now resident only in Melbourne and other parts of Victoria (Pizzey, 1980). Introduced to New Zealand in 1862, it is now among the most numerous birds in the country and is present on most offshore and outlying islands north to the Kermadecs and south to Campbell Island (Falla *et al*, 1981). The Song Thrush was recorded in Vanuatu by MacMillan in the 1930s as a vagrant from New Zealand. This is noted in Diamond and Marshall (1977b).

Australian Robins, Whistlers and allies   *Pachycephalidae*
The members of this family which also belong to the larger group of Australo-Papuan insect-eaters, are often included in the family Muscicapidae though the Australian Robins are sometimes placed in a separate family, Eopsaltridae, as in Beehler et al *(1986). Characteristic features are the round, thick-set head and the small rictal bristles at the base of the bill (which help in catching insects). They are sometimes given the name 'thick-heads'.*

There are 2 representatives of this family in Vanuatu, the Scarlet Robin, genus Petroica, *and the Golden Whistler, genus* Pachycephala. *They are small insectivorous birds but take their prey in different ways. The robins catch insects in flight and also on the ground, where they drop on their prey. They seem to prefer the rainforest but may visit partly cleared areas where they are relatively tame and friendly. The whistlers have a stocky body and short, rather heavy bill with a shrike-like hook at the tip. They are usually found in the canopy or the substage of the forest where they search for insects on twigs and branches, picking and gleaning. The robins and whistlers are solitary birds, usually seen singly, in pairs or family parties but occasionally in mixed feeding flocks.*

92. **Scarlet Robin**   *Petroica multicolor*   PLATE 14
French name: Rossignol à poitrine rouge

IDENTIFICATION

Length about 11 cm. This small, dark chunky bird, with upright stance, scarlet breast and white forehead cannot be mistaken for any other species in Vanuatu. Five races occur in the islands and these differ in the amount of sexual dimorphism. *Adult male:* typically, upperparts sooty-black except for the conspicuous white forehead, prominent white wingbar and white outer tail shafts. Upper throat black; breast and belly scarlet red; rest of underparts greyish-white. Iris: brown. Bill: short and black. Legs and feet: black. *Adult female:* rufous to grey-brown above; forehead, wingbar and outer tail dull white; throat greyish-brown; breast paler red, rest of underparts greyish-white. *Immature:* resembles adult female but is duller, with little red apparent and buff instead of white markings. *Juvenile* is streaked and mottled brown and buff.

In 3 races the males are brown above and dull like the females but can be distinguished by the pure white spot on the forehead and the greater depth and extent of scarlet on the breast and belly:

P. m. soror from the Banks Islands

P. m. feminina from Emae, Efate, Nguna and Emau

P. m. cognata from Erromango

The other 2 races follow the general description above:

P. m. ambrynensis from Gaua, Mere Lava, Santo, Malo, Malakula, Maewo, Ambae, Ambrym, Paama, Lopevi, Epi, Tongoa and Tongariki

P. m. similis from Tanna and Aneityum. See Mayr (1934).

DISTRIBUTION AND STATUS

The Scarlet Robin is widely distributed from Australia including Norfolk Island, through the southwest Pacific islands to the Solomons, Fiji and western Samoa. In Vanuatu it is common but not numerous on most islands. Its preferred habitat is the substage of the indigenous forest so that it is now uncommon or absent in lowland areas where forests have been indiscriminately cleared for development.

FIELD NOTES

The Scarlet Robin is among the smallest Vanuatu birds. It mainly inhabits the forests, heavy growth along creeks and other mature vegetation almost from sea-level to the highest mountains, but may visit partly cleared areas, village gardens, cacao and coffee plantations adjoining the forest. Strongly territorial, it is usually seen singly or in pairs and once a pair has been located it can generally be found again in the same area though there seem to be some local movements outside the breeding season. The robins can be elusive with their habit of flitting silently and unobtrusively about the shaded forest. They apparently feed mainly in the substage, often close to the ground or on it, but they also visit the canopy. They watch for prey from a branch or other vantage point then dart out after flying insects or suddenly pick one acrobatically from a tree trunk or branch, hover to pluck one from a leaf or drop to the forest floor to pick up an insect amongst the leaf litter, then rise again to a perch. This cycle may be repeated again and again accompanied by characteristic movements, a frequent rapid flicking of the drooped wings and tail. The Scarlet Robin is often rather trusting and inquisitive and may come as close as a metre to inspect an intruder or even accompany someone along a forest track for a distance; if the nest is approached however, it may nervously flick the wings and tail and snap the bill. Flight is rarely sustained for long and has a fluttering quality.

VOICE

The contact call is a plaintive, faint yet carrying twitter 'teet-teet' frequently repeated. It also has a weak and sometimes sharp alarm call 'tchee-zteazeazea'. The melodious song, often given at dawn, is a series of pleasant whistling notes in quick cadence, 'twee-weeweeweet', either subdued or surprisingly loud for such a small bird.

FOOD

It takes mainly insects and their larvae, also spiders, small worms and grubs.

NEST AND BREEDING

The nest is a beautifully compact little cup of plant fibres neatly bound together with spiderwebs and coated liberally with green moss and lichen. It is lined with plant down, feathers or hair. It is placed in a tree fork, hollow stump or horizontal limb of a tree at any height from low over the ground to the lower canopy. The nest blends so well with the mossy, lichen-covered background that it can easily be overlooked. The 2-3 eggs are pale blue-white and speckled and blotched with shades of grey or brown, often forming a zone at the larger end. The male and female join in rearing the young. The breeding season is from October to January but some nests have also been found in July. The Scarlet Robin is parasitised by the Fan-tailed Cuckoo.

93. Golden Whistler   *Pachycephala pectoralis*   PLATE 14
Other names: Common Golden Whistler, Thickhead
French name: Siffleur d'or

IDENTIFICATION

Length 16.5 to 17 cm. A robust bird with a round, thick head, and strong shrike-like bill. The male is one of the most attractively coloured birds in Vanuatu. *Adult male:* crown and sides of the head slightly glossy, black extending in a band around the upper breast; nape yellow extending around the neck to breast and abdomen; rest of upperparts olive-green; wings black with feathers edged dull olive-green; tail black. Throat pure white; rest of underparts deep golden-yellow. Iris: red-brown. Bill, legs and feet: black. *Adult female:* very different to adult male; head brownish-grey; back, wings and tail dull brownish-olive. Throat greyish-white; faint indication of a brownish or greyish breast band; abdomen buff to yellowish, vent pale yellow. Bill: brownish-black. *Immature:* resembles female but throat is often lightly mottled brown and the iris is brown. Young males have more rufous in the plumage; edges of wing feathers and sides of the head are tinged rufous and, apparently, there is a further transitional stage with increasingly mottled black on head, white on throat and yellow on the underparts. Much has yet to be learned about the stages before the final moult to bright adult plumage.

According to Mayr (1945) 6 races were described from Vanuatu, mainly based on subtle differences in the intensity, extent or lack of certain colours in the female plumage which, although noted in museum specimens, are not apparent in the field. In *P.p.banksiana* (from Vanua Lava, Gaua, Maewo and Pentecost), *P.p.intacta* (from Santo, Malo, Ambae and Malakula), *P.p.brunneipectus* (from Ambrym, Paama, Lopevi, Epi, Tongoa, Tongariki and Emae) and *P.p.efatensis* (from Efate, Nguna and Emau) the differences have since been considered too slight for validity as separate races and Galbraith (1956) has combined them in a single race, *P.p.intacta*. The other races at present accepted are *P.p.chlorura* from Erromango and *P.p.cucullata* from Aneityum.

A similar species, the Mangrove Whistler *P.melanura*, occurs in southwest New Guinea to the Bismarck Archipelago and in Australia but has not yet been recorded in Vanuatu. It has a distinctly longer bill, brighter more orangey-yellow underparts, a broader black breast band, a more extensive yellow collar and yellow on the rump; tail is shorter, jet black. It prefers coastal and island thickets and mangroves.

The Golden Whistler lays two blotched eggs in a deep cup-shaped nest

DISTRIBUTION AND STATUS

Throughout the full range of the Golden Whistler, more than 70 geographical races have been described. It occurs in Java through New Guinea (mountain forest and island forest habitats) to the Solomons, Santa Cruz and Loyalty Islands and is widespread and common in the southwest Pacific from Australia to Fiji and Samoa. In Vanuatu it is common to very common nearly everywhere.

FIELD NOTES

The Golden Whistler inhabits forests, secondary growth, open wooded country, plantations and gardens from sea level to the highlands. It is apparently more common in dense secondary growth or forests in the lowlands. Whistlers usually forage in the lower branches of the canopy, the substage of the forest, the tangled thickets of the secondary growth or shrubs and on occasions may even be seen on the ground. When feeding their movements are slow and deliberate in search of insects, gleaned mostly from the foliage and branches, searching between leaves, probing into cavities and crevices or under loose bark. They hop from branch to branch or fly short distances from one tree to another and sometimes hawk after flying insects. The birds have a characteristic upright stance but they are usually heard more often than seen; their musical calls are generally the first indication of their presence. They prefer to stay under cover and may sit still for long periods. They are perhaps the loudest and most persistent songsters in the wooded areas. The best time to hear them is when they are foraging in groups of up to 5 or more birds and appear to call to and answer each other in the canopy. The whistlers are usually seen alone or in pairs but may be found in mixed feeding flocks with other flycatchers and white-eyes. They apparently wander a great deal locally in the non-breeding season.

VOICE

The Golden Whistler is a gifted songster, calling more persistently at the beginning of the breeding season. The penetrating call though varied is characteristic, a succession of loud clear and melodious whistling notes 'cheer-chee-chee-cheeoweet' ending with an upward 'whip-crack' which may be repeated over and over again. The 'chee' note is uttered slowly and may be repeated a number of times or given once whereas the 'cheeoweet' note is delivered rapidly and has an explosive quality. The song varies somewhat between individuals and probably also from island to island with local populations developing their own dialects. It also has a number of short, soft contact calls and harsh alarm notes.

FOOD

Insects and their larvae are taken, also grubs, spiders and some berries.

NEST AND BREEDING

A cup-shaped nest is built of loosely interwoven fine twigs, plant stems and rather large leaves. It is placed in the fork of a tree, low bush or tangled growth up to 6 m above the ground but mostly much lower. The nest is about 95 to 110 mm in diameter and 120-130 mm deep outside and about 35 × 65 mm inside. Usually 2, occasionally 3 oval eggs (24 × 18 mm) are laid. The eggs are cream to pale ochre, blotched with shades of dark red-brown concentrated in a ring at the larger end. Both adults build the nest and share incubation and the duties of rearing the young. The breeding season is from August to January.

Monarch Flycatchers *Monarchidae*

This family has certain affinities with the families Pachycephalidae and Rhipiduridae and is sometimes classed with them as subfamilies of a larger group Muscicapidae. *The family Monarchidae comprises some 87 species and has a wide distribution in Australia, New Guinea and the tropical Pacific. It includes the genera* Monarcha, Pomarea, Clytorhynchus, Myiagra *(sometimes given family status,* Myiagridae*) and* Neolalage. *These flycatchers range from 12 to 20 cm in size with relatively short legs and longish tail. They have small heads, the strong bill may be flattened and the rictal bristles are prominent. The monarch flycatchers are active birds, mainly confined to forest or thickly wooded habitats.*

Three species are known to occur in Vanuatu. The Southern Shrikebill (genus Clytorhynchus*) and the Vanuatu Flycatcher (*Neolalage*) gather their insect prey mainly by hopping through the branches and gleaning from leaves and twigs, but also, infrequently,* *flying out to catch insects on the wing. The Broad-billed Flycatcher and related species (genus Myiagra) have 'typical' flycatcher habits. They sit upright on branches and dart out after flying insects, returning to their perch after each capture.*

94. Southern Shrikebill *Clytorhynchus pachycephaloides* PLATE 14
French name: Gobe-mouches brun

IDENTIFICATION
Length 19 cm. A fairly large, dull-coloured flycatcher with a characteristic, massive wedge-shaped bill, long and vertically compressed, with a shrike-like hook at the tip. *Adult male and female* are alike but the female is paler: rufous-brown to olive-brown above with broad white tips on the lateral tail feathers; lighter and more greyish below, sometimes with buffish wash on sides. Iris: ochre to brown. Bill: bluish-grey, tip whitish. Legs and feet: lead-grey. *Immature:* as adult but much duller, bill brownish.

DISTRIBUTION AND STATUS
This species is confined to New Caledonia and Vanuatu. The race *grisescens*, described above, occurs throughout Vanuatu from Erromango northwards (Mayr, 1933b). It is uncommon in the southern islands but more numerous in the north. On some islands, as on Efate, it is apparently restricted to the highlands and its absence from the lowlands could be due to the indiscriminate clearing of forests for development. On Santo it also inhabits forests near the coast.

FIELD NOTES
The Southern Shrikebill may be found feeding at any height up to the lower canopy but the most dense and gloomy parts of the tangled forest are apparently the more favoured habitat. It has a characteristic foraging method and, although it is rather an elusive bird, it is usually noticed when it noisily investigates dead vegetation, rustles dead leaves, pulls tangled vine tendrils apart, probes rotten wood and prises off loose bark with the massive bill. It is usually seen singly or in pairs, travelling through the middle to upper parts of the forest. It rustles its way methodically up a tree, hopping from branch to branch, gleaning insects from leaves, vine tangles or trunk, then flies in short, slightly undulating swoops to another tree. It rarely catches insects on the wing and only occasionally descends to the ground. Medway and Marshall (1975) note that on Erromango it was observed in mixed feeding flocks with other predominantly insect-eating passerines.

VOICE
The melodious but somewhat melancholy song can often be heard in the darker parts of the forest. The song varies considerably and consists of long drawn-out whistling sounds in cadence. It also has a harsh, rasping scolding note.

FOOD
A wide range of insects and grubs are taken, probably also caterpillars and small fruits. It is also said to eat lizards.

NEST AND BREEDING
The nest is a deep cup of very thin twigs, plant fibres, rootlets, tendrils and leaves,

generally lined with fine fibres and decorated on the outside with pieces of bark. It is usually well camouflaged in a fork of a tree or a tangle of vines in the forest substage. The 2 eggs are white or pale salmon-coloured and blotched or spotted with reddish-brown, particularly at the larger end where a ring may be formed. The breeding season is from September to January.

95. Broad-billed Flycatcher *Myiagra caledonica*   PLATES 14, 19
French name: Gobe-mouches à large bec

IDENTIFICATION
Length about 16 cm. A small restless bird with a very broad, flat bill flanked by long, stiff rictal bristles. Male and female are very different but both have a slight erectile crest. *Adult male:* upperparts, throat and upper breast black with a greenish gloss; rest of underparts white. Iris: brown. Bill: leaden-blue, tipped black. Legs and feet: bluish-grey. *Adult female:* upperparts dark grey, with a narrow white eye-ring; wings and tail brownish; back olive-brown. Throat and upper breast ochraceous-orange, rest of underparts white. *Immature:* resembles female but is duller with buff edging on dark feathers. The young male gradually changes to adult plumage and in the transition is increasingly mottled black losing the brown and orange. Two races occur in Vanuatu:

   M. c. marina from Efate northwards is slightly smaller than

   M. c. melanura from Erromango, Tanna and Aneityum.

DISTRIBUTION AND STATUS
The Broad-billed Flycatcher is also found on Rennell Island in the Solomons, in the Loyalty Islands and New Caledonia. It is a common species throughout Vanuatu though it has not yet been recorded on Paama and Tongariki. See Mayr (1933b) and Galbraith and Galbraith (1962).

FIELD NOTES
Most often found singly or in pairs, their frequent calls and active nature readily attract attention. They apparently prefer open woodland, mangroves, secondary growth, the edges of plantations and gardens near human habitations and are more common near the coast than in the mountains. In the forest they feed in the canopy but in more open country they feed at all heights. These birds seem to be always on the move and are usually seen darting from branch to branch or perching briefly, with erect stance, on the lookout for insects. They launch into the air to capture insects, assisted by the well-developed rictal bristles on both sides of the gape, then return to the perch. They hunt for insects through the treetops and high shrubs and may pick from the foliage but take most of their insect food on the wing. They also hover to pick insects from leaves. During all this activity they call often, erect the small crest frequently and when perched, particularly when agitated, the tail is quivered rapidly and continuously in typical *Myiagra* fashion. They are not difficult to observe as they perch openly and betray their presence by their rasping contact calls. The birds generally fly directly and in a leisurely way but may zig-zag through the branches with tail slightly spread. Out of the breeding season they may be seen in mixed foraging flocks with other flycatchers and white-eyes.

VOICE

The characteristic contact call of the Broad-billed Flycatcher, a short, harsh rasping or grating 'zweat' is repeated frequently and especially given when excited or annoyed. The song is a moderately loud, musical repeated whistling 'tweeee' or 'tooweeee'. It also has a series of beak-clapping sounds.

FOOD

Insects are taken, including various flies, butterflies, moths, flying termites and ants, cicadas, grasshoppers, small beetles, dragonflies and probably also spiders and caterpillars.

NEST AND BREEDING

Courtship display has been observed on several occasions. A male appeared to be very excited, with crest raised, body rigid and tail spread like a fan, while uttering a rapid series of musical notes 'tweet' or 'teweet'. A display was recorded in mid-September when both male and female, perched some distance apart on a large horizontal branch, excitedly began to utter their sharp, rasping calls, with crest raised, wings drooped and tail fanned, at the same time turning in circles. The female stayed in the same place but the male moved slowly towards the female and once the male reached the female both birds flew away together. Richard Pickering observed similar courtship behaviour on 3 June 1982 during which a piercing whistle was also given and there was some attempt at mating (Naika 16:12).

The nest is an inconspicuous compact cup (42 × 30mm inside) of fine plant fibres, strips of bark and rootlets bound with spiderwebs and decorated or camouflaged outside with lichen and flakes of bark. It may be placed from 3 m above the ground up to the canopy, sometimes in an exposed position on dead parts of a horizontal limb or in a fork. The 2-3 eggs are white to pale buff and blotched with light brown and grey, usually in a central belt or concentrated at the larger end. Both adults build the nest, incubate the eggs and feed the young. Incubation takes about 18 days and the young fledge 17 to 19 days after hatching. This species is sometimes parasitised by the Fan-tailed Cuckoo. The breeding season is probably from August to December/February.

96. Vanuatu Flycatcher *Neolalage banksiana*   PLATE 14
Other name: Buff-bellied Flycatcher
French name: Gobe-mouches de Vanuatu
Local name: Zai'Zari in the mountain village of Nokovula, Santo

IDENTIFICATION

Length about 15 cm. A striking, slightly glossy black, white and golden-coloured bird. *Adult male and female:* crown, back and base of the tail black; wings black with a broad light golden-yellow band. Upper throat, face and sides of the head white; breast band black; abdomen, rump, the underside of the tail feathers and the tip of the tail light golden-yellow. Iris: brown. Bill: black. Legs and feet: leaden-grey. The female is duller than the male. *Immature:* similar pattern to adult but much duller, the black colours are brownish, the white colours are greyish and the golden-yellow whitish. This species might be confused with the male Golden Whistler but the white face,

The nest of the Vanuatu Flycatcher is made of vine tendrils, rootlets and thin twigs with
no lining

black pectoral band and the light golden-yellow markings on wings and tail are
diagnostic and distinguish the Vanuatu Flycatcher from all other birds in Vanuatu.

DISTRIBUTION AND STATUS

This endemic species, confined to Vanuatu, is found from Efate northwards and has
been recorded on Vanua Lava, Santo, Malo, Maewo, Ambae, Pentecost, Malakula,

Ambrym, Epi and Efate and it is common to very common. It is the sole species in the genus *Neolalage*, the only endemic genus in the Vanuatu archipelago.

FIELD NOTES

The Vanuatu Flycatcher occurs in a variety of wooded habitats from the lowland up to about 1,200 m. It is usually seen singly or in pairs, sometimes in small parties in the forest and in adjoining secondary growth, dense humid scrub, borders of overgrown plantations and in village gardens. When foraging this rather active bird moves unhurriedly through the substage and lower canopy of the forest and other shady areas, hopping from branch to branch or making short slow flights, and only occasionally ascending to the canopy. The body is held in a horizontal position as it gleans its prey from the vegetation, infrequently attempting to capture insects on the wing. The quiet and unobtrusive Vanuatu Flycatcher is not always conspicuous but it may be present in mixed feeding flocks in the forest and the observer may, with some luck, then see this shy flycatcher. Writing about this species on Efate, Richard Pickering notes that 'you will not see it unless you go into some forest' though 'the area of bush does not have to be very big' and it 'is common in the trees on the Tagabe Cliffs behind the Agricultural School' and is 'usually seen in small groups, often with Spotted Fantails and white-eyes' (Naika 8:9).

VOICE

The Vanuatu Flycatcher is not a vocal bird. The most characteristic call is a low, mournful drawn-out trill 'treereeeeee'. When alarmed a harsh angry 'tzea' or 'tzea tzeazeazea', repeated once or several times may be uttered and it is said to have a melodious song.

FOOD

Many kinds of insects and their larvae are taken, probably also spiders.

NEST AND BREEDING

The conical nest (about 65 × 45 mm outside and 30-40 mm deep) is made entirely of vine tendrils, rootlets and thin twigs and has no lining. It is placed in an upright fork of a small tree in a dark place in the substage of the forest from 2 to 5 m above the ground. The clutch consists of 2 conical eggs which are pale cream to matt white and usually freckled with red-brown to purple, particularly at the larger end where the spots are bigger. Some eggs are all light except for an indistinct ring of spots at the broader end. The Vanuatu Flycatcher is particularly sensitive to interference with its nest and, like many other species, will desert the nest if it is handled. The breeding season is from August to December/January.

Fantails   *Rhipiduridae*

Fantails are a group of about 39 species of small to medium-sized passerines, from 14 to 20 cm in length, with a long, rounded fan-shaped tail, moderately broad bill and prominent rictal bristles. They are sometimes included in other family groupings of flycatchers or treated as a subfamily (Rhipidurinae or even Monarchinae) of Muscicapidae. It is generally accepted that further study of the relationships within these groups is required. In fantails, male and female plumage is alike in most species with predominantly sombre colours of grey, brown, black and rufous with some white. Young birds are not spotted but feathers on the upperparts may have buff to cinnamon tips. Two species of fantail flycatchers, the Grey or Collared Fantail and the Spotted Fantail, occur in Vanuatu. They are easily distinguished by their relatively short legs, very small bill and feet, short but wide drooping wings, long, cocked-up and more or less fanned tail and their restless movements. They are arboreal and frequent either the shady substage of the forest or the thickets along the forest edge where they flit from branch to branch, fluttering against the foliage with jerky movements to dislodge insects, or performing aerial manoeuvres to capture insects in flight. They have a tinkling call-note and a short melodious song which they repeat frequently. They are usually confiding and inquisitive and may follow an observer for some distance, scolding and flirting the tail and they have been known to enter houses.

The various flycatchers in Vanuatu are usually the more common and conspicuous birds in the forest and along the forest edge, and several species usually comprise a large proportion of the mixed flocks that are typical of the tropical forest.

97. Grey Fantail *Rhipidura fuliginosa brenchleyi*   PLATE 13
Other name: Collared Fantail
French name: Rhipidure à collier
Bislama name: Nasiksik

IDENTIFICATION

Length 14 to 15 cm. A small bird with long, well-spread fan tail and restless movements. *Adult male and female:* crown dark grey with a conspicuous broad white stripe over the eye and another over the ear-coverts; upperparts slate-grey, more blackish on the tail; outer tail feathers are narrowly tipped white and the wings have 2 inconspicuous white bars. The white throat is separated from the ochraceous-buff underparts by a narrow black breast band. Iris: brown. Bill: upper mandible black, lower mandible light horn-colour. Legs and feet: brown. *Immature:* duller than adult, the white markings on head and wings are tinged buff and the feathers on the upperparts tipped buff. The Grey Fantail may be confused with the Spotted Fantail but differs in smaller size, grey back, white wingbar, lack of spots on the breast and black band sharply dividing the white throat and buff abdomen.

DISTRIBUTION AND STATUS

The Grey Fantail is found in Australia (6 races) and New Zealand (3 races), New Caledonia, the Loyalty Islands and the Solomons. Beehler *et al* (1986) suggest that it might occur as a migrant from Australia in southern New Guinea. The race *brenchleyi*, described above, is common throughout Vanuatu though there are no records for Makura, Aniwa and Tanna. The same race is also found on San Cristobal in the Solomons.

FIELD NOTES

The Grey Fantail is unmistakable with wings drooped, and long fan tail which is constantly flicked from side to side, up and down, spread or closed. These birds seem to be always moving, flitting about restlessly from branch to branch and when they settle for a moment on a twig they turn from side to side jerkily or dart out in whirling flight to take an insect in the air. Now and again these dainty birds break into their short pleasing song or with a sharp twittering are off to another tree, with direct and

Two young Grey Fantails almost ready to fly. The nest is a neat cup with typical tail of thin plant strips hanging beneath

jerky flight, to start their dancing routine again. They are arboreal, but just as frequently seen in low scrub as in the high trees and they may descend to the ground for a short visit. They may be found in all types of wooded habitat, though rarely in the dense forest. They are more numerous around clearings in the forest or the forest edge, in mangroves, parkland and shrub thickets, cultivated land and even in gardens close to human habitations. They are usually seen singly or in pairs. Being rather inquisitive, they can be approached closely and often respond to an imitation of their call. They appear to be somewhat nomadic in the non-breeding season and may join feeding flocks with other flycatchers and white-eyes.

VOICE

The call-note is a single short 'chip', which is repeated rapidly when the bird is agitated. The short, high-pitched, melodious song, composed of a series of short twittering notes is usually given from a perch and often repeated.

FOOD

Small insects are taken, generally on the wing.

NEST AND BREEDING

The nest (about 50 mm across and 30 mm deep with walls 5 mm thick) is a neat cup of plant fibres, strips of soft bark and fine grasses, liberally bound with spiderwebs and with a tail hanging beneath which may be up to 150 mm long. It is placed on a thin, horizontal fork of a tree or vine, usually low in the substage but some have also been found up to about 10 m. Normally 2 but sometimes 3 eggs are laid (16 × 13 mm), weighing from 1.25 to 1.5 gm. The eggs are dull white with dark and pale brown blotches all over, sometimes forming a zone at the larger end. Both parents share incubation and feed the young. The Grey Fantail may be parasitised by the Fan-tailed Cuckoo. The breeding season extends from September to January/February.

98. Spotted Fantail *Rhipidura spilodera spilodera* PLATE 13
Other name: Streaked Fantail
French name: Rhipidure tacheté

IDENTIFICATION

Length 17 cm. A restless little bird with long fan tail and distinctive black spotting on the breast. *Adult male and female:* upperparts dark, greyish on head and tail, brownish on back and wings with a broad white eyestripe and a short white line behind the eye. Underparts whitish, lighter on the throat; lower throat and breast have numerous, partly concealed triangular blackish spots; flanks washed buffy-ochraceous. Lateral tail feathers have white edges and tips. The wings are short and wide. The small bill is relatively broad and is fringed with well-developed bristles on each side of the gape. Iris: brown. Bill: upper mandible black, lower mandible whitish-horn colour. Legs and feet: brown. *Immature:* like adult but duller, with a shorter tail; dark feathers have buff tips. The Spotted Fantail may occur in the same localities as the Grey Fantail but differs in larger size, spotted plumage, the colour of back and wings and in behaviour and preferred habitat.

DISTRIBUTION AND STATUS

The Spotted Fantail occurs in the Loyalty Islands, New Caledonia and in Fiji where 3 endemic races are found. Pratt *et al* (1987) note that the bird is streaked rather than spotted and that the intensity of colour in the plumage varies geographically. The race *spilodera*, described above, is found throughout Vanuatu from Efate northwards (Mayr 1931c). It is common in suitable habitats but not as numerous as the Grey Fantail.

FIELD NOTES

This relatively tame and inquisitive bird is easily recognised by its spotted breast and by the long rounded fan tail which is usually kept moving from side to side, up and down, spread into a fan from time to time and closed again. The wings are drooped as it hops about and when at rest the body and tail are swayed almost constantly from side to side. This restless, active bird does not dart so much from branch to branch (like the Grey Fantail) but captures insect prey in short erratic flights, returning to the same perch many times. It is arboreal, apparently preferring the shady substage of the forest or the lower canopy but occasionally visits the ground. It frequents the true forest, the forest edge and thickets at all altitudes but appears to be more common in mountain forest and is infrequently found in partly cleared forest or gardens. It is usually seen singly or in pairs and tends to be sedentary though at times it may join loosely formed feeding flocks of white-eyes, whistlers and other flycatchers and travel with them for a distance. The Spotted Fantail is one of the more conspicuous of the small forest birds and if observers pass through its territory will harangue them with scolding calls and often follow them for a short distance before disappearing again into the tangled undergrowth.

VOICE

The call-note is a short, tinkling sound and it also has sharp scolding chirping notes when agitated. The melodious, short twittering song consists of four or more distinct syllables and is usually given from a perch.

FOOD

Many kinds of insects are taken, usually captured on the wing.

NEST AND BREEDING

Fantails have a characteristic nest with a long tapering tail, sometimes more than 15 cm long, trailing beneath. The neat cup nest of the Spotted Fantail is tidily built of plant fibres, fine grass or some vine tendrils liberally bound with spiderwebs. It is placed on a thin, often horizontal fork or branch generally fairly low in the substage but sometimes in the lower canopy. The 2 whitish eggs are marked with light brown blotches, concentrated at the broader end. Both adults incubate the eggs and rear the young. The breeding season is normally from October to January but some nests have been found as early as June. There are possibly 2 broods in a season.

Australian Warblers *Acanthizidae*
There are about 66 species in 8 genera in this recently described Australasian family of small insectivorous, arboreal or terrestrial birds. The family comprises 4 main groups, mouse warblers, thornbills, gerygones (sometimes known as fairy warblers), and scrubwrens. They

occur from Thailand and the Philippines through New Guinea and the southwest Pacific islands to Australia, which has approximately 41 species, and New Zealand. Until recently they were often included in the family Sylviidae, the so-called Old World Warblers but it is now accepted by many authorities that the Acanthizidae have evolved independently (Beehler et al, 1986; Simpson and Day, 1989).

The 2 warbler species of Vanuatu do not have much more in common with each other than their small size and thin bill. The arboreal Fantail Warbler, Gerygone flavolateralis, *has been recorded from most islands in the archipelago whereas the Thicket Warbler,* Cichlornis whitneyi, *skulks in the dense undergrowth of the forests of Santo and is reluctant to fly.*

The gerygones are a well-defined group with 8 species in New Guinea and 11 in Australia. They are dainty birds, very active and gregarious, frequently joining mixed-species feeding flocks working their way through the foliage of woodland trees. The second species here included in the family Acanthizidae is the Thicket Warbler. Discovered in 1926 on Santo in montane forest, the life history and habits of this secretive bird are not well known and it has not been found elsewhere in Vanuatu. It has some of the characteristics of the false babblers, Pomatostomatidae, a small Australasian family of 5 species but is much smaller than most and does not appear to be gregarious. This species may be more closely related to the scrubwrens, genus Sericornis *in the family Acanthizidae and until more taxonomic and behavioural studies have been made it seems best to place* Cichlornis *in this family.*

With few exceptions the Australian warblers are dull-coloured, mainly in shades of grey, brown and olive-green, sometimes washed with yellow. Male and female are usually alike or similar in colour. They have thin pointed bills with rictal bristles and all live primarily, some exclusively on insects. They build domed nests which are sometimes very elaborate or pendulous. All are probably sedentary and most species have a pleasing song.

99. Fantail Warbler *Gerygone flavolateralis correiae* PLATES 13, 19
French name: Fauvette à ventre jaune

IDENTIFICATION
Length about 10 cm. One of the smallest and most drab birds in Vanuatu, dark above and lighter below, with a short tail. *Adult male and female* are alike but the female is paler: upperparts appear olive; head olive-grey with an indistinct white stripe on either side of the forehead and an incomplete narrow white eye-ring; wings and tail olive-brown with subterminal white spots on the lateral tail feathers. Throat whitish-grey: flanks and abdomen lemon-yellow; rest of underparts pale grey. Iris: red. Bill: black, short and straight. Legs and feet: black. *Immature:* the entire underparts are yellowish. The Fantail Warbler differs from the 2 species of white-eyes in Vanuatu by the smaller size, narrow eye-ring and the white spots on the tail. It differs from the female and immature honeyeaters in the shape of the bill, the lack of red in the plumage and the red colour of the iris.

DISTRIBUTION AND STATUS
The Fantail Warbler with 4 endemic races is known to occur only on Rennell Island in the Solomons (*G.f.citrina*), in New Caledonia (*G.f.flavolateralis*), the Loyalty Islands (*G.f.lifuensis*) and in Vanuatu where the race *correiae* is relatively common in suitable habitat.

Various changes in distribution have been documented in Vanuatu. Of the numerous 19th century collectors who worked in the group, none recorded the Fantail Warbler though collections were made in some central, northern and southern islands. The first Vanuatu records are those of the Whitney Expedition, which in 1926-7 collected this species on Vanua Lava, Gaua, Ambae, Malakula, Ambrym, Lopevi, Epi, and Emae but not on the 23 other islands including Malo and Santo, visited by them. Furthermore, none of the collectors and observers on Santo in the period from 1922 to 1945 reported the Fantail Warbler there and the Whitney collectors explicitly mentioned in their field notes that it was absent. The first records for Santo are by the author in 1961, by Diamond in 1969 and by the Royal Society Expedition in 1971. Peter Kaestner who visited Santo 14-17 June 1985 and travelled 12-15 km inland from Ipayato on the southern coast and up to 600 m noted that it was 'fairly common in the forest' (Naika 19:7). The author also made the first observation on Malo and Diamond and Marshall (1976) note that it has also been recorded on Maewo and Pentecost. However during the same period this species has not been found again on Vanua Lava, Ambae, Ambrym, Epi, and Emae despite the earlier Whitney records and it has yet to be recorded on any island in Vanuatu south of Emae though it reappears in the Loyalty Islands and in New Caledonia. Diamond and Marshall (1977b) assume that since the Vanuatu population is an endemic race it was not absent from the whole archipelago in the 19th century but only from those islands visited by the collectors at that time. It seems likely that the Fantail Warbler colonised Vanua Lava, Malakula, Ambrym and Epi between the late 1800s and 1926, colonised Santo between 1945 and 1961, Malo between 1926 and the 1960s and may have disappeared again from Ambae, Ambrym, Epi, Emae and Vanua Lava between 1926 and the 1960s.

FIELD NOTES

The Fantail Warbler may be found at all altitudes and in many different habitats; the forest, secondary growth, open park-like areas, scrub and village gardens. Diamond and Marshall (1977b) found it from sea-level to at least 1,600 m. It is usually solitary but sometimes seen in pairs or family parties and occasionally with other species in loose feeding flocks which it follows for some distance. It searches for small insects, quietly but vigorously, flitting through the branches and clinging to the foliage, close to the ground as well as in the canopy. As it feeds it moves systematically from one tree or bush to another, gleaning insects along stems or under leaves and sometimes taking them in flight, hovering with rapid wingbeats about the foliage. It is not conspicuous and although feeding birds keep in communication with soft twittering, it may easily be overlooked. It is often only the song which reveals its presence.

VOICE

These warblers twitter softly 'tawee' or 'hawee' when feeding, presumably for contact. The little song, an unmistakable series of musical liquid and undulating notes, 'twee-wee-heet' or 'hee-weetaweet', is uttered slowly while the bird flits about and is often repeated incessantly for long periods.

FOOD

Many kinds of insects are taken and their eggs, larvae and pupae.

NEST AND BREEDING
The nest is a compact pear-shaped dome having a side entrance, usually hooded, near the top. The length is usually between 20 and 25 cm, including a tail which may be from 6 to 12 cm long. It is constructed from plant fibres, rootlets, soft bark and mosses bound together with spiderwebs and lined with soft plants and some feathers. It is suspended from a slender stem of vines, usually from one to 5 m above the ground. The 2-3 eggs are white or buff, marked with brown. The Fantail Warbler is a favourite host-species of the Shining Bronze-Cuckoo. The breeding season is from September to January/February.

100. Thicket Warbler   *Cichlornis whitneyi*   PLATES 13, 19
French names: Fauvette de Santo, Fauvette des buissons
Local name: Zizileri – in Nokovula village at the foot of Mount Tabwemasana, Santo

IDENTIFICATION
Length about 16.5 cm. A skulking, slender ruddy-brown bird with rather long legs and tail. *Adult male and female* are alike but the female is paler: head brown, darker on the crown, with a conspicuous, straight buffish eyebrow and dark patch through the eye; upperparts rufous-brown, wings and tail dark brown. Underparts are rich buff-brown, lighter on the throat. The wings are short and rounded and the tail long and graduated. Iris: brown. Bill: black or blackish-brown. Legs and feet: black. *Immature:* has not been described.

DISTRIBUTION AND STATUS
This species of Thicket Warbler is only known to occur in the mountain forests of two islands in the southwest Pacific, Santo in Vanuatu and Guadalcanal in the Solomons. It was first discovered on Santo in 1926 and in the early 1950s a second race, *C.w.turipavae*, was found on Guadalcanal (Galbraith and Galbraith, 1962). In Vanuatu it is common within its limited range. Two other species of Thicket Warbler have since been described, *C.grosvenori* in 1958 from the Whiteman Mountains of New Britain (Naika 10:15), and *C.llaneae* in June 1979 from the mountains of Bougainville Island in the Solomons (Hadden, 1983).

FIELD NOTES
The Thicket Warbler apparently prefers to live mainly in the dense, low vegetation of the primaeval mountain forest, on the dryer Santo west coast, rarely occurring below 700m above sea level and more commonly around 1,200m. Medway and Marshall (1976) found this species near Hog Harbour on Santo, at an altitude of 160m, indicating that 'this warbler is not confined to montane elevations' but it was 'less common there than at Nokovula'. It is usually found singly, in pairs or family parties. It is probably sedentary, the favoured haunt being the more humid parts of the forest and the edges of wetter gullies. In such places these active birds spend most of their time close to the forest floor, moving quietly, rummaging through leaf litter, probing into moss or soft soil, turning over small objects or picking up insects from leaves, twigs, liane tangles and so on. They also examine the bark of trees and probe into crevices. Shy and secretive, they are difficult to observe as they keep to the dense undergrowth, seldom showing themselves. If disturbed they may fly away low over the

forest floor but usually conceal themselves among the ground cover and utter loud alarm calls. The sharp, drawn-out alarm call is often the first indication of their presence. The calling bird scurries about like a rodent in the dense tangle of ferns, stems and moss covered boulders. It usually keeps out of sight but may be seen at intervals, for just a few seconds, often with its tail partly cocked up and slightly fanned. The Thicket Warbler is apparently reluctant to fly and, when forced to, will rapidly cross the open space from one gully edge to another or just travel a few metres before landing again in low vegetation.

VOICE

Usually when approached too closely or alarmed a series of piercing, scolding notes, rapidly delivered and of equal or descending pitch 'tzwee-zweeweeweewee' may be rapidly repeated. This explosive alarm call is very distinctive and cannot be confused with anything else in its range. It probably also has softer contact calls and a musical song but these have not been described. The vigorous alarm calls of the Thicket Warbler are among the most characteristic sounds of the Santo highland rainforest.

FOOD

Many kinds of small insects, worms, and spiders are taken and possibly small snails.

NEST AND BREEDING

Nothing is known of the role of male and female in nest building, incubation of the eggs and feeding the young. The nest has been described as dome-shaped and placed low down in thick vegetation, often under a rock or fallen branch.

Honeyeaters *Meliphagidae*

The 170 or so species of honeyeaters in about 38 genera form one of the largest and most characteristic bird families in the Australo-Papuan region. They are found mainly in Australia and New Guinea (which both have about 66 species), but their range has extended as far as the Lesser Sundas and Bali in Indonesia, New Zealand, the southwest Pacific islands and Hawaii. Most honeyeaters are rather dull-coloured in various shades of olive-green, grey or brown, but others have attractive, boldly patterned plumage with bright red or yellow and white. Among the larger honeyeaters are species that have patches of bare skin, wattles, casques or ornamental tufts of feathers about the head or neck. Honeyeaters vary in size from about 8 to 32 cm and the sexes are usually alike in plumage though in some species the female is markedly smaller or less attractively coloured. However, all have the typical honeyeater-look, rather streamlined body, fairly long, strong legs and slender medium to long, downcurved bill, though the tail may be short or quite long. The pointed beak and long extensible tongue, with sides that curl up to form a tube and the tip broken up into stiff fibres forming a brush, are highly adapted for probing into flowers and collecting nectar. The honeyeaters however, do not feed exclusively on nectar and, although flowering trees provide most of the food for many species, they all eat insects and may take soft fruits or berries. When feeding from blossoms, the birds may take up any position, even hanging upside down. They also feed on the wing, especially the small species, scanning the leaves for insects or hovering before blossoms which they could not otherwise reach, but they usually sit down to their meals perching on, or in front of, the flowers. Honeyeaters find a good part of their insect diet in flowers, in conjunction with nectar but also forage among the leaves and branches hunting like some flycatchers. The honeyeaters are important as pollinators of many indigenous plants and an interesting relationship exists between a number of these plants and various species of the honeyeater family. These trees and shrubs are known as ornithophilous which literally means 'bird-loving' and their flowers are shaped to facilitate pollination by nectar-sipping birds.

Honeyeaters are largely arboreal. Some species live in the lowland or mountain forest while others occur in plantations or open savannah country and a few are common visitors in village and city gardens. Quite a few species are nomadic following the flowering of indigenous trees and shrubs. They are vigorous on the wing and have an undulating flight. Many species are gregarious, others are quarrelsome and pugnacious and will attack any other bird that ventures too close. Most species are highly vocal with distinctive calls. Some have extraordinarily loud or raucous calls while others have very pleasant notes or musical songs and some are competent mimics, imitating the songs of other birds. With few exceptions their nests are cup-shaped, usually placed in the fork of a branch in trees or bushes but occasionally pendulous. Most lay 2-3 eggs, white, sometimes tinted pink or buff, with markings of darker shades.

The honeyeaters are represented in Vanuatu by 3 common and conspicuous species. The endemic Vanuatu Mountain (White-bellied) Honeyeater is found mainly in the mountains of the central and northern islands. The most frequently seen is the Silver-eared Honeyeater and on some islands also, the brightly coloured Cardinal Honeyeater. The voice is diagnostic for each species. Medway and Marshall (1975) state that where all three honeyeaters exist together, in the coastal strip at Malakula, there is no evidence of interaction and they 'are obviously separated by size, feeding niche and other behavioural characters'.

101. Vanuatu Mountain Honeyeater   *Phylidonyris notabilis*   PLATES 9, 20
Other name: White-bellied Honeyeater
French name: Méliphage des montagnes
Bislama name: Long fala mouth blong hill
Local name: Pearye or Petyea – in the mountain villages around the foot of Mount Tabwemasana, Santo

IDENTIFICATION

Length 18 to 21.5 cm, the female is probably smaller. A medium-sized honeyeater, dark above and light below with a strongly downcurved bill. *Adult male and female:* crown black; face and forehead black with white spots which form a more or less distinct stripe over the eye; rest of upperparts rufous or olive-brown. Throat greyish-white; lower breast and abdomen pure white, sides of the breast and flanks have numerous long thin brownish streaks; underwing pale rufous. Iris: brown. Bill: black, slender and strongly curved. Legs and feet: bluish-grey. *Immature:* similar to adult but duller with light streaks above and lacking the dark streaks below. Two races with slight differences in plumage have been separated in Vanuatu:

P. n. notabilis from Ureparapara, Vanua Lava, Santo and Ambae
P. n. superciliaris from Maewo, Pentecost, Malakula, Ambrym, Paama and Epi.
This species was formerly in the genus *Guadalcanaria* (Salomonsen, 1967).

DISTRIBUTION AND STATUS

The Vanuatu Mountain Honeyeater is endemic to Vanuatu. It is found on the larger islands in the central and northern parts of the group and was formerly thought to be restricted to the highlands. On Santo, Medway and Marshall (1975) encountered it from 850m at the head of the Apuna Valley up to 1,100m near Nokovula, but not in the lowlands. However, some birds have been seen by the author on the west coast of Santo close to the village of Kerepua in sea-level forest and one was mist-netted in mangroves in the coastal strip on Malakula (Medway and Marshall, 1975). In Vanuatu it is common and widely distributed within its range and is fully protected by law. A similar species occurs particularly in the mountains of New Caledonia and 5 species in the same genus occur in Australia, mainly around the south and east coasts, in coastal heaths and woodlands.

FIELD NOTES

This species, the largest of the Vanuatu honeyeaters, is generally found in the highlands from about 450m and above. The call of this handsome white-bellied honeyeater is one of the most characteristic sounds of the highlands, carrying far through the forest and it is one of the opening calls of the dawn chorus. While it is still dark one bird calls and others join in until the forest is filled with their ringing flute-like notes. This extremely active, rather sociably inclined species may be seen singly, in pairs or small parties, either high up in the trees or low down in the undergrowth, vigorously darting about the foliage and inspecting the blossom for nectar or hunting for insects, stopping only to utter its call from time to time. Like most honeyeaters it also makes short wheeling flights in pursuit of passing insects. The birds characteristically search quickly for nectar in one bloom after another then fly rapidly and gracefully from tree to tree. Unlike other honeyeaters the Vanuatu Mountain Honeyeater does not appear to be aggressive in behaviour towards its own kind in the wild or in captivity. In an aviary in Port Vila a group of five birds indulged in many types of communal activities, feeding, bathing and even roosting together, either side by side tightly along a perch or huddled closely on top of a nest box.

VOICE

The Vanuatu Mountain Honeyeater is a very vocal bird with a great range of ringing calls which are frequently repeated and sometimes strung together to make a song. One of their first calls in the dawn chorus is a powerful 'tyau' or 'tyjau'. Other noticeable calls are a loud, usually prolonged 'toowyt', a less often heard, moderately loud, somewhat plaintive 'teewee' and the harsh alarm call 'tchea'. The birds sometimes sit on some exposed branch and sing their rich series of pleasant, flute-like notes and whistles; 'teewee-twytwyttee' or 'teewee-teeeeeeee' and 'teewy-teewy-zwyt'. They probably also imitate the calls of other birds they hear.

FOOD

The diet is varied and includes nectar, pollen, insects, spiders and probably juicy fruits.

NEST AND BREEDING

Neither the nest nor the eggs have been found by any of the ornithologists that have studied the species. However, the nest has been described by the Santo mountain people as being cup-like, containing 2 light coloured eggs and has usually been found from September to January.

102. Silver-eared Honeyeater   *Lichmera incana*   PLATE 9
French name: Méliphage à oreillons gris
Bislama name: Long fala mouth

IDENTIFICATION
Length 15.5 to 17 cm, the female is noticeably smaller than the male! A featureless drab-coloured, slender bird with a long tail and slightly downcurved bill. *Adult male and female:* crown dark grey; ear-coverts silver-grey; back, wings and tail olive-green. Throat ash-grey with somewhat scaly pattern; rest of underparts dusky light grey, slightly washed with olive. Iris: light grey. Bill: black. Legs and feet: bluish-grey. *Immature:* similar to adult but paler and lacks silver-grey on ear-coverts. Flavistic individuals are known from Efate. A further record is noted in *Naika* (16:12) from Hermon Slade of 'a bright canary yellow honeyeater' feeding from garden flowers with 'other normal-coloured honeyeaters' who were 'apparently acting rather aggressively towards it'. It was first seen on 13 November 1984 and he 'continued to see' it until at least June 1985 (Naika 18:13).

DISTRIBUTION AND STATUS
This species is restricted to the Loyalty Islands, New Caledonia and Vanuatu. Some

The nest of the Silver-eared Honeyeater is a deep cup of grasses, plant fibres, leaves and spiderwebs suspended from a thin forked branch

authorities list 2 races, *flavotincta* and *griseoviridis* from Vanuatu (Salomonsen, 1966 and 1967). Mayr (1945) noted that *L. i. flavotincta* occurred in central Vanuatu; Malakula, Ambrym, Paama, Lopevi, Epi, Tongoa, Tongariki, Emae, Makura, Efate, Nguna, and Emau and in southern Vanuatu on Erromango. Medway and Marshall (1975) note that this species was also recorded from Tanna by Ramsay in 1879. Three other species in the genus *Lichmera* occur in New Guinea and one of these, the Brown Honeyeater *Lichmera indistincta*, also occurs in the Lesser Sundas and in Australia (where, according to Pizzey (1980), it is widespread on the mainland and many coastal islands). In Vanuatu the Silver-eared Honeyeater is common and widespread.

FIELD NOTES

It is a conspicuous bird in almost all habitats at low or moderate altitudes, forest, secondary growth, mangroves, scrub and gardens in villages and towns. Although it feeds from a great variety of flowers it shows a strong preference for the nectar in young blooms in coconut plantations which is available the whole year round. These honeyeaters are also common in other agricultural areas and suburban gardens where they are usually seen when visiting the flowers of hibiscus, ornamental ginger bushes, banana plants and lantana shrubs. They are restless noisy birds drawing attention to themselves by their loud cheery calls. They are almost constantly on the move from the scrub layer to the treetops searching vigorously for nectar in blossom and for insects among the leaves and branches. They also hover in front of flowers or catch flying insects in quick aerial dashes. When the captured insect is large it is stunned on a perch, in kingfisher fashion. Richard Pickering (Naika 10:15) notes a record of a honeyeater of this species hovering in front of a spider's web to pick off trapped insects. He observed this behaviour several more times and on one occasion a honeyeater had 'become completely enmeshed in spider's web' and was 'struggling in a strait-jacket of gossamer' but it presumably disentangled itself as it had gone a little later (Naika 16:12). The honeyeaters are most often seen singly or in pairs but when a favourite food tree is in bloom the honeyeaters gather from several kilometres around and groups of 10 to 30 birds will feed noisily from daylight to dusk, often together with white-eyes, Cardinal Honeyeaters and lories. They are territorial and pairs usually stay in the same area for many years aggressively keeping away other birds of their own species. The birds are largely sedentary, their only known movements being local in search of blossoming trees.

VOICE

They call regularly but are particularly vocal in the morning and evening. Almost all their call-notes are loud and often harsh. Their main call is a rather loud 'tchoo-tchoo-tchoo'. They also have a sparrow-like 'cheelp-cheelp' and a musical warbled song and are fair imitators of other bird species. They are the first birds to announce the coming of day with their calls which start well before dawn.

FOOD

Their diet consists of nectar, pollen, insects, spiders and probably some fruits. The young are raised mainly on a diet of insects and spiders.

NEST AND BREEDING

The nest, a small deep cup of grasses, plant fibres and a few small leaves lined with soft materials (inner diameter 55 mm), is held together by spiderwebs and fastened at the rim to a thin forked branch of bush or tree from 2 to 12 m above the ground. It is sometimes so finely constructed that the contents may be seen through it. Usually 2 eggs are laid, matt white marked with a few pale reddish-brown spots, often only at the larger end. Apparently both sexes build the nest and share the rearing duties. Incubation takes about 14 days and the young leave the nest about 12 days later. The breeding season is normally from about October to January/February but nests containing young birds have been found as early as June.

103. Cardinal Honeyeater *Myzomela cardinalis* PLATE 9
French name: Sucrier cardinal

IDENTIFICATION
Length 11 to 12.5 cm. A small bird with a long thin downcurved bill and short tail. The sexes are very different: the male in scarlet and black is one of the most strikingly coloured birds in Vanuatu while the female is dull brown with some traces of scarlet. *Adult male:* head, breast, middle of back and rump scarlet; lores and rest of plumage black, slightly glossy. Iris: brown. Bill: black. Legs and feet: black with yellow soles of the toes. *Adult female:* much duller than the male; the black is replaced by olive-grey or olive-brown, darker above, lighter below. The scarlet is duller and almost entirely replaced by olive-brown except for some scarlet on the upper throat, crown and back. *Immature:* similar to female but with the red plumage further reduced; only the throat and crown are washed with scarlet and the gape is yellow. The size, brilliant plumage and long bill make the male unlikely to be confused with any other bird in Vanuatu. Females and immatures might be mistaken for species with similar, more or less olive plumage, but can be distinguished by the longer, curved bill, the scarlet wash on crown and upper throat and the absence of white on the forehead, around the eye and on the tail. In Vanuatu the Cardinal Honeyeater is often likened to and called a hummingbird because of the small size, brilliant colours of the male and the habit of feeding on nectar. Although they do resemble the hummingbirds of the New World in some ways, the birds are quite different in structure and they are not closely related to each other.

DISTRIBUTION AND STATUS
The Cardinal Honeyeater occurs in a number of races in the eastern Solomons, Santa Cruz Islands, the Loyalty Islands and Samoa. In Vanuatu 2 races are recognised:
   M. c. tenuis is found on all islands from Efate northwards and the larger
   M. c. cardinalis on Erromango, Tanna and Aneityum.
It is common, but on some islands it is apparently restricted to the highlands or at least is more numerous there (Koopman, 1957). A similar species occurs with various races in several Micronesian islands and another endemic species has recently been recognised on Rotuma Island in Fiji. On the basis of museum specimens these were all once thought to be races of the Cardinal Honeyeater but Pratt *et al* (1987) consider that they should be given separate species status because of their morphological and vocal differences and geographic isolation.

FIELD NOTES

The Cardinal Honeyeater is a bird of the true forest but it has a wide habitat tolerance and may be encountered on the forest edge, in secondary growth, mangroves, open park-like country, coconut plantations and suburban gardens wherever there are flowering trees or shrubs. It can be found from the coastal lowlands up to the highest mountain tops on most islands but on Efate at least, it is only occasionally seen in the lowlands and it is noticeably more numerous in the mountainous interior on all islands. In the forest these restless birds flit through the middle and upper levels of the forest or lower down but apparently prefer tall flowering trees. They are usually seen singly, but gather in considerable numbers when favourite indigenous trees are in full bloom. They are locally nomadic, apparently more so than the other honeyeater species. Populations may be reduced to a few isolated individuals where they were once numerous or large numbers may appear in an area from which they have been absent for long periods if nectar in abundance is available. When a flock of Cardinal Honeyeaters feeds in a flowering tree the contrast between the blossoms and the brilliant black and red plumage of the males as they dart about the vegetation is a thrilling sight indeed. They are very acrobatic and tumble, hover or hang upside down to reach blossoms in the least accessible places, chase insects through the foliage or dart out from the branches to catch insects on the wing. A bird of this species has also been known to become entangled in a spider's web, presumably when attempting to pick off trapped insects (Naika 19:7). The Cardinal Honeyeater is one of the most aggressive of all the Meliphagidae. When feeding in flocks the rowdy little birds quarrel constantly among themselves and seem to spend as much time chasing one another and other small birds away from the blooms as they do feeding. This chasing can culminate in violent fights when the two adversaries jump at each other and may tumble to the ground in a tangle of feathers, claws and beaks. While attacking they keep up a shrill twittering note. Both sexes engage in this behaviour but the fights usually last only a few seconds. The flight of the Cardinal Honeyeater is rapid, direct and mostly over short distances only.

VOICE

They are vocal birds but the voice is not as strong as that of the other two honeyeaters in Vanuatu. A characteristic sharp, high-pitched 'tzwee' or 'tzeer' is uttered almost constantly as they flit vigorously through the foliage. The last note is especially given when the birds are angry. They also have a short, melodious jingling song 'tzeewyt-tzeewyt--tweet-weet-tweet', repetitive and usually performed from a high perch. The song is more lively during the breeding season.

FOOD

The diet consists of nectar, pollen, small insects and spiders.

NEST AND BREEDING

The nest of the Cardinal Honeyeater has only seldom been discovered and this suggests that, like many canopy birds, they nest mainly in the tops of tall trees in a site well hidden by leaves. It is a small cup-shaped nest built of fine roots and spiderwebs fastened at the rim to a thin fork of a branch or a vine and may be from 3 m upwards. Usually 2 eggs are laid, rarely more, white marked with pale red-brown. The female apparently does most of the nest building and incubation but the male helps in rearing the young. Incubation takes 12 to 14 days and the nesting period lasts about the same time. As far as is known the breeding season is from September to December/January.

White-eyes or Silvereyes   *Zosteropidae*
This family is made up of about 82 species which range throughout Africa, across southern Asia to the islands of the Pacific, north to China and Japan and south to Australia and New Zealand. White-eyes are much alike. They are small birds from 8 to 15 cm long, with a slender pointed, slightly curved bill, medium long, square tail, strong legs and, like honeyeaters, a lightly brush-tipped tongue. Their only conspicuous feature, which gives the family its name, is the narrow circle of silver-white feathers around the eye, though this varies somewhat and is yellow in one species and missing in others. Their plumage colour ranges from prevailing olive-green, yellow and grey to brown and grey in some island populations. Male, female and immature have similar plumage. White-eyes are arboreal, extremely active and restless birds, and often travel in large flocks except when breeding.

In the Pacific islands white-eyes do not appear to be particularly strong fliers and some populations show a high degree of differentiation into an incredible number of races. In contrast some white-eyes have a strong tendency to migrate or disperse in flocks and have established themselves on remote islands more successfully than any other passerines. In the 1850s the Silvereye (Grey-backed White-eye) Zosterops lateralis *from Tasmania colonised New Zealand, travelling over 1,930 km, and has since become the commonest landbird there (Campbell and Lack, 1985). Recent banding studies of Silvereyes in eastern and southern Australia (over 100,000 birds banded) have shown in the past 20 years that in autumn some populations, previously thought to be sedentary or only locally nomadic, undertake long journeys in flocks of several hundred birds (Simpson and Day, 1989).*

Some species frequent the treetops of the true forest, but others prefer the edges of the forest, secondary growth or plantations, mangroves and gardens. They have twittering and chirruping call-notes. Their melodious song, a sequence of distinct notes with slurs and trills, often repeated may be diagnostic for each species. The food comprises insects, nectar, berries and some fruits. The small, neat cup-shaped nest is usually woven onto a fork of a branch in a bush or tree. The clutch consists of 2-4 light to dark blue eggs.

This widespread family is represented in Vanuatu by 2 common species, the Vanuatu White-eye and the Grey-backed White-eye (Silvereye) which are easy to distinguish. Both species frequently form loose, trailing flocks, sometimes mixed, the birds keeping in contact with each other with their almost continuous high-pitched calls. The ecological separation of the 2 species is not clear cut. Habitat preference and altitude seem to be involved but there is some habitat overlap and both species, for example, are seen in gardens at Port Vila. It is apparent that the Vanuatu White-eye is the generalised species found in any habitat, though it is commoner in the forests and at higher altitudes, whilst the Grey-backed White-eye seems to be absent from the true closed forest and common in disturbed habitats (Diamond and Marshall, 1977a). Their liking for lantana berries Lantana camara *has helped to spread this introduced plant.*

104. Vanuatu White-eye *Zosterops flavifrons* PLATES 9, 20
Other names: White-eye, Yellow White-eye, Yellow-fronted White-eye
French name: Zosterops de Vanuatu   or locally: Lunettes
Bislama name: Nalaklak (used for both species of white-eyes in Vanuatu)

IDENTIFICATION
Length 11.5 to 12.5 cm. A small entirely yellowish-green bird with a conspicuous white eye-ring and a short slender bill. *Adult male* has a broad silvery-white eye-ring; upperparts olive-yellow or yellow-green. Forehead and underparts rich yellow. Iris: brown. Bill: dark tip; upper mandible brown, lower mandible light horn-colour. Legs and feet: lead-grey. *Adult female* has similar plumage but is paler, particularly the yellow on the head and underparts. *Immature* is similar to adult but all colours are much paler and the eye-ring is narrower. Seven races, 6 of which were described between 1929 and 1937, have been separated in Vanuatu (Mayr, 1945). They differ in the amount of yellow in the plumage:

Z. f. gauensis from Gaua

Z. f. perplexa from Vanua Lava, Mere Lava, Maewo, Ambae, Pentecost, Ambrym, Paama, Lopevi, Epi, and Tongoa

Z. f. brevicauda from Malo and Santo

Z. f. macgillivrayi from Malakula

Z. f. efatensis from Efate and Erromango

Z. f. flavifrons from Aniwa and Tanna

Z. f. majuscula from Aneityum.

Z. f. gauensis, *efatensis* and *flavifrons* are yellowish-olive above, have a yellow forehead and are bright yellow below. The 4 other races are darker above with a little yellow on the forehead and are more greenish below.

The Vanuatu White-eye can be distinguished from all other greenish-yellow birds in Vanuatu by the bright yellow forehead and the distinctive ring of white feathers around the eye. It is less sturdy than the Grey-backed White-eye (Silvereye) with which it often associates, lacks the grey back and has more yellow in the plumage and also, has a slightly higher-pitched contact call.

DISTRIBUTION AND STATUS
The endemic Vanuatu White-eye is perhaps the most numerous bird in the group. It occurs on almost all islands but has not yet been recorded on Ureparapara and Mota Lava. It is common to abundant, especially in the mountains. Possibly related species occur in Fiji, the Loyalty Islands and New Caledonia (Mees, 1969).

FIELD NOTES
The Vanuatu White-eye is found in forests and all other types of habitat from the lowlands to the mountains where there is sufficient tree or shrub growth. They are also one of the common native birds seen in plantations, on other agricultural land and around suburban gardens. They are very active, searching vigorously through the foliage for insects and other food, low down in shrubs or high up in the trees but infrequently on the ground. In the treetops these little birds would be hard to detect if they did not incessantly utter their rather monotonous contact calls. They are found in pairs or small parties but outside the breeding season gather and wander locally,

The neatly woven nest of the endemic Vanuatu White-eye is usually attached at the rim to leaf stems or a thin horizontal fork

often in fairly large noisy flocks, sometimes in the company of whistlers, fantails, flycatchers and honeyeaters. When disturbed they fly off, still calling to each other, to start foraging afresh in another tree, usually close by. If sustained, flight is rapid and slightly undulating.

VOICE
The almost constant contact call is a short, high-pitched 'chip-chip' or 'tzeep-tzeep'. It also has a pleasant warbling song often repeated.

FOOD
The Vanuatu White-eye has a mixed diet of insects, their eggs and larvae, spiders, berries, fruits, nectar and probably also small buds and seeds. It is fond of lantana berries, chilli fruits and all kinds of soft, sweet wild figs; ripe but uncollected paw-paw fruits are usually hollowed out.

NEST AND BREEDING
The small neatly woven cup (60 × 55 mm outside and about 55-66 mm deep from the rim) is made of fine grass, thin bark shreds and spiderwebs occasionally lined with a few feathers and fine vegetable fibres. It is attached at the rim to a thin horizontal fork or two leaf stems from about 2.5 m above the ground upwards. Three whitish-blue eggs are laid (17 × 14 mm). Both parents care for the young and probably more than one brood is raised in a season. The breeding season is from September to January or March.

105. Grey-backed White-eye   *Zosterops lateralis*   PLATE 9
Other names: Silvereye, White-eye, Grey-breasted White-eye
French name: Zosterops à dos gris   or locally: Lunettes

IDENTIFICATION

Length 13 to 13.5 cm. Larger than the preceding species, a yellow-green and grey bird with a broad white eye-ring. *Adult male and female:* head, wings and rump yellowish-olive; mantle and back grey. Chin and throat greenish-yellow, clearly separated from the brownish-grey of the breast and flanks, giving the impression that the whole head is yellowish; middle of abdomen white; undertail-coverts greyish-white or with a yellowish tinge. Wing and tail feathers brown, edged with olive-yellow. The broad white eye-ring is bordered with blackish feathers. Iris: light brown. Bill: blackish-brown. Legs and feet: lead-grey. The female is slightly paler. *Immature:* similar to adult but all colours are duller and the eye-ring is feebly developed. The 3 races found in Vanuatu differ mainly in the amount of grey on the back and the extent of black below the eye:

Z. l. valuensis from Mota Lava in the Banks Islands has almost no grey on the warbler-like green back

Z. l. vatensis from Erromango northwards, including the Banks and Torres islands, with the exception of Mota Lava, is intermediate in colour

Z. l. tropica from Aniwa and Tanna has much grey on the back and much black below the eye.

This species is distinguished from the Vanuatu White-eye in all races by the more greenish plumage, grey back and tawny flanks and slightly sturdier build.

DISTRIBUTION AND STATUS

This widespread species occurs in Australia, New Zealand, and Pacific islands to New Caledonia, the Loyalty Islands and Fiji. It was introduced to the Society Islands from New Zealand in 1939 and later to the Tubuai Islands. The Grey-backed White-eye is found on most islands in Vanuatu but has not yet been recorded on Aneityum or Futuna. It is common but not nearly as numerous as the Vanuatu White-eye. See Mees (1969) for discussion.

FIELD NOTES

These vigorous and restless white-eyes may be encountered in a wide variety of habitats; secondary growth, the edges of forests, scrubland, mangroves, plantations and other agricultural land but are uncommon or absent in the high mountains and the true forest. They commonly visit suburban gardens. They forage at any height from the ground to the canopy, typically in small flocks, gleaning insects from leaves and branches, probing flowers for nectar and taking ripe berries. When on the move these unobtrusive small birds utter their plaintive, short contact call almost continuously. After the breeding season the birds congregate in small flocks and wander locally, at times in company with whistlers, flycatchers and the other white-eye. Their flight, though jerky and uneven is strong and fast.

VOICE

In flocks the Grey-backed White-eye maintains contact with an almost continuous high-pitched, drawn-out rather peevish 'cheew' or 'tzee'. It also has a melodious song.

Pizzey (1980) describes it as a 'surprisingly loud beautiful warbling territorial song of rapid succession of high-pitched notes and trills, warbles and slurs'. It also has a 'quiet or autumn sub-song that includes mimicry'.

FOOD
Similar to the Vanuatu White-eye, the varied diet consists of insects, spiders, softer berries, fruits and nectar. Favourite fruits are lantana, chilli and the soft sweet wild figs and it also hollows out ripe paw-paw fruits.

NEST AND BREEDING
The nest is a small, somewhat untidy cup (65 × 60 mm) mainly of fine grasses and rootlets with some spiderwebs, moss and lichen, lined with softer materials. Both sexes build the nest which is suspended by the rim from an almost horizontal fork or branch in dense foliage, from 2 to 14 m above the ground. The 2-4 eggs (17 × 13 mm) are pale blue to green and incubation takes about 12 days. Both sexes incubate and feed the young which leave the nest when 11 to 13 days old. The breeding season is from August to January/February and probably 2 broods are raised in a season.

Finches *Fringillidae*

The term 'finch' in the past has been used generally for any small seed-eating songbirds with a stout bill and their family has included 11 subfamilies. Following Campbell and Lack (1985) the family Fringillidae here comprises the subfamilies of Fringillinae with 3 species including the well-known Eurasian chaffinch and brambling and Carduelinae with about 122 species, found in North and South America, Africa and Europe, several of which have been introduced to Australia and New Zealand. Finches in this family have similar skull structure, 9 large primary feathers and 12 rectrices. One other family characteristic is that only the female builds the nest and incubates the eggs. They are small birds, from 11 to 19 cm long, with a short, conical, heavy bill showing considerable adaptation according to the method of extracting and shelling the various types of seeds in the diet. They have a plump body, relatively short wings and undulating flight. The colour of plumage varies, some being cryptically coloured with streaked plumage while others are brightly coloured or have prominent patches on shoulder, wing or tail. Many species are sociable and are frequently encountered in small to large flocks. Some finches, like the domestic canary, because of their bright colours and melodious song have been bred in captivity for centuries or, at least, kept in cages as pets. Most species eat seeds but some also eat insects and buds or fruit and in some agricultural and fruit growing regions they are considered to be pests.

No members of the finch family are resident in Vanuatu but there is one record of a male Redpoll, collected in March 1961 on Aneityum.

106. Redpoll   *Carduelis flammea cabaret*   PLATE 15
French name: Tarin à front rouge

IDENTIFICATION AND FIELD NOTES
Length 11 to 12 cm. A small streaked bird with a short conical bill and slightly forked tail. *Adult male:* forehead blackish, top of head dark crimson-red; upperparts light brown streaked blackish on the centres of feathers; hindneck and sides of the head

paler; rump reddish, streaked blackish-brown; wings and tail feathers dark brown edged light brown; in flight wings show a buff double wingbar. Sides of face light brown; chin black; throat and breast rose-pink; abdomen white. Iris: yellow-brown. Bill: dark brown. Legs and feet: brown. *Adult female:* similar to male but lacks red on breast and rump. *Immature:* like the female but has no red on the crown, less black on the chin and has more dark streaks on throat and breast. A similar race *C.f.flammea*, is larger and paler and has white (not buff) wingbars.

The Redpoll has adapted to a variety of habitats, forests, farmlands and all types of open country. It may feed in trees or close to or on the ground eating the seeds of trees, grasses, sedges and of many sorts of wild flowers. It also eats the buds of plants and takes insects. It commonly forages in flocks, even during the breeding season, and has a distinctive, staccato, metallic flight call, 'chi-chi-chi-chi-chi'. The song is a melodious short trill. The breeding season in New Zealand is from September to January.

DISTRIBUTION AND STATUS

The Redpoll is naturally a northern hemisphere species, breeding in northern temperate regions and the arctic and wintering in Europe as far south as the Mediterranean with similar migrations in North America and Asia. In the eastern Pacific it is a rare vagrant to Hawaii (Pratt *et al*, 1987). In 1862 a shipment of these birds, which contained individuals of the 2 races described above, was released in New Zealand and they have subsequently become established throughout the islands. *C.f.flammea* type individuals now comprise 10-15% of the population there but the two types are interbreeding. The Redpoll is rather rare in North Island, mostly breeding at higher altitudes but a few breed on the coast in areas of sand dunes and scrub. It is very common in South Island at all altitudes up to 1,600m and has colonised the subantarctic islands (Falla *et al*, 1981). There is one record for Vanuatu of a male Redpoll collected close to Anelghowat on Aneityum in March 1961. This bird may have been a straggler from New Zealand or a bird which had escaped from a passing ship.

Sparrows *Passeridae*
This family includes about 30 species in 3 genera, the true sparrows, genus Passer *with about 16 species, the rock sparrows,* Petronia *and the snow finches,* Montifringilla. *In some ways they resemble the finches and in others the weaver birds, family Ploceidae and these relationships are still being studied. Sparrows are small birds, 10 to 20cm long, similar in shape to finches with a thick conical bill for eating seeds but they are generally dull-coloured with mainly brown or grey plumage. They have various harsh chirping calls but no real song. The majority are birds of open country, some inhabiting the mountains, rocky scrub or grasslands while others prefer agricultural regions or have adapted to urban situations. Many are gregarious and nest colonially making bulky nests, sometimes domed, in holes or crevices in rocks, trees or buildings. Some species are found in the tropical regions of Africa while others occur widely in Europe and Asia. One species, the House Sparrow, has spread or been introduced to most parts of the world.*

In Vanuatu the House Sparrow can be found in small numbers in and around Port Vila on Efate and possibly at Luganville on Santo.

107. House Sparrow *Passer domesticus* PLATE 15
French name: Moineau domestique

IDENTIFICATION
Length 14 to 15 cm. A plump, bold and noisy bird with a short, stout bill and a notched tail. *Adult male* in breeding plumage: crown ashy-grey; nape and sides of the neck dark chestnut; back chestnut with black streaks; median wing-coverts chestnut broadly edged white showing as a bar in flight; rump grey and tail brown. Cheeks grey-white; throat and upper breast black forming a bib; rest of underparts light grey. Iris: brown. Bill: blackish. Legs and feet: brown. In non-breeding plumage the head pattern and the lower part of the black bib are obscured by buff tips to the feathers and the bill is yellow-brown. *Adult female and immature* are alike: head pale brown with a prominent buff-white eyestripe back from the eye; upperparts pale earth-brown, streaked with black and rufous on the upper back; wings dark brown, variegated with rufous and with a thin white wingbar; throat and rest of underparts pale grey-brown, paler on the belly. Bill: yellow-brown, lighter in the immature.

DISTRIBUTION AND STATUS
This species originated in Eurasia and Africa. It has spread widely or been introduced and is now present in all countries except Japan and China and some isolated island groups. Several shipments were released in Australia and New Zealand in the 1860s. It is not known whether the House Sparrow was introduced to Vanuatu deliberately, or came by accident with an assisted passage by boat. It may have been first introduced by Europeans who brought birds from New Caledonia.

The earliest reference to the House Sparrow in Vanuatu comes from a note in *Naika* (17:12) that the leader of the Whitney Expedition, which was in Vanuatu in 1926-27, had written in his journal that the House Sparrow was common in Vila. It was well established there by 1959 and when Richard Pickering surveyed the northern edge of House Sparrow colonisation of Port Vila in 1982, he found that 'it had not quite reached B P Tebakor though birds were fairly well established at Anabrou'. Before and since then odd birds or pairs had been seen 'near the Anglican Church at Tagabe, at Tam's Store and at the Agricultural College and once at Bauerfield Airport terminal'. In June 1984 a pair was in residence among the buildings at Tagabe Agricultural Station (Naika 14:10). This pair was seen carrying nest material in September 1984 and later that year 4 birds were seen, 'one male and three which could be either females or juveniles' (Naika 16:13). It can be expected that in the future, its range will be extended as Vila and the other towns expand.

FIELD NOTES
This noisy little bird may be seen singly or in pairs but is usually found in small parties perched in trees or on houses or hopping about on the ground looking for food. It is surprisingly wary. Flight is swift and undulating but it seldom flies far. In Vanuatu it lives close to human habitations or other buildings, and has not intruded into agricultural areas or the natural vegetation.

VOICE
It has a variety of harsh chirping notes, 'tchirp' or 'chissick'. Sometimes these notes are strung together but the noise could not be described as a song.

FOOD

It eats seeds of many kinds and in many cereal growing regions of the world it is classed as a pest. It also eats buds and fruit and may peck at flowers but usefully takes aphids and other small insects. The nestlings are fed mainly on insects for the first 6 to 10 days. The House Sparrow regularly takes scraps of food or kitchen waste thrown out and visits chicken yards to eat grain or other food provided for the poultry.

NEST AND BREEDING

The nest is a bulky, dome-shaped structure with a side entrance, built of grass, rags, paper and any other material available, lined with feathers. It is placed in a crevice in a building, often the eaves of a house, or in thick bushes or trees. The 3-6 eggs are greyish-white, blotched with brown and grey. Both adults share in nest-building, incubating the eggs and rearing the young. The breeding season is apparently from September to February and probably at other times if conditions are suitable. It is said to breed from July to April in New Caledonia.

Waxbills, Mannikins and allies *Estrildidae*

This large Old World family with about 130 species in 28 genera, originated in Africa and has spread through Asia to Australia, Melanesia and Polynesia. It is composed of small, seed-eating birds with a short thick bill and thin graduated tail, pointed in some species. They are similar in aspect to finches and are often called the 'estrildid finches'. Plumage varies considerably, some being extremely ornamental, with scarlet, blue or orange patches, some with contrasting colours or patterned with white spots. Male and female usually have similar plumage but the female is duller. They probably pair for life and most species have elaborate courtship displays. When breeding, most species also eat insects; some parrotfinches take fruit. Most nest in small trees or bushes, others in tall grass or reeds and the nest is an untidy structure, domed with a side entrance, sometimes lined with feathers. Usually 4-6 white eggs are laid. Both sexes build the nest, share incubation and the care of the young. They are very attractive small birds, often kept in cages, and they are easy to breed in captivity.

This family is represented in Vanuatu by 8 species in 5 genera. Two of these, the Red-browed Firetail and the Red Avadavat have both been recorded only once and are of uncertain status. Possibly these birds escaped from an aviary and it would be interesting to know if there have been any further sightings. Four species, the Common Waxbill, the mannikins and the Red-throated Parrotfinch are known to have been introduced either intentionally or through aviary escapes. In this context it must be strongly underlined that the release of exotic fauna is highly undesirable, from a conservation and an economic point of view, as a vigorous, opportunistic introduced species may become a strong competitor for the indigenous wildlife of Vanuatu and may become a pest by damaging grain or fruit crops. The other 2 species are parrotfinches, genus Erythrura *which are local races of species native to islands in the tropical and southwest Pacific.*

108. Common Waxbill *Estrilda astrild* PLATES 15, 16
French name: Astrild gris   or locally: Bengali

IDENTIFICATION

Length 11 cm. A small slender bird with a bright red bill and a rather long graduated tail. *Adult male:* grey-brown above, greyer on the crown, with a broad, crimson stripe from the bill, through the eye. Underparts pale grey, slightly washed with pink, with a crimson patch in the middle of the abdomen; vent and undertail-coverts black. The entire plumage except for the throat is finely barred blackish-brown. Iris: brown. Bill: orangey-red, with a glossy wax-like sheen. Legs and feet: black. *Adult female:* the whole plumage is paler than the male; the red patch on the belly is less extensive and duller. *Immature:* similar to female but with little or no red and only faint barring. The bill is black but nestlings have a pair of white papillae on each side of the gape which are joined by a thick black membrane.

DISTRIBUTION AND STATUS

This species is very widely distributed in tropical and southern Africa and has been introduced in several other countries and to some Pacific islands including Tahiti and New Caledonia. In Vanuatu escaped aviary birds first became established in Port Vila on Efate and found the conditions so ideal that they spread rapidly, following the major roads, to country areas. It is common in suitable habitat. The date of introduction is not known but by 1959 Waxbills could be seen in open rough grass, in scrub and by the roadsides throughout Efate, mainly in the lowland. The Common Waxbill was also introduced in Santo. Medway and Marshall (1975) noted that by 1971, the 'introduced population that was present on Santo in 1944 (Scott 1946) appeared to be extinct'.

FIELD NOTES

In Vanuatu the Common Waxbill inhabits grassland interspersed with groups of trees or bushes and has become a typical inhabitant of gardens and suburbs. The birds feed by climbing up and down grass stems collecting seeds or hopping about on the ground eating fallen seeds. When a bird is moving or excited the tail is constantly flicked up and down and from side to side. When disturbed they rise up uttering short high-pitched calls then drop quickly into concealment in the grass or settle in nearby shrubs and trees where they completely disappear from view for a while. They are highly gregarious and out of the breeding season wander about in small flocks of several dozens. They usually fly in tight formation and are capable of very sharp simultaneous turns. Within the flocks the pairs keep together and social preening is apparently restricted to partners.

VOICE

The contact call is a soft, short nasal 'tjeek' or 'tzep'. The song is simple, a high-pitched 'tzetzechree' often repeated.

FOOD

Mainly ripe and half-ripe seeds of different grasses are taken and some insects, particularly during the breeding season.

NEST AND BREEDING

The nest is spherical (23 to 28 cm long, 13 cm high and 10 to 12 cm wide) with a long downwards pointing entrance tunnel of green or dry grass and is lined with finer grass and sometimes a few feathers. It is placed in high grass or thick foliage in bushes or trees, often less than 3 m above the ground. It may also be placed amid the aerial roots of banyan trees. At times a second rudimentary nest, without an entrance tunnel, is built on top of the true nest. The 5-7 eggs are pure white. Both parents take turns to incubate the eggs which hatch after 11 to 12 days. The young fledge 18 to 21 days after hatching but may return to sleep in the nest for several more days. The breeding season is from August to December/February.

109. Red-browed Firetail *Neochmia temporalis*
Other name: Red-browed Waxbill (*Estrilda/Emblema temporalis*)
French name: Astrild à cinq couleurs

IDENTIFICATION AND FIELD NOTES
Length 11 to 12 cm. An olive-green and grey bird with a conspicuous red eyebrow and red rump. *Adult male and female:* head blue-grey with a thick scarlet stripe from the base of the bill over the eye; back and wings olive-green with a lighter yellow-olive shoulder patch; rump scarlet, tail black and tapering. Underparts pale grey. Iris and bill: scarlet. Legs and feet: yellowish-flesh colour. *Immature:* brownish above and buff below with a blackish bill and no scarlet on the head; scarlet rump is prominent. This species is unlikely to be confused with the Common Waxbill with which it often associates in the Pacific; the olive and grey plumage with no barring and the red rump are diagnostic.

Usually seen in flocks, in Australia it inhabits the forest edge or thickets interspersed with grassland whereas in the Pacific it is more likely to be seen in grassland, at the roadside close to settlements or in gardens. The voice is a thin high squeak or chattering notes in flocks. Pizzey (1980) describes the flight as erratic and bouncing.

DISTRIBUTION AND STATUS
A native of Australia where it mainly inhabits the wide coastal strip, bordered by the mountains, from Adelaide to the Torres Strait. This species was introduced to the Society Islands in the 1800s and subsequently to the Marquesas where it is common but not so numerous as the Common Waxbill (Pratt *et al*, 1987). Mayr (1945) noted that it was introduced to New Caledonia and was 'common in grasslands' but this was most probably based on an error as *Estrilda astrild* is the only known waxbill there. The only record for Vanuatu is of 'a small party of Red-browed Waxbills' seen in 1988 by John Edge 'on the flat ground at the top of the track' (presumably the track between the Hospital and the Intercontinental Hotel), at Port Vila on Efate (Naika 29:28).

110. Red Avadavat *Amandava amandava*
Other names: Red Munia, Strawberry Finch
French names: Bengali rouge, Astrild rouge

IDENTIFICATION AND FIELD NOTES
Length 11 cm. A small plump finch of Asian origin with a bright red bill and red rump. The male and female are very different and the male, alone of the estrildid finches, moults after breeding. *Adult male in breeding plumage:* red-brown above patterned with

small white spots on back and wing-coverts; rump red. Crimson below, liberally spotted white on the sides of the upper breast and flanks. In non-breeding plumage the male is much duller, resembling the female. Bill: glossy bright red. Legs and feet: brown. *Adult female:* olive-green above with a dark stripe through the eye; wings and tail dark olive-brown; wings patterned with small white spots; rump dark red. Pale olive-yellow below, darker on the flanks, undertail-coverts buff. *Immature:* similar to female but duller.

In countries where it is common it is usually seen in small flocks feeding in grassland or along roadside verges, often close to towns or villages. It has a twittering contact call. It is highly gregarious and may be seen in flocks with other species.

DISTRIBUTION AND STATUS

The Red Avadavat occurs in India and through southeast Asia to the Lesser Sundas and has been introduced to many other countries, including the Philippines. It was brought to Fiji in the early 1900s and has become established there. It is now common to abundant on Viti Levu and Vanua Levu (Pratt *et al*, 1987). The only record for Vanuatu is of 'a party of a dozen Red Avadavats' seen on Efate in 1988 in the same place, and possibly at the same time, as the Red-browed Firetail (Naika 29:27).

111. Chestnut-breasted Mannikin *Lonchura castaneothorax*   PLATE 15
French name: Donacole à poitrine châtaine

IDENTIFICATION

Length 10 cm. A small, plump bird with a black face, stout blue-grey bill and a pointed tail. *Adult male and female:* crown, nape and hindneck grey with dark streaks; back and wing-coverts dark cinnamon-brown; wing feathers greyish-brown; rump and uppertail-coverts straw to brownish-yellow; central pair of tail feathers straw-yellow, the rest brown with yellow margins. Lores, ear-coverts and throat black; foreneck and breast pale chestnut, separated from the white abdomen by a variable black breast band; flanks scalloped black; thighs and undertail-coverts black. Iris: brown. Bill: light bluish-grey. Legs and feet: leaden-grey. According to some authors the black breast band is narrower in the female but such differences are subject to considerable individual variation and there seem to be no plumage characters for sexing the birds with certainty. *Immature:* dark olive-brown above; cheeks olive-brown with white streaks; chest brownish-buff; rest of underparts whitish-buff.

DISTRIBUTION AND STATUS

A native of Australia, where it breeds in the north and east and on northern offshore islands, and New Guinea, it was introduced to the Society Islands in the 1800s where it is now common and to the Marquesas (Pratt *et al*, 1987). Pizzey (1980) notes that it has also been introduced to Tahiti and New Caledonia. In Vanuatu this species became established around the town of Luganville on Santo after escaping from an aviary (the date has not been recorded). In 1972 a few birds were seen in the suburban gardens of Luganville and a family group on short seed-bearing grasses on the west coast near the village of Kerepua. It has spread to suitable habitats in the coastal lowland and the foothills.

FIELD NOTES

It inhabits grassy park-like country, reed beds, plantations, paddocks, gardens and the fringe of villages but rarely ventures into the town. The Chestnut-breasted Mannikin is usually seen in pairs, family parties or small flocks, feeding on seeds. It is quite tame and can be approached closely. It may feed on the ground but apparently prefers to pick seeds from the seed-heads of tall grasses while climbing nimbly among the upright stalks.

VOICE

The main call is a low, soft bell-like 'tet' or 'tee', uttered frequently in flight and when feeding in flocks. The high-pitched, lengthy song is barely audible from only a short distance away.

FOOD

The diet consists mainly of ripe and half-ripe seeds of wild grasses and herbaceous plants. In agricultural areas, however, it may switch almost entirely to cultivated grasses such as rice, cereals, millet and sorghum. In Australia it has become a minor pest in rice-growing regions. During the breeding season it takes some insects, such as flying termites.

NEST AND BREEDING

The nest (14 cm in diameter) is made of coarse grasses and lined with softer grass. It is globular in shape, slightly depressed laterally, with a small entrance hole at the side which may be protected by a hood. It is placed in tall grass, reeds, dense scrub or low bushes. The clutch consists of 4-6, occasionally 8 white eggs. In Australia this species may breed in any month of the year but in Vanuatu apparently between September and January.

112. Black-headed Mannikin *Lonchura malacca* PLATE 15
Other names: Chestnut Munia, Chestnut Mannikin
French name: Donacole à tête noire

IDENTIFICATION

Length 11 cm. A small plump bird with an all black head, heavy blue-grey bill and a short pointed tail. *Adult male and female:* head, nape, throat and breast black. Rest of plumage chestnut-brown except for black belly and undertail-coverts; the tail is tinged with orange. Iris: brown. Bill: blue-grey. Legs and feet: dark grey. *Immature:* pale brown above and buff below. The chestnut plumage could appear red in flight and be confused with the male Red Avadavat, but note the blue-grey bill.

DISTRIBUTION AND STATUS

A native of southeast Asia from India to the Philippines, it has been introduced in several other countries. In Vanuatu it has become established in and around the town of Luganville on Santo after escaping from an aviary in about 1960, 'spontaneously extending to Auta Plantation, Aore, about 1965' (Medway and Marshall, 1975). In 1971 they saw the Chestnut Munia 'only in these two places'.

FIELD NOTES

The Black-headed Mannikin frequents areas of grass and reeds among scattered trees and bushes, the margins of swamps, mangroves and cultivations. It is highly social, forming flocks in which all members perform the same actions simultaneously and close together. It feeds mostly by landing high on grass stems and gathering half-ripe seeds as it climbs among the stalks but also closer to the ground.

VOICE

The contact call is a shrill, short 'teep'. It also has a soft drawn-out song.

FOOD

It eats mainly half-ripe seeds from a variety of plants. During the breeding season it probably also takes insects.

NEST AND BREEDING

The nest is made of coarse grass, lined with fine grass and is oval with a side entrance tunnel. It is placed in tall grass or low bushes from 0.5 to 2 m above the ground. The clutch varies from 4-8 white eggs. The breeding season is probably from September to January.

113. Red-throated Parrotfinch   *Erythrura psittacea*   PLATE 15
French name: Diamant psittaculaire

IDENTIFICATION

Length 11 to 11.8 cm. A small green finch with red face, conical bill and pointed reddish tail. *Adult male:* grass-green except for the bright crimson-red forehead, face, throat and breast; rump and tail rust-red. Iris: brown. Bill: black. Legs and feet: horn-colour to brown. *Adult female:* similar but according to some authors, slightly duller; the red on the head is less extensive; abdomen is tinged ochraceous. However such differences could be subject to considerable individual variation or age and there seem to be no plumage characters for sexing the birds with certainty. *Immature:* much duller, with little or no red. As in all parrotfinches the nestlings have a peculiar set of dark spots and lines inside the mouth and, on each side of the gape, two phosphorescent blue papillae which are joined together by a thick yellow membrane. See Ziswiler, Güttinger and Bregulla (1972) for biology, ethology and discussion.

DISTRIBUTION AND STATUS

The Red-throated Parrotfinch is a native of New Caledonia where it is common. In Vanuatu, a small group of these finches escaped or were released from an aviary in about 1966 and were first found in plantations around Port Vila. Since then they have only been seen occasionally and may have died out. They have also been observed on Emae but apparently have not become established.

FIELD NOTES

In New Caledonia this parrotfinch may be seen mainly in the lowlands and less often in the mountains. It frequents grasslands and other open areas, the forest edge, forest glades, plantations, pastures, roadside verges and gardens. It is usually seen in pairs, family groups or small flocks. These birds are nomadic, their movements being governed by the availability of food.

VOICE

The short contact call is a single or double-noted 'tzee' or 'tzeet', uttered frequently, especially during flight. The song consists of a series of trills.

FOOD

The diet consists mainly of the ripe and half-ripe seeds of grasses, many species of herbaceous plants and casuarina seeds. During the breeding season it probably also takes insects.

NEST AND BREEDING

The nest is a sphere made of grass, leaves and moss, with a side entrance. It is often placed low down in dark places such as rock or tree hollows, amongst the exposed roots of fallen trees or trees in banks, or in small caves and very occasionally between branches in bushes or trees. The clutch consists of 3–6 white eggs and the eggs hatch after about 13 days. The young leave the nest 18 to 22 days later and are independent about 2 weeks after fledging. The breeding season is from September to January.

114. Blue-faced Parrotfinch *Erythrura trichroa cyaneifrons* PLATES 15, 22
Other names: Blue-faced Parrot Mannikin, Blue-faced Finch
French name: Diamant tricolore de Kittlitz

IDENTIFICATION

Length 11.2 cm. A small emerald-green finch with blue face, conical bill and pointed reddish tail. *Adult male:* forehead, front of crown to behind the eye and face deep violet-blue bordered by a variable band of green tinged golden-olive; upperparts bright grass-green, primaries and outer secondaries brown edged green; rump and long central pair of tail feathers rust-red, outer tail feathers brown tinged dull red on the outer webs. Underparts bright green. Iris: brown. Bill: black. Legs and feet: dark brown. *Adult female:* according to some authors is similar to the male but all colours are less bright; the blue on the crown is less extensive and does not reach behind the eye; the abdomen is tinged ochraceous. However, such differences could be due to considerable individual variation or age and there seem to be no plumage characters for sexing the birds with certainty. *Immature:* dull green above with little or no blue on the forehead or face; breast, abdomen and undertail-coverts pale ochraceous. The bill is pale greyish-brown and the feet yellowish-brown. The nestlings have two phosphorescent blue papillae joined together by a thick yellow membrane on each side of the gape. The immature might be mistaken for the immature Royal Parrotfinch but differs in having a distinctly thinner dark bill and less blue and no red on the head. See Ziswiler, Güttinger and Bregulla (1972) for biology, ethology and discussion.

DISTRIBUTION AND STATUS

This wide-ranging finch is found from Queensland in Australia to Sulawesi and the Moluccas, New Guinea where it occurs mainly in the hills and mountains 750 to 3,000 m (Beehler *et al*, 1986), the Caroline Islands and Palau in Micronesia and in

Melanesia. Pratt *et al* (1987) note that it is fairly common in the east Carolines but is hard to find on Palau. It is present on Guadalcanal in the Solomons. The race *cyaneifrons*, described above, occurs on Lifu and Mare in the Loyalty Islands and in Vanuatu on Gaua, Ambae, Ambrym, Lopevi, Efate, Nguna, Emau, Erromango, Tanna and Aneityum. It is generally rather uncommon but is common to abundant on some islands like Efate, where the favourable factor which has permitted their increase is habitat modified through the development of pastures. Medway and Marshall (1975) imply that it is surprising that this species has never been found on Santo or Malakula, which both have extensive suitable habitat.

FIELD NOTES

The Blue-faced Parrotfinch is found in open habitats. It frequents the forest edge, savannah, village gardens, plantations, pastures, roadside verges, sports fields and town gardens and openings or clearings in the true forest from sea level up to at least 1,200m. Like all granivorous species it must also have access to a supply of fresh water. It may be encountered singly but is more often seen in pairs, family parties or flocks. It is nomadic and its movements are governed by the availability of food supplies. In areas with a plentiful supply of ripening seed large flocks of 200 or more birds may quickly gather, to disappear just as rapidly once the seeds have been eaten. They feed by expertly climbing grass stems to take seeds from the spike or by jumping up and pulling the spike down to extract them. They also hop over the ground in tight groups searching for fallen seeds. When feeding in open grassland, the birds like to keep near scattered trees or bushes. If disturbed they fly to the nearest cover only to return to the same spot, a short while later, after much nervous calling. When in flocks they synchronise many of their actions and keep relatively quiet. Silence is broken only by their contact calls. Flight is fast with rapid wingbeats and the sustained flight is undulating. There has been a considerable increase in numbers on some islands during the past 25 years or so, where forest clearance for pasture and agricultural developments has created more of the open countryside favoured by this species. The planting of introduced grasses has enormously expanded their food supply. Richard Pickering noted that flocks were attracted to the observation plots of upland rice at Tagabe Agricultural Station and harvested 'a fair proportion of the grain' (Naika 19:10). The provision of stock watering places has further aided their success.

VOICE

The contact call is a short high-pitched single note 'tzeet' or 'tzee'. At regular intervals during flight a double-noted 'tzeet-tzeet' is uttered, often even when moving just a few metres. The alarm call is a loud, sharp 'treeee'. The song consists of a series of high-pitched trills that fall and rise towards the end. Fledglings pursue their parents with an incessant, imploring, penetrating 'tchreeee'.

FOOD

It mainly eats ripe and milky seeds of grasses and other plants, favourite foods being the seeds of the indigenous grass *Cyrtococcum trigonum* and some of the exotic grasses like the Guinea Grass *Panicum maximum*. In the first few days of life the nestlings are probably fed partly on insects.

NEST AND BREEDING

This species has a courtship display which usually takes place in the treetops. The male, with trilling calls, chases the female for long periods from tree to tree before finally catching her. During copulation the male holds the female by the head or neck feathers with his beak. In Vanuatu the Blue-faced Parrotfinch has apparently switched mainly to hole-nesting. It usually breeds in small hollows in limestone cliffs and between rocks covered with dense vegetation or in hollows in trees and between branches. Inside the hollow a small and often rather rudimentary nest is built with thin walls made of grass, leaves and vines. The percentage of traditional nests built in a bush, tree or amid the aerial roots of the giant fig tree is probably low. The clutch is 4-6 white eggs and the young hatch after about 12 to 15 days. The young leave the nest about 25 days later but are fed by both parents for a further two weeks. Two or three broods are raised during the breeding season. The majority of pairs breed during October to February/March but odd pairs can be found nesting before or after this period.

115. Royal Parrotfinch *Erythrura cyaneovirens* PLATES 15, 22
Other name: Red-headed Parrotfinch
French name: Diamant royal
Local names: Tabut – on Tongoa and Emae
Batukira – in the mountain village of Nokovula, Santo

IDENTIFICATION

Length 11 to 12 cm. A small, compact glossy blue-green finch with a bright red head, thick black bill, red rump and tail. *Adult male:* crown and side of the head bright crimson-red; back and wings variable blue-green; rump bright crimson-red; tail rust-red. Throat and breast blue; rest of underparts green, more or less washed with blue. Iris: brown. Bill: black. Legs and feet: light brown. *Adult female* has noticeably less blue in the plumage. *Immature:* plumage is generally dull with no blue on the throat and breast; head is dull blue, sometimes with a few red feathers; the bright yellow bill darkens gradually to black. Nestlings have two pairs of large, glossy blue papillae either side of the gape, joined together by a thick yellow membrane, which are still visible for some days after leaving the nest. Adult plumage is apparently acquired within the first year. Three races were originally separated in Vanuatu on the amount of blue in the plumage:

E. c. regia from Gaua, Santo, Ambae, Pentecost, Malakula, Ambrym, Paama, Lopevi, Epi, Tongoa and Emae was described as having some blue on the back and much blue on the abdomen, especially in the adult male.

E. c. efatensis on Efate and *E. c. serena* on Aneityum (described by Mayr in 1931) were stated to have a blue nape and breast and green back and abdomen. However, more recent studies indicate that they are not reliably distinguishable. This work and the proposed 'sinking' (inclusion) of the races *efatensis* and *serena* in the one race, *regia*, are discussed in Ziswiler, Güttinger and Bregulla (1972).

DISTRIBUTION AND STATUS

This species is confined to Savaii and Upolu islands in Samoa, where it is uncommon

(Pratt et al, 1987), and Vanuatu, where, in addition to the islands listed above it may also occur on several more islands in the north of the group. It is uncommon on Efate but more numerous in suitable habitats in most of the northern islands and fairly common on Tongoa and Emae. The present relatively high number of individuals on these small islands is presumably due to an increase in food supply, throughout the year, from the considerable number of different species of fig trees that have become established, in the many partly cleared areas and the thinned out forests, on the higher parts of the islands. However the number of birds could decrease in coming decades if the natural forest-cover further diminishes in size (and with this the number of fig trees) as the land is taken over for various developments. This is especially likely on Tongoa with its high human population. On Aneityum the species may be present in very small numbers or even extinct. During a survey by the author in 1961 no parrotfinches were found. A second survey in 1971 also failed to find any of these birds but reported that their searches were not exhaustive enough to confirm the extinction of this species on Aneityum (Medway and Marshall, 1975). The species may have become rare or extinct in part at least because most of the natural forests were cut in commercial operations resulting in severe environmental damage.

A similar species, common in Fiji is the Red-headed Parrotfinch *Erythrura pealii*, which is treated by some authors as a race of *Erythura cyaneovirens*. However, it is a more generalist feeder, described by Pratt et al (1987) as feeding on grass seeds near the ground or on flowers, buds and insects in trees, and it may be found in a variety of habitats including city parks and gardens. It is not a specialised tree-feeding finch of the montane rainforest like the Royal Parrotfinch of Samoa and Vanuatu. Please refer to Ziswiler, Güttinger and Bregulla (1972) for separate species status of *E. pealii*, the biology and ethology of parrotfinches and discussion.

FIELD NOTES
These beautiful finches are generally confined to the highlands and mountains and rarely descend to the lowlands. On smaller islands like Tongoa and Emae it is possible to find them from 50m upwards but on islands with high mountains they are more likely to be found from the upland forest to the highest peaks and are rare or even absent in the lowlands. They inhabit most types of wooded country with fig trees; forest, savannah, plantations and village gardens. They prefer to feed in the canopy and only come to the ground to drink. They are difficult to observe as they can only be seen easily among the higher branches of trees or flying high overhead when they come into the more open areas. Flight is strong and undulating. Being the most solitary of all the finches in Vanuatu they are usually encountered alone or in pairs but small groups may gather in fig trees with ripening fruits, each bird arriving and departing alone. The characteristic contact call usually gives their presence away.

VOICE
The usual call is a single or double note, 'tzeet' or 'tzee' at long intervals when feeding, but more often and at regular intervals in flight. The alarm call is a high-pitched, drawn-out 'treeeeee'. The song consists of a series of high trills. The calls of the Royal Parrotfinch are similar to those of the Blue-faced Parrotfinch but the contact call appears to be somewhat shorter in this species.

FOOD
The staple diet is the seeds of wild figs and it also takes some insects, their larvae and eggs which are found in the flesh and between the seeds of the fruit. To reach the seeds, the bird tears at the pulp of the fig with its thick, strong bill until the seeds are exposed. The fruit may still be attached to the tree or may be taken to a larger horizontal branch where it is held down by one foot while the fruit is cut open. Apparently, insects account for only a small percentage of the diet. See Ziswiler, Güttinger and Bregulla (1972) for investigation of nutrition within the genus and discussion.

NEST AND BREEDING
The bulky nest (about 30cm in diameter) is made of coarse materials, broad blades of grass, leaves and bark for the outer walls and softer grass for the inner walls. The nesting chamber is relatively large, approximately 12 × 10cm. The nest is spherical with a short entrance tunnel and often has a loose tail, which may be up to 60cm long, hanging beneath. It is built in a fork of a tree (frequently not well hidden) or in the middle of a tangle of small branches and twigs which may then be used to form part of the nest walls. It is usually about 10m or more above the ground but some nests have been found as low as 3m. The clutch consists of 4-6 pure white eggs. Occupied nests have been found in March and April though most pairs apparently breed from September to January.

Starlings and Mynahs *Sturnidae*

This family, comprising about 110 species in 25 genera, is found almost throughout the world. Starlings are a well-defined group of vigorous, active medium-sized birds of Old World origin. They are sturdy with a sharp, straight or slightly downcurved bill and strong legs and feet. Some are crested or have prominent wattles or bare patches of skin on the head. The tail is usually short and square though it is rounded or longer and tapering in a few. They generally have dark plumage, black, brown or grey, sometimes brightly marked with white, yellow or red, or with a metallic sheen in some species. Most starlings are found in open country, some around human habitation and only a few in indigenous forest. They may live in trees or on the ground, except for some aberrant African species, the oxpeckers, genus Burphagus, *which have adapted to living with and on large animals. The diet is varied, predominantly fruit, insects, and worms but some take pollen, nectar and seeds and those living near towns also take kitchen waste. In some countries they are classed as pests of fruit and cereal crops, whereas in others they are encouraged because they eat insect pests. Many species are gregarious and gather in flocks of tremendous size, often roosting together on trees or on buildings when they can become a nuisance. They tend to be nomadic and temperate zone species migrate and winter in flocks. Their flight is swift and direct. Most do not hop on the ground but walk with a wading gait. Starlings are generally noisy and aggressive, chattering to one another continuously in flight or when roosting and using a variety of harsh notes or musical whistles. Several rank high as mimics. In captivity the imitation of human speech rendered by the asiatic Hill Mynah* Gracula religiosa *is far superior to that of most parrots. The majority of starlings and mynahs build bulky nests in cavities in trees, cliffs or sometimes buildings but some build massive covered nests of sticks and twigs. One Australasian species, the Metallic Starling* Aplonis metallica, *nests colonially and weaves a large hanging nest of plant fibres in the treetops. The eggs are usually clear blue-green but are white in a few species or marked with brown. The size of the clutch varies from 2 to 9 and breeding behaviour varies considerably within the family.*

The two native starlings of Vanuatu are the endemic Santo Mountain Starling and the Rusty-winged Starling which is restricted to 2 island groups in Melanesia. There is one reference in the literature to the presence of the European Starling in Vanuatu, the Indian Mynah has been introduced on some islands in the group and in 1988 there were 2 possible sightings of the Papuan (Yellow-faced) Mynah.

116. Santo Mountain Starling *Aplonis santovestris* PLATE 12
Other names: Mountain Starling, Vanuatu Mountain Starling
French name: Stourne des montagnes
Local name: Mataweli – in the mountain village of Nokovula, Santo

IDENTIFICATION
Length 17 to 18 cm. An inconspicuous rufous-brown starling of the forest understorey, compact, with a stout bill and short tail. *Adult male:* crown blackish-brown; back brown; lower back and rump rufous-chestnut; wings and tail blackish-brown. Throat brownish; rest of underparts warm rufous-brown. Iris: milky-white. Bill, legs and feet: blackish-brown. *Adult female:* similar but has generally duller rufous plumage. The immature has not been described though a 'male – possibly juvenile – in non-breeding condition' which was 'similar except for a very slightly paler throat and a smaller size in general to the female' was collected in 1933 in the Mount Tabwemasana region (Harrisson and Marshall, 1937).

DISTRIBUTION AND STATUS
This interesting endemic species is confined to its mountain refuge in the cloud forest on the highest peaks of Santo where it is probably moderately common. The type specimen in the British Museum was collected at 4,000 ft (about 1,200 m), on Mount Watiamasan in northwest Santo during the Oxford University Expedition in 1933-34. In 1961 the Santo Mountain Starling was seen by the author about 17 times on the slopes of Mount Tabwemasana well above Nokovula village. However, some of these sightings during three weeks could possibly refer to the same bird. Village people present at that time at Nokovula said that they also encountered this species fairly regularly in the Mount Kotamtam and Tawuloaba area. Even when assuming that this starling is not uncommon in its specialised habitat, the limited extent of the cloud forest makes this, nevertheless, the rarest of the endemic species in Vanuatu. A similar species, the Pohnpei Mountain Starling *Aplonis pelzelni*, which is endemic to Pohnpei in the Caroline Islands, is an endangered species. It was last reliably sighted in 1956, though surveys were made in 1976, 1978 and 1984, and it is possibly extinct (Pratt *et al*, 1987). *Addendum:* Santo Mountain Starling p.274.

FIELD NOTES
The Santo Mountain Starling is one of the least known birds in Vanuatu and little information has been gathered on the birds' habits since their discovery. Singly or in pairs, it frequents the undergrowth of the heavily mossed cloud forest aptly described by Harrisson and Marshall (1937) as 'a dripping world of mists and rotting vegetation,

of scarlet "Flame-trees", tree ferns, patches of tough *Pandanus*-palm, and above all, a luxuriant flora of mosses, tree-creepers, and epiphytic orchids and pitcher plants.' They describe the bird as 'unobtrusive and solitary, and sub-terrestrial in that it is rarely observed higher than fifteen feet (5 m), and is completely at home among the rotting stumps and mossy lower foliage.' 'In the bush it sits silently on low boughs and stumps, flitting swiftly away through the dripping foliage when disturbed.' Flight is rather quick and direct with rapid wingbeats.

VOICE

The calls were described as 'a thin hissing note and an unemotional harsh Thrush-like call' (Harrisson and Marshall, 1937). The call has been described more recently by the Nokovula village people as short and moderately loud 'tzeetzeetzee' or separate notes 'tzee-tzee-tzee', which may be uttered when perched or in flight.

FOOD

It takes fruit, seeds and insects.

NEST AND BREEDING

The nest is built in a hole in a tree, close to the ground. Two white eggs are laid. Nothing further has been recorded about breeding behaviour or the breeding season.

117. Rusty-winged Starling   *Aplonis zelandicus rufipennis*   PLATE 12
French name: Stourne aux ailes rousses
Local name: Woohia – in the mountain village of Nokovula, Santo

IDENTIFICATION

Length 19.5 cm. A medium-sized arboreal, rather dull-coloured starling with a heavy bill and short tail. *Adult male and female:* grey-brown above, blackish on the head with black lores; wings dark brown with a bright rufous-chestnut patch on the primary coverts; rump rufous-brown; tail brown. Greyish-brown below with a buffish tone, lighter on the abdomen; vent pale rufous-brown. Iris: black. Bill, legs and feet dark brown. The immature has not been described. See Mayr (1942a) and Baker (1951) for affinities in Micronesia.

DISTRIBUTION AND STATUS

This species, with 3 races, is restricted to the Santa Cruz Islands and northern and central Vanuatu. The 2 Santa Cruz races differ mainly in having darker underparts. In Vanuatu the race *A. z. rufipennis* occurs on Ureparapara, Vanua Lava, Gaua, Mere Lava, Santo, Ambae, Pentecost, Malakula, Ambrym, Paama and Lopevi. On most islands it is more common in the highlands or even restricted to them. The apparent altitude preference may depend on the island's topography; on smaller flatter islands it may be found in wooded gardens at lower altitudes but on larger islands it is primarily an upland forest species and is uncommon or even absent in the lowlands. On Santo it is relatively common at around 1,000 m and on Vanua Lava it was sighted once close to the coast.

FIELD NOTES

The Rusty-winged Starling is principally a bird of the forest but may be seen in secondary growth, and partly cleared areas. It flies and bounds through the trees with vigorous movements, keeping most often to the lower canopy but it may also descend to the substage. It is usually found singly or in pairs, though several birds may gather to feed in a fruiting tree. In the dense forest it is more likely to be heard than seen.

VOICE

The call heard most often is a short, melodious 'zee-twee' or 'twee', frequently repeated. It also has a jumble of metallic whistles which may be repeated for quite long periods.

FOOD

Presumably it eats mostly fruits and seeds but it has also been seen gleaning insects from the foliage. Several birds examined had been feeding mainly on fruits.

NEST AND BREEDING

Very little has been recorded about the breeding behaviour. According to the village people it nests in tree holes, usually high above the ground. The breeding season is probably from August to December/January.

118. European Starling *Sturnus vulgaris*
Other name: Common Starling
French name: Etourneau sansonnet

IDENTIFICATION AND FIELD NOTES

Length 22 cm. A stocky, short-tailed blackish bird with a bustling gait and distinctive flight silhouette. Male and female are alike and both moult after breeding. *Adult breeding:* head and body blackish with green and purple gloss, back and rump speckled buff; wings and tail blackish edged with buff. Bill: yellow, sharply pointed. Legs and feet: dull pink. *Adult non-breeding:* body plumage heavily spotted with white and buff which is gradually lost through abrasion. Bill: dusky-yellow. *Immature:* dull grey-brown, paler below with a brown bill.

It flies directly and fast showing the characteristic triangular wingspread and short tail. It often travels in flocks which perform aerial manoeuvres, especially over communal roosting sites. Calls are various, including loud whistles and squeaks. The song is elaborated from calls, with trills and twittering and often includes imitations of other species' songs.

DISTRIBUTION AND STATUS

A native of Eurasia, it has been introduced deliberately to many countries and is now one of the world's most numerous birds. In Australia it is widespread in the southeast while in New Zealand it is abundant almost everywhere, including the offshore islands and it is found in large numbers on Norfolk Island and the Kermadecs (Falla *et al*, 1981). The only reference to the European Starling in Vanuatu comes from a letter published in *Ibis* (99:129) in 1957 from A J Cain and I C J Galbraith which contains the statement that 'Neither *Sturnus vulgaris* nor *Passer domesticus*, seen by us in the New Hebrides , have been recorded from the Solomons'. There have been no recent records in Vanuatu, though it could occur as a vagrant. Beehler *et al* (1986) note that it has twice been recorded in the Port Moresby area of New Guinea as a vagrant from Australia.

119. Indian Mynah *Acridotheres tristis*   PLATE 12
Other names: Common Mynah, Indian House Mynah
French name: Martin triste   or locally: Merle des Moluques

IDENTIFICATION
Length 24 to 25 cm. A robust, raucous black and brown bird with large white wing patches, conspicuous in flight. *Male and female* are alike: head black, very slightly crested on nape, with a large patch of bare yellow skin around and behind the eye; throat blackish-grey; back, breast and flanks cocoa-brown; lower belly and undertail-coverts white; wings blackish with a large white patch at the base of the primaries; tail rounded, blackish with a broad white tip. Iris: red-brown, flecked white. Bill, legs and feet: bright yellow. *Immature:* similar to adult but duller; bill and feet: brownish. The rich brown colour, conspicuous yellow wattles on the face, large white wing patch and white-tipped tail distinguish the Indian Mynah from the other starling species in Vanuatu. It is also larger and darker than the Rusty-winged Starling.

DISTRIBUTION AND STATUS
The Indian Mynah has been deliberately introduced from southeast Asia to many of the southwest Pacific islands in attempts to control insect pests of plants and possibly cattle. Some introductions have led to declines in populations of indigenous species of birds through competition, particularly for nest-sites, as in the Solomons, New Caledonia and Fiji. It is said to have been introduced to Vanuatu in the 1880s when a ship carrying caged birds to Fiji was wrecked at Lenakel on Tanna (Medway and Marshall, 1975). It is now well established on Tanna and has spread northwards to Efate and Epi and to Paama where it is present only at Liro (Richard Pickering pers. comm. 1985). It has also been recorded on Malo and Aore and is found on Santo west to Ipayato. The population has not increased to pest proportions in Vanuatu though it does compete for nest sites with the native hole-nesting parrots and the Rusty-winged Starling.

FIELD NOTES
This species is conspicuous because of its close association with humans and its garrulous nature. It is found in gardens, backyards and on rubbish tips in towns and villages, in plantations, on cattle stations, in other agricultural areas and in open country. Since it was introduced to Vanuatu, its spread on islands seems to have followed the major roads and as more forests are cleared, the range of this species is slowly expanding. It is mainly seen in scattered pairs, family groups or flocks, either feeding on the ground or perching on trees, fences or roof tops. Pairs always appear 'self-confident' and perky as they walk about with rapid, bouncy steps, stopping occasionally to pick up food or utter loud calls. The last syllables of these 'songs' are, 'invariably accompanied by a quaint, stiff bobbing of the head, generally close in front of the mate' (Whistler 1941). Grazing animals are often attended by these mynahs which ride on the backs of the cattle and horses to pick up parasitic insects. They also forage fearlessly around the feet of the animals for insects that have been disturbed in the grass. Being pugnacious, these birds quite frequently engage in fights where the adversaries jump at each other in a screaming and clawing match. Such fights may involve two individuals, pairs or several birds together. In the non-breeding season,

they often gather in feeding parties. If disturbed when feeding they rise with loud alarm calls. Flocks gather in the evening at communal roosts in dense groves of trees.

VOICE

The Indian Mynah is a noisy bird with a varied repertoire of loud, raucous calls, unmusical screeching, chuckling and squawking mixed with softer chatterings. It also has tuneful whistles and it attempts to mimic other birds. Whistler (1941) notes that, at 'intervals during darkness, short bursts of chattering are to be heard' from roosting flocks.

FOOD

An omnivorous bird with no particular food preferences, it may feed mainly on insects and fruits in agricultural areas but in towns it scavenges in the streets and on rubbish tips.

NEST AND BREEDING

Mynahs are territorial at least during the breeding season and may pair for life. Both males and females participate in complex displays of stylised bowing and jumping, which are thought to be important in the formation and maintenance of the pair-bond. Counsilman (1977) gives detailed descriptions of the displays of the Indian Mynah. The nest is an untidy and often large mass of assorted materials such as grass, leaves, feathers, twigs, rags, paper, plastics or pieces of rope. It is placed in almost any available cavity in trees, walls or roofs of houses. The 3-6 eggs (about 31 × 22 mm) are pale blue to greyish-green. The breeding season is from October to February/March and pairs may raise more than one brood in a season.

120. Papuan Mynah *Mino dumontii*
Other names: Yellow-faced Mynah, Orange-faced Grackle
French name: Merle de Papouasie

IDENTIFICATION AND FIELD NOTES

Length 25 cm. A heavily built, black bird with a mostly orange head, white rump and belly and small white wing patches. *Adult male and female:* head black on the lores, crown and nape with a large bare orange patch around the eye; back and wings black with a bluish gloss and a narrow white bar across the primaries, noticeable in flight; rump white and tail black; breast black, centre of belly yellow, undertail-coverts white. Iris: orange. Bill: bright yellow, stout and sharply pointed. Legs and feet: yellow. *Immature* has a similar plumage pattern but is duller.

The Papuan Mynah is much less conspicuous than the Indian Mynah because it inhabits wooded areas, especially the edges of forests. It feeds on fruit and sometimes catches swarming insects. Call-notes are varied and distinctive, usually loud, low-pitched and guttural, described as a polysyllabic croak by Beehler *et al* (1986). This mynah often perches in trees and calls frequently for long periods.

DISTRIBUTION AND STATUS

This species is found throughout most of New Guinea from sea level to 750 m and occasionally to 1,500 m. It also inhabits the Bismarck Archipelago and the Solomons (Beehler *et al*, 1986). In Vanuatu, two observers reported on at least one possible record on Efate in 1988. Euan Macdonald had brief glimpses of an orange-headed bird with a group of Indian Mynahs at Mele while John Edge repeatedly heard 'an irritating bird with a loud monotonous two-note call' and had glimpses of black and orange high up in the dense foliage (Naika 29:28). From memory of the call in the Solomons, he believed it could be this species.

Woodswallows or Swallow-shrikes   *Artamidae*

The Artamidae are neither swallows nor shrikes but a peculiar family which apparently originated in Australia where 6 of the 10 known species occur. They are small to medium-sized chunky birds (12 to 19 cm in length) with long pointed wings, a fairly long, stout slightly downcurved bill and wide gape, and a medium-length square or notched tail. Plumage is usually a mixture of black, grey and white colours, except for one partly chestnut species, and is dense, soft and finely textured. The Artamidae are the only passerine family to have powder-down feathers, the tips of which break up into a fine powder, and this imparts a bloom to the plumage. The sexes are alike or nearly so. They are aerial birds and feed almost entirely on insects caught on the wing, though at least one species also takes insects from foliage or the open ground. Some ornithologists consider the woodswallows to be the best fliers of all the songbirds. Their flight is diagnostic, exceedingly graceful, often interrupted by long periods of gliding, and some of the larger species are even able to soar in thermals.

  Woodswallows can be found in many types of habitat, desert, open scrub or partly wooded country according to the species and some may be seen hawking insects over forest clearings or along the forest edge. They are common throughout most of their range and conspicuous as they are noisy, pugnacious and highly gregarious. They often gather to roost at night in some crevice or on a bare branch huddled together in tight bunches. During the day they can be identified from a long distance perched together on some vantage point, flicking their tails up and down and from side to side. From there, the birds fly out individually to catch passing insects and then spiral around in soaring circles for a few moments before returning. They build saucer-shaped nests, sometimes flimsy structures of fine grasses, fibres and feathers though twigs and roots are often used. Nests may be built on branches of trees or bushes, at the base of the leaves on a palm tree, in a tree cavity or on cliffs. Most species nest colonially. The 2-4 eggs are white to buff and are usually spotted around the larger end. Both parents take part in rearing the young but in some species, birds other than the parents may help to feed the nestlings. This family is represented in Vanuatu by a single widespread species.

121. White-breasted Woodswallow   *Artamus leucorhynchus tenuis*   PLATE 14
Other names: Swallow-shrike, White-rumped Woodswallow
French name: Langrayen à ventre blanc   or locally: Hirondelle Busière

IDENTIFICATION
Length 16 to 17 cm. A plump-bodied, black and white bird with distinctive soaring flight and a characteristic upright posture when perched. *Adult male and female:* head and upperparts slate-black except for the white rump. Chin and throat slaty-black; rest of underparts white. The wings are long and pointed and when folded project beyond the tail; underwing pale grey. The tail is slightly notched. Iris: red-brown. Bill: light grey-blue with a black tip, longish, almost conical and slightly downcurved. Legs and

feet: grey-blue, short and strong. *Immature:* like the adult but slightly mottled; the dark plumage feathers are tipped light grey and the throat also has some white. Iris is light brown and the bill brownish.

The White-breasted Woodswallow can be distinguished from the trillers by the black throat and the absence of white on the wing. It sometimes looks like a stout-bodied swallow but the flight is much slower, more direct, less erratic and marked by long stretches of soaring. It also differs from the Pacific Swallow by the white rump and by the black (not chestnut) forehead and throat.

DISTRIBUTION AND STATUS

This species has a wide distribution in a number of races from Australia through Indonesia to India, New Guinea and the Philippines in the north and through New Caledonia, the Loyalty Islands and Vanuatu to Palau in Micronesia and to Fiji. See Stresemann (1940). In Vanuatu the race *A. l. tenuis* occurs from the Banks Islands south to Aneityum though Medway and Marshall (1975) failed to find it on Erromango and Tanna. It is moderately common on all islands. Recent records, one of which comments on the remarkably graceful flight of this species are both from Efate (Naika 11:6 and 29:28).

FIELD NOTES

This interesting species is most often seen hawking insects over forest clearings, the forest edge, park-like areas or any other type of open partly wooded country in lowland and highland regions. It may be observed sitting quietly on an exposed perch, often with 6 or more birds huddled closely together and may roost in a swarm at night. The White-breasted Woodswallow feeds mostly on insects caught by dashing out from a perch as they fly past but may also search high in the air for prey. Flight is very graceful, brief bursts of rapid wingbeats alternating with long periods of gliding, for which it is well adapted with long almost triangular-shaped wings. It is conspicuous when foraging in flocks which centre their activity around a lookout with a good all-round view, such as a dead branch in a tall lone tree, the top of a palm tree, telephone wires or any other high exposed perch. Individual birds dash out in pursuit of an insect, seizing it in the bill in a sweeping pass and often spiralling around before returning to the perch. Smaller insects are usually swallowed whole; larger prey is transferred to the feet and picked apart with the bill. Like many other species, the White-breasted Woodswallow is mainly active in the early morning and late afternoon and is quiescent during the heat of the day. It is quite vocal when perched or flying and chatters as it feeds, maintaining contact with the group. Predators are mobbed with strident aggressive calls and it has even been observed to swoop at cats. It is relatively sedentary but may wander locally. It is rarely seen on the ground. When perched, this species has a conspicuous habit of tail-swivelling; if a bird is excited or alarmed it moves its tail up and down and the tail may be rotated, often partly fanned.

VOICE

The frequent contact call between pairs or groups is a soft twittering chatter. It also has harsh warning notes and a mobbing call. It is said to have a complex, soft, pleasing song.

FOOD

All kinds of flying insects are taken including butterflies, grasshoppers and beetles. Some birds kept in an aviary for several months for observation also took large dead insects from their food dish.

NEST AND BREEDING

The nest is a cup of plant fibres, fine twigs and rootlets placed in the tree canopy in a fork, on top of a broken projecting stump of branches, in the shallow cavity of a broken branch or high in a crevice in a cliff. The clutch consists of 2-3 eggs which are white or creamy-white, blotched and speckled with purplish-brown often at the larger end in a circle. Both sexes take part in incubating the eggs and rearing the young which stay with their parents for many weeks after fledging. It is not known if this species has any co-operative breeding behaviour in Vanuatu. The breeding season is normally from August to January though one nest with young in July has been reported.

Addendum:

116. Santo Mountain Starling   *Aplonis santovestris*

An expedition to find the Santo Mountain Starling, initiated by the Vanuatu Natural Science Society, took place from 17-26 August 1991. Three members, Thorkil Casse, Michael Wylie and Geoff Boon, were accompanied by Robin Deamer, a ni-Vanuatu student, 2 visiting ornithologists, Jim Reside and Peter Montgomery, and local guides from Ipayato. They confirmed the presence of a small population of this species in the cloud forest on Peak Santo (Vanuatu Weekly, 14.09.91 page 10).

In 3½ days nine separate sightings were made, all in the locality of the Peak Santo summit (1,704m) and summit ridge (above 1,400m). Five observations were of two birds together, presumed to be a pair, the other 4 were of single birds. The observers could not establish how many individual Mountain Starlings were present. Two birds were caught in mist-nets; measurements and a description of one were taken. 'Once the pair were caught in the mist-nets, no more were caught, which may have meant they were the only pair on the top'. Generally the birds were seen in the upper shrub and sub-canopy layers from 3 to 6m with 3 observations in the canopy (10m). Two birds were seen feeding on tree berries. Flight was fast and direct through the trees. Four types of call were heard: 'a high even pitched cheep/whistle, repeated often' as a contact call when perched or in flight; a loud, twittering song, made from a perch; 'soft, two-syllable clicking calls, made by members of a pair when close to each other'; and an alarm call, a 'loud harsh rapid-fire whistle/cheep', heard when 'a pair' were startled. (pers comm Euan Macdonald, October 1991 – from a report to the VNSS).

Glossary

aberrant: deviation from the type; divergent; exceptional
adaptive radiation: the development of different forms from an original stock, each adapted to a different environment or way of life; ecological divergence
adult: breeding birds or those with breeding capabilities
allopreening: preening of one bird by another, usually the mate
aquatic: growing or living in or near water; associated with water
arboreal: living in trees
Australasian region: Australia, New Zealand, New Guinea and Pacific Islands
axillaries: the feathers growing from the axilla or 'armpit', covering the junction of underwing and body
bars or barring: transverse lines or marks on the plumage
canopy: the closed upper part of the forest shading the understorey
carpal joint: wrist, forward 'bend' in the wing when folded
cere: bare, soft, sometimes swollen fleshy covering at the base of the upper mandible in which the nostrils open as in hawks, doves and parrots
clutch: the number of eggs laid during one breeding attempt
'commic': name applied to grey and white terns in the genus *Sterna* when specific identification is doubtful
convergent evolution: the evolution of similar features in unrelated animals as they adapt to a similar environment or way of life
conspecific: of the same species
cosmopolitan: found in many or all parts of the world
crepuscular: active at twilight; appearing, feeding or flying at dusk
crest: a plume or tuft of feathers on the head
cryptic: concealing, as in the colour of plumage adapted for concealment
culmen: the ridge along the top of the upper mandible from the base of the feathers to the tip
diagnostic: of value in identifying or classifying a particular species
dimorphism (sexual): distinct colour of plumage, shape or size between sexes
diurnal: active in the daytime
echolocation: the ability to navigate by emitting high-frequency sounds and then picking up the echoes from surrounding objects
eclipse-plumage: inconspicuous non-breeding plumage of male ducks, usually of short duration
ecology: the study of living things in relation to their surroundings
ecosystem: system of interacting organisms in a particular habitat

endemic: occurring naturally in a restricted area and not found elsewhere
established: an introduced species which is breeding successfully in the wild
estuary: area subject to tidal influence at the mouth of a river
ethology: science of animal behaviour or character formation
evolution: the process by which new forms or species develop
eyebrow: stripe over the eye; superciliary
eyestripe: stripe through the eye
fledged: fully feathered; able to fly
fledgling: young bird that has left the nest but may not be independent
flight feathers: primaries and secondaries
frugivore: fruit-eating
gape: the wide open mouth; the fleshy angle at the base of the open bill, often brightly coloured in nestlings
gradated or graduated: gradually increasing or decreasing in length or width as in the tail
gular: relating to the throat
habitat: the particular environment in which a species of bird lives
hackles: long, narrow feathers, usually in the neck region
herbivore: animal which feeds on plants
indigenous: a native of or belonging naturally to a certain island or area
immature: refers to a young bird in any plumage before it is fully adult
insectivorous: insect-eating
invertebrate: without a backbone or spinal column
iridescent: shiny colour which may change according to the viewing position
juvenile: refers to a young bird in the first plumage after the natal down
kleptoparasitic: a species that lives by robbing other species of their prey
knob: fleshy fold of skin at the base of the upper mandible as in some pigeons
lores: area between the eyes and the base of the bill
marsh: an area of land with low herbage which is frequently overflowed with fresh or saltwater
mandible: the upper or lower half of the bird's bill; sometimes of the lower mandible only
maxilla: upper mandible; upper section of the bill
melanistic: having an excess of black or dark brown pigment in plumage or eggs
migrant: used of species that move seasonally between breeding and non-breeding areas
mollymauks: common name for the smaller species of albatross in the southern oceans
monotypic: including only a single species
montane: higher elevation and the tops of the mountains
moult: renewal of plumage, usually annually; dropping old feathers as the new feathers grow
Neotropical: zoogeographical region of Central and South America
New World: the Americas
niche: all conditions in the environment to which a species is adapted and in which it can survive

nomadic: wandering; applied to species with irregular movements
nominate: the first named race of a particular species (when a second race is described the species name is repeated in the name of the nominate race)
nuchal: pertaining to the hindneck as in nuchal collar, nuchal plumes
Old World: geographical region, as the palearctic
omnivorous: having a varied diet of animal and vegetable matter
ochraceous: golden yellow-brown
palearctic: of the arctic and temperate regions of Europe, North Africa and northern Asia
papillae: small projections on the tongue or at the base of the gape as found in the nestlings of the estrildid finches
pectoral band: distinctively coloured band of feathers across the breast
pelagic: of the open sea; oceanic; (of birds that come to land only to breed)
phase (morph): different form or colour within the species, mostly of plumage as 'light/dark phase' or 'light/dark morph'
plumage: all the feathers or down covering the bird's body
phylogeny: the history of the evolution of an animal group
polyandrous: having more than one male mate at the same time
polytypic: a species with two or more races
precocious: advanced development or behaviour for its age
primaries: the long outer flight feathers of the wing attached to the bones of the 'hand'
rectrices: the tail feathers; a single horizontal row of quills (12 in most species)
resident: of a species which remains in the same area
rictal: of the gape
rufous: reddish-brown or rust colour
scapulars: feathers along the dorsal shoulder covering the base of the wing
secondaries: the inner flight feathers of the wing, attached to the 'forearm'
sedentary: non-migratory
sonagraph: a machine used to analyse bird song which produces a visual representation (time on the horizontal axis, frequency on the vertical)
spangled: with bright, glossy spots in the plumage
speculum: a metallic or brightly coloured patch or band across the wing, usually on the secondaries or tips of the upperwing-coverts, which contrasts with the surrounding wing colour
streamers: elongated tail feathers
striated: streaked with lines of darker or lighter colour along the body
substage: region within a forest extending from ground-level to middle height
superciliary: eyebrow; stripe above the eye
subterminal: near the tip, as in subterminal bar on the tail
suffused: spread lightly or indistinctly with another colour
swamp: ground saturated with water with some trees or shrubs
terrestrial: living mainly at or near ground level
thigh: upper leg, usually feathered
ubiquitous: present everywhere
understorey: the part of the forest under the canopy

vagrant: a wanderer; a bird found outside its normal range, perhaps disorientated by cyclones or other adverse weather conditions

vent: the area surrounding the cloaca which includes the openings of the anus and the oviduct and sometimes the undertail-coverts

vermiculations: marked with close, fine wavy lines

vernacular names: common names used in a country or region

vestigial: well developed in ancestors but reduced to a vestige; of little use

vinaceous: wine-red

wattle: a naked fleshy flap or area of skin, usually on the head

wingbar: a distinct band of contrasting colour seen on the extended wing, usually formed by the tips of the wing-coverts

wrist: carpal joint, the 'bend' in the wing

zoogeography: the distribution of animals

Bibliography

Amadon, D: *Birds collected during the Whitney South Sea Expedition.* (1942a) 49. Notes on some non-passerine genera, 1. *American Museum Novitates* (1175).
— (1942b) 50. Notes on some non-passerine genera, 2. *AMN* (1176).
— (1943) 52. Notes on some non-passerine genera, 3. *AMN* (1237).
— (1970) Taxonomic categories below the level of genus: theoretical and practical aspects. *J. Bombay Nat. Hist. Soc.* 67:1-13.
Austin, O L jr: (1967) *Birds of the World.* Paul Hamlyn, London.
Bock, W J: (1956) A generic review of the family *Ardeidae* (Aves). *AMN* (1779).
Baker, J R & Harrisson, T H: (1936) The season in a tropical rain-forest (New Hebrides) Part 1 Meteorology. *J. Proc. Linn. Soc. Lond.*; Zool. 39:443-462.
— Marshall, A J & Harrisson, T H: (1940) The season in a tropical rain-forest Part 5 Birds (Pachycephala). *J. Proc. Linn. Soc. Lond.*; Zool. 41:50-70.
Baker, R H: (1951) The Avifauna of Micronesia, its origin, evolution and distribution. *Univ. Kansas Publ. Mus. Nat. Hist.* 3:1-359.
Barritt, M K: (1976) A visit to Hunter and Matthew Islands, two little known islands in the Hunter Island Ridge, south-east by east of the New Hebrides chain, by HMS *Hydra*, surveying ship, 26th June 1974. *Sea Swallow* 25:13-15.
Beehler, B M, Pratt, T K & Zimmerman, D A: (1986) Birds of New Guinea. Princeton University Press, Princeton NJ.
Bell, R S: (1912) Breeding habits of the White Tern *Gygis alba* on the Kermadecs Group. *Emu* 12 (1):26-30.
Bennett, R M: (1972) Forest conservation and reserves: in 'South Pacific Conference on National Parks and Reserves', Sydney.
Bourne, W R P & Warham, J: (1966) Geographical variation in the Giant Petrels of the genus *Macronectes*. *Ardea* 54:45-67.
Bregulla, H L: (1972) Proposed reserves on Efate and the Reef Islands: in 'South Pacific Conference on National Parks and Reserves', Sydney.
Brookfield, H C & Hart, D: (1966) *Rainfall in the Tropical Southwest Pacific.* ANU Canberra.
Brown, L & Amadon, D: (1968) *Eagles, Hawks and Falcons of the World.* McGraw Hill, New York.
Cain, A J: (1954) Subdivisions of the genus Ptilinopus (Aves, Columbidae). *Bull. Br. Mus. nat. hist. Zool.* 2:267-284.
— (1955) A revision of some parrots. *Ibis* 97:432-479.
Campbell, B & Lack, E (eds): (1985) *A Dictionary of Birds.* Poyser, Calton & Buteo, Vermillion.

Collett, R: (1892) On a collection of birds from Tongoa, New Hebrides. *Forhandlinger i Videnskabs-selskabet i Christiana* No.13, 11 p.

— (1898) On a second collection of birds from Tongoa, New Hebrides *Christiana videnskabs-selskabs forhandlinger* No.6, 7 p.

Condon, H T & McGill, A R: (1952) *Field Guide to the Waders.* The Bird Observers Club, Melbourne, Victoria.

Conroy, J W H: (1972) Ecological aspects of the biology of the Giant Petrel *Macronectes giganteus* in the maritime Antarctic. *British Antarctic Survey Sci. Rep.* 75.

Counsilman, J J: (1977) Visual displays of the Indian Myna during pairing and breeding. *The Babbler* 1:1-13. Queensland, Australia.

Cramp, S & Simmons, K E L: (eds) (1977-1985) *The Birds of the Western Palearctic,* Vols I to IV. Oxford University Press, Oxford.

Crome, F H J & Brown, H E: (1979) Notes on social organisation and breeding of the Orange-footed Scrubfowl *Megapodius reinwardt. Emu* 79:111-119.

Delacour, J: (1954-64) *The Waterfowl of the World.* Country Life, London.

— (1966) *Guide des Oiseaux de la Nouvelle-Calédonie et de ses dépendances.* Editions Delachaux et Niestlé, Neuchâtel.

Diamond, J M: (1975) The island dilemma: lessons of modern biogeographic studies for the design of natural preserves. *Biol. Conserv.* 7:129-146.

— , & Marshall, A G: (1976) Origin of the New Hebridean Avifauna. *Emu* 76:187-200.

— , & Marshall, A G: (1977a) Niche Shifts in New Hebridean Birds. *Emu* 77:61-72.

— , & Marshall, A G: (1977b) Distributional Ecology of New Hebridean Birds: A Species Kaleidoscope. *J. Anim. Ecol.* 46:703-727.

— , & Veitch, C R: (1981) Extinctions and introductions in the New Zealand avifauna: cause and effect? *Science* 211:499-501.

Dorst, J: (1954) Le pélican à lunettes aux Nouvelles-Hébrides. *L'Oiseau et la Revue française d'Ornithologie* 24:149-151, Paris.

— (1974) *The Life of Birds.* Weidenfeld and Nicholson, London.

Dorward, D F: (1962) Comparative biology of the White Booby and the Brown Booby spp. at Ascension Island. *Ibis* 103b:174-220 and

— Behaviour of boobies *Sula* spp. *Ibis* 103b:221-234.

Du Pont, J: (1976) *South Pacific Birds.* Del. Mus. Nat. Hist., Monograph No.3, pp.218.

Falla, R A: (1976) Notes on the Gadfly Petrels *Pterodroma externa* & *P.e. cervicalis. Notornis* 23:320-322.

— , Sibson, R B and Turbott, E G: (1981) *A Field Guide to the Birds of New Zealand.* Collins, London.

Fisher, J: (1951) *Watching Birds.* Penguin Books, London.

Forshaw, J M: (1973) *Parrots of the World.* Lansdowne Press, Melbourne.

Friedmann, H: (1968) The evolutionary history of the avian genus *Chrysococcyx. Bull. US natn. Mus.* 265.

Frith, H J: (1956) Breeding habits in the family Megapodiidae. *Ibis* 98:620-640.

— (1967) *Waterfowl in Australia.* Angus and Robertson, Sydney.

Galbraith, I C J: (1956) Variation, relationships and evolution in the *Pachycephala pectoralis* superspecies (Aves, Muscicapidae). *Bull. Br. Mus. nat. hist. Zool.* 4:131-222.

— , & Galbraith, E H: (1962) Land Birds of Guadalcanal and the San Cristobal group,

Eastern Solomon Islands. *Bull. Br. Mus. nat. hist. Zool.* 9:1-86.
Garnett, M C: (1984) Conservation of Seabirds in the South Pacific Region: A Review, in *Status and Conservation of the World's Seabirds*, eds. J P Croxall, P G H Evans & R W Schreiber, ICBP Technical Publication No.2: 547-558.
Gilliard, E T: (1958) *Living Birds of the World*. Hamish Hamilton, London.
Goodwin, D: (1960) Taxonomy of the genus *Ducula*. *Ibis* 102:526-535.
— (1970) *Pigeons and Doves of the World*. 2nd ed. British Museum (Natural History), London.
Greenway, J C: (1967) *Extinct and Vanishing Birds of the World*. Dover, New York.
Hadden, D: (1983) A new species of Thicket Warbler *Cichlornis* (Sylviinae) from Bougainville Island, North Solomons Province PNG. *Bull. Brit. Orn. Club* 103:22-25.
Hall, B P: (1974) *Birds of the Harold Hall Australasian Expeditions*. British Museum (Natural History), London.
—, & Moreau, R E: (1970) *Atlas of Speciation of African Birds*. British Museum (Natural History), London.
Halliday, T: (1978) *Vanishing Birds – their Natural History and Conservation*. Hutchinson, Australia.
Hancock, J & Kushlan, J: (1984) *The Herons Handbook*. Croom Helm, London.
Harper, P C & Kinsky, F C: (1978) *Southern Albatrosses and Petrels*. Price Milburn, Wellington.
Harrison, P: (1983) *Seabirds: An Identification Guide*. Croom Helm, London.
Harrisson, T H: (1935) The Birds of Espiritu Santo. *Geographical Journal*. 85:225-227. London.
— (1942) Note on some ritually important birds, in Layard, J *Stone men of Malekula* 751-753. London.
—, & Marshall, A J: (1937) Description of a new species of *Aplornis*. *Bull. Brit. Orn. Club* 57:148-150.
—, & Marshall, A J: (1941) The comparative economy of closely related birds on an island and a continent. *Emu* 40:310-318. Melbourne.
Heather, B D: (1966) *A Biology of Birds – with particular reference to New Zealand birds*. Orni. Soc. of New Zealand, Wellington.
Hinde, R A: (1961) *Behaviour*, ch. xxiii, in *The Biology and Comparative Physiology of Birds*, by A J Marshall (1961).
Hindwood, K A: (1942) The birds of Lonf Reef. *Proc. Roy. Zool. Soc. NSW.* 1941-42:14-33.
Imber, M J: (1985) Origins, phylogeny and taxonomy of the gadfly petrels *Pterodroma* spp. *Ibis* 127:197-229.
Immelmann, K, Steinbacher, J & Wolters, H E: (1964) Vögel in Käfig und Voliere – Prachtfinken. Vierzehnte Lieferung, *Estrilda astrild*. 302-323. Verlag Hans Limberg, Aachen.
Johnsgard, P A: (1965) *Handbook of Waterfowl Behaviour*. Cornell University Press, Ithaca.
Jouventin, P, Martinez, J & Roux, J P: (1989) Breeding biology and current status of the Amsterdam Island Albatross *Diomedea amsterdamensis*. *Ibis* 131:171-182.
Keast, A: (1985) Tropical Rainforest Avifaunas: an Introductory Conspectus, in

Conservation of Tropical Forest Birds, eds. A W Diamond & T E Lovejoy, ICBP Technical Publication No. 4:3-31.

King, A S & McLelland, J: (1975) *Outlines of Avian Anatomy*. Balliere Tindall, London.

King, W C: (1967) *Seabirds of the Tropical Pacific Ocean*. Smithsonian Institution, Washington DC.

— (1985) Island Birds: Will the Future Repeat the Past?, in *Conservation of Island Birds*, ed. P J Moors, ICBP Technical Publication No.3:3-15.

Koopman, K: (1957) Evolution in the genus *Myzomela* (Aves, Meliphagidae) *Auk* 74:49-72.

Landsborough Thomson, A (Ed.): (1964) *A New Dictionary of Birds*. Nelson, London.

Layard, E L: (1880) Notes of a collecting trip in the New Hebrides, the Solomon Islands, New Britain and the Duke of York Islands. *Ibis* 4th series: No.4:290-309.

—, & Layard, E L C: (1878) Notes on some birds collected and observed by E Leopold C Layard in the New Hebrides. With remarks by the Rev. Canon Tristram. *Ibis* 4th series: No.2:267-280.

—, & Layard, E L C: (1881) Notes on the avifauna of New Caledonia and the New Hebrides. With remarks by Rev. Canon Tristram. *Ibis* 5:132-139.

Lister, M: (1962) *A Glossary for Bird Watchers*. Phoenix House, London.

Madge, S & Burn, H: (1988) *Wildfowl: an identification guide to the ducks, geese and swans of the world*. Christopher Helm, London.

Marchant, J, Prater, T & Hayman, P: (1986) *Shorebirds: An Identification Guide to the waders of the world*. Croom Helm, London.

Marshall, A G: (1973) A start to nature conservation in the New Hebrides. *Biol. Cons.* 5(1):67-69.

—, & Medway, Lord: (1976) A mangrove community in the New Hebrides, southwest Pacific. *Biol. J. Linn. Soc.* 8:319-336.

Marshall, A J: (1961) *The Biology and Comparative Physiology of Birds*. Academic Press, New York and London.

Mayr, E: *Birds collected during the Whitney South Sea Expedition*.

— (1931a) 12. Notes on *Halcyon chloris* and some of its subspecies. *American Museum Novitates*. (469).

— (1931b) 13. A systematic list of the birds of Rennell Island with description of new species and subspecies (refers to possible relatives of *Gerygone flavolateralis*) *AMN* (486).

— (1931c) 16. Notes on fantails of the genus *Rhipidura*. *AMN* (502).

— (1932a) 18. Notes on Meliphagidae from Polynesia and the Solomon Islands. *AMN* (516).

— (1932b) 19. Notes on the Bronze Cuckoo *Chalcites lucidus* and its subspecies. *AMN* (520).

— (1933a) 24. Notes on Polynesian flycatchers and a revision of the genus *Clytorhynchus* Elliott. *AMN* (628).

— (1933b) 25. Notes on the genera *Myiagra* and *Mayrornis*. *AMN* (651).

— (1933c) 26. Notes on *Neolalage banksiana* (Gray). *AMN* (665).

— (1934) 29. Notes on the genus *Petroica*. *AMN* (714).

— (1937a) 32. On a collection from Tanna, New Hebrides. *AMN* (912).

– (1937b) 33. Notes on New Guinea birds. 1. *AMN* (915).
– (1938) 38. On a collection from Erromanga, New Hebrides. *AMN* (986).
– (1940) 49. Notes on New Guinea birds. 6. *AMN* (1056).
– (1941a) 47. Notes on the genera *Halcyon, Turdus* and *Eurostopodus*. *AMN* (1152).
– (1942a) 48. Notes on the Polynesian species of *Aplonis*. *AMN* (1166).
– (1942b) *Systematics and Origin of species*. Columbia University Press, New York.
– (1945) *Birds of the Southwest Pacific*. Macmillan, New York.
– (1945a) Bird conservation problems in the Southwest Pacific. *Audubon Mag.* 47:29-282.
– (1949a) Notes on the birds of Northern Melanesia, 2. *Am. Mus. Novit.* (1417).
– (1949b) Artbildung und Variation in the *Halcyon-chloris*-Gruppe, pp.55-60 in *Ornithologie als biologische Wissenschaft* eds. E Mayr & E Schutz, Universitätsverlag, Heidelberg.
–, & Amadon, D: (1941) Birds collected during the Whitney South Sea Expedition, 46. Geographical variation in *Demigretta sacra* (Gmelin). *Am. Mus. Novit.* (1144).
–, & Amadon, D: (1951) A classification of recent birds. *AMN* 1496:1-42.
–, & Ripley, S D: (1941) Birds collected during the Whitney South Sea Expedition, 44. Notes on the genus *Lalage* Boie. *AMN* (1116).
Medway, Lord: (1966) Field characters as a guide to the specific relationships of swiftlets. *Proc. Linn. Soc. Lond.* 177:151-172.
– (1975) The nest of *Collocalia v. vanikorensis*, and taxonomic implications. *Emu* 75:154-155.
–, & Marshall, A G: (1975) Terrestrial vertebrates of the New Hebrides: origin and distribution. *Phil. Trans. R. Soc. Lond.* B.272:423-465.
–, & Pye, J D: (1977) Echolocation and the systematics of swiftlets, pp.225-238 in *Evolutionary ecology* eds. B Stonehouse & C M Perrins, Macmillan, London.
Mees, G F: (1969) A systematic review of the Indo-Australian Zosteropidae (Part III). *Zool. Verh. Leiden.*, 102.
Moors, P J: (1985) Eradication Campaigns against *Rattus norvegicus* on the Noises Islands, New Zealand, using Brodifacoum and 1080, in *Conservation of Island Birds*, ICBP Tech. Pub. No.3.
Murphy, R C: (1936) *Oceanic Birds of South America*. Two vols. The Macmillan Company & American Museum of Natural History, New York.
Naika: Journal of the Vanuatu Natural Science Society Vols 1-33 1980-90 VNSS PO Box 944, Port Vila, Vanuatu.
Oldfield, S: (1987) *Fragments of Paradise: a guide for conservation action in the UK dependent territories*. Pisces, Oxford for BANC.
Olson, S: (1973) A classification of the Rallidae. *Wilson Bull.* 85:380-416.
Parker, G J: (1968) Notes on the avifauna of Efate, New Hebrides. *Elepaio* 29:46-68.
Parker, S: (1967) Some eggs from the New Hebrides, south-west Pacific. *Bull. Br. Orn. Club* 87:90-91.
Perrins, C M consultant: (1990) *The Illustrated Encyclopaedia of Birds*. Headline, London and ICBP, Cambridge.
Peters, J L: (1937) *Check-list of birds of the world*, 3. Harvard University Press, Cambridge, Massachusetts.

Pettingill, O S jr: (1985) *Ornithology in Laboratory and Field: Fifth Edition*. Academic Press, London.
Pickering, R: (1981) *Annotated Checklist of the Birds of Vanuatu*. Vanuatu Natural Science Society, Miscellaneous Publication No.1.
Pizzey, G: (1980) *A Field Guide to the Birds of Australia*. Collins, Sydney.
Prater, A J, Marchant, J H & Vuorinen, J: (1977) *Guide to the identification and ageing of Holarctic Waders*. Guide No.17, BTO, Tring.
Pratt, H D, Bruner, P L & Berrett, D G: (1987) *The Birds of Hawaii and the Tropical Pacific*. Princeton University Press, Princeton NJ.
Prŷs-Jones, R P & Peet, C: (1980) Breeding periodicity, nesting success and nest site selection among Red-tailed Tropicbirds *Phaethon rubricauda* and White-tailed Tropicbirds *P. lepturus* on Aldabra Atoll. *Ibis* 122:76-81.
Ramsay, E P: (1877) Description of a supposed new species of Fruit Pigeon from Malacola, one of the New Hebrides Islands; proposed to be called *Ptilinopus corriei*. *Proc. Linn. Soc. NSW* 1:133.
— (1879) Notes on a small collection of birds from the New Hebrides, with a description of a new species of *Merula*. *Proc. Linn. Soc. of New South Wales* 3:336-339.
Ripley, S D: (1941) Notes on the genus *Coracina*. *Auk* 58:381-95.
—, & Birckhead, H: (1942) Birds collected during the Whitney South Sea Expedition, 51. On the fruit pigeons of the *Ptilinopus purpuratus* group. *Am. Mus. Novit.* (1192).
Roberts, B B: (1940) The life cycle of Wilson's Petrel *Oceanites oceanicus* (Kuhl). *British Grahamland Expedition 1934-37, Sci. Reps.* 1:141-194.
Roper, D S: (1983) Egg incubation and laying behaviour of the Incubator Bird on Savo. *Ibis* 125:384-389.
Rösler, G & Rösler, R: (1975) *Die Taube-Wildtauben*. VEB Deutscher Landwirtschaftsverlag, Berlin.
Salomonsen, F: (1966) Preliminary descriptions of new honey-eaters (Aves, Meliphagidae). *Breviora* (254).
— (1967) Family Meliphagidae, Honeyeaters, in *Peters Check-list of birds of the world*: 338-450.
Schodde, R: (1977) Survey of the Birds of southern Bougainville Island, Papua New Guinea; contribution to Papua Ornithology VI, CSIRO tech. paper.
Schreiber, R W & Ashmole, N P: (1970) Seabird breeding seasons on Christmas Island, Pacific Ocean. *Ibis* 112:363-392.
Sclater, P L: (1880) On the birds collected in Tongatabu, the Fiji Islands, Api (New Hebrides) and Tahiti by Dr O Finsch CMZS with notes and additions by P L Sclater FRS. *Challenger Expedition Zool.* 8:34-58.
Scott, P: (1972) *A Coloured Key to the Wildfowl of the World*. The Wildfowl Trust, Slimbridge.
Scott, W E: (1946) Birds observed on Espiritus Santo, New Hebrides. *Auk* 63:362-368.
Serventy, D L, Serventy, V & Warham, J: (1971) *The Handbook of Australian Seabirds*. A H & A W Reed, Sydney.
Sharpe, R B: (1900) On a collection of birds by Captain A M Farquhar, RN, in the New Hebrides. *Ibis* (7) 6:337-351.

Sibley, F C & Clapp, R B: (1967) Distribution and dispersal of Central Pacific Lesser Frigatebirds *Fregata ariel. Ibis* 109:328-337.
Simpson, K & Day, N: (1989) *Field Guide to the Birds of Australia.* Christopher Helm, London.
Smith, G A: (1975) Systematics of Parrots. *Ibis* 117:18-67.
Smith, S: (1945) *How to study birds.* Collins, London.
Steere, J B: (1894) On the distribution of genera and species of non-migratory land-birds in the Philippines. *Ibis* [1894]: 411-420, London.
Storer, R W: (1963) Courtship and mating behaviour and the phylogeny of the grebes. *Proc. XIII International ornithological Congress*:562-569.
Stresemann, E: (1940) Die Vögel von Celebes, III. Systematik und Biologie. *J. Orn., Lpz.* 88:1-35.
— (1950) Birds collected during Capt. James Cook's last expedition (1776-1780). *Auk* 67:66-88.
Swanson, N M & Merritt, F D: (1974) The breeding cycle of the Wedge-tailed Shearwater on Mutton Bird Island, NSW. *The Australian Bird Bander* Vol.12, No.1:3-9.
Tickell, W L N: (1962) The Dove Prion *Pachyptila desolata* Gmelin. *Falkland Islands Dependencies Survey Scientific Reports,* 33.
— (1968) The biology of the Great Albatrosses. *Diomedea exulans* and *Diomedea epomophora.* Antarctic Research Series, Vol.12:1-55, *Antarctic Bird Studies,* Washington DC.
Todd, D: (1982-83) Pritchard's Megapode on Niuafo'ou Island, Kingdom of Tonga. *WPA Journal* VIII:69-88.
Tristram, H B: (1876) Notes on a collection of birds from the New Hebrides. *Ibis* 3rd series: No.6:259-267.
— (1879) Notes on collections of birds sent from ... and the New Hebrides by E L Layard. *Ibis* 4th series: No.3:180-195.
— (1879) On a collection of birds from the Solomon Islands and New Hebrides. *Ibis* 4th series: No.3:437-444.
Tuck, G & Heinzel, H: (1978) *A Field Guide to the Seabirds of Britain and the World.* Collins, London.
Ulrich, S, Ziswiler, V & Bregulla, H L: (1972) Biologie und Ethologie des Schmalbindenloris, *Trichoglossus haematodus massena* Bonaparte. *Zool. Garten, NF. Leipzig* 42, 1/2, S.51-94.
Voous, K H: (1977) List of Recent Holarctic Bird Species – Passerines. *Ibis* 119:223-250 & 376-406.
Warham, J: (1956) Observations on the birds of Pelsart Island. *Emu* 56:83-93.
Warner, D W: (1951) A new race of the cuckoo, *Chalcites lucidus* from the New Hebrides islands. *Auk* 68:106-107. Cambridge, Mass.
Watson, J B: (1908) The behaviour of Noddy and Sooty Terns. Paper from Tortugas Laboratory of Carnegie Institute, Washington, 2:187-225.
Wattel, J: (1973) *Geographical Differentiation in the genus Accipiter.* Nuttall Orn. Club, Cambridge, Massachusetts.
Weightman, B: (1989) *Agriculture in Vanuatu – A Historical review.* The British Friends of Vanuatu, Cheam, Surrey, SM2 6ER.

Welty, J C: (1962) *The Life of Birds*. W B Saunders, Philadelphia.

Whistler, H: (1941) *Popular Handbook of Indian Birds* 3rd edition. Gurney and Jackson, London.

Witherby, H F *et al*: (1940-41) *The Handbook of British Birds*. Five vols. H F & G Witherby, London.

Ziswiler, V, Güttinger, H R & Bregulla, H L: (1972) Monographie der Gattung Erythrura Swainson, 1837 (Aves, Passeres, Estrildidae). *Bonn. zool. Monogr.* (2).

Index of birds and places

Figures in italic indicate colour plate numbers; those in bold type refer to the species accounts.

Acanthizidae, 238
Accipiter fasciatus, 5, 49, **123**
Accipitridae, 122
ACCIPITRIFORMES, 122, 127
Acridotheres tristis, 12, 47, **270**
Actitis hypoleucos, 150, **156**
Aerodramus spodiopygius, 11, 47, **204**
— *vanikorensis*, 11, **206**
Aigle de mer à dos rouge, 123
Aigrette des récifs, 111
Albatros hurleur, 81
— royal, 81
Albatross, Amsterdam Island, **80-81**
—, 'Great', 80
—, Royal, *1*, **80-81**
—, Wandering, **80-81**
Albatrosses, 80
Alcedinidae, 207
Amandava amandava, **258**
Ambae, 22, 24, 28-9, 78, 92, 102, 118, 121, 139, 143, 180, 191, 194, 209, 216, 222, 226-7, 233, 240, 243, 250, 263-4, 268
Ambrym, 22, 24-5, 28, 34, 139, 143, 180, 191, 194, 196, 205, 216, 222, 226-7, 234, 240, 243, 246, 250, 263-4, 268
Amok, 179
Anabrou, 255
Anas gibberifrons, *4*, **119-20**
— *platyrhynchos*, **116-17**
— *superciliosa*, *4*, 16, 49, 111, **117-19**
Anatidae, 115
Anatinae, 116
Aneityum, 22, 24-5, 29, 32, 34, 38-40, 47, 69, 84, 92, 94, 96, 99, 104, 111, 118, 124, 128, 139, 141, 143, 176, 183, 191, 200, 205, 209, 216, 220, 226-7, 231, 247, 250, 252-4, 263-5, 273
Anelghowat, 141, 254
Aniwa, 22, 24, 29, 32, 47, 114, 128, 176, 183, 194, 196, 216, 235, 250, 252
Anous minutus (tenuirostris), **168-9**
— *stolidus*, 2, **167-8**
ANSERIFORMES, 115
Aore, 27, 116, 121, 260, 270

Aplonis santovestris, 12, 48, **267-8**, 274
— *zelandicus*, 12, 48, **268-9**
Apodidae, 201
APODIFORMES, 201
Ardea (Egretta) sacra, 3, 16, **111-13**
— *novaehollandiae*, 3, **110-11**
Ardeidae, 109
Arenaria interpres, 7, **152**
Artamidae, 272
Artamus leucorhynchus, 14, 49, **272-4**
Astrild à cinq couleurs, 258
— gris, 256
— rouge, 258
Atchin, 22, 28
Autour australien, 123
Avadavat, Red, 256, **258-9**
Aythya australis, 4, **121-2**

Banks Islands, 24, 27, 36, 47, 70, 84-86, 91-98, 121, 161, 180, 191-2, 198, 209, 220, 226, 252, 273
Barge rousse, 156
Batukira, 264
Bauerfield Airport, 150, 156, 216, 255
Bécasseau à col rouge, 158
— à queue pointue, 157
— tacheté, 158
Bengali, 256
— rouge, 258
Big fala dak dak, 117
— — green Pijin, 175
— — hawk, 125
Bligh, 222
Blongios vert, 114
Boobies and Gannets, 96
Booby, Blue-faced or White, 100
— Brown, *1*, 44, **97-99**, 101, 105
— Masked, *1*, 97-9, **100-1**
— Red-footed, *1*, 44, 97, 98, **99-100**, 105
Bosunbird, Golden or White-tailed, 107
—, Red-tailed 106
Burhinidae, 146
Busard australien, 125

Butorides striatus, 3, **114-5**

Cacomantis pyrrhophanus, 10, 47, **194-5**
Calidris acuminata, **157-8**
— *melanotos*, **158**
— *ruficollis*, **158-9**
Campephagidae, 217
Canard à sourcils, 117
— colvert, 116
— japonais, 102
Carduelis flammea, 15, **253-4**
Carpophage de Baker, 180
— pacifique, 177
Chalcophaps indica, 8, 17, 47, **184**
Charadriidae, 148
CHARADRIIFORMES, 144
Charadrius bicinctus, 148, 150
— *leschenaultii*, 150
— *mongolus*, **150-51**
— *veredus*, **151**
Charmosyna palmarum, 9, 46, 64, **191-2**
Chevalier à croupion gris, 155
— à pieds courts, 154
— cendré, 154
— guignette, 156
— voyageur, 155
Chouette, 199
Chrysococcyx lucidus, 10, 47, **195**
Cichlornis whitneyi, 13, 19, 47, 239, **241**
CICONIIFORMES, 108
Circus approximans, 5, 49, **125-7**
Clytorhynchus pachycephaloides, 14, **230-31**
Col marron, 121
Collier blanc, 181
Collocalia esculenta, 11, 202, **203-4**
Colombe à longue queue, 183
— turvert, 184
Columba livia, 170
— *vitiensis*, 8, 17, 49, **181-3**
Columbidae, 171
COLUMBIFORMES, 170
Cook Reef, 54
Coq Bankiva or sauvage, 136
CORACIIFORMES, 207
Coracina caledonica, 12, 49, 64, **217-8**
Cormoran pie, 102
Cormorant, Little Pied, 4, 16, 44, **101-2**
Cormorants, 101
Coucou à éventail, 194
— cuivré, 195
Courlis courlieu, 153
— de Sibérie, 153
Crake, Spotless, 6, 47, 49, **140-41**
—, White-browed, 6, 49, **142-3**
Crakes, 137

Crane, Blue, 110
—, Nankeen, 113
Cuckoo, Fan-tailed, 10, 46, **194-5**, 227, 232, 237
—, Long-tailed New Zealand, 10, 46, **197-8**
—, Shining Bronze-, 10, 47, **195-7**, 241
Cuckoo-shrike, Melanesian, 12, 49, 64, **217-18**
Cuckoo-shrikes, 217
Cuckoos, 193
Cuculidae, 193
CUCULIFORMES, 193
Curlew, Australian, 153
—, Far Eastern, **153**
Curlews, 151

Dabchick, 78
Dedenga, 191
Denga, 191
Diamant psittaculaire, 261
— royal, 264
— tricolore de Kittlitz, 262
Diomedea amsterdamensis, **80-81**
— *epomophora*, 1, **80-81**
— *exulans*, **80-81**
Diomedeidae, 80
Donacole à poitrine châtaine, 259
— à tête noire, 260
Dotterel, Eastern or Oriental, 151
Dotterels, 148
Dove, Green-winged Emerald or Emerald Ground, 184
— Green-winged Ground, 8, 17, 47, 49, **184-6**, 187-8
— Red-bellied Fruit, 8, **172-5**, 177, 186
— Rock, 170
— Rufous-brown Cuckoo-, 183
— Rufous-brown Pheasant-, 8, 17, 47, 49, **183-4**
— Santa Cruz Ground, 8, 17, 184, **186-8**
— Tanna Ground, 49
— Vanuatu Fruit, 8, 52, 172, 174, **175-7**
— Yellow-headed Fruit, 175
Doves, 171
Duck, Australian Grey, 117
— — White-eyed, 4, 116, **121-2**
— Pacific Black or Black, 4, 16, 49, 111, **117-19**, 121
Ducks, 115
Ducula bakeri, 8, 17, 47, **180-81**
— *pacifica*, 8, 48, **177-180**

Ebau, 100
Echenilleur de Mélanésie, 217
— de Polynésie, 218
— Pie, 220
Efate, 21-2, 24-5, 28, 31-4, 36-8, 40, 49, 53-5, 69, 78, 83-4, 90-92, 100-102, 105, 111, 116,

118, 120-1, 123-4, 128, 130, 132, 136, 139, 141, 143, 148, 150-52, 155-60, 163-4, 167, 169, 179, 182, 189, 191, 194, 196, 198, 201, 205, 209, 211, 216, 219-20, 222, 224, 226-7, 230-31, 233-4, 238, 245-8, 250, 254, 257-9, 263-5, 270, 272-3
Effraie des clochers, 199
Egret, Reef, 111
Emae, 28, 32, 139, 143, 189, 191, 194, 205, 216, 219, 222, 226-7, 240, 246, 261, 264-5
Emau, 28, 139, 143, 196, 219, 226-7, 246, 263
Epi, 22, 24, 28, 32, 40, 87, 139, 143, 191, 194, 196, 205, 216, 219, 222, 226-7, 234, 240, 243, 246, 250, 264, 270
Erakor Island, 29, 112, 160
Eratap, 29, 36
Erromango, 22, 24, 29, 32, 38, 42, 47, 49, 54, 64, 69, 87, 114, 118, 121, 128, 139, 141-3, 194, 196, 200, 205, 209, 216-18, 220, 222, 226-7, 230-31, 246-7, 250, 252, 263, 273
Erythrura, 256
— *cyaneovirens*, 15, 22, 64, **264-6**
— *psittacea*, 15, **261-2**
— *trichroa*, 15, 22, **262-4**
Esacus magnirostris, 7, 45, **146-7**
Estrilda astrild, 15, 16, **256-8**
Estrilda/Emblema temporalis, 258
Estrildidae, 256
Etourneau sansonnet, 269
Eudynamis taitensis, 10, 46, **197-8**

Falco peregrinus, 5, 49, **128-130**
Falcon, Peregrine, 5, 49, **128-130**
Falconidae, 127-8
FALCONIFORMES, 127
Falcons, 128
Fantail, Grey or Collared, 13, 49, **235-7**, 238
—, Spotted or Streaked, 13, 234, 235, **237-8**
Fantails, 234
Faucon pélerin, 128
Fauvette à ventre jaune, 239
— de Santo, 241
— des buissons, 241
Finch, Blue-faced, 262
—, Strawberry, 258
Finches, 253
Firetail, Red-browed, 256, **258**, 259
Flycatcher, Broad-billed, 14, 19, 49, 195, 230, **231-2**
—, Buff-bellied, 232
—, Vanuatu, 14, 49, 229, **232-4**
Fou à pattes rouges, 99
— à ventre blanc, 97
— masqué, 100

Fowl, Red Jungle or Wild, 6, 47, 49, 131, 135, **136-7**
Fowls, 135
Fregata ariel, 1, 44, **104-5**
— *minor*, **103-4**
Frégate du Pacifique, 103
Fregatidae, 102
Fregetta grallaria, 94
— *tropica*, **93-4**
Frigatebird, Great, **103-4**
—, Least or Lesser, 1, 44, 103, **104-5**
Frigatebirds, 102
Fringillidae, 253
Futuna, 22, 24, 29, 47, 128, 143, 176, 189, 194, 196, 220, 252

Gallicolumba santaecrucis, 8, 17, **186-8**
GALLIFORMES, 130-31
Gallinule, Purple, 143
Gallirallus philippensis, 6, 21, 49, **138-40**
Gallus gallus, 6, 47, **136-7**
Gaua, 22, 24, 27, 32, 78, 114, 118, 121, 126, 128, 142, 180, 182, 194, 196, 200, 222, 226-7, 240, 250, 263-4, 268
Gerygone flavolateralis, 13, 19, 47, 196, **239-41**
Goat Island, 54, 87
Gobe-mouches à large bec, 231
— brun, 230
— de Vanuatu, 232
Godwit, Bar-tailed, 150, **156-7**
—, Eastern Bar-tailed, 156
Godwits, 151
Golden Plover, 156
Goshawk, Brown or Australian, 5, 49, **123-5**
Goshawks, 123
Grackle, Orange-faced, 271
Gravelot de Mongolie, 150
— oriental, 151
Grebe, Australian, 4, **78-9**
Grèbe australien, 78
Grebes, 77
Grive musicienne, 224
GRUIFORMES, 137
Gull, Silver or Red-billed, **159-60**
Gulls, 159
Gygis alba, 2, **169-70**

Haematopodidae, 147
Haematopus longirostris, 45, **147-8**
— *ostralegus*, 147
Halcyon chloris, 12, 18, 49, **208-11**, 212-13
— *farquhari*, 12, 18, 49, **212-14**
Haliastur indus, 123
— *sphenurus*, 123
Hardhead, 121

Harrier, Swamp or Australasian, 5, 49, 123, **125-7**
Harriers, 122
Hawk/Harrier, Marsh, 125
Hawks, 122
Héron à face blanche, 110
— de Nuit, 113
Heron, Eastern Reef or Reef, 3, *16*, **111-13**
—, Green-backed or Striated, 114
—, Little (Mangrove), 3, **114-15**, 147
—, Rufous or Nankeen Night, **113-14**
—, White-faced, 3, **110-11**
Herons, 109
Heteroscelus brevipes, **154-5**
— *incanus*, 7, **155**
Hidaway Island, 160, 167
Hiomatokara, 212
Hirondelle Busière, 272
— du Pacifique, 215
Hirundo tahitica, *11*, 49, **215-7**
Hiu, 27, 32, 38, 215
Hog Harbour, 241
Hoknaet, 199
Honeyeater, Cardinal, *9*, 48-9, 243, 246, **247-9**
—, Silver-eared, *9*, 48-9, 243, **245-7**
—, Vanuatu Mountain or White-bellied, *9*, *20*, 48, **243-4**
Honeyeaters, 242
Huîtrier de Finsch, 147
Hunter Island, 21, 24, 29, 99, 104, 107

Incubator Bird, *6*, 54, 131, **132-5**
Ipayato, 123, 240, 270, 274
Iririki Island, 28, 148

Kerepua, 147, 244, 259
Kingfisher, Vanuatu or Chestnut-bellied, *12*, *18*, 49, **212-13**
—, White-collared, *12*, *18*, 49, **208-11**, 212-13
Kingfishers, 207
Kite, Brahminy or Red-backed, **123**
— Whistling, 123
Kites, 122
Koel à longue queue, 197
Kolivu, 22
Koroliko, 87

Laika Island, 28, 54, 69, 87, 89, 107
Lake Halékar, 22
— Halewogh, 22
— Lakua, 22
— Letas, 22
— Manaro, 22
— Naléma, 22
— Otas, 22

— Siwi, 54, 117, 121, 128, 141-2, 216
— Vui, 22
Lakes, Little and Great Duck-, 54, 111, 121
Lalage leucopyga, *12*, 49, **220-21**
— *maculosa*, *12*, **218-20**
L'Alcyon à collier, 208
— à ventre roux, 212
Langrayen à ventre blanc, 272
Larus novaehollandiae, **159-60**
Latuba, 187
Lenakel, 270
Lichmera incana, *9*, 48, **245-7**
Limosa lapponica, 150, **156-7**
Liro, 270
Loh, 27, 215
Loltong, 42
Lonchura castaneothorax, *15*, **259-60**
— *malacca*, *15*, **260-61**
Long cou, 111
— fala mouth, 245
— — mouth blong hill, 243
— — tel, 183
Longfala neck, 111
Longtel, 183
Longue queue, 183
Lopevi, 22, 24-5, 28, 37, 178, 189, 191, 194, 196, 200, 216, 222, 226-7, 240, 246, 250, 263-4, 268
Lorikeet, Green Palm or Vanuatu, *9*, 46, 48, 53, 64, **191-3**
—, Rainbow, *9*, *17*, 48-9, **189-91**, 192
Loriquet des palmiers, 191
Lory, Coconut or Rainbow, 189
Lowiakamak, 117
Luganville, 22, 35, 157, 254, 259-60
Lunettes, 250, 252

Macronectes giganteus, **82-3**
— *halli*, 83
Macropygia mackinlayi, *8*, *17*, 47, **183-4**
Maewo, 24, 28, 32, 78, 139, 143, 180, 191, 216, 222, 226-7, 233, 240, 243, 250
Makura, 28, 143, 176, 178, 200, 203, 220, 235, 246
Mala, 125
Malakula, 22, 24-5, 28, 31-2, 36-8, 53, 64, 69, 114, 118, 128, 136, 139, 143, 161, 163, 179, 191, 194, 196, 205, 209, 212, 216, 218-19, 222, 226-7, 233, 240, 243-4, 246, 250, 263-4, 268
Malapoa, 55, 91
Mallard, **116-7**, 118
Malo, 27, 64, 78, 108, 121, 128, 139, 143, 192, 194, 205, 212, 216, 218-19, 222, 226-7, 233, 240, 250, 270

Man of War bird, 103-4
Mannikin, Black-headed or Chestnut, *15*, **260-61**
—, Blue-faced Parrot, 262
—, Chestnut-breasted, *15*, **259-60**
Mannikins, 256
Manutu, 180
Maramarei, 191
Marouette fuligineuse, 140
Martin pêcheur, 208
— — des îles du nord, 212
— — rouge, 212
Martin triste, 270
Martinet à croupion blanc, 204
— de Vanikoro, 206
— soyeux, 203
Maskelyne Islands, 22, 28, 32, 161, 163
Mataso Island, 22, 28, 54, 98, 104
Mataweli, 267
Matthew Island, 21, 24, 29, 99, 105, 161, 165-6
Mégapode, 132
Megapode, Niuafo'ou, 135
Megapodes, 131
Megapodiidae, 131
Megapodius freycinet layardi, 6, 54, **132-5**
— *reinwardt*, **132-5**
— *pritchardii*, 132, 135
Melanesian Graybird, 217
Mele, 36, 105, 156, 158, 160, 167, 216, 272
Méliphage à oreillons gris, 245
— des montagnes, 243
Meliphagidae, 242
Mere Lava, 22, 24, 27, 84, 86, 91, 126, 215, 226, 250, 268
Merle de Papouasie, 271
— des îles, 222
— des Moluques, 270
Metoma, 22, 27
Milan brahmane, 123
Mino dumontii, **271-2**
Moineau domestique, 255
Monarch Flycatchers, 229
Monarchidae, 229
Monument Rock, 54, 98, 104, 108
Moso, 28, 32, 41
Mota Lava, 27, 32, 126, 194, 250, 252
Mouette australienne, 159
Munia, Chestnut, 260
—, Red, 258
Myiagra caledonica, *14*, *19*, 49, 195, **231-2**
Mynah, Indian or Common, *12*, 47, 267, **270-71**, 272
—, Papuan (Yellow-faced), 267, **271-2**
Mynahs, 266
Myzomela cardinalis, *9*, 48, **247-9**

Nalaklak, 250
Namalau, 132
Nambilak, 138
Nambiru, 143
Narabut, 136, 182
Nasiko, 208
Nasiksik, 235
Nasiviru, 189
Natarua, 181
Naufa, 111
Nautou des îles, 177
— des montagnes, 180
Nawemba, 177
— blong hill, 180
Neochmia temporalis, **258**
Neolalage banksiana, *14*, 49, **232-4**
Nesofregetta fuliginosa, 44, 93, **94-5**
Nguna, 28, 139, 143, 194, 196, 216, 219, 226-7, 246, 263
Noddi à cape blanche, 168
— niais, 167
Noddies, 159
Noddy, Black, White-capped or Lesser, **168-9**
—, Common or Brown, 2, **167-8**
—, White, 169
Nokovula, 180, 186, 191, 193, 212, 232, 241, 244, 264, 267-8
Numenius madagascariensis, **153**
— *phaeopus*, 7, 150, **153-4**
Nycticorax caledonicus, **113-4**
Nyroca austral, 121

Oceanites oceanicus, **93**
Oceanitidae, 92
Oedicnème des récifs, 146
Owl, Barn, 5, 49, 50, **199-201**
Oystercatcher, Eurasian, 147
—, South Island Pied, 45, **147-8**
Oystercatchers, 147

Paama, 24, 28, 35, 37, 178, 191, 194, 200, 216, 219, 222, 226-7, 231, 243, 246, 250, 264, 268, 270
Pachycephala pectoralis, *14*, 49, **227-9**
Pachycephalidae, 225
Pachyptila desolata, **86-7**
— *salvini*, 87
— *vittata*, 87
Paonangisu, 40
Parrotfinch, Blue-faced, *15*, 22, 50, **262-4**, 265
—, Red-throated, *15*, 256, **261-2**
—, Royal or Red-headed, *15*, 22, 49, 64, 262, **264-6**
Parrots, 188
Passer domesticus, *15*, 47, **255-6**, 269

Passeridae, 254
PASSERIFORMES, 213
Pearye, 243
Pelecanidae, 95
PELECANIFORMES, 95
Pelecanus conspicillatus, **96**
Pelican, Australian, **96**
Pélican australien, 96
Pelicans, 95
Pentecost, 22, 24, 28, 32, 42, 139, 143, 180, 191, 216, 222, 227, 233, 240, 243, 250, 264, 268
Perruche des cocotiers, 189
Petite Frégate, 104
Petrel, Antarctic Giant-, **82-3**
—, Collared, 44, 84
—, Gould's, 44, **85**
—, Hall's Giant-, 83
—, Slender-billed, 90
—, Tahiti, 2, 44, **83-4**
—, White-necked or White-naped, 44, 84, **86**
—, White-winged or Collared, 44, **84-5**
Pétrel à nuque blanche, 86
— aux ailes blanches, 84
— de Gould, 85
— de Tahiti, 83
— de Wilson, 93
— géant, 82
— tempête à gorge blanche, 94
— — à ventre noir, 93
Petrels, 81
Petroica multicolor, *14*, 195, **225-7**
Petyea, 243
Phaéthon à queue blanche, 107
— à queue rouge, 106
Phaethon lepturus, 2, 44, **107-8**
— *rubricauda*, 2, 44, **106-7**
Phaethontidae, 105
Phalacrocoracidae, 101
Phalacrocorax melanoleucos, *4*, *16*, 44, **102**
Phasianidae, 131, 135
Phylidonyris notabilis, *9*, *20*, 48, **243-4**
Pigeon à gorge blanche, 181
— vert à tête jaune, 175
— vert à tête rouge, 172
Pigeon, Pacific Imperial, *8*, 48-9, 174, 177, **178-80**, 181-2
—, Rock, 170
—, Vanuatu Mountain or Baker's Imperial, *8*, *17*, 47-8, 52, 178, **180-81**
—, White-throated or Metallic Wood, *8*, *17*, 49, 178, **181-3**
Pigeons, 171
Pimo, 186
Plongeur, 78
Plover, American Golden, 150

—, Double-banded, 148, 150
—, Eastern Golden or Lesser Golden, 149
—, Greater Sand, 150
—, Grey, 148-9
—, Large-billed Shore, 146
—, Mongolian or Lesser Sand, **150-51**
—, Oriental or Eastern Sand, **151**
—, Pacific Golden, 7, **149-50**, 151, 158
Plovers, 148
Pluvialis dominica, 150
— *fulva*, 7, **149-50**
— *squatarola*, 148, 149
Pluvier doré, 149
— mongol, 150
— oriental, 151
Podicipedidae, 77
PODICIPEDIFORMES, 77
Poliolimnas cinereus, *6*, 49, **142-3**
Pongkil, 42
Porphyrio porphyrio, *6*, 49, **143-4**
Port Vila, 21-2, 25, 35, 144, 148, 150, 156, 159-60, 216, 244, 249, 254-5, 257-8, 261
Porzana tabuensis, *6*, 47, **140-41**
Poule sultane, 143
Prion, Antarctic or Dove, **86-7**
—, Broad-billed, 87
—, Lesser Broad-billed, 87
Prion Colombe, 86
Prions, 81
Procellariidae, 81
PROCELLARIIFORMES, 79
Pseudobulweria rostrata, 2, 44, **83-4**
Psittacidae, 188
PSITTACIFORMES, 188
Pterodroma brevipes, 85
— *externa*, 44, **86**
— *leucoptera*, 44, **84-5**
Ptilinopus greyii, *8*, **172-5**
— *tannensis*, *8*, **175-7**
Ptilope de Grey, 172
— de Vanuatu, 175
Puffin à bec grêle, 90
— à queue pointue, 87
— d'Audubon, 91
— volage, 90
Puffinus gavia, 2, 44, **90-91**
— *lherminieri*, 44, **91-2**
— *pacificus*, 44, **87-9**
— *tenuirostris*, 82, 88, **90**
Punampioni, 187

Rail, Buff-banded or Banded, *6*, *21*, 49, **138-40**
—, Sooty, 140
—, White-browed, 142
Rails, 137-8

Râle à bandes, 138
— à sourcils blancs, 142
Red Nasiko, 212
Redpoll, *15*, **253-4**
Reef Islands, 22, 27, 36, 54, 98
Rhipidura fuliginosa, *13*, 49, **235-7**
— *spilodera*, *13*, **237-8**
Rhipidure à collier, 235
— tacheté, 237
Rhipiduridae, 234
Robin, Scarlet, *14*, 195, **225-7**
Robins, Australian, 225
Rossignol à poitrine rouge, 225

Sandpiper, Common, 150, **156**
—, Grey-rumped, 154
—, Pectoral, 157, **158**
—, Sharp-tailed, **157-8**
Sandpipers, 151
Santo, 21-2, 24-5, 27, 29, 31-2, 34, 36, 38-9, 47-9, 64, 69, 78, 80, 111, 114, 118, 121, 123, 128, 139, 143, 147, 157, 179-80, 184, 187, 191-4, 196, 205, 212, 215-16, 218-19, 222, 226-7, 230, 232-3, 239-41, 243-4, 250, 254, 257, 259-60, 263-4, 267-8, 270, 274
Sarcelle grise, 119
Scolopacidae, 151
Scrubfowl, 132
Scrubfowl, Orange-footed, 135
Sea Eagle, 123
— Hawk, 103, 104
Seagull, 159
Shag, Little, 102
Shearwater, Audubon's or Dusky-backed, 44, **91-2**
—, Fluttering, 2, 44, **90-91**
—, Short-tailed, 82, 88, **90**
—, Wedge-tailed, 44, **87-9**, 90
Shearwaters, 81
Shepherd Islands, 24, 28, 54, 108, 191
Shrikebill, Southern, *14*, 229, **230-31**
Siffleur d'or, 227
Sikraptak, 132
Silvereye, 249, 252
Silvereyes, 249
Skraptak, 132
Smole fala dak dak, 119
— — green Pijin, 172
Sot leg, 184
Sparrow, House, *15*, 47, 254, **255-6**
Sparrowhawks, 123
Sparrows, 254
Starling, European or Common, 267, **269**
—, Rusty-winged, *12*, 48, 267, **268-9**, 270
—, Santo Mountain or Vanuatu Mountain, *12*,

47-9, **267-8**, 274
Starlings, 266
Sterna anaethetus, **165-6**
— *bergii*, **166-7**
— *dougallii*, **162-3**
— *fuscata*, 44, 161, **164-5**
— *hirundo*, **162**
— *sumatrana*, 2, 44, **163-4**
Sterne à nuque noire, 163
— blanche, 169
— bridée, 165
— de Dougall, 162
— fuligineuse, 164
— huppée, 166
— pierregarin, 162
Stint, Red-necked or Rufous-necked, **158-9**
Stone-curlew, Beach, 146
Storm-Petrel, Black-bellied, **93-4**
—, Polynesian, 44, 93, **94-5**
—, Samoan or White-throated, 94
—, White-bellied, 94
—, Wilson's, **93**
Storm-Petrels, 92
Stourne aux ailes rousses, 268
— des montagnes, 267
STRIGIFORMES, 198
Sturnidae, 266
Sturnus vulgaris, **269**
Sucrier cardinal, 247
Sula dactylatra, 1, 97, **100-101**
— *leucogaster*, 1, 44, **97-9**
— *sula*, 1, 44, 97, **99-100**
Sulidae, 96
Swallow, Coast, House or Welcome, 215
—, Pacific, *11*, 49, **215-17**, 273
Swallow-shrikes, 272
Swallows, 214
Swamphen, 137
—, Purple, 6, 49, **143-4**
Swiftlet, Glossy, 203
—, Grey-rumped or Grey, 204
—, Uniform (Vanikoro), *11*, 202, 204-5, **206**
—, Vanikoro, Island or Lowland, 206
—, White-bellied, *11*, 202, **203-4**, 205
—, White-rumped, *11*, 47, 202, **204-5**
Swiftlets, 201

Tabut, 264
Tachybaptus novaehollandiae, *4*, **78-80**
Tagabe, 216, 234, 255, 263
Tanna, 22-4, 29, 36-8, 47, 49, 54, 69, 85, 92, 94, 116-18, 120-21, 128, 139, 141-3, 179, 194, 200, 205, 209, 216, 220, 222, 226, 231, 235, 246-7, 250, 252, 263, 270, 273
Tarin à front rouge, 253

Tasmanian Muttonbird, 90
Tattler, Grey-tailed or Polynesian, 154
—, Siberian, **154-5**
—, Wandering, 7, 154, **155**
Teal, Grey, *4*, 118, **119-20**
Teouma, 111
Tern, Black-naped, *2*, 44, **163-4**
—, Bridled or Brown-winged, 164, **165-6**
—, Common or Eastern Common, 162
—, Great Crested, **166-7**
—, Noddy, 167
—, Roseate or Graceful, **162-3**
—, Sooty or Wideawake, 44, 161, **164-6**
—, White or Fairy, *2*, **169-70**
Terns, 159, 160
Thick-knee, Beach or Reef, 7, 45, **146-7**
Thick-knees, 146
Thickhead, 227
Thion Island, 22, 27, 32
Thrush, Island, *13*, 49, 221, **222-4**
—, Song or English, 221, **224-5**
Thrushes, 221
Tinakula, 187
Toga, 27, 215
Tongariki, 28, 126, 143, 178, 200, 203, 216, 220, 226-7, 231, 246
Tongoa, 28, 87, 92, 107, 128, 139, 143, 191, 216, 219, 226-7, 246, 250, 264-5
Torres Islands, 21-2, 24, 27, 32, 34, 39, 41, 47, 69, 114, 176, 183, 191, 200, 209, 215, 220, 252
Tourne-pierre, 152
Tourterelle, 184
Tourterelle de Santa-Cruz, 186
Trichoglossus haematodus, *9*, *17*, 48, **189-91**
Triller, Long-tailed, *12*, 49, 219, **220-21**
—, Polynesian, *12*, **218-20**
Trillers, 195, 217
Tropicbird, Red-tailed, *2*, 44, **106-7**
—, White-tailed, *2*, 44, **107-8**
Tropicbirds, 105
Turdidae, 221
Turdus philomelos, **224-5**
— *poliocephalus*, *13*, 49, **222-4**
Turnstone, Ruddy, 7, **152**

Tyto alba, *5*, 49, **199-201**
Tytonidae, 199

Ureparapara, 24, 27, 32, 40-41, 98, 114, 176, 180, 194, 205, 222, 243, 250, 268
Utupua, 187

Vanua Lava, 22, 24-5, 27, 32, 34, 114, 139, 180, 194, 196, 200, 222, 227, 233, 240, 243, 250, 268
Vao, 22, 28
Vini, 191
Vusi, 147

Wael dak dak, 117
Warbler, Fantail, *13*, *19*, 47, 49, 196-7, **239-41**
—, Thicket, *13*, *19*, 47, 239, **241-2**
Warblers, Australian, 238
Waxbill, Common, *15*, *16*, **256-8**
—, Red-browed, 258
Waxbills, 256
Whimbrel, 7, 150, **153-4**, 156
—, Asiatic, 153
Whistler, Golden or Common Golden, *14*, 49, 225, **227-9**, 232
—, Mangrove, 227
Whistlers, 225
White-eye, Grey-backed or Grey-breasted, *9*, 249-50, **252-3**
—, Vanuatu, *9*, *20*, 249, **250-51**, 253
—, Yellow or Yellow-fronted, 250
White-eyes, 249
Woodswallow, White-breasted or White-rumped, *14*, 49, **272-4**
Woodswallows, 272
Woohia, 268

Zai'Zari, 232
Zizileri, 241
Zosteropidae, 249
Zosterops à dos gris, 252
— de Vanuatu, 250
Zosterops flavifrons, *9*, *20*, **250-51**
— *lateralis*, *9*, 249, **252-3**